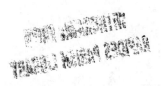

ADAM KARLIN
REGIS ST. LOUIS

WASHINGTON, DC
C I T Y   G U I D E

Corinthian pillars of the majestic Capitol Columns Garden, United States National Arboretum (p109)

RICK GERHAR

In 1968, U and 13th Sts NW were burning. Thousands of African Americans protested Dr Martin Luther King Jr's assassination during the worst race riots in Washington, DC's history.

Forty years later, in November 2008, anarchy ruled the same address. But this time white and brown mixed with black. If folks were crying, it was for joy; if they were making a ruckus, it was from all the hugging, singing and dancing: Barack Obama, the new president of the United States, had carried Washington, DC by 92.9%.

U St was unrecognizable from 1968. The ghetto was gone. Now, black- and white-owned businesses competed to give locals the best of the American urban experience. The U St Corridor, including Columbia Heights, Petworth, Shaw and other once-neglected neighborhoods, was a flag bearer for the new Washington, DC. So while they celebrated everywhere in this town, the party was poignant here, a place that grew from riot's heart into revitalized neighborhood. If Obama, the mixed-race wunderkind, was *someone* Washingtonians loved, U St was *somewhere* Washington could be: also multiracial, also an unlikely success story, also enamored with Hope and Change.

Still: cities aren't built by single places, people or strokes of history. The celebrations that accompanied that evening broke out over Barack, but they couldn't have occurred without 40 years of hard work and occasional heartache, four decades of the evolution of this town from bureaucracy surrounded by ghetto into one of the most diverse, vibrant metropolises in America.

WASHINGTON, DC LIFE

Washington, DC is undergoing the largest changes, in terms of demographics and development, of its recent history. Once roughly 73% black, that number is now around 56%, yet at the same time the remaining African American population is better educated and more prosperous than ever before. African

'Washington, DC contains within it every facet of the American experiment'

Americans are no longer necessarily leaving town as the District grows, and the District is growing – new high-end condos and their accompanying arts, eateries and nightlife are appearing in parts of Washington that were once boring at best, blight at worst.

The American government, for good or ill, is a larger entity than it has ever been, and as such it has attracted a surfeit of talent from around the world to this, its home base. At the same time, the government of Washington, DC has been trying to integrate that growth into the city itself, to create partnerships and a capital that is also a community. The effort is enormous; its failure would be heartbreaking, and its potential for success is exciting in a very raw way. What Washington, DC will become remains to be seen, and travelers, long a backbone of the capital economy, will have a loud voice in the direction this town chooses to take.

This is not the Washington, DC you've heard of. It is not just the monuments and the museums, or the White House, or the 'hood. It is a city where the lines between all of the above have blurred, a town where class and race, once abstract Berlin Walls that kept the District as divided as any concrete partition, are crumbling. It's a complicated, controversial, easily stereotyped gem that contains within it every facet of the American experiment: immigrants, politicians, community organizers, students, gangsters, journalists, volunteers, soldiers, our soil and our soul.

JEAN-PIERRE LESCOURRET

Unmistakably DC: a luminous Capitol building (p77) presiding over Pennsylvania Ave

HIGHLIGHTS

GREGG NEWTON/CORBIS

THIS AMERICAN CITY

Washington, DC is what America has been, remains and is becoming. The capital captures the highs and lows, beauty and grit, and ultimate vision of the American experience. The abstracts of our national unconscious take on solid, symbolic form on these streets.

LEE FOSTER

BRENT WINEBRENNER

❶ **National Archives** Three documents sturdy enough to support a nation (p89)

❷ **Lincoln Memorial** Lincoln's monument is also a Civil Rights icon (p55)

❸ **Vietnam Veterans Memorial** A stark reminder of war's real cost (p56)

❹ **Smithsonian American Art Museum** The national aesthetic: raw, exciting, unmissable (p90)

❺ **Independence Day** Celebrate the nation's birthday in its capital (p15)

4

MARK PETERSON/CORBIS

NIGHTLIFE

The residents of the nation's capital like to throw down. Sink beers with a senatorial aide; get sweaty on a Ghanaian dance floor; trade shots with an ambassador's daughter and treat her to a freak show on H St. Just don't go home early.

DAN HERRICK

1 **Raven** Where $20 buys about a barrel of Schlitz (p182)

2 **18th Street** Drink till the nightclubs blur into one shot (p179)

3 **Marvin** One of the best outdoor decks in the city (p184)

4 **Atlas District** Punk minigolf, Belgian beer halls, circus sideshows (p176)

5 **Wonderland** Edgy, awesome, anchoring up-and-coming Columbia Heights (p183)

JUSTIN MATHEWS

JASON COLSTO

FOOD

Throw together a few young professionals, the north–south culinary fault line and one of the most diverse immigrant diasporas in the country (plus a lot of comped business lunches) and you get: some damn fine grub. Polish your knife and dig into DC.

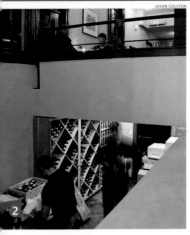

JASON COLSTON

DAN HERRIC

1 Hitching Post Split some fried chicken with the neighbors (p166)

2 Cork Wine Bar Small plates, great wine and neighborhood ambience (p163)

3 Ben's Chili Bowl As iconic to locals as the White House (p163)

4 Fish Wharf Open the Old Bay and crack some crabs (p155)

5 Minibar at Café Atlantico Push the envelope of culinary possibility (p158)

SHAWN THEW/EPA/CORBIS

JUSTIN MATHEWS

① **National Museum of American History** Interactivity aids in understanding the past (p59)

② **Newseum** Multimedia flash meets hands-on interactive everything (p61)

③ **National Museum of Natural History** Enough dinosaurs to restart the Cretaceous (p58)

④ **National Zoological Park** Pandas, otters, apes and elephants in Woodley Park (p116)

⑤ **United States National Arboretum** An amazing urban green space made for rompin' (p109)

COURTESY OF THE SMITHSONIAN INSTITUTION

DC FOR KIDS

We love your kids. Seriously. Can we take them to the museums? The monuments? How about a ride on the National Mall carousel, or a day in our many parks? There's a lot little ones can love, laugh at, and perhaps most importantly, learn from in the capital.

MEHGAN MURPHY /SMITHSONIAN'S NATIONAL ZOO

MARK NEWM

THE CAPITAL REGION

The area surrounding Washington, DC is a collage of landscapes that are crucial to national geography and memory. Explore historical battlefields, miles of marsh and the backbone of the earliest Western frontier, and in the process, what it means to be an American.

KRAIG LI

❶ **Manassas National Battlefield Park** The best-preserved 19th-century landscapes in America (p222)

❷ **Chesapeake Bay** America's loveliest estuary: glinting tidewater and lush forests (p229)

❸ **Shenandoah National Park** The Appalachians dramatically frame the Eastern Seaboard (p225)

❹ **Baltimore** Working-class, hard-partying town an hour north of DC (p227)

❺ **Mount Vernon** Escape to George Washington's elegant old Virginia digs (p220)

MARK NEWM

CONTENTS

THE AUTHORS

Adam Karlin

Adam Karlin was born in Washington, DC and raised two hours south of the city in Southern Maryland, where the Potomac and Patuxent rivers spill into the Chesapeake Bay. Besides field trips, he never properly explored the capital until he started covering crime and politics in nearby Prince George's County – this following a period of (still simmering) wanderlust, when he worked as a journalist and editor in every inhabited continent on Earth. Lonely Planet has generously helped him continue his expeditions, and he has worked on roughly 20 Lonely Planet guidebooks. In the midst of all this, Adam is also a local boy, and DC and the DC metro region always feel international enough, yet comfortably cozy, to be something like home.

ADAM'S TOP DC DAY

This is hard, as there are so many different ways to enjoy DC. Do I want a museum kind of day? An episode of epicurean excess? Choices, choices. Regardless, let's assume it's summer, when the days are hot and the nights are silky humid in that perfect mid-Atlantic way.

I'll start the morning on Capitol Hill with a slug of coffee and some breakfast in Eastern Market (p152), then head over to the Library of Congress (p80) to check out whatever excellent special exhibition it's got on. Then I wander up to the Smithsonian American Art Museum (p90), where I can easily pass a day lost in contemplation. Being in a cerebral mood, I'll roll up to U St, where I sit and write in Busboys & Poets (p164). When the day reaches that right point and the summer sunset burnishes the District lavender and the air feels like a kiss, I meet up with friends for drinks and dinner at either next-door Eatonville (p164) or nearby Cork Wine Bar (p163). If we've got a good edge going, we might head up to Marvin (p184) for an alfresco drink, or to Columbia Heights to get ripped in the Raven (p182) or Red Derby (p183). Depending on the mood of the group (do we wanna dance or hit the links?), we either stumble over to Wonderland (p183) or catch a cab to the H Street Country Club (p175) for some sloshed minigolf. I should probably go home now. But before I do, I want to see my Washington from the hill on 14th St NW that Cardozo High School sits on. From here, the city spills under me like stars, and the jazz in its soul erupts like steam from the sidewalks.

Contributing Author
REGIS ST. LOUIS

An avid news junkie and admirer of all things strange and political, Regis was destined for a long and tumultuous relationship with that elusive spirit of Washington, DC. No matter the season, he finds the city of grand design and big ideas (if sometimes small-minded bureaucrats) a fascinating place to roam.

He has written over two dozen guides for Lonely Planet, and his articles have appeared in the *Los Angeles Times* and the *Chicago Tribune* among other publications. He lives in New York City.

GETTING STARTED

Washington, DC offers ample rewards to the traveler with a well-planned itinerary. Catching a lively festival, booking seats at one of DC's world-class theaters, and reserving that elegant room with a view are just a few things to keep in mind when planning the big DC trip. A well-planned itinerary will also help you maximize your time, though do leave some room for unscheduled exploring of the city's many captivating streets.

Washington, DC can be an expensive city to visit, though free museums, affordable dining options and inexpensive transport on the Metro help lesson the blow to your budget.

WHEN TO GO

The best time to visit DC is generally autumn (September to October), when the summer crowds have dissipated along with the scorching heat. Spring (April to May), which brings flowering blossoms and clear blue skies, is also a fine time to visit, though it's one of the busiest times in DC. Summer is even busier, when tourists arrive in droves, and the days can be exceptionally hot and humid, especially in July and August. If you plan to travel then, plan your outings to take advantage of the cooler mornings and late afternoons, heading inside to much-needed air-conditioning (museums and other sites) during the midday heat.

Winter can be unpredictable with crisp clear afternoons followed by days of gray, frigid weather when no one cares much for venturing outdoors. Although the temperatures hover in the mid 40s (6°C to 8°C), the city does receive occasional snowstorms – and even a mild dusting of snow can bring the city to a halt. For average temperatures and rainfall, see p241.

FESTIVALS & EVENTS

The biggest party in town is the quadrennial Inauguration Day, where millions celebrate (and millions more gnash their teeth) as the incoming President assumes (or re-assumes) high office. For those who'd rather not wait until 2013, Washington throws a year-round line-up of festivals and parades, including the famous Cherry Blossom Festival, the massive multicultural Smithsonian Folklife Festival and the concert- and fireworks-filled Independence Day when the nation celebrates its birthday.

On federal holidays, banks, schools, government offices and some attractions close; transportation runs on a Sunday schedule. For a list of public holidays, see p243.

For more on events and festivals, check out the Washington Post (www.washingtonpost.com),

Washington City Paper (www.washingtoncitypaper.com), washington.dc.eventguide.com and Cultural Tourism DC (www.culturaltourismdc.org).

January
MARTIN LUTHER KING JR'S BIRTHDAY
The legacy of one of America's greats lives on each year at concerts, films and the recitation of King's famous 'I have a dream' speech on the Lincoln Memorial (p55) steps. His birthday is commemorated on the third Monday in January and the weekend just prior. A highlight is the children's concert 'Sweet Honey in the Rock', staged by the Washington Performing Arts Society (www.wpas.org).

February
BLACK HISTORY MONTH
www.smithsonianeducation.org
The Smithsonian museums organize an impressive array of special events and cultural programs. Gallery walks, photography exhibitions, plays and other events happen throughout the month.

CHINESE NEW YEAR
www.chinatownchamber.us
Bringing a bit of fire to the cold winter is the annual Chinatown parade, which lights up the neighborhood with dancing dragons and firecrackers. The parade (scheduled around the lunar calendar – meaning it sometimes falls in late January) happens around H and I Sts between 6th and 8th Sts.

WASHINGTON DC INTERNATIONAL WINE & FOOD FESTIVAL
☎ 800-343-1174; www.wine-expos.com/wine/dc
Local and celebrity chefs gather at this Epicurean gathering amid the winter

gloom. Expect an eclectic range of global fare, mouthwatering wines from all corners of the globe and demonstrations by celebrated chefs.

OUR CITY FILM FEST
www.yachad-dc.org/OurCityFilmFestival.shtml
This film fest admirably focuses on showing the works of local talent.

DC FASHION WEEK
www.dcfashionweek.org
Held in February and September, this week-long event often brings an eclectic array of emerging talent and lesser-known international designers to the fore – a recent line-up included designers from Nigeria, Iran and Pakistan. Most shows are open to the public, though some require ticket admission.

March

ST PATRICK'S DAY
www.dcstpatsparade.com
Dancers, bagpipers, marching bands and assorted merrymakers share the Irish love along Constitution Ave NW (from 7th to 17th Sts) at this big annual event. The parade is held on a Sunday, either on or preceding March 17.

ENVIRONMENTAL FILM FEST
☎ 202-342-2564; www.wjff.org
This film fest attracts both documentaries and feature films.

SMITHSONIAN KITE FESTIVAL
☎ 202-633-3030; www.kitefestival.org
On the last Saturday of March, the skies near the Washington Monument (p55) come alive with colors as kite lovers fill the mall. There are a number of awards ('beauty in the air,' 'best kite-maker,' 'best tricks' etc) that add to the excitement. This usually kicks off the Cherry Blossom Festival.

NATIONAL CHERRY BLOSSOM FESTIVAL
☎ 877-442-5666; www.nationalcherryblossom festival.org
The grandest of Washington's annual events, the Cherry Blossom Festival in late March and early April celebrates spring's arrival with hundreds of performances and special exhibitions, plus boat rides in the Tidal Basin, evening walks by lantern light, cultural fairs and a parade. Aside from the gorgeous blossoms themselves, the highlight is undoubtedly the Japanese Street Festival (www.sakuramatsuri.org), where kimono-clad dancers, *taiko* drummers, martial-arts masters and dozens of food vendors draw big crowds. The two-week event also commemorates the gift of 3000 cherry trees by Tokyo's Mayor Yukio Ozaki in 1912 to the city of Washington. Today over 750,000 people attend the festival.

CHERRY BLOSSOM 10-MILE RUN
☎ 301-320-3350; www.cherryblossom.org
If you prefer your blossoms rushing past in a riot of pinks and whites, sign up for the 10-mile run held during the festival. The race loops around the Tidal Basin and along the Potomac, and winners receive cash prizes. There's also a 3-mile (5km) run/walk and a 1km children's run. Registration begins in December (and fills up quickly for the 12,000 spots).

April

WHITE HOUSE EASTER EGG ROLL
1600 Pennsylvania Ave
A White House tradition since 1878, the Easter Egg Roll attracts some 30,000 families from across the US for storytelling, games, music and dance. The big event (aside from hearing the President read a fairy tale to three- to six-year-olds) is the massive egg hunt, featuring 13,000 hard-boiled eggs. It's held on the South Lawn.

SMITHSONIAN CRAFT SHOW
☎ 888-832-9554; www.smithsoniancraftshow.org; 1st fl, Smithsonian Castle, 1000 Jefferson Dr SW; admission $15
In mid- to late April, some 120 American craft makers display works in categories that include basketry, ceramics, furniture, glass, jewelry, mixed media, paper, wearable art and wood. The juried show features both new and established artists, and all works are for sale.

SHAKESPEARE'S BIRTHDAY
☎ 202-544-7077; www.folger.edu; 201 E Capitol St
On the nearest Sunday to April 23, the Folger Shakespeare Library & Theatre (p82) celebrates the Bard's birthday (nearly 450

years ago) with jugglers, jesters, music, singing, dancing and free birthday cake. It's particularly popular among families.

FILMFEST DC
☎ 202-724-5782; www.filmfestdc.org
Featuring over 70 films from across the globe, DC's FilmFest showcases new and avant-garde cinema at venues around the city. In addition to film screenings, there are guest appearances by directors and other special events. Filmfest is held over 10 days from mid- to late April.

May
PASSPORT DC
www.passportdc.org
One of Washington's newest and more innovative festivals, Passport DC is a chance to peer inside some of the city's grandest and least-visited gems, when many embassies throw open their doors to the public for two weeks in early May. Expect music, crafts, dancing and cuisine from each country hosting.

GAY BLACK PRIDE
☎ 202-737-5767
The nation's largest annual Gay Black Pride celebration takes place on the Memorial Day weekend and draws some 100,000 participants from across the country. Don't miss it if you're in town during this lovely spring season.

ROLLING THUNDER RIDE FOR FREEDOM
☎ 908-369-5439; www.rollingthunder1.com
The Harley Davidson contingent of Vietnam vets commemorates Memorial Day (last Monday of May) with a ride along the National Mall to draw attention to the POWs and MIAs who were left behind. The ride begins at the Pentagon and ends at the Vietnam Veterans Memorial (p56) and draws nearly one million spectators and participants.

June
CAPITAL JAZZ FEST
☎ 301-780-9300; www.capitaljazz.com; Merriweather Post Pavilion, Columbia, Maryland; 1-/3-day pass $40/140
On one weekend in early June, Jazz Fest comes to the capital – or at least near it.

Held 28 miles northeast of DC, the event features big-name and up-and-coming stars playing jazz and soul on two stages. The Hilton Columbia Hotel hosts the after-hours party.

CAPITAL PRIDE
☎ 202-719-5304; www.capitalpride.org
Some 250,000 descend on the nation's capital for the city's festive gay pride holiday. The parade along Pennsylvania Ave to the Mall is the focal point, although there are also film screenings and performances, plus many bars and clubs host special events. It's held in early to mid-June.

DANCE AFRICA DC FESTIVAL
☎ 202-269-1600; www.danceplace.org; Dance Place, 3225 8th St NE
This festival showcases traditional African dance along with dance from the African diaspora. Held at Dance Place (p192), the festival has ticketed indoor shows, free outdoor performances, tasty street food and an African-style marketplace. It's held in mid-June.

LAWYERS HAVE HEART 10KM RACE
☎ 703-248-1713; www.runlhh.org
Lawyers help the American Heart Association raise money by sweating it out and running a 10km loop around Georgetown's Washington Harbor (p192). The race, which is also popular with nonbarrister types, attracts thousands of runners each year and has raised nearly $6 million. It is held in early June.

SMITHSONIAN FOLKLIFE FESTIVAL
☎ 202-633-6440; www.festival.si.edu
For 10 days before Independence Day, this extravaganza celebrates international and US cultures on the Mall in front of the Smithsonian Castle (p62). The fest features folk music, dance, crafts, storytelling and ethnic fare, and it highlights a diverse mix of countries each year.

BARBECUE BATTLE
☎ 301-860-0630; www.bbqdc.com; Pennsylvania Ave, btwn 9th & 14th Sts; admission $10
The must-see event for all barbecue lovers takes place in late June and features independent teams and restaurateurs competing

for $40,000 in prizes for serving up the best barbecue. In addition to tender ribs, chicken and sausage, you'll find live bands, cooking demonstrations, celebrity chefs and kiddie toys.

DC CARIBBEAN CARNIVAL
www.dccaribbeancarnival.org
On the last weekend in June, 300,000 people show up for island revelry on Georgia Ave. The highlights are live bands, food vendors, craft stalls and a brilliantly colorful parade (between Missouri Ave and Barry Pl).

July & August
INDEPENDENCE DAY   July 4
July 4 commemorates the adoption of the Declaration of Independence in 1776. Huge crowds gather on the National Mall to watch marching bands parade along Constitution Ave, attend the Smithsonian Folklife Festival (opposite) and listen to the Declaration read from the steps of the National Archives (p89). Nightfall brings a concert on the steps of the Capitol (performed by the National Symphony Orchestra) followed by the grand finale, the nation's largest fireworks show. Keep in mind that the crowds are huge – some 800,000 at last count.

VIRGIN FESTIVAL
The biggest show around is the annual Virgin Festival (that's the Richard Branson-type, not some Roman temple ceremony), held every August in Merriweather Post Pavilion in Columbia, MD, 30 miles northeast of the city. In 2009 the line-up featured

---

the Flaming Lips, Red Hot Chili Peppers and The Killers.

SCREEN ON THE GREEN
In summer, one of DC's favorite traditions is this movie festival. Held Monday nights at sundown between mid-July and mid-August, it features a different Hollywood classic each week in the National Sculpture Garden (p61).

DC RESTAURANT WEEK
www.washington.org/restaurantwk
Held in late August, DC Restaurant Week features over 170 of the capital's best restaurants offering three-course lunches (for around $21) and dinners (around $36). This is a great way to experience Washington's fine-dining scene at excellent prices.

September
KENNEDY CENTER OPEN HOUSE ARTS FESTIVAL
☎ 202-467-4600, 800-444-1324; www.kennedy-center.org
In early to mid-September, the Kennedy Center kicks off its new season with this all-day arts festival. Each year the Center showcases a different region and its cultural heritage, staging music, dance, theater, performance art and more. In 2009, the theme was circus and street performers, complete with acrobats, a 'musical instrument petting zoo,' an Afro-Funk orchestra and storytelling. Geared to all ages, the Arts Festival is popular with families.

FIESTA DC
☎ 202-232-4393; www.fiestadc.org; 14th St NW btwn Spring & Columbia Rds, Columbia Heights
One of the main events of Hispanic Heritage Month (which runs mid-September to mid-October), this Latino parade features colorful floats, world music, twirling dancers, pounding drum corps, craft stalls and, perhaps most importantly, Latin American food. The parade is held on the last Sunday in September in Columbia Heights (Map pp106–7).

DC FASHION WEEK
www.dcfashionweek.org
Held twice a year, DC Fashion Week hosts a lineup of runway shows, networking

---

SUMMER IN THE CITY
Summer nights are sultry and set aside for concerts, most of which are free. Events run from Memorial Day to the Labor Day weekend (late May to early September).

- National Zoological Park (p116) Free concerts every Thursday evening.
- Jazz in the Garden Every summer from 7pm, in the National Sculpture Garden (p61).
- Military Music The marine corps, air force, army and navy bands perform at 8pm most weeknights on the steps of the Capitol on alternating days in summer.

parties and the occasional free outdoor event when international fashionistas descend on the capital. Check the website for the dates and times. It's also held in February (p13).

DC BLUES FESTIVAL
☎ 301-322-4808; www.dcblues.org
In late August or early September, the all-volunteer DC Blues Society sponsors a free, day-long festival of top local blues acts at Rock Creek Park's Carter Barron Amphitheater (p190).

DCSHORTS
☎ 202-393-4266; http://dcshorts.com
This film fest is a great collection of short films from across the world.

ADAMS MORGAN FESTIVAL
www.adamsmorgandayfestival.com; 18th St NW btwn Columbia & Florida Sts
DC's biggest (and longest-running) neighborhood festival takes over 18th St NW on the weekend after Labor Day with live bands (playing jazz, funk, rock and world music) on two stages, craft stalls, a cultural stage (featuring poetry, theater and dance) and those all-important food vendors.

October

TASTE OF GEORGETOWN
www.tasteofgeorgetown.com
Thirty of Georgetown's best restaurants get experimental, innovative and, best of all, affordable. Wine pairings and live music enhance the value of this early to mid-October event.

REEL AFFIRMATIONS
☎ 202-986-1119; www.reelaffirmations.org
The best of new gay, lesbian, bisexual and transgender films the world over can be viewed at this fest in mid-October. The festival also runs late-night camp films, lively parties and a women's filmmaker brunch.

MARINE CORPS MARATHON
☎ 800-786-8762; www.marinemarathon.com
Known as the people's marathon, this popular road race takes in some of DC's iconic scenery. The course winds along the Potomac, takes in Georgetown, the entire length of the Mall, the Tidal Basin and Arlington Cemetery. It's held on the last Sunday in October.

HIGH HEEL DRAG RACE
17th St NW, btwn Church & Q Sts
Traditionally held on the Tuesday before Halloween (October 31), the High Heel Drag Race brings revelers out in droves to fête this riotously fun event in the gay district. Outrageously dressed divas strut their stuff before large crowds, then line up for a no-holds-barred sprint down 17th St. An informal block party, with more colorful mayhem, ensues. The race starts at 9pm, but show up by 6pm or 7pm to get a prime viewing spot.

November & December

WASHINGTON JEWISH FILM FESTIVAL
☎ 202-777-3248; www.wjff.org
In late November/early December, this festival explores and celebrates contemporary Jewish-American themes.

NATIONAL CHRISTMAS TREE & MENORAH LIGHTING
www.nps.gov/whho/national_christmas_tree_program.htm
In early December, the president brings on the holiday cheer by switching on the lights to the national Christmas Tree. The president does the honors for the National Menorah as well – also held in December. Live bands and choral groups play holiday music, which adds to the all-round good cheer. It all happens on the Ellipse (p67), the expansive park located on the south side of the White House. Apply for free tickets two months in advance; otherwise you'll be watching proceedings through the fence.

COSTS & MONEY

Washington, DC is in the middle of the pack when it comes to cost-of-living indexes among big American cities. You'll spend less traveling and staying in DC than you would in New York City, San Francisco, LA and even Chicago. That said, the city can still set you back a fair bit unless you're actively economizing.

As elsewhere in the world, the biggest expense will be for accommodations. On average, single travelers who stay in a B&B or midrange hotel, eat at least one meal a day out and take in a bit of nightlife and entertainment can expect to spend upwards of $200 or so per day. Couples can anticipate paying a bit more – something in the daily range of $250 and up. For those on tight budgets, there are plenty of ways to cut costs, from sleeping in a hostel to eating at low-key restaurants and limiting entertainment options.

Breaking things down a bit: midrange accommodations, including three-star hotels and B&Bs, average around $120 to $200 per night for a room in a central neighborhood. Going up a notch, starting around $250, you can stay in a boutique hotel or heritage inn with obvious style and charm. At $350 per day and up, the city's luxury hotels are at your disposal. On the low-end of the scale, it's possible to bunk in a hostel dorm bed for around $26 per day.

Keep in mind that you'll have to pay tax on top of that which will add another 14.5% to the bill. Some places include the tax in their prices. Do inquire if you're not sure.

When it comes to eating, prices vary widely. A midrange restaurant meal with two courses and a drink will start around $25 at lunchtime and $35 for dinner per person – plus tax and tip (which adds another 30% or so to the bill). If you're dining at one of the city's trendier places, count on spending at least twice that amount. Those on tight budgets can economize by frequenting diners, delis and inexpensive ethnic restaurants – where you can have a meal for around $10.

Food and lodging aside, Washington provides many ways to save money. Free federal sites and museums, along with free concerts and summer festivals make for an inexpensive way to take advantage of the city. Other good ways to experience DC without the expense are by attending gallery openings, free summertime movie screenings on the Mall (or free screenings at the Mary Pickford Theater, p194) and by keeping an eye out for free cultural events at the Smithsonian. Happy hours offer good value for eating and drinking, and many upscale restaurants have prix-fixe and pre-theater menus that are fine value.

Do browse online for accommodations specials – Trip Advisor (www.tripadvisor.com), Orbitz (www.orbitz.com), Expedia (www.expedia.com) and their ilk

HOW MUCH?

bottle (8 oz) of mineral water in supermarket $1.25

pint of Samuel Adams $6

dinner for two at Zaytinya $65

chili dog at Ben's Chili Bowl $4

Metro ticket across town $1.65

ticket to see the Washington Wizards $12-60

live show at Blues Alley $20-35

Washington Post $0.75

Obama 'Hope' souvenir t-shirt $18

movie ticket $10

often have competitive rates that you won't receive just walking in off the street (or even by phoning). And, of course, online bidding sites (such as www.priceline.com and www.hotwire.com) can also save you big.

INTERNET RESOURCES

In addition to the DC-specific listings on sites like Chowhound (www.chowhound.com), Yelp (www.yelp.com), Daily Candy (www.dailycandy.com) and Craigslist (www.craigslist.org), the following are all good sites for preparing for the Washington experience:

http://map.mapnetwork.com/destination/dc Interactive downtown map.

www.amandamc.blogspot.com Excellent blog about the local dining scene, covering organic markets, restaurant openings, notable chefs and more.

www.artdc.org Local arts scene.

www.congressionalbadboys.com Fun Congressional scandal stories.

www.culturaltourismdc.org Events, tours and information.

www.dc.gov Local government.

www.dc.metromix.com More food and fun.

www.dcfoodfinder.org Map of farmer's markets and community gardens.

www.dcist.com A nifty blog about all-things DC, covering gossip, film openings, arts and culture, along with plenty of stuff of little interest to those outside the capital.

www.dcnites.com Nightlife.

www.dcsocialite.com Social events blog.

www.downtowndc.org Good gateway.

ADVANCE PLANNING

Those who have an aversion to strict schedules and fixed itineraries can do just fine traveling impulsively and unstructured in DC. If you have specific, must-see goals in mind, however, it's key to make advanced arrangements.

It goes without saying that you'll need to book a room in advance. The same goes for anything else that might be in high demand, from dining at a much-touted restaurant to theater tickets for an acclaimed production. For restaurant reservations, you can use the free online OpenTable (www.opentable.com) system. A good site for buying half-priced tickets to upcoming theater, dance and music performances is TicketPlace (www.ticketplace.org). The well-known Ticketmaster (www.ticketmaster.com) sells tickets to citywide events.

DC throws some impressive free events that are well worth attending, but require you to book well in advance – notably the lightings of the national Christmas tree and national Menorah (p16) and the Easter Egg Roll (p13). Also, if you plan to participate in the Marine Corps Marathon (p16) or the Cherry Blossom 10-Mile Run (p13), sign up well ahead.

If you're planning to rent a car for excursions out of town, it's wise to make advance arrangements, especially on holiday weekends when many rental-car agencies suffer a chronic shortage of automobiles.

Before you leave, you can start becoming well versed in upcoming goings-on by subscribing to email bulletins like Daily Candy (www.dailycandy.com) and perusing listings in the Washingtonian (www.washingtonian.com).

www.thenaturalcapital.blogspot.com Outdoor resources.

www.politico.com Independent website with great coverage of the American political scene from Washington insiders.

www.wamu.org WAMU, local NPR affiliate.

www.washington.org Official tourism site with useful links.

www.washingtonian.com Excellent insight into DC culture with features on dining, entertainment, shopping and local luminaries.

www.washingtoncitypaper.com City Paper – edgy weekly.

www.washingtonpost.com The city's oldest and most widely read daily paper covers news, arts, sports and nightlife in the capital.

HISTORY
EARLY SETTLEMENT

Before the first European colonists sailed up from Chesapeake Bay, Native Americans, primarily the Piscataway tribe of the Algonquian language group, made their home near the confluence of the Potomac and Anacostia Rivers. As many as 10,000 Piscataway inhabited the region, living a sustainable hunter/gatherer/trader lifestyle when the explorers arrived. The first recorded white contact with the Piscataway was in 1608 by the English Captain John Smith, who set out from Jamestown colony to explore the upper Potomac.

Relations with the peaceful Piscataway were amicable at first, but soon turned ruinous for the Native Americans. Vulnerable to European sicknesses, many Native Americans succumbed and their numbers were reduced by half within 25 years. In mid-century, the Piscataway suffered further losses from entanglements in the Indian Wars between the English and the more hostile Susquehannock and Powhatan tribes. By 1700, the few remaining Piscataway migrated out of the region to Iroquois territory in Pennsylvania and New York.

The first European settlers in the region were traders and fur trappers, who plied the woodlands beyond the Allegheny Mountains, often working with local Algonquin communities. English and Scots-Irish settlers followed, turning the forests into farmland. With the founding of Maryland, soul-saving Jesuits arrived to convert the locals.

By the late 1600s, expansive agricultural estates lined both sides of the Potomac. These tidewater planters became a colonial aristocracy, dominating regional affairs. Their most lucrative crop was the precious sotweed – tobacco – which was tended by African indentured servants and slaves. The river ports of Alexandria and Georgetown became famous for their prosperous commercial centers.

FIGHT FOR INDEPENDENCE

In the 1770s, growing hostilities with Britain led the colonies (now calling themselves states) to draft the Declaration of Independence, severing ties with Britain. In 1775, the Continental Congress issued a declaration outlining the colonists' reasons for fighting the British. Perhaps the most empowering section of the declaration stated that Americans were 'resolved to die free men rather than live as slaves.' Also, as a prelude to impending armed conflict, Congress established America's first navy, then appointed a clandestine panel to seek assistance from European nations in the struggle for independence.

After word of the first battles taking place in Massachusetts, Britain's King George III issued a Proclamation of Rebellion, declaring the colonies to be in open rebellion against the crown. Those who issued the declarations were essentially traitors as far as the king was concerned. And if the drive for independence failed, they could all be hanged.

At the outset of the war, the colonies faced tremendous obstacles. The colonial leaders' belief in their ultimate success was both visionary and utterly improbable. They had neither a professional

TIMELINE

1608	1791–92	1800
Piscataway people, who live in the area around the Potomac and Anacostia Rivers, encounter Captain John Smith on his journey up the Potomac – a word that may mean 'trading place' in Algonquin.	The site for the new federal capital is chosen and the initial stone is laid for the Executive Mansion (later named the White House).	Congress convenes in the new capital for the first time. Despite the grandeur of L'Enfant's plan, the capital remains a sparsely populated, muddy frontier town.

top picks

BOOKS ON DC HISTORY

- *Black Georgetown Remembered,* Kathleen M Lesko, Valerie Babb and Carroll R Gibbs (1991) From Native American village to bustling tobacco port to slave town to colonial town, this great narrative tells the story of Georgetown from the very beginning.
- *Capital Speculations: Writing and Building Washington, DC,* Sarah Luria (2005) Portrait of the political, social and even literary meanings inscribed in the capital over the centuries.
- *Katharine Graham's Washington,* edited by Katharine Graham (2002) Fascinating collection of essays by and about the Washington experience, by presidential insiders, novelists, journalists, socialites and humorists.
- *On this Spot: Pinpointing the Past in Washington, DC,* Paul Dickson and Douglas Evelyn (1992) A photographic, cartographic journey around DC, where historic events took place.
- *Team of Rivals: The Political Genius of Abraham Lincoln,* Doris Kearns Goodwin (2005) Pulitzer Prize–winning novel about one of the great men of all time. (It's what Obama was reading before taking office.)
- *The Birth of the Nation: A Portrait of the American People on the Eve of Independence,* Arthur Schlesinger (1968) Colonial life vividly portrayed.
- *Washington Burning,* Lee Standiford (2008) Describes the early days of Washington, from L'Enfant's original design to the incineration in 1814 and subsequent rebuilding.
- *Washington Goes to War,* David Brinkley (1996) An intriguing book by an astute newsman who vividly describes the inner workings of Washington – past and present.

army nor navy – only a ragtag group of poorly trained militiamen fighting against the most powerful army and navy on the planet. The king expected a quick suppression of the revolt.

Instead, the British faced off against George Washington, a highly skilled and charismatic military tactician whose courage under fire (in the French and Indian War) was well known. Washington was appointed commander in chief of the 20,000-odd men – a number that would swell to more than 200,000 by the war's end.

Incredibly, the war would rage on for eight years, with more soldiers dying from disease and exposure during the long bitter winters than from battle wounds. The war also brought other European powers into the fray, with France providing arms and munitions – and eventually troops and naval power.

Despite numerous losses – and many times when the dispirited colonial troops seemed on the verge of annihilation – Washington's army prevailed. The British surrendered at Yorktown in 1783 and later ceded all formerly British-held territories to the American colonies.

A VISIONARY NEW CITY

Following the Revolutionary War, the fledgling US Congress launched a search for a permanent home. The Constitution, ratified in 1788, specified that a federal territory, no greater than 10 sq miles, should be established for the nation's capital. Northerners and southerners both wanted the capital in their territory, and archrivals Thomas Jefferson (a Virginian) and Alexander Hamilton (a New Yorker) struck a compromise, agreeing to construct a new city on the border between north and south. The precise location was left up to the newly inaugurated and wildly popular President George Washington.

Washington chose a sight some 20 miles from his own Mount Vernon estate (p220) – a place he loved and knew well. The site on the Potomac proved a strategic location for commerce and river traffic, and politically pleasing to both Northern and Southern concerns. Maryland and Virginia agreed to cede land to the new capital.

1814	1835	1860
As the War of 1812 rages, British troops attack the fledgling capital, destroying many public buildings (including the White House and the Capitol). President Madison flees to Virginia.	Issue of slavery is dividing the nation. The Snow Riots erupt in Washington, with white mobs attacking blacks. In response, congress passes laws restricting blacks' economic rights.	Abraham Lincoln is elected president. The South secedes from the Union and war is declared. Washingtonians live in constant fear of attack from rebels, camped across the river in Virginia.

WASHINGTON IN THE AGE OF DEMOCRACY

To most visitors in the first half of the 19th century, the city was more a desolate provincial outpost than a dynamic urban center. Washington may have been the seat of federal government, but the states were the real players in political power and economic wealth. Governor Morris, a prominent New Yorker, acidly observed: 'We only need here houses, kitchens, scholarly men, amiable women and a few other trifles, to possess a perfect city.'

The city's rough-hewn appearance was, at least partially, intended. Thomas Jefferson disliked formal displays of power and privilege, and dispensed with the ceremonial pomp of the Washington and Adams presidencies. He was known to greet foreign dignitaries in his slippers. Another champion of the common man, President Andrew Jackson celebrated his inauguration with a raucous open-house party, at which inebriated guests made off with White House furnishings. This sort of official humility tempered – to some extent – the aristocratic pretensions of Washington high society.

Over drinks at Suter's tavern in Georgetown, Washington persuaded local landowners to sell their holdings to the government for $66 an acre. In March 1791 the African American mathematician Benjamin Banneker and surveyor Andrew Ellicott mapped out a diamond-shaped territory that spanned the Potomac and Anacostia Rivers. Its four corners were at the cardinal points of the compass, and it embraced the river ports of Georgetown and Alexandria (the latter eventually returned to Virginia). Pierre Charles L'Enfant, a French officer in the Revolutionary War, sketched plans for a grand European-style capital of monumental buildings and majestic boulevards. It was named the 'Territory of Columbia' (to honor Christopher Columbus), while the federal city within would be called 'the city of Washington'.

L'Enfant, despite his great vision for the city, would be dismissed within a year. He refused to answer to anyone aside from Washington, and when he challenged the commissioning authority above him, he was eventually fired. Nevertheless, his plan for the city would play a major role in its eventual design – and no one, aside from Washington, had a greater influence upon its development. After Washington fired his planner, land speculators grabbed prized properties and buildings sprang up haphazardly along mucky lanes. In 1793, construction began on the President's House and the Capitol, the geographic center points of the city. In 1800, John Adams became the first president to occupy the still uncompleted mansion. His wife Abigail hung the family's laundry in the East Room. The city remained a half-built, sparsely populated work in progress.

City residents for their part still associated themselves with the states from which they'd come. This began to change in 1801 when DC residents lost the right to vote in Virginia and Maryland elections. According to the Constitution, Congress alone would control the federal district, which intentionally or not, disenfranchised District residents. In 1820, DC held its first mayoral and city council elections, which voters took part in – though this would not always be the case.

WAR OF 1812: WASHINGTON BURNS

In the early 19th century, the young nation had yet to become a formidable force in world affairs. US merchants and seamen were regularly bullied on the high seas by the British Navy. Responding to congressional hawks, President James Madison declared war in 1812. In

1862	1864	1865
Washington becomes an army camp as the Civil War continues. President Lincoln issues the Emancipation Proclamation, freeing all slaves. By the end of the Civil War, some four million African Americans will be freed.	The war comes to Washington when the Confederate army attacks Fort Stevens – the only battle fought on capital soil. The Union army prevails.	The Confederate army surrenders. Five days later Lincoln is assassinated. Andrew Johnson takes office and does little to help newly freed blacks. For his incompetence, he is impeached and nearly removed from office.

retaliation for the razing of York (Toronto) by US troops, the British assaulted Washington. Work was barely complete on the Capitol in August 1814, when redcoats marched into Washington and sacked and burned the city's most important buildings (but left private houses largely unharmed). President Madison fled to the Virginia suburbs. Upon returning, the president took up temporary residence in the Octagon (p69), the home of Colonel John Tayloe, where he ratified the Treaty of Ghent, which ended the war. He remained here until the refurbishing of the White House was complete.

Although the British were expelled and the city rebuilt, Washington was slow to recover. A congressional initiative to abandon the dispirited capital was lost by just nine votes.

SLAVERY IN THE FEDERAL CITY

When Congress first convened in Washington in 1800, the city had about 14,000 residents. It was even then a heavily African American populated town: slaves and free blacks composed 29% of the population. Free blacks lived in the port of Georgetown, where a vibrant African American community emerged. They worked alongside and socialized with the city's slaves.

Since its introduction in Jamestown colony in 1619, slave labor had become an essential part of the regional tobacco economy. In 1800, more than half of the nation's 700,000 slaves lived in Maryland and Virginia. The capital of America's slave trade at that time, Washington, DC, contained slave markets and holding pens. Slavers conducted a highly profitable business buying slaves locally in DC and selling them to Southern plantations.

The city's slave population steadily declined throughout the 19th century, while the number of free blacks rose. They migrated to the city, establishing their own churches and schools.

Washington, DC, became a front line in the intensifying conflict between the North and South over slavery. The city was a strategic stop on the clandestine Underground Railroad, shuttling fugitive slaves to freedom in the northern states. The abolitionist movement fueled further racial tensions. In 1835, the Snow Riots erupted as white mobs set loose on black Washingtonians. When the rampage subsided, legislation was passed restricting the economic rights of the city's free blacks. At last, Congress outlawed the slave trade in Washington in 1850; the District Emancipation Act abolished slavery outright in 1862.

THE CIVIL WAR & ITS AFTERMATH

The 1860 election of Abraham Lincoln meant that the office of president would no longer protect Southern interests in the increasingly irreconcilable rift over slavery. Rather than abide by the electoral outcome, Southern secessionists opted to exit the Union, igniting a horrific four-year war that would leave over half a million dead. Washington was a prized target and the frontlines of fighting often came quite near the capital. Indeed when the war began, city residents (including Lincoln) remained fearful of a siege from the Confederates, whose campfires were visible just across the Potomac in Virginia. Had Maryland joined the Confederate side – and it very nearly did – the capital would have been completely isolated from the North, with disastrous results for the city and country. A ring of earthwork forts was hastily erected, but Washington saw only one battle on its soil: Confederate General Jubal Early's unsuccessful attack on Fort Stevens in northern DC, in July 1864. Nevertheless, Washingtonians lived in constant anxiety, as bloody battles raged nearby at Antietam, Gettysburg and Manassas (p222).

1865–67	1870–80	1901
After the war, Congress establishes the Freedman's Bureau to help former slaves transition to free society. In 1867 Howard University, the nation's first African American university, is founded. Blacks compose nearly half the city's population.	Washington experiences a postwar boom, with a growth in commerce and a doubling of population. Board of Public Works 'Boss' Shepherd helps modernize the city with paved streets, sewers, gaslights and parks.	The McMillan Commission unveils a new plan for the rapidly growing capital. L'Enfant's original design is revived, which beautifies the Mall with clean lines and impressive monuments, reclaims marshlands and solidifies the grandeur of Washington.

FROM SLAVE TO STATESMAN: FREDERICK DOUGLASS

Born Frederick Augustus Washington Bailey in 1818 on a slave plantation along Maryland's Eastern Shore, Frederick Douglass is remembered as one of the country's most influential and outstanding black 19th-century leaders.

In 1838, at 20 years old, he escaped wretched treatment at the hands of Maryland planters and established himself as a freeman in New Bedford, Massachusetts, eventually working for abolitionist William Lloyd Garrison's antislavery paper, the *Liberator*. His years as a slave had led Douglass to a profound personal truth: 'Men are whipped oftenist who are whipped easiest.' After his escape, he took his new last name from a character in the Sir Walter Scott book, *The Lady of the Lake*. Largely self-educated, Douglass had a natural gift for eloquence. In 1841, he won the admiration of New England abolitionists with an impromptu speech at an antislavery convention, introducing himself as 'a recent graduate from the institution of slavery,' with his 'diploma' (ie whip marks on his back). The Massachusetts Anti-Slavery Society hired Douglass, and he traveled the free states as an energetic spokesman for abolition and the Underground Railroad.

Douglass' effectiveness so angered proslavery forces that his supporters urged him to flee to England to escape seizure and punishment under the Fugitive Slave Law. He followed their advice and kept lecturing in England until admirers contributed enough money ($710.96) to enable him to purchase his freedom and return home in 1847.

Douglass then became the self-proclaimed 'station master and conductor' of the Underground Railroad in Rochester, New York, working with other famed abolitionists like Harriet Tubman and John Brown. In 1860, Douglass campaigned for Abraham Lincoln, and when the Civil War broke out, helped raise two regiments of black soldiers – the Massachusetts 54th and 55th – to fight for the Union.

After the war, Douglass went to Washington to lend his support to the 13th, 14th and 15th Constitutional Amendments, which abolished slavery, granted citizenship to former slaves and guaranteed citizens the right to vote. He later became US marshal for Washington and the US minister to Haiti (the country's first black ambassador).

In 1895, Douglass died at his Anacostia home, Cedar Hill, now the Frederick Douglass National Historic Site (p83). His funeral was held at DC's historic Metropolitan AME Church, 1518 M St NW, where one speaker mourned him in words that illustrated what Douglass had meant to black Washington: 'Howl, fir tree, for the Cedar of Lebanon has fallen.'

As the war raged on, soldiers, volunteers, civil servants and ex-slaves flooded into the capital. Within three months of the first shots fired at Fort Sumter, over 50,000 enlistees descended on the capital to join the Union Army. Throughout the war, Washington would serve as an important rearguard position for troop encampments and supply operations. Among those who spent time here were local resident Matthew Brady, whose compelling photographs provide a vivid document of the war. Poet Walt Whitman was also a Washington resident then, volunteering at a makeshift hospital in the converted Patent Office – today the National Portrait Gallery (p90); his poem 'The Wound Dresser' is based on his experiences tending the injured and dying. This building, incidentally, also hosted President Lincoln's inauguration ball, after his re-election in 1865.

Lincoln's second term would be short-lived. One month later – and five days after Confederate General Robert E Lee surrendered to Union General Ulysses S Grant at Appomattox – Lincoln was assassinated by John Wilkes Booth in downtown Washington at Ford's Theatre (p91).

The Civil War had a lasting impact on the city. The war strengthened the power of the federal government, marking the first efforts to conscript young men into military service and to collect income tax from private households. Warfare brought new bureaucracies, workers and buildings to the capital. Between the war's start and end, the city's population nearly doubled to more than 130,000. One of the largest influxes of newcomers was freed blacks.

1916–19	1920s	1931
WWI attracts thousands of people to Washington for the administration of the war. Following the armistice, decommissioned soldiers and civilians look for work, and festering racial tensions lead to the violent race riots of 1919.	Women win the right to vote in 1920. The '20s also see an African American cultural boom, led by Ella Fitzgerald and native son Duke Ellington; U St becomes known as the Great Black Way.	The Great Depression devastates the country. In 1931 Hunger Marchers protest in the capital followed by encampments of 20,000 jobless WWI vets known as the Bonus Army.

Vice-president Andrew Johnson, a southerner from Tennessee, assumed the presidency following Lincoln's death, but did little to help the freed African Americans; he even vetoed the first Civil Rights bill (indeed scholars rate him among the country's worst presidents). Congress, however, did attempt to help blacks make the transition to free society, and in 1867 Howard University, the nation's first African American institute of higher learning, was founded. By this time, blacks composed nearly a quarter of the population.

Washington's economy was bolstered by a postwar boom. Although in some ways a Southern city, Washington was already part of the commercial networks of the north. The B&O Railroad connected the city via Baltimore to the industry of the northeast; while the Chesapeake and Ohio Canal opened a waterway to the agriculture of the Midwest. In 1871, President Ulysses S Grant appointed a Board of Public Works to upgrade the urban infrastructure and improve living conditions. The board was led by Alexander Shepherd, who energetically took on the assignment. He paved streets, put in sewers, installed gaslights, planted trees, filled in swamps and carved out parklands. But he also ran over budget by some $20 million and was sacked by Congress, who reclaimed responsibility for city affairs. 'Boss' Shepherd was the closest thing that DC would have to self-government for 100 years.

TURN OF THE AMERICAN CENTURY

As the 1900s began, the US asserted itself on the world stage, competing with Europe to extend its influence overseas. With the Spanish-American War and Theodore Roosevelt's presidency, the US had entered the Age of Empire.

In 1900, Senator James McMillan of Michigan formed an all-star city-planning commission to makeover the capital, whose population now surpassed a quarter-million. The McMillan plan effectively revived L'Enfant's vision of a resplendent capital on par with Europe's best cities. The plan proposed grand public buildings in the beaux arts style (see DC Beaux Arts Buildings, p38), which reconnected the city to its neoclassical republican roots, but with an eclectic flair. It was impressive, orderly and upper class. The plan entailed an extensive beautification project. It removed the scrubby trees and coal-fired locomotives that belched black smoke from the National Mall, and created the expansive lawn and reflecting pools that exist today.

The Mall became a showcase of the symbols of American ambition and power: monumental tributes to the founding fathers; the enshrinement of the Declaration of Independence and Constitution in a Greek-style temple; and the majestic Memorial Bridge leading to Arlington National Cemetery, hallowed ground of the nation's fallen warriors. Washington had become the nation's civic center, infused with the spirit of history, heroes and myths. The imagery was embraced by the country's budding political class.

The plan improved living conditions for middle-class public servants and professionals. New 'suburbs,' such as Woodley Park and Mt Pleasant, offered better-off residents a respite from the hot inner city, and electric trolleys crisscrossed the streets. Of course, the daily life of many Washingtonians was less promising. Impoverished slums like Murder Bay and Swamppoodle stood near government buildings, and about 20,000 poor blacks still dwelled in dirty alleyways.

A WORLD AND A CITY AT WAR

Two world wars and one Great Depression changed forever the place of Washington in American society. These events hastened a concentration of power in the federal government in general

1932–35	1941–44	1963
Roosevelt is elected president. His New Deal programs put people to work, and Washington sees a host of construction projects, including the National Archives and the Supreme Court.	The expanding federal government and its wartime bureaucracy lead to another population boom. More big projects are bankrolled, including construction of National Airport and the Pentagon.	Martin Luther King Jr leads the Civil Rights march on the National Mall. He delivers his 'I have a dream' speech on the steps of Lincoln Memorial before a crowd of 200,000.

and the executive branch in particular. National security and social welfare became the high-growth sectors of public administration. City life transformed from Southern quaintness into cosmopolitan clamor.

WWI witnessed a surge of immigration. The administration of war had an unquenchable thirst for clerks, soldiers, nurses and other military support staff. By war's end, the city's population was over half a million.

The 1920s brought prosperity to Washington and other parts of the country. In 1927, the city held its first Cherry Blossom Festival, which showcased the newly blossoming beauty along the riverfront, and civic pride grew as work begun by the McMillan Commission continued. The free-spending days wouldn't last. The stock market crash of 1929 heralded the dawn of the Great Depression, the severe economic downturn that had catastrophic implications for many Americans. As more and more lost their jobs and went hungry, people turned to Washington for help. Thousands gathered in Hunger Marches on Washington in 1931 and 1932; they were followed by some 40,000 protesters (17,000 jobless WWI vets and their families) who set up makeshift camps throughout the city, waiting for Congress to award them cash payment for service certificates issued in bonds – they became known as the Bonus Army. President Hoover ordered the US Army to evacuate them, and the troops attacked their encampments, killing several and wounding hundreds of others.

Franklin Roosevelt's New Deal extended the reach of the federal government. In regards to the Bonus Army, Roosevelt offered them work in the Civilian Conservation Corps and later building highways in the Florida Keys – unfortunately they were there when a category 5 hurricane swept through and over 200 veterans were killed. Federal regulators acquired greater power to intervene in business and financial affairs. Dozens of relief agencies were created to administer the social guarantees of the nascent welfare state. In Washington, New Deal work projects included tree planting on the Mall and the construction of public buildings, notably the massive National Archives and the Supreme Court.

The Great Depression didn't really end until the arrival of WWII, when Washington again experienced enormous growth. A burgeoning organizational infrastructure supported the new national security state. The US Army's city-based civilian employee roll grew from 7000 to 41,000 in the first year of the war. The world's largest office building, the Pentagon, was built across the river as the command headquarters. National Airport (today Reagan National) opened in 1941.

THE COLD WAR

The Cold War defined much of US foreign – and to some degree, domestic – policy in the decades following WWII. The United States' battle with the USSR was not fought face to face, but through proxy clients like Korea, Vietnam, Cambodia, Mozambique and Afghanistan – all were pawns in the geopolitical, economic and ideological battle. Red fever swept the US, as Washington organized witch hunts, like those investigated by HUAC (the House Committee on Un-American Activities), which aimed to blacklist communist subversives. Senator Joseph McCarthy also spread fear and paranoia, by stating there were communist spies and sympathizers operating inside the federal government. US presidents from Eisenhower to Reagan invoked the domino theory (if one country turns communist the next one will follow until a whole continent topples like a set of dominoes) – and used it as a justification to go to war.

1968	1969–71	1974
Martin Luther King Jr is assassinated in Memphis; Washington and other cities erupt in violence. Twelve people are killed in the ensuing riots, with small businesses torched. Some 13,000 troops are called in to quell the violence.	As the disastrous war in Vietnam claims thousands of American lives, many citizens come to Washington to protest, Over 500,000 march in 1969, followed by hundreds of thousands more in 1970 and 1971.	Five burglars working for President Nixon are arrested breaking into the Democratic campaign headquarters at the Watergate Hotel. The ensuing brouhaha and senate investigation leads to President Nixon's resignation.

Some citizens and communities even built special underground shelters (stocked with canned food and bottled water) as a refuge in the event of nuclear war.

The Cuban Missile Crisis, which took place over 12 days in October 1962, brought the United States and the Soviet Union perilously close to nuclear war, and some historians believe that without the effective diplomacy of John F Kennedy and Secretary of State Robert McNamara, the nation would have gone to battle. (Frighteningly, the US Joint Chiefs of Staff all advocated a pre-emptive, full-scale invasion.) Luckily, the president resisted using force while allowing Soviet President Nikita Khrushchev to withdraw the missiles without losing face.

During the Cold War, many covert battles were waged on foreign soil. Perhaps the most famous was the Iran-Contra affair in the 1980s, during Ronald Reagan's tenure as president. Staff in his administration, along with the CIA, secretly and illegally sold arms to Iran, a US enemy, and then used the proceeds to finance the Contras, an anti-communist guerilla army in Nicaragua.

The Cold War furthered the concentration of political power in Washington-based bureaucracies. It attracted new breeds of policy specialists – macro-economists, international experts and social engineers. They comprised a better-educated and more prosperous middle class. This trend continued unabated until the Reagan presidency. Even then, the foundations of 'big government' proved too firm to undermine. Candidate Reagan vowed to abolish the Commerce Department once elected. Not only did the bureaucracy survive his tenure, but it constructed a fabulous new office building, ironically named for Reagan himself.

SEGREGATION & THE CIVIL RIGHTS MOVEMENT

In the early 20th century, Washington adopted racial segregation policies, like those of the South. Its business establishments and public spaces became, in practice if not in law, 'whites only.' The 'progressive' Woodrow Wilson administration reinforced discrimination by refusing to hire black federal employees and insisting on segregated government offices.

Following WWI, decommissioned soldiers returned en masse from the front, bringing to a head festering racial tensions in society. In the steamy summer of 1919, the tinderbox ignited when a white mob marched through the streets attacking at random black residents with bricks, pipes and, later, guns. In the following two days, whites and blacks alike mobilized and the violence escalated. President Wilson called in 2000 troops to put an end to the chaos, but by then nine people had been killed (dozens more would die from their wounds) and hundreds injured. It was but a foreshadowing for more chronic race riots in the future.

In response, organized hate groups tried, without much success, to organize in the capital. In 1925, the Ku Klux Klan marched on the Mall. Nonetheless, Washington was a black cultural capital in the early 20th century. Shaw and LeDroit Park, near Howard University, sheltered a lively black-owned business district, and black theater and music flourished along U St NW, which became known as the Great Black Way – Washington's own version of the Harlem Renaissance. Southern blacks continued to move to the city in search of better economic opportunities. Between 1920 and 1930, Washington's black population jumped 20%. Citywide segregation eased somewhat with the New Deal (which brought new black federal workers to the capital) and WWII (which brought lots more).

In 1939, the DC-based Daughters of the American Revolution barred the black contralto Marian Anderson from singing at Constitution Hall. At Eleanor Roosevelt's insistence, Anderson

1975	1976	1981
Following the Home Rule Act passed in 1973, disenfranchised Washingtonians are finally given the right to effectively govern themselves. The city's first mayoral election is held, with voters electing Walter Washington – DC's first African American mayor.	Metrorail opens to serve the growing suburban community, with lines that will eventually cover more than 100 miles. Despite intense lobbying by the automobile industry, several destructive freeway projects through the city are never realized.	Washington, like other American cities, enters a period of urban blight. Reagan survives an assassination attempt outside the Washington Hilton. The attack permanently disables press secretary James Brady, who becomes a leading advocate for gun control.

instead sang at the Lincoln Memorial before an audience of 200,000. That was the beginning of the growing movement toward equality – though the struggle would be long with demonstrations, sit-ins, boycotts and lawsuits.

Parks and recreational facilities were legally desegregated in 1954; schools followed soon thereafter. President John F Kennedy appointed the city's first black federal commissioner in 1961. The Home Rule Act was approved in 1973, giving the city some autonomy from its federal overseers. The 1974 popular election of Walter Washington brought the first black mayor to office. The capital became one of the most prominent African American–governed cities in the country.

Washington hosted key events in the national Civil Rights struggle. In 1963, Reverend Martin Luther King Jr led the March on Washington to lobby for passage of the Civil Rights Act. His stirring 'I have a dream' speech, delivered before 200,000 people on the steps of the Lincoln Memorial, was a defining moment of the campaign. The assassination of Reverend King in Memphis in 1968 sent the nation reeling. Race riots erupted in DC – and in over 100 other American cities. The city exploded in two nights of riots and arson (centered on 14th and U Sts NW in the Shaw district). Twelve people died, over 1000 were injured and hundreds of mostly black-owned businesses were torched. White residents fled the city en masse, and downtown Washington north of the Mall (especially the Shaw district) faded into decades of economic slump.

The legacy of segregation proved difficult to overcome. For the next quarter-century, white and black Washington grew further apart. By 1970, the city center's population declined to 750,000, while the wealthier suburbs boomed to nearly three million. When the sleek, federally funded Metrorail system opened in 1976, it bypassed the poorer black neighborhoods in favor of linking downtown with the largely white suburbs.

DECAY & DECLINE

By the end of the 1960s no one could ignore the declining situation in Vietnam, a conflict the US had entered in the 1950s. President Lyndon Johnson, who was lauded for his ambitious Civil Rights and social programs, sank his reputation on the disastrous war in Vietnam. Americans mobilized by the hundreds of thousands to protest against a bloody and wholly unnecessary war.

The political upheaval that began in the 1960s continued unchecked into the next decade. The year 1970 marked the first time DC was granted a nonvoting delegate to the House of Representatives. Three years later the Home Rule Act paved the way for the District's first mayoral election in more than a century.

These were two rare positives in an otherwise gloomy decade. The city's most famous scandal splashed across the world's newspapers when operatives of President Nixon were arrested breaking into the Democratic National Committee campaign headquarters at the Watergate Hotel (p70). The ensuing cover-up and Nixon's disgraceful exit was not a shining moment in presidential history.

Meanwhile, life on the streets was no more glorious, as neighborhoods continued to decay; crack-cocaine hit District streets with a vengeance and housing projects turned into war zones. By the late 1980s, DC had earned the tagline of 'Murder Capital of America'. In truth, urban blight was hitting most American cities.

1990–94	1999	2000
In 1990, Mayor Marion Barry is arrested after being videotaped smoking crack. His arrest angers supporters, who decry the FBI 'entrapment'. In 1994, after his release from prison, Barry is re-elected to a fourth term.	The Monica Lewinsky scandal breaks; Bill Clinton becomes the first president since Andrew Johnson (in 1868) to be impeached. Washingtonians elect the sober, less-controversial Anthony Williams as the city's fourth mayor.	Washington's real-estate boom is underway, with gentrification transforming formerly black neighborhoods. George W Bush is elected president in a much-disputed election.

Jimmy Carter became president in 1977. A 'malaise' marked his tenure. Gas prices, unemployment and inflation all climbed to all-time highs. The taking of American hostages in Iran in 1979, and his perceived bungling of their release, effectively ended his political career. In November 1980, Ronald Reagan, a former actor and California governor, was elected president.

Reagan, who was ideologically opposed to big government, nevertheless presided over enormous growth of bureaucratic Washington, particularly in the military-industrial complex.

Local politics entered an unusual period when Marion Barry, a veteran of the Civil Rights struggle, was elected mayor in 1978. Combative and charismatic, he became a racially polarizing figure in the city. On January 18, 1990, Barry and companion, ex-model Hazel 'Rasheeda' Moore, were arrested in a narcotics sting at the Vista Hotel. The FBI and DC police arrested the mayor for crack-cocaine possession resulting in his memorable quote: '…set up…bitch set me up,' see also p45.

When Barry emerged from jail, his supporters, believing he'd been framed, re-elected him to a fourth and lackluster term. As city revenues fell under his term, Congress lost patience and seized control of the city, ending yet another episode in Home Rule.

THE 21ST CENTURY

The 2000 presidential election went off with a history-making glitch. On election night, November 7, the media prematurely declared the winner twice, based on exit-poll speculations, before finally concluding that the Florida race outcome was too close to call. It would eventually take a month before the election was officially certified. Numerous court challenges and recounts proceeded after Al Gore lost to George W Bush, despite winning the popular vote.

Despite much back and forth and a final intervention by the Supreme Court, Gore eventually gave up, grew a beard and proceeded into political obscurity until 2006 when he popped up in media gossip circles again with the release of his environmental blockbuster documentary, *An Inconvenient Truth*. Gore was once again in the spotlight when the film won an Oscar in 2007; later that year, the former vice-president shared the Nobel Peace Prize with the Intergovernmental Panel on Climate Change.

On September 11, 2001, 30 minutes after the attack on New York's World Trade Center, a plane departing Washington Dulles International Airport bound for Los Angeles was hijacked and redirected toward Washington. Speculation was that the hijackers' primary objective was the White House, but they opted for a more exposed target. The plane crashed into the Pentagon's west side, penetrating the building's third ring. Sixty-six passengers and crew, as well as 125 Pentagon personnel, were killed in the suicide attack.

Like most Americans, Washingtonians had no living memory of war on their territory. The shock of terrorism deeply scarred the nation's public psyche.

In the wake of the attack, prominent media and political figures received lethal doses of anthrax in the mail. Several congressional staffers were infected and two DC postal workers died. Though unsolved, the anthrax mailings were eventually attributed to a domestic source.

Over a three-week period in the autumn of 2002, area residents were once again terrorized by unseen assailants. A pair of serial snipers went on a shooting spree in the Washington suburbs; 10 people were dead and thousands frightened before the snipers were finally apprehended by police.

2001	2005	2008–09
Planes hijacked by terrorists destroy the World Trade Center in New York and crash into the Pentagon. A fourth plane, probably intended for the capital or the White House, crashes in Pennsylvania.	As Montreal weeps, Washington receives a new professional baseball team, the Washington Nationals (and former Expos). President George W Bush is sworn in to his second term. Protests over the war in Iraq continue.	Barack Obama becomes the first African American President in US history. His agenda after taking office is ambitious: rescue the faltering US economy, reform the problematic healthcare system and address the escalating war in Afghanistan.

Following these incidents, Washington experienced increasing security measures and declining tourism – though visitor numbers eventually rebounded. And since then, the city has regained its vitality, while losing none of its vigilance over what *might* happen.

Meanwhile president Bush's tenure in office was marred by controversy on many fronts. The war in Iraq – launched in 2003 under the pretense of seizing Iraq's (nonexistent it turns out) stockpiles of weapons of mass destruction – raged until the end of his second term, and sent the government deeply into debt. Bush was also criticized for the bungling of Federal relief efforts to victims of Hurricane Katrina – which devastated New Orleans in 2005. Even Republicans were reluctant to be associated with Bush, his approval ratings plummeting to a historic low (around 22%) by the time he left office.

The election of 2008 featured one of the most hotly debated (and most expensive) presidential contests in American history. In the end, Barack Obama, who seemed an unlikely candidate, won the election and immediately entered history as the first African American to be elected president.

Americans turned out in huge numbers for inauguration day in 2009. On a cold day in January, over one million crowded the mall to watch the 45th president taking the oath of office. Obama, who ran on a platform of hope and change in an era of increasingly divisive American politics, set to work immediately. Following the financial meltdown in 2008, the Obama administration pumped money into the flailing economy. He also took on the growing crisis in Afghanistan, although his biggest challenge – an issue that some analysts say he's staked his presidency on – is the complicated issue of health-care reform (currently some 40 million Americans lack health care, and the US remains the only industrialized nation not to provide universal healthcare for its citizens).

At press time, Obama was weathering attacks from both liberals and conservatives: 'too much big-government spending' according to some Republicans, 'too much compromising to Republicans' according to some Democrats.

ARTS

Washington is the showcase of American arts, home to such prestigious venues as the National Gallery and the Kennedy Center. The National Symphony Orchestra and the National Theatre, meanwhile, host top-notch music and theater to represent the nation. The result is that Washington's arts scene – where it is most visible and most acclaimed – is national rather than local in scope.

It is a blessing for local culture vultures, for sure. Access to the nation's (and the world's) top artists and musicians is reserved for residents of only a few cities; DC is among them because it was deemed appropriate for a political capital.

Often overlooked, however, is another arts scene – a scene representative of DC and not necessarily the USA. It is edgier, blacker, more organic and more experimental. It is colored by the experiences of the city's African American and immigrant populations, lending diversity and ethnicity. It dances around the edges of the more conservative national scene and discreetly tests its boundaries. The Arena Stage, the Corcoran Gallery and Dance Place are examples of the innovative, experimental venues that draw on local talent and themes in their productions. Loads of smaller art galleries and community theaters around the city contribute to the vibrant arts scene. For venue details, see the Arts chapter (p188).

MUSEUMS & ART GALLERIES

Visual arts in DC has three faces: the vast holdings of the National Gallery of Art (p58) and the Smithsonian Institution (see Thank You, James, p61); the private collections and special exhibits at the Corcoran Gallery of Art (p66) and the Phillips Collection (p95); and the wealth of small commercial galleries supporting local, national and international artists.

The first hardly needs an explanation. The National Gallery of Art comprises two buildings filled with paintings, sculpture, photography and decorative arts from the Middle Ages to the present. The Smithsonian Institution operates the Freer Gallery, the Hirshhorn Museum & Sculpture Garden, the National Museum of African Art, the National Museum of American Art, the National Portrait Gallery (p90), the Renwick Gallery (p66) and the Sackler Gallery (p60) – an impressive collection to be sure. From ancient handicrafts to modern sculpture, the scope of the works at these national museums is vast.

The Corcoran and the Phillips are private museums that were built from the collections of philanthropic art lovers. The Corcoran Gallery has a renowned collection of 20th-century American prints, photography and painting. The Phillips Collection holds impressionist and modern masterpieces from both Europe and America. Both museums host special exhibits to lure visitors off the National Mall and into their decked-out halls.

The city has been pumping substantial sums of money into the arts lately. Over the last decade over $1.5 billion has been spent renovating or constructing new museums and memorials. Especially pertinent to art lovers was the superb, six-year, $283-million renovation of the old Patent Office Building, home to the National Museum of American Art and the National Portrait Gallery. Aside from the two museums, the building is now home to a unique conservation facility with floor-to-ceiling glass windows that allow visitors to view art conservators at work.

Small Galleries

Lesser known, but no less important, DC is riddled with grassroots art galleries. Many are owned or operated by the artists themselves. This scene has blossomed since the 1990s, fuelled by DC's reinvigorated neighborhoods and increasingly cosmopolitan population. It is no longer a given that a talented artist will flee to New York to make it big. Some names to look out for on the DC art scene include Colby Caldwell, Steve Cushner, Sam Gilliam, Ryan Hackett, Jae Ko and Nancy Sansom Reynolds. DC can boast bona fide art districts in Dupont Circle and Downtown. The Old Torpedo Factory (p124) in Old Town Alexandria is also an incredible conglomeration of creative minds. These are the places to see the face of DC art at its most pure.

LITERATURE

Washington's literary legacy is, not surprisingly, deeply entwined with American political history. The city's best-known early literature consists of writings and books that hammered out the machinery of American democracy. From Thomas Jefferson's *Notes on the State of Virginia* to James Madison's *The Federalist Papers* and Abraham Lincoln's historic speeches and proclamations, this literature fascinates modern readers – not only because it is the cornerstone of the US political system, but because of the grace and beauty of its prose. Skill with the pen is, alas, no longer a notable characteristic of US presidents.

Apart from politicians' writings, 19th-century Washington literature was created primarily by authors and journalists who resided here only temporarily, drawn to DC by circumstance, professional obligation or wanderlust. Walt Whitman's *The Wound Dresser* and *Specimen Days* and Louisa May Alcott's *Hospital Sketches* were based upon the authors' harrowing experiences as Civil War nurses at Washington's hospitals. Mark Twain had an ill-starred (and short) career as a senator's speechwriter, memorialized in *Washington in 1868*.

Frederick Douglass (1818–95), the abolitionist, editor, memoirist and former slave (see From Slave to Statesman: Frederick Douglass, p23), is one of Washington's most respected writers. His seminal antislavery works *The Life & Times of Frederick Douglass* and *My Bondage & My Freedom* were written in DC, where Douglass lived on Capitol Hill and in Anacostia.

Henry Adams (1838–1918), grandson of President John Adams, often invited DC's literati to salons at his mansion on Lafayette Sq, which became the literary center of the day. His brilliant *Democracy* was the forerunner of many political-scandal novels of the 20th century. His later autobiography, *The Education of Henry Adams,* provides a fascinating insider's account of Washington high society during this period.

In the early 20th century, another salon often took place across town at 15th and S Sts in Shaw. Artists and writers often gathered here, at poet Georgia Douglas Johnson's home, which became the center of the Harlem Renaissance in DC. Her guests included African American poets Langston Hughes and Paul Dunbar.

Another member of this circle was Jean Toomer, author of *Cane.* Not a novel in the traditional sense, Toomer's seminal work is part poetry, part prose and part play. The book – while lacking a continuous plot or defined characters – is among the strongest representations of Harlem Renaissance literature.

BACKGROUND ARTS

In DC, the Harlem Renaissance is sometimes called the New Negro movement, named after the famous volume by Howard University professor Alain Locke. *The New Negro* – the bible of the Renaissance – is a collection of essays, poems and stories written by Locke and his colleagues. The writing is energetic and subversive; as a snapshot of the Renaissance and the African American experience it is invaluable.

Throughout the 20th century, Washington literature remained a deeply political beast, defined by works such as Carl Bernstein and Bob Woodward's *All the President's Men* (1974) and John Kennedy's *Profiles in Courage* (1955). Perhaps the most eloquent poem about DC is Robert Lowell's *July in Washington*, written about the poet's participation in a 1968 political protest.

Many more purely literary writers have appeared on the scene, too. The contemporary writer who is best able to capture the streets and sounds and sights of DC in his writing is Edward Jones. His National Book Award nominee, *Lost in the City* (1992) is an incredible collection of 14 stories set in inner-city DC in the 1960s and 1970s. Each recounts a tale of an individual facing the complexity of city life in a strangely hopeful way. The portrayal of the city – like the characters themselves – is real and raw.

Marita Golden is a modern African American writer whose novels about contemporary African American families dealing with betrayal, loss, growth and reconciliation have attracted a loyal following. *The Edge of Heaven* (1997) is set in DC, where an accomplished 20-year-old student confronts her confusion about reuniting with her parents upon her mother's release from four years in prison.

Paul Kafka-Gibbons addresses the touchy subject of marriage in his second novel, *Dupont Circle* (2001). From the title (and setting), you might guess the subject is gay marriage, but the novel does not exclude anyone. Intertwining plots revolve around three couples – only one is gay but all three are untraditional – who deal with the expectations and realities of being in a relationship. Kafka-Gibbons won the Los Angeles Times Book Prize for his first novel *Love <Enter>* (1997), which does not take place in DC, but his second novel has not been as well received.

Native Washingtonian Gore Vidal often aims his satirical pieces squarely at his hometown. His six-volume series of historical novels about the American past includes *Washington, DC* (1967), an insightful examination of the period from the New Deal to the McCarthy era from the perspective of the capital. *The Smithsonian Institution* (1998) is a fantastical historical account of a 13-year-old boy who travels through time to save the world. Readers who can throw all caution to the wind and follow Vidal without skepticism will enjoy the weird and wonderful ride.

Advise and Consent (1959) is Allen Drury's fictional account of Alger Hiss' nomination as Secretary of State under Franklin D Roosevelt. The novel brilliantly portrays the conflicting personal and political motivations of his characters – an eye-opening revelation of what goes on inside the US Senate.

top picks

WASHINGTON, DC IN LITERATURE

- *American Tabloid* by James Ellroy (1994) A favorite of historical fiction, this epic tells one version of the Camelot years and the conspiracy to end all conspiracies – the assassination of JFK. It manages to work the Mafia, rogue CIA agents, ruthless Cubans, J Edgar Hoover, Howard Hughes, drugs, and a couple of cops and FBI guys into one crazy story.

- *Advise and Consent* by Allen Drury (1981) A compelling fictional account of personalities and politics in the US Senate.

- *The Dream Keeper and Other Poems* by Langston Hughes (1996) A collection of poignant poems written especially for kids.

- *Hits Below the Beltway* by Dave Barry (2002) Not exactly literature, but still a hilarious account of history and politics by one of America's best-loved columnists.

- *Lost in the City* by Edward Jones (2003) Evocative short stories about people and places in DC.

- *Sammy's Hill* by Kristin Gore (2005) A story of life and love on Capitol Hill. Told through the eyes of 26-year-old Samantha Joyce, a self-deprecating health-care policy advisor to an Ohio senator. Gore, aside from being the former vice-president's daughter, is best known for her comedic writing on shows like *Saturday Night Live*.

BACKGROUND ARTS

Good writers search out conflict to give their stories significance and drive, but for many, the battles on the Hill are too bloodless. So they cross the Anacostia or venture up Rhode Island Ave into Northeast. This task of digging into DC's underclass has often been upheld by authors of the crime and noir genre, and *D.C. Noir* (2006), a collection of short stories edited by George Pelecanos, is as good an introduction to this world (literary and actual) as you'll find. As a bonus, the collection funnels some of the city's finest contemporary writing talent, including Kenji Jasper and Jennifer Howard, into one book. Pelecanos himself is one of the city's best scribes, an author who peppers his work with geographic references visitors can learn from and insiders can appreciate. *Right as Rain* (2001) and *The Night Gardener* (2006) are both excellent examples of his work, lessons on and adventures in DC's hard edge, and ripping good reads to boot.

The capital also generates a huge amount of short stories. Some of our favorites have been written by former *Washington Post* reporter Ward Just. His collection *The Congressman Who Loved Flaubert* (1973) is as dry, tragicomic, intelligent and human a rendering as you'll find of the Hill, as is his novel *Echo House* (1997).

Much of DC's best literary canon is nonfiction, direct commentary on America itself and, often, penned by her first citizens. Here we're specifically referring to the letters and speeches of presidents like Thomas Jefferson and Abraham Lincoln, whose works possess both insight and a depth of prose we're hoping a certain Mr Obama can match (critics from *Time* to *The Guardian* have called *Dreams of My Father* (1995) the best memoir by a major American politician in decades). In the meantime, while we've seen great reads that illuminate both DC's politics and predators, we're still awaiting the writer who can capture what Washington is becoming, a city still marked by divisions between haves and have-nots but not defined by them (if ever it was) either.

On a less elevated note, DC has also inspired thousands of potboilers. Tom Clancy, a northern Virginia resident and creator of innumerable right-wing thrillers, sometimes features Washington's apocalyptic destruction – see *Debt of Honor* (1994) and *Executive Orders* (1996) for much President-and-Congress offing. Along those lines, conspiracy theorists will find a selection of DC-related titles to fuel the imagination. Dan Brown's recent *The Lost Symbol* (2009) brings his Harvard 'symbologist' to the nation's capital on a suspenseful – if formulaic – journey into the hidden secrets of DC's coded (Freemason-filled) history.

DC has also been the setting for chick lit in the past years – even Al Gore's daughter, Kristin Gore, penned a novel, *Sammy's Hill* (2004). The most popular book of this genre is probably Jessica Cutler's salacious *Washingtonienne* (2005), which is an only slightly fictionalized tell-all about her Capitol Hill sexual liaisons. Cutler was fired from Senator Mike DeWine's (R-Ohio) office after the online blog she kept for friends about 'the presidential appointee who gives her cash after each tryst' exploded into the city's scandal of the month.

For a fine profile of the Washington literary scene, check out David Cutler's *Literary Washington: A Complete Guide to the Literary Life in the Nation's Capital* (1989).

MUSIC

Only in the capital can national orchestras coexist with rebellious punk, all under the rubric of the local music scene. That military marches and soulful go-go both reached their peaks under the watchful eye (and attentive ear) of DC fans is tribute to the city's electric – if eclectic – music scene.

In the early 20th century, segregation of entertainment venues meant that black Washington had to create its own arts scene – so it created one far more vibrant than anything white Washington could boast. Jazz, big band and swing flourished at clubs and theaters around DC and particularly in the Shaw district. Greats such as Duke Ellington (p34), Pearl Bailey, Shirley Horne, Johnny Hodges and Ben Webster all got their start in the clubs of U St NW. Today this district is reviving as new clubs and theaters open in the historic buildings in the area. After 30 years of neglect, the renowned Bohemian Caverns (p183) now hosts local soul-jazz music. But other venues in the area – like the Black Cat (p183) and the 9:30 Club (p183) – are now DC's premier venues for modern rock, blues and hip-hop. Shaw is not a re-creation of a historical fantasy: it is an organic area, shaped not only by its history but also by modern musical movements.

The scene at these venues is varied, but not particularly unique to DC. The exception – where DC really stands out musically – is where it builds on its local roots in go-go and punk. Go-go is an infectiously rhythmic dance music combining elements of funk, rap, soul and Latin percussion, which stomped onto the city scene in the 1970s. These days, go-go soul blends with hip-hop and reggae's rhythm – everybody dance now! Clubs playing 1980s dance and lounges with mellow house and trance are equally popular.

DC's hardcore take on punk, embodied by such bands as Fugazi and Dag Nasty, combined super-fast guitar with a socially conscious mindset and flourished at venues in the 1990s. Arlington-based Dischord Records, one of the country's most successful small labels, grew out of the punk scene and remains a fierce promoter of local bands. Check out *Banned in DC*, a photo book by Cynthia Connolly that documents the Washington punk scene of the 1970s and '80s. While punk is no longer the musical force it once was, its influence on grunge and other modern genres is undeniable. Local bands such as Dismemberment Plan and Dog Fashion Disco carry the post-punk torch.

Showing off its southern roots, DC has spawned some folk and country stars of its own, too, including Emmylou Harris, Mary Chapin Carpenter and John Fahey (who named his seminal folk record label Takoma for Takoma Park, his boyhood home). Folksy keyboardist Bruce Hornsby is a native of nearby Williamsburg, VA.

Popular African American R&B and soul artist Roberta Flack was raised in Arlington, VA. Before establishing her music career, she was the first black student teacher in an all-white school in posh Chevy Chase, Maryland. She was discovered at a respected Capitol Hill jazz club, Mr Henry's, where the owners eventually constructed an elaborate stage for her.

In the alternative rock area, nationally known acts include Jimmie's Chicken Shack, which got its start playing at the now-defunct WHFStival, formerly one of the biggest music festivals on the east coast.

---

top picks

WASHINGTON, DC PLAYLIST

Every city has a soundtrack, and DC is no exception. However, there is a noticeable lack of songs about the city – no one seems to leave their heart in Washington. The following playlist is a mixture of songs about DC and songs by Washington artists.

- '1 Thing' by Amerie
- 'Are You My Woman?' by the Chi-Lites
- 'Banned in DC' by Bad Brains
- 'Bustin' Loose' by Chuck Jones
- 'Chocolate City' by Parliament
- 'Do Right' by Jimmie's Chicken Shack
- '(Don't go back to) Rockville' by R.E.M.
- 'Don't Worry about the Government' by Talking Heads
- 'He Thinks He'll Keep Her' by Mary Chapin Carpenter
- 'Idiot Wind' by Bob Dylan
- 'I'm Just a Bill' by School House Rock
- 'It Don't Mean a Thing (If it Ain't Got that Swing)' by Duke Ellington
- 'Killing Me Softly with His Song' by Roberta Flack
- 'Radio King Orchestra' by Radio King Orchestra
- 'Red Dirt Girl' by Emmylou Harris
- 'Rock Creek Park' by The Blackbyrds
- 'Run Joe' by Chuck Jones
- 'The Way It Is' by Bruce Hornsby
- 'Waiting Room' by Fugazi
- 'Washington Bullets' by The Clash
- 'We the People' by Chuck Jones

PERFORMING ARTS

The capital's most visible musicians are the big boys – those from the weighty cultural landmarks like the National Symphony Orchestra (NSO; p192) and the Washington Opera (p193). For the most part, they are not doing anything new. At the NSO, directed by Leonard Slatkin, classical means classical. Placido Domingo directs the Washington Opera. Repertoire and productions tend to lean toward the traditional side but are technically sound – highlighted by special occasions when Domingo conducts or sings. Diva Denyce Graves, graduate of the local Duke Ellington School of Performing Arts, occasionally graces its stage and thrills her hometown audiences.

A national orchestra of sorts is the Marine Corps Marching Band, based at the Marine Barracks (p84) in Southeast DC. Back in the late 19th century, military marching-band music reached its apotheosis (such as it was) in the work of John Philip Sousa, who directed the Marine Corps

THE DUKE

'My road runs from Ward's Place to my grandmother's at Twentieth and R, to Seatan Street, around to 8th Street, back up to T Street, through LeDroit Park to Sherman Avenue,' wrote DC's most famous musical son, jazz immortal Edward Kennedy 'Duke' Ellington (1899–1974), describing his childhood in Washington's Shaw district. In the segregated DC of the early 20th century, Shaw hosted one of the country's finest black arts scenes – drawing famed actors, musicians and singers to perform at venues like the Howard Theatre and Bohemian Caverns (p183) – so the Duke took root in rich soil.

As a tot, Ellington purportedly first tackled the keyboard under the tutelage of a teacher by the name of Mrs Clink-scales. He honed his chops by listening to local ragtime pianists like Doc Perry, Louis Thomas and Louis Brown at Frank Holliday's T St poolroom. His first composition, written at 16, was the 'Soda Fountain Rag'; next came 'What You Gonna Do When the Bed Breaks Down?' The handsome, suave young Duke played hops and cabarets all over black Washington before decamping to New York in 1923.

There, Ellington started out as a Harlem stride pianist, performing at Barron's and the Hollywood Club; but he soon moved to the famed Cotton Club, where he matured into an innovative bandleader, composer and arranger. He collaborated with innumerable artists – including Louis Armstrong and Ella Fitzgerald – but his most celebrated collaboration was with composer/arranger Billy Strayhorn, who gave the Ellington Orchestra its theme, 'Take the "A" Train,' in 1941. Strayhorn worked with Duke throughout his life, collaborating on later works like *Such Sweet Thunder* (1957) and *The Far East Suite* (1964).

Ellington's big-band compositions, with their infectious melodies, harmonic sophistication and ever-present swing, made him one of the 20th century's most revered American composers and his ability to craft arrangements highlighting the singular talents of his musicians made him the foremost bandleader of his time. His huge volume of work – more than 1500 pieces – is preserved in its entirety at the Smithsonian Institution in his old hometown.

For more on the Duke, check out his witty memoir *Music Is My Mistress*, which details his DC childhood and later accomplishments.

Marching Band for many years (and was born and buried nearby). In this era of amped-up patriotism, this genre remains alive and well: the band still performs his work today.

A great resource for information about the contemporary local music scene is the DC Music Network (www.dcmusicnet.com).

THEATER & COMEDY

Political comedy and theater are regular fixtures of the DC arts scene. Ford's Theatre (p91) – site of Lincoln's assassination – holds its place in time by presenting traditional, Americana-themed productions. If you're looking for comedy, then head to the Ronald Reagan Building and International Trade Center downtown to catch a performance by the capital's foremost comedy troupe, the Capitol Steps Political Satire (p193). The group cuts up exclusively with biting satire of the goings-on in the White House and on Capitol Hill.

Such theatrical ventures certainly have their place in the nation's capital. There is more, however, to theater in DC. Most Broadway shows will eventually find their way to the National Theatre (p191) or the Kennedy Center (p190). The Arena Stage (p190), home to one of the country's oldest troupes, was the first theater outside of New York to win a Tony and continues to stage diverse productions by new playwrights. Over the course of 25 years, smaller companies like Studio Theatre (p191) have established a strong presence. For almost as long, the Source Theatre (p191) has hosted the Annual Washington Theater Festival, a platform for new plays, workshops and the insanely popular 10-Minute Play Competition held in June. The Folger Shakespeare Library & Theatre (p190) gives new perspective to the Bard. The edgy Woolly Mammoth Theatre Co (p191) and the multicultural Gala Hispanic Theatre (p191) have moved to larger theaters.

What's exciting on the DC theater scene is the proliferation of brand-new companies and community theaters, stepping into the empty spaces that their predecessors have left behind. Acting guilds and theater groups are popping up on every stage in Shaw, Dupont Circle and Capitol Hill, pressing the limits of what theater can do. For example, heritage-based companies, such as Asian Stories in America and Theater J (p191), are highlighting the works of various ethnic groups. And the District of Columbia Arts Center (DCAC; p191) hosts the innovative Playback, where the audience provides stories to fuel the plot on stage.

CINEMA & TV

Hollywood directors can't resist the black limousines, white marble, counterintelligence sub-terfuges and political scandal that official Washington embodies. But local film buffs offer up two complaints about all this attention. First, unofficial Washington – the real place where real people live – might as well be Waikiki; few films are set anywhere other than Capitol Hill and it's a rare movie character that does not live in Georgetown (unless they live in the White House). Second, even the movies about official Washington fail to capture how the personalities and politics really work. Then again, since when does Hollywood capture how anything *really* works?

Hollywood's favorite theme for a Washington movie is the political naïf who stumbles into combat with corrupt capital-veterans. Such is the story in the preeminent Washington film *Mr Smith Goes to Washington,* in which Jimmy Stewart and his troop of 'Boy Rangers' defeat big, bad government and preserve democracy for the rest of the country. This theme reappears in the 1950 hit *Born Yesterday,* as well as the less lauded but still funny *Dave, Legally Blonde 2* and *Being There.*

For sheer ridiculousness on this same subject we loved the smartness hidden behind the oft-black humor in both *Bullworth* (Warren Beatty and Halle Berry) and *Head of State* (Chris Rock).

Another popular theme for DC-based cinema is the total destruction of the nation's capital by aliens (perhaps some wishful thinking on the part of the West Coast). The best of this genre is *The Day the Earth Stood Still,* both for its underlying pacifist message and its off-Mall DC scenes. Adaptations of this theme include the Cold War–era *Earth vs Flying Saucers* and the Will Smith vehicle *Independence Day.*

DC is a popular setting for political thrillers – action-adventure fans might enjoy *In the Line of Fire* (Clint Eastwood as a savvy secret-service agent protecting the president), *Patriot Games* (Harrison Ford as a tough CIA agent battling Irish terrorists), and *No Way Out* (Kevin Costner as a navy officer out-racing Russian spies). All of them are entertaining, especially the scenes of DC's famous sites.

A twist on this action-packed genre goes like this: unwitting-but-wise hero discovers a dangerous state secret and so must outwit intelligence forces to save the day. In *The Pelican Brief,* law student Julia Roberts discovers the conspiracy behind the death of two Supreme Court justices, resulting in a whirlwind flight from and fight against the FBI. Most of this film – based on the John Grisham novel – takes place in New Orleans, but there are a few shots of Georgetown. Essentially the same storyline is played out in *Enemy of the State,* except lawyer Will Smith takes on the ultra-mysterious National Security Agency right here in the capital. Both of these entertaining films have suspense-filled plots and well-developed characters, even if the themes are trite.

For a lighter look at intelligence, *The Man with One Red Shoe* is a silly, spoofy story of an unsuspecting musician (Tom Hanks) who is mistaken for a CIA mole. It's good for some laughs and some glimpses of the city. Theodore Flicker's 1967 *The President's Analyst* (James Coburn) has become a political cult classic. The leading man plays the president's psychiatrist who gets into all sorts of trouble with various spies and thugs who are trying to find out what he knows.

The finest satire of the Cold War has to be Stanley Kubrick's 1964 *Dr Strangelove.* Based at the Pentagon, the plot revolves around a power-mad general who brings the world to the brink of annihilation because he fears a communist takeover of his 'precious bodily fluids.'

Real-life intrigue has been the subject of more than one DC film. *All the President's Men* is based on Carl Bernstein and Bob Woodward's first-hand account of their uncovering of the Watergate scandal (a young Robert Redford and Dustin Hoffman are brilliant as the reporters.) This film's only disappointment is that it does not take the insiders' account to its completion, but concludes – anticlimactically – with the 1973 *Post* headlines recounting the end of the story.

In 2005, George Clooney directed and starred in the highly praised *Good Night, and Good Luck.* Shot in black and white, it is a stark account of how CBS reporter Edward R Murrow and his producer Fred W Friendly exposed and helped bring down one of the most controversial American senators, Joseph McCarthy.

The only movies where the politician is a good guy are those depicting the US president: *Air Force One, The American President, Primary Colors, Thirteen Days* – all entertaining but idealistic

top picks

MUST-SEE DC CINEMA

- *Mr Smith Goes to Washington* (1939) The quintessential Washington, DC political drama of the little guy, portrayed by Jimmy Stewart at his most…American, standing up to all those big, bad special interests.

- *All the President's Men* (1976) The excellent drama that follows the Watergate investigation of Bob Woodward and Carl Bernstein, in which some little guys really did bring down some big, bad special interests – the Nixon presidency.

- *The Exorcist* (1973) Still one of our favorite scary movies; see what happens when a little girl in Georgetown gets possessed by the demon Pazuzu.

- *Bulworth* (1998) Warren Beatty plays a Democratic senator who takes a contract out on his own life and then finds himself liberated to finally say the truth he's been holding back all his life.

- *Spy Game* (2001) While not exclusively set in DC, this is one of the better what-it's-like-to-work-for-the-CIA thrillers out there, and includes some excellent atmospheric shots of the capital.

- *Legally Blonde 2* (2003) Reese Witherspoon gives us the chick flick take on the last-honest-American-cleaning-up-the-capital genre.

- *Head of State* (2003) Chris Rock plays a DC alderman (municipal councilman) who ends up running for, and winning, president of the United States. Smarter commentary than you might think.

- *Wedding Crashers* (2005) Owen Wilson and Vince Vaughn strike a blow for testosterone in this buddy movie about DC divorce lawyers sleeping their way through capital-area wedding bashes.

- *Talk to Me* (2007) See the other side of DC in this ripping biopic of local radio DJ and ex-con Ralph 'Petey' Green, who hosted one of the city's most popular morning shows during the racially charged 1960s and '70s.

portraits of the Chief Executive facing various crises. A variation on this theme is *Wag the Dog,* a hilarious parody of presidential-election spin: a presidential advisor (Robert De Niro) hires a Hollywood producer (Dustin Hoffman) to 'produce' a war in order to distract voters from an unfolding sex scandal. This marriage of Hollywood and Washington results in the cleverest satire of national politics to date.

Arguably the best – most realistic, most captivating – Washington movie is Otto Preminger's *Advise and Consent,* based on Allen Drury's novel by the same name. For its portrayal of the US political system at work, complete with personalities and processes, this film is a must-see. Interesting tidbit: the DC scenes include the first in Hollywood history that were shot in a gay bar.

In 2004, controversial left-wing filmmaker Michael Moore released *Fahrenheit 9/11,* a documentary slamming the Bush administration, in particular its handling of September 11 and the Iraq war. Much of it is filmed in DC. It won top prize at the Cannes Film Festival and went on to become the most successful documentary in history – it opened first in a select few cinemas nationwide, but seats sold so quickly the movie was released in most major cinemas across the country.

Only a select few films set in Washington, DC, are not about politics. The horrific highlight is undoubtedly *The Exorcist,* the cult horror flick set in Georgetown. The creepy long staircase in the movie – descending from Prospect St to M St in reality – has become known as the Exorcist Stairs (p75). Another classic Georgetown movie is the 1980s brat pack flick *St Elmo's Fire.* Demi Moore and Judd Nelson's characters are supposed to be Georgetown graduates, but the college campus is actually the University of Maryland in College Park (although there is the key scene shot in the popular Georgetown bar the Third Edition). For its excellent acting and suspense-filled storyline (and not a few shots of the nation's capital at its finest), *A Few Good Men* is an excellent Washington, DC, movie.

Slam, a 1998 docudrama, is one of the most powerful DC movies we've seen. It tells the story of Ray Joshua, a gifted young (and jobless) MC trapped in a war-zone DC housing project known as Dodge City. Ray copes with the despair and poverty of his neighborhood by creating haunting poetry.

Film fans that want the lowdown on every movie ever shot in DC should read *DC Goes to the Movies* by Jean K Rosales and Michael R Jobe.

Portrayals of DC on TV range from national capital to murder capital. One of the best recent efforts was the Sundance Channel's 2006 six-part, documentary miniseries entitled *The Hill.* The show, which follows congressman Robert Wexler (D-FL) and his staff, on and off Capitol Hill, plays like a cross between *CNN* and MTV's *Laguna Beach.*

The semipopular Geena Davis vehicle, *Commander in Chief* is modeled after the now off-the-air (but once wildly popular) *The West Wing*. The first few seasons of *The West Wing*, which starred Martin Sheen as the beneficent, liberal president ('the best president we've ever had,' fans claimed), when Alan Sorkin was still writing for the show, were truly brilliant and are well worth renting on DVD.

The District, which had a four-year run from 2000 to 2004 (now available on DVD), is about the other side of DC – the dangerous, crime-ridden streets that are far (symbolically if not geographically) from the White House. Craig Nelson plays the chief of police, who uses unconventional means to fight crime in the capital. The drama is inspired by the real-life experiences of one of its creators, New York Deputy Police Commissioner Jack Maple.

ARCHITECTURE

Washington's architecture and city design are the products of its founding fathers and city planners, who intended to construct a capital city befitting a powerful nation. The early architecture of Washington, DC was shaped by two influences: Pierre Charles L'Enfant's 1791 city plan (p20), and the infant nation's desire to prove to European powers that its capital possessed political and artistic sophistication rivaling the ancient, majestic cities of the Continent.

The L'Enfant plan imposed a street grid marked by diagonal avenues, roundabouts and grand vistas. He had in mind the magisterial boulevards of Europe. To highlight the primacy of the city's political buildings, he intended that no building would rise higher than the Capitol. This rule rescued DC from the windy, dark, skyscraper-filled fate of most modern American cities.

In an effort to rival European cities, Washington's early architects – many of them self-taught 'gentlemen architects' – depended heavily upon the Classic Revival and Romantic Revival styles, with their ionic columns and marble facades (witness the Capitol, p77, and Ford's Theatre, p91). Federal-style row houses dominated contemporary domestic architecture and still line the streets of Capitol Hill and Georgetown.

Other fine examples from the Federal period are the Sewall-Belmont house (p82) and the uniquely shaped Octagon Museum (p69). The colonnaded Treasury Building (p67), built by Robert Mills in the mid-19th century, represented the first major divergence from the L'Enfant plan, as it blocked the visual line between the White House and the Capitol. Mills also designed the stark, simple Washington Monument (p55), another architectural anomaly (and not only because it is 555ft high, taller than the Capitol). Later, other styles would soften the lines of the cityscape, with creations like the French-inspired Renwick Gallery (p66), designed by James Renwick.

At the turn of the 20th century, the McMillan plan revived many elements of the L'Enfant plan. It restored public spaces downtown, lent formal lines to the Mall and Capitol grounds, and added more classically inspired buildings, such as the beaux arts Union Station (p81). During this period, John Russell Pope built the Scottish Rite Masonic Temple, which was modeled after the mausoleum at Halicarnassus, as well as the National Archives (p89).

Classicism came to a screaming halt during and after WWII, when war workers flooded the city. Temporary offices were thrown onto the Mall and new materials developed during wartime enabled the construction of huge homogenous office blocks. Slum clearance after the war – particularly in Southwest DC – meant the wholesale loss of old neighborhoods in favor of modernist boxes, such as the monolithic government agencies that currently dominate the ironically named L'Enfant Plaza.

Washington architecture today is of uncertain identity. Many new buildings, particularly those downtown, pay homage to their classical neighbors while striving toward a sleeker, postmodern monumentalism.

A handful of world-renowned architects have left examples of their work in the city. The National Gallery of Art (p58) is a perfect example. Franklin Delano Roosevelt opened the original building, designed by John Russell Pope, in March 1941. Now called the West Building, Pope's symmetrical, neoclassical gallery overwhelms the eye at first glimpse (approach it from the Mall for the more powerful experience). Two wings lacking external windows stretch for 400ft on either side of the main floor's massive central rotunda, which has a sky-high dome supported by 24 black ionic columns. In the center are vaulted corridors leading off to each wing, which

top picks

DC BEAUX ARTS BUILDINGS

Senator McMillan's Plan (1901–02) picked up where L'Enfant's became largely unrealized by reconstructing the face of the nation's monumental core in the beaux arts style suitable of a powerful nation. Here are some of the best examples of this eclectic French-inspired style that is so DC.

- Historical Society of Washington, DC (p92) Former uses include the DC Public Library and the City Museum.
- Corcoran Gallery of Art (p66) Described by Frank Lloyd Wright as 'the best designed building in Washington, DC,' fittingly, it is the city's first museum of art.
- Meridian International Center (p103) A limestone chateau by John Russell Pope.
- Willard Inter-Continental Hotel (p205) Fabled hotel where the term lobbyist originated, from the men who prowled the lobby in search of political prey.
- Union Station (p81) The archetypical example of the neoclassical beauty and grandeur of beaux arts during the age of railroads.

end with an internal skylight and fountain and plant-speckled garden court.

The East Building of the gallery is perhaps even more spectacular. Designed in 1978 by famed architect IM Pei, the ethereal structure is all straight modern lines that create a triangular shape. The building design was initially difficult to conceive, as Pei was given a strange shaped block of land between 3rd and 4th Sts. He solved the problem by making only the marble walls permanent. The rest of the internal structure can be shaped at will, according to the size of various temporary exhibitions. The design is striking, resembling the Louvre in Paris, with pyramidal skylights rising out of the ground (look up from the ground floor of the museum and you'll see a glassed-in waterfall).

Other famous buildings include Mies van der Rohe's Martin Luther King Jr Memorial Library (p91) and Eero Saarinen's Washington Dulles International Airport (p235). Plans are underway for the Corcoran Gallery of Art (p66) to expand with a fantastic addition designed by Frank Gehry. Gehry is famed for his work on Bilbao's Guggenheim museum.

Sometimes appalling and sometimes awesome, the architecture of this unique city tells much about American political ideals and their occasionally awkward application to reality. The National Mall of today is a perfect example. The western half of the Mall is a straightforward place, a graceful mix of sleek modern creations and neoclassical marble temples disguised as memorials. The eastern side is an entirely different story, a mishmash of sometimes awesome and sometimes appalling architecture.

Speaking of appalling, the 1964 National Museum of American History (p59) is possibly the Mall's ugliest piece of architecture – a giant concrete box with huge projecting panels on its facade. The neoclassical National Museum of Natural History (p58), c 1911, is much less of an eyesore. Appealing marble arches and columns add character.

One of the most comely museums on the Mall is the newish National Museum of the American Indian (p60), opened in 2004. Designed by Canadian architect Douglas Cardina, it is a curving, almost undulating glass-and-stone building with brown earthy hues and a terraced facade. It sort of brings the Southwest to Washington and successfully updates ancient Native American architectural creations.

The American Indian Museum's neighbor, the National Air and Space Museum (p58) is much less pleasing to look at. It's an unremarkable 700ft-long squat marble spread.

The Hirshhorn Museum (p59) further south along the Mall is a concrete cylindrical creation rising on 15ft stilts above a sculpture-thick plaza. The 1974 Gordon Bunshaft building has been called everything from a spaceship to a doughnut.

The Smithsonian Institution Building (p62), locally known as the Castle, is our favorite building on the Mall. Dating from 1855, it was designed by James Renwick and features striking Gothic towers and battlements.

Between the Castle and the Hirshhorn Museum one stumbles across the 1881 Arts and Industries Building, which is sadly closed indefinitely. It was the second public construction on the Mall and has a Victorian energy about it, with a jaunty pattern of polychromatic brick and tile.

The National Museum of African Art (p60) and the Arthur M Sackler Gallery (p60) are modern designs, conjured up by the same Boston architectural firm and opened in 1987. The two, made from embroidered, granite-and-limestone cubes, are connected via an underground walkway.

AMBASSADORIAL ARCHITECTURE & ANECDOTES

Some of Washington, DC's most interesting buildings, by dint of design or history, are her many embassies, mainly concentrated in the Dupont Circle area and Upper Northwest. Note that you'll generally have to appreciate these buildings from the outside; for an embassy walking tour see p99.

- The Indonesian Embassy (2020 Massachusetts Ave NW) is a beautiful enough building built in a curving baroque style, but what's really of note here is a historical party thrown by 19th-century mining baron Thomas Walsh, where 325 guests knocked back 480 quarts of champagne, 288 fifths of scotch, 48 quarts of cocktails, 40 gallons of beer and 35 bottles of miscellaneous liqueurs (according to the *New York Times* archives).
- Perhaps the most striking diplomatic building in the city is the Embassy of Italy Chancery (3000 Whitehaven St NW). This starkly geometric structure is actually fashioned to resemble the District itself – the layout of the building resembles a giant diamond cut by a glass atrium, meant to resemble the curving flow of the Potomac.
- There are Victorian gems and super-sleek manses strutting all across the world of Washington embassy architecture, but for modernity so simple it's almost Zen, look no further than the Scandinavians. The Danish Embassy (3200 Whitehaven St NW), stark simple and beautiful, was designed by Vilhelm Lauritzen and includes the Danish ambassador's residence.
- Resembling a floating box-like final level of a video game, the Embassy of Kuwait Chancery (3500 International Dr NW) is one of the most futuristic buildings in the District.
- Although it can be difficult to immediately appreciate, the Embassy of Bangladesh Chancery (3510 International Dr NW) has one of the more innovative facades in the District. Because water is such an important feature of the Bangladeshi landscape, the inverted roof gable is meant to resemble a water lily, while the interior, composed of different grades of slate and other materials, brings to mind a riverbed.
- Located in Southeast Asia, traditional houses in Brunei are simple stilt structures built over water. The deceptively modern-looking Embassy of Brunei (3520 International Court NW), with its posts and pitched roof, is inspired by these rustic designs.

Dating from 1923, Charles A Platt's Freer Gallery of Art (p60) is an Italianate palazzo constructed with granite and marble, and linked to the Sackler Gallery by an underground passageway.

ENVIRONMENT & PLANNING
THE LAND

DC stands at a pivotal place upon the fall line, the exact point where the coastal plain intersects with the higher, rockier piedmont plateau. Most of Downtown and Southeast DC lie on the delta formed by the joining of the Potomac River and its smaller tributary, the Anacostia River. The federal city was sited here precisely because of this geographic anomaly: it is the last navigable point on the Potomac, which city founders deemed important for trade. Just north of here at Great Falls, the river tangles itself in a series of cliffs and crags, impeding the progress of ships.

In the city, the high ground defined by the fall line proved an attractive setting for the mansions of Washington's wealthy residents – it runs through Georgetown and follows Kalorama Rd. The southern, monumental part of Washington around the Mall is coastal lowland smoothed out by seasonal flooding of the Potomac and Anacostia Rivers. To control flooding in the 19th century, developers created landfills like West Potomac Park and dredged the Washington Channel.

Washington, DC is a small city with wide sidewalks and few highways, making it an ideal city for walking.

GREEN DC

Today Washington, DC is a uniquely green city. Hundreds of acres of protected parks and wetlands make a good home for urban wildlife, including small woodland creatures and aquatic animals like raccoons, turtles, salamanders, beavers, white-tailed deer, weasels, muskrats, foxes and opossums. Olmstead's 2000-acre Rock Creek Park is a particularly attractive habitat. Cardinals, pileated woodpeckers and wood thrushes also flit around here.

The mixed woodlands of DC parks are fetching in springtime, when forsythia, fruit trees – especially cherries and crab apples – and wildflowers (violets, bluebells, wild orchids, chicory and trilliums) burst into a pale-pastel rainbow of blooms. Also native to the city, sometimes in near-virgin stands, are tulip poplars, red-and-white oaks, sycamore, elm, willow, dogwood, beech, hickory and pine.

The waterways and wetlands surrounding the city attract waterfowl and other feathered friends. Hundreds of bald eagles and ospreys nest along the Potomac south of Washington and along the Patuxent River to the east. Kenilworth Gardens, in Northeast DC, is thick with wading great blue herons, red-winged blackbirds and bitterns. In 2000, Mayor Anthony Williams announced a major riverfront redevelopment and cleanup effort that will, hopefully, spur revitalization of the Anacostia as a natural and recreational resource.

URBAN PLANNING & DEVELOPMENT

Since the 1970s, DC's population has declined, as residents have moved up and out to burgeoning suburbia. DC's outlying areas are some of the fastest growing in the nation; suburban sprawl and the accompanying automobile dependence have resulted in traffic problems and air pollution. In recent years, the local government responded with innovative transportation solutions: expanding the Metrorail, adding and enforcing designated lanes for High Occupancy Vehicles (HOVs), and allowing bicycles on trains and buses are all ways of encouraging commuters to leave their car keys at home.

The economic upswing in the 1990s sparked investment in Washington neighborhoods, especially Downtown. Projects such as the MCI Center (a huge arena that hosts major sporting events and big-name rock concerts) and the Convention Center are the backbone of the ongoing revitalization in the area. New additions like the National Museum of the American Indian and the National WWII Memorial promise to continue to draw visitors to the Mall. Since September 11, 2001, local government has placed more importance on security concerns when developing public works projects.

MEDIA

The media in DC really means only one thing: the *Washington Post*. Widely read and widely respected, the local daily is considered among the nation's top newspapers. Its competitor, the *Washington Times*, is owned by the Unification Church and provides an unsurprising, more conservative perspective. However, many are saying these days the *Post* seems more conservative than ever. The national newspaper *USA Today* is based across the Potomac in Arlington, VA. Several TV programs are also based in DC, including the PBS *News Hour* with longtime host Jim Lehrer, CNN's *Larry King Live* and all of the major networks' Sunday morning news programs.

The *Post*, of course, is famed for its role in the uncovering of the Watergate scandal in the early 1970s. Budding reporters Bob Woodward and Carl Bernstein traced a break-in at the Watergate Hotel to the top ranks of the White House administration. Then editor and local legend Ben Bradlee took a risk in supporting the investigation and publishing the stories. The discoveries eventually forced the resignation of President Richard Nixon.

Also based in DC is National Public Radio (NPR), the most respected commercial, non-profit free radio network in the nation. Popular shows include *Morning Edition, All Things Considered* and *The Diane Rehm Show*. NPR's offices are in the heart of the Downtown redevelopment project.

As the news capital of the free world (and home to thousands of reporters from all over the US, not to mention the world), Washington media is dominated by the big boys; however, smaller independent voices, both digital and print, help energize the scene. For many reporters, getting to report in DC is like getting to Mecca. Positions at bigger papers and especially TV stations are coveted. As a result there are some very good reporters working for the smaller outlets, biding their time until they break the story of a lifetime and move on to greener pastures, so it's not unheard of for the little guy to grab the big scoop here. The Drudge Report (www .drudgereport.com), an online publication, is a perfect example. It broke the Monica Lewinsky story in the late 1990s.

Washington, DC has some excellent sources of independent media. The **City Paper** (www.washingtoncitypaper.com) keeps an alternative but informed eye on local politics and trends. Another valuable source for local and national events is the **DC Independent Media Center** (www.dc.indymedia.org). Smaller rags filled with juicy Hill gossip include the **Hill** (www.hillnews.com) and **Roll Call** (www.rollcall.com).

To get the scoop on Washington political gossip and humor head to **Wonkette: The DC Gossip** (www.wonkette.com), which also has links to local blogs (Washingtonienne – see p30 – was outed here). You can also catch up on DC celebrity sightings – Sam Donaldson waiting for a cab, the Bush twins downing shots at an unhip bar. Don't worry if you've never heard of some of the names before, some of these folks are *only* famous in Washington – this is a city where CNN anchors are kind of akin to rock stars.

If you're looking for some side-splittingly funny, but decidedly left-wing political cartoon humor, check out www.markfiore.com. The artist, whose work has appeared in newspapers across the country (and who is a former staff cartoonist for the *San Jose Mercury News*), does hilarious, yet thought-provoking, weekly animated skits that take aim at the Washington ruling elite.

More details on Washington's newspapers (p244), radio (p246) and television (p246) are in the Directory.

FASHION

DC has long been a suit-and-tie kind of town, and visitors are often stunned by the number of well-coiffed men and women (from young to old) packing into dark and dingy dives where the smell of smoke and grease is thick for happy-hour cocktails. It's also a fashionable town, and just because the bar looks better suited to work boots and jeans, you're likely to see lots of Blahnik heels, Chanel suits and Louis Vuitton carryalls. For the minority of Washingtonians who can afford it, fashion is an important component of life. Status symbols like expensive cars and even more expensive mansions are the norm in the quiet, elegant, old-money neighborhoods scattered throughout Northwest and the neighboring Virginia suburb McLean. (Quite a few Supreme Court Justices live on the same quiet street in McLean, just spitting distance from the CIA, which is also in the neighborhood. We suppose it's a good choice if you're looking for protection.) Maryland's ritziest zip code, Potomac 20854, has houses so big they are nothing short of embarrassingly ostentatious.

For the fabulous and rich, anything goes fashion-wise as long as it shows up in next season's *Vogue*. For the fabulous and broke, vintage shops selling anything designer are hot. Most of Washington wears a suit to work. In the African American community, dress ranges from haute couture to street wear, with baggy pants and expensive sneakers still dominating the male fashion trend.

LANGUAGE

DC's English is as varied as the city itself. You'll hear plenty of accents and slang from New York, the Midwest, Southern USA and California among the residents of this transient US city, as well as the urban dialect of its African American neighborhoods. Diplomatic and immigrant communities add pockets of multilingualism to the city – you'll hear more Spanish than English in Mt Pleasant and lots of Amharic in Adams-Morgan's African restaurants; Vietnamese is the lingua franca in suburban Virginia's 'Little Saigon.'

Washington, DC bureaucrats – who seem to spend their days crafting acronyms, abbreviations and neologisms – make their own peculiar contributions to DC's language. It is only in Washington that you will hear acronym-laden constructions like, 'If HR 3401 passes, everyone under GS-10 at HUD and HHS will be SOL' and bureaucratic phraseologies like 'non-means-tested entitlement,' 'soft money' and 'what the meaning of *is* is.'

Politics and Washington, DC, are more than peanut butter and jelly or milk and cookies. Think more along the lines of 'water' and 'livable planet': the two simply don't exist without each other. Bureaucracy, compromise, republicanism, democracy, and checks and balances are all concepts that influence DC in ways that run far deeper than job climate and social scene. Take location: the American capital was built on a swamp to satisfy regional politics. Northerners and Southerners agreed, it may have been a malarial swamp, but it was *centrally* malarial. The grid and wagon-wheel layout of the city also draws from the idea of a well-ordered, easily navigable Republic (gotta love the irony that the design conceals America's Escher-like bureaucratic apparatus). In short, to embrace this town, you have to breathe its air, and that's politics: from smoke-and-dagger backrooms to the massed voice of protest and everything in between.

MOVERS, SHAKERS, LIFERS, PLAYERS

DC, unlike so many other world capitals, is rarely boring, and it owes its excitement to its population. This isn't sleepy Canberra or baffling Brasilia; this is the capital of the free world, and it likes to recruit top talent. Yes, there're gray bureaucrats, but in the USA you'd be hard pressed to find a greater concentration of young, motivated individuals, all clawing up the career ladder.

Start at the bottom of the totem pole with pages, high-school students nominated by their congressmen and senators to hand-deliver important documents. Next comes interns: these overworked, underpaid (if paid at all) youngsters can be menial coffee-grabbers or influential speechwriters, and often wear both hats at once. They're also notorious party people, with women sometimes (and chauvinistically) referred to as 'skinterns' for their sometimes skimpy business outfits and occasional Lewinsky-esque dalliances.

Lucky interns become staff, which often means the same job with marginally better pay. Official staff positions may run from policy research ('So what does privatizing social security entail?') to press spokesperson ('The senator doesn't necessarily advocate closing down nursing homes') to letter writing ('Senator Crookshanks is sorry to hear your grandmother's retirement community has been closed…').

By their 30s, political peons have either burned out, earned senior staff roles, or been selected as potential elective material and primed for office in home constituencies. Or they become lobbyists. Lobbyists are (often very highly) paid advocates for a particular cause, and someone who has survived a decade of DC is often well-positioned (and cynical) enough to join their ranks.

So do these hard-driving, highly opinionated, often politically at-odds types get along outside of the office? When they do catch a break, the answer is often: yes. Although some politicos believe in no fraternizing with the enemy, the fact of the matter is Americans have a genius for compromise, and you can't compromise with people you hate. It's not all lovey-dovey, but it's not unheard of for a Republican research analyst to grab a beer, catch a Washington Nationals' baseball game, and even split an apartment with a Democratic Senate staffer.

The jobs described aren't limited to congressional offices either – DC also headquarters think tanks, NGOs, lobbying firms, the World Bank and embassies, to name a few. All kinds of Type A intelligentsia roll through here: students at some of the best universities in America; activists campaigning out of their central headquarters; and foreign diplomats, young and old, navigating the power networks of their own countries.

UNDERSTANDING AMERICAN POLITICS

Everyone knows Americans do things differently – spelling, measuring, sports – and the democratic process is no exception. Now, some of you may sneer, 'What democratic process?' and start comparing American presidents to fascist dictators, but the fact is that this is the longest-running Republic in the world. On top of that, while the American system was unique in its inception, it has been emulated by governments across the globe, notably in Latin America and Eastern Europe. But the difference runs way beyond organization to philosophy. Whereas many governments exist to protect their citizens, the American model focuses on protecting citizens' *rights* – or at least it's supposed to.

SEPARATION OF POWERS

Some may ask, 'What's the difference?' The best answer probably comes from journalist HL Mencken, who summed up many Americans' feelings toward a nanny state: 'The urge to save humanity is almost always a false face for the urge to rule it.' Americans are by and large paranoid about their government. The entire country was founded by anti-authoritarian colonists, while the Civil War was fought over how much power Washington, DC, could exert over the states (among other things). Obsessed with keeping government in check, the founding fathers devised a system that disperses power through three branches that all have the ability to smack each other down.

You can visit those branches starting on Capitol Hill, where the legislative branch, better known as Congress, convenes. Put simply, Congress writes laws. There are two bodies assigned to this task: the House of Representatives and the Senate. In the House, the number of representatives (also known as congressmen and women) is split proportionally by state population. The next census to determine the size of the House takes place in April 2010 (the numbers generally change every decade). As of this writing, there were 438 representatives in the House; Wyoming, the least-populated state, had one, and California, with the largest population, had 53. There are 100 senators: two for each state, a way of giving smaller states equal footing with more populous ones. Congress not only writes laws, it can also impeach the president, determine the jurisdictional limits of courts and vote out its own members.

Behind the Capitol dome is the Supreme Court, whose 12 justices are appointed by the president to life terms. The court's job is to determine how true to the constitution laws are. Arguably the weakest branch, its influence is still crucial to the democratic process. While the public face of many causes in America are crowds of protestors, actual change is often practically affected through the courts, from the Supreme on down. This was the case with the Scopes Trial, which allowed evolution to be taught in public schools, the African American Civil Rights movement and the continuing battle for gay marriage.

A little ways down Pennsylvania Ave sits the White House, where the president heads the executive branch. Unlike a prime minister, the president is both head of state and head of government, and possesses the power to veto (override) Congress' bills, pardon criminals, and appoint a cabinet, judges and ambassadors. But the position isn't quite as powerful as some might think. Many media analysts argue that in a short-attention-span world, it's just easier for everyone to understand a one-person office versus a 538-seat Congress – and assume the former holds the reigns of power.

On the other side, some scholars have argued the presidency has been increasing in power to the point that it is no longer a co-equal branch of government. Historian Arthur Schlesinger Jr made the most famous argument for this position in a book whose title is synonymous with overarching executive power: *The Imperial Presidency*. The arguments over how powerful the president truly is could fill several libraries. What we can say for certain is a stubborn Congress can make a president's life hell. George W Bush's efforts to privatize social security were squashed by a Democratic Congress. A few years later (and as of this writing), while Barack Obama's party still controls the executive and both houses of Congress, a strongly organized Republican opposition has been able to stymie many of the president's health-care reform efforts.

Finally, while the powers are separated, they are not isolated from each other. The founding fathers figured that each branch's ability to check its partners would generate a healthy tension. This uneasy equality makes compromise a necessity for movement on the issues, and is the true bedrock of American politics.

THE ELECTORAL COLLEGE

Americans vote most of their leaders into office, but not the president (in a similar vein, under a parliament voters elect a party that then selects the prime minister). Instead, they vote for electors, a group of individuals who make up the semi-shadowy Electoral College. It is the college and its electors who actually pick the president every four years. Although a candidate's name appears in voting booths, individual votes go to the electors, whose votes are supposed to reflect the will of the public.

Every four years candidates push for the magic number of electors that will give them over half the votes needed for victory. The states, along with Washington, DC, get as many electors as they have senators and representatives. The number of electors will have changed by the time you read this guidebook, as the census that will determine the size of Congress will take place in April 2010. As of this writing, California tops the list with 55 electors, and Wyoming bottoms out at three. The game is winner-takes-all: when a party wins a state, it gets every one of the electoral votes.

Here's how the system works. Let's say it's election day in a state inhabited by 100 people, represented by 10 electors. Come game day, 60 people vote for candidate Smith (or more accurately, for his electors), and 40 for candidate Brown. Although the votes split 6:4, Smith's party takes them all and comes 10 electoral votes closer to victory.

The system was founded for several reasons. Firstly, direct democracy was pretty much considered mob rule in the 1700s; electors were supposed to mollify the base instincts of the people. In addition, the college is supposed to guarantee geographically fair elections. If candidates focused on the popular vote, rather than the states, campaigns (and their promises) would largely be directed at big cities on the coasts. Because every state gets two electors to complement their senators, even the small ones can command election attention.

The counter argument is: 'So what?' Politics are not as regional as they once were, and the concerns of the coasts often overlap those of the heartland. There are also questions of how democratic the college is. Technically, electors can vote how they want, although none have recently gone against their constituents' will. Plus, is it fair for Wyoming, with a population

MALL OF JUSTICE

Washington, DC is not just the center of government, it is also the center of demonstration. What the Capitol is to conventional politics, the National Mall is to protest politics. The Mall has long provided a forum for people who feel that they or their issue have been shut out by the establishment. Peace-loving war veterans, long-skirted suffragettes, civil-rights activists, shrouded white supremacists, tractor-driving farmers and million-mom marchers have all staged political pageants on the Mall over the years. Following are some of the great moments in American protest politics:

- Bonus Army (1932) – WWI veterans, left unemployed by the Great Depression, petitioned the government for an early payment of promised bonuses for their wartime service. As many as 10,000 veterans settled in for an extended protest, pitching tents on the Mall and the Capitol lawn. President Hoover dispatched Douglas MacArthur to evict the 'Bonus Army.' In a liberal display of force, the veterans were routed and their campsites razed.
- 'I Have a Dream' (1963) – The Civil Rights movement was the most successful protest movement, effectively employing boycotts and demonstrations. Reverend Martin Luther King's stirring speech, delivered from the steps of the Lincoln Memorial to 200,000 supporters, remains a high point in the historic struggle for racial equality.
- Anti-War Protests (1971) – The Vietnam War aroused some of the most notable episodes of protest politics. In April 1971, an estimated 500,000 Vietnam veterans and students gathered on the Mall to oppose continued hostilities. Several thousand arrests were made.
- AIDS Memorial Quilt (1996) – Lesbian and gay activists drew more than 300,000 supporters in a show of solidarity for equal rights under the law and to display the ever-growing AIDS quilt, which covered the entire eastern flank of the Mall from the Capitol to the Washington Monument.
- Million Mom March (2000) – A half-million people convened on the Mall on Mother's Day, to draw attention to hand-gun violence and to influence Congress into passing stricter gun-ownership laws.
- Bring Them Home Now Tour (2005) – At least 100,000 protestors demanded the withdrawal of American soldiers from Iraq. They were met with 400 counter-protestors who support a continued American presence. Both sides are led by families who have lost loved ones in the war.
- Barack Obama's Inauguration (2009) – While not a protest, Obama's swearing in as president is believed to be the largest public gathering in the history of the city, with attendance estimates ranging from 850,000 to 1.8 million people.

WASHINGTON'S SITES OF SCANDAL, SEDUCTION & SKULDUGGERY

Washington media loves a good scandal (and some argue spends too much time trying to sniff one out). We offer here only a brief primer on some of the city's best-known scandal sites.

- Scandal Central: Watergate – Towering over the Potomac banks, this chi-chi apartment-hotel complex has lent its name to decades of political crime. It all started when Committee to Re-Elect the President (CREEP) operatives were found here, trying to bug Democratic National Committee headquarters. Thus was launched Woodward and Bernstein's investigation, which would eventually topple Nixon.
- Swimming for It: Tidal Basin – In 1974, Wilbur Mills, 65-year-old Arkansas representative and chairman of the House Ways & Means Committee, was stopped for speeding, whereupon his companion – 38-year-old stripper Fanne Foxe, known as the 'Argentine Firecracker' – leapt into the Basin to escape. Unfortunately for Mills' political career, a TV cameraman was there to film the fun.
- What's Your Position, Congressman?: Capitol Steps – John Jenrette was a little-known South Carolina representative until he embroiled himself in the bribery scandal (dubbed Abscam after Abdul Enterprises Ltd, the faux company set up by the FBI to offer money to members of Congress in return for political favors). Jenrette's troubles were compounded when his ex-wife Rita revealed to *Playboy* that she and her erstwhile husband used to slip out during dull late-night congressional sessions for an alfresco quickie on the Capitol's hallowed marble steps. (And that's not all.)
- Smoking Gun: Vista Hotel – It was in room No 727 that former DC mayor Marion Barry uttered his timeless quote: '...set up...bitch set me up!' when the FBI caught him taking a friendly puff of crack cocaine in the company of ex-model (and police informant) Hazel 'Rasheeda' Moore. The widely broadcast FBI video of his toke horrified a city lacerated by crack violence, but didn't stop it from re-electing Barry in 1994. (The Vista has since changed its name to the Wyndham Washington Hotel.)
- Suicidal Tendencies: Fort Marcy Park – The body of Vince Foster, deputy counsel to president Clinton and Hillary Clinton, was found in this remote Mclean, Virginia, park in 1993. Foster was dead from a bullet shot to the head. Investigations by both the Park Police and the FBI determined that the death was a suicide, but conspiracy theories abounded among right-wing pundits.
- Stool Pigeon Sushi: Pentagon City Food Court – It was by the sushi bar that Monica Lewinsky awaited Linda Tripp, her lunch date (and betrayer) who led Ken Starr's agents down the mall escalators to snag her up for questioning in the nearby Ritz-Carlton Hotel. Who knew a food court could provide such a media fiesta?

of 532,000 and three electoral votes, to have parity with Montana – population 967,000 and same number of electors?

One recommendation, which sounds like winning the Golden Snitch in quidditch, is to keep the Electoral College but give the popular vote-winner 100 electoral votes, essentially guaranteeing their victory. However, attempts to reform the system are notoriously failure-prone.

To learn more about the college (and the debate), check the Federal Election Commission (www.fec .gov) website.

THE MEDIA & WASHINGTON

Besides Israel and the Occupied Territories, it's hard to imagine an area that packs so many journalists into such a small space (keep in mind DC's population, within the city limits, is only 592,000). Journalists and politicians have been, through the course of this city's history, fellow travelers, arch enemies, jilted ex-lovers and tense rivals.

But probably the best analogy is 'uncomfortable bedfellows.' Politics is a game of public perception, and the gatekeepers of that opinion are the media. Politicians – even the ones who publicly lambaste journalists – must maintain a working (although not necessarily good) relationship with the press corps. On the other hand, reporters must ostensibly be merciless, brutally honest and somehow removed from the politicians they cover. In reality, to gain access to the sources they require for their stories, relationships are forged between profiler and profiled.

We should stress this situation isn't unique to Washington– every beat reporter in the world eventually runs into the dilemma of getting to know a subject well and then having to present that subject negatively. But they say where you stand is where you sit, and many DC reporters have been sitting inside the Washington bubble for years.

And Washington can be a bubble. The same faces appear in the same hearings and conferences day after day, at lunches, after-work drinks and lectures. Politicians (although they'd rarely admit it) often become closer to reporters and across-the-aisle opponents than their own constituents. The boat the ship of state sails on can be small, and when someone rocks it, everyone notices. Sometimes good journalism can suffer as a result. Glenn Greenwald, a constitutional lawyer and columnist for Salon (www.salon.com), is perhaps the most prolific commentator on the DC press corps' reluctance to cover their backyard too critically.

The local media scene is still one of the most vibrant in the world. Even as American newspapers shut their doors and lay off staff, online reporting and new media trends are increasingly in evidence here. One thing this town is good at is figuring out new ways to convince people of something, fresh methods of conveying a message. Every congressman seems to have a Twitter feed these days.

But at the end of the day, no matter what medium the message is expressed in – magazine piece or Facebook link – its first steps are a conversation in a Capitol Hill pub, a press conference in the Hart Building, or a leak whispered in a Rosslyn parking garage. In other words, the shape of the national conversation is inimical to its origin. The topics of the great American debate are set here, and as such the media and its accompanying three-ring circus will always be a part of this city's scene.

LOBBYISTS

'Lobbyist' is one of the dirtiest words in the American political lexicon, yet its meaning is fairly innocuous. Essentially, a lobbyist is someone who makes a living advocating special interests. This isn't Europe, where causes form their own party and seek power through a parliamentary coalition. Here the agenda-pushers directly thrust their message onto elected officials.

Lobbying is traditionally dated to the late 19th century, but took off as a vital component of American politics during the money-minded 1980s. Most politicos see lobbyists as a necessary evil, and while it's the rare politician who admits to being influenced by them, everyone understands their importance: lobbyists are the go-betweens in a city built on client-patron relationships. For better or worse, they have become a vital rung on DC's power ladder.

Labor unions and tree-huggers, gun nuts and industrialists; every group gets its say here through the work of well-paid and connected advocates. Lobbying ranks, largely based on K St (to the point that the two terms are synonymous), are swelled by those who know how to navigate the complex social webs of the capital; some watchdogs estimate as many as 40% of former congressman rejoin the private sector as lobbyists. In a city where getting anything done is often based on personal relationships, a lobbyist can be worth far more than, say, an embassy with rotating staff. Indeed, many countries keep embassies for ritual value and leave the real legwork of diplomacy to DC lobbying firms.

Wining, dining, vacation packages and the art of giving all of the above without violating campaign contribution laws is a delicate dance. Every year legislation is introduced to keep lobbyists off the floor of Congress (figuratively and sometimes literally), but lobbyists are probably too ingrained into the political landscape to ever be completely removed from it.

DEMOCRACY IN ACTION

One of the great paradoxes of American politics is how simultaneously accessible and shut off the system is. Visitors can walk into congressional hearings dressed in jeans and a T-shirt and address their elected representatives, in public, with barely any security screening at all. Mass protests have rocked the foundations of government and seared themselves on the national psyche forever. Yet most of the decisions that influence American government are made between small groups of well-connected policy wonks, lobbyists and special interests who are mainly concerned with perpetuating their own organizations.

Americans believe changing the system requires going to DC and coming face to face with their elected officials (there's even a cinematic subgenre devoted to the idea, from *Mr Smith Goes to Washington* to *Legally Blonde 2*). On a grand scale, the equation is partly true.

Large protests, often held on the National Mall (p44), can shift public perception a few points towards a particular cause. But smaller delegations usually require lots of money and clout to affect change.

It's maddening, but the surface of the process is surprisingly open to travelers. Check www. house.gov and www.senate.gov to get the schedules for congressional committee hearings (call ahead to the numbers provided, as some meetings are closed to the public). Passes for Capitol tours and public viewings of Congress are doled out on a first-come, first-served basis starting at 9am on weekdays, at a kiosk on the southwest corner of the Capitol grounds (1st St and Independent Ave SW); go to www.aoc.gov/cc/visit/index.cfm for more details.

Commonwealth visitors may be surprised at how courteous politicians here are in formal, public debate. The decorum is especially strange considering how highly Americans prize informality, but a lot of stock is placed on addressing officials as 'The respected gentleman,' and 'My respected colleague from [insert state here].' That entire system received a shock in September 2009, when during a speech to the joint houses of Congress, Barack Obama was interrupted by congressman Joe Wilson, R-South Carolina, who yelled 'You lie!' in the midst of a speech. Such outbursts are unheard of here, and prompted a huge debate on a congressional censure of Wilson.

POLITICALSPEAK 101

Here's a primer on some head-scratching political terms you may hear thrown about:

filibuster – the art of delaying the passage of a bill by talking it to death; now used to refer to any sort of painful wait. Longest ever: Strom Thurmond's 24-hour, 18-minute rant to block the (successful) passage of the 1957 Civil Rights Act.

-gate – any kind of scandal, named for the Watergate hotel, the nexus of the events that led to Richard Nixon's resignation in 1974. Other examples include: Monicagate (for Monica Lewinsky, the intern whose novel use of cigars earned her a 'favored' place in the Oval Office) and Katrinagate (the mismanagement that crippled the emergency response to Hurricane Katrina in 2005).

gerrymander – when elected officials redraw electoral boundaries for their own benefit, named for the weird, salamander-like shape of a replotted Massachusetts district created by Elbridge Gerry in 1812.

pork barrel – hitching funding (often for dams, roads and airports) to a popular bill that has no relation to the funded projects. For instance: millions of dollars for new bridges tacked onto a bill that deals with lobbying reform.

red state/blue state – a term for the American political divide that references the electoral map display used by news services during national elections. One of the stated theme's of Barack Obama's politics has been a 'purple America,' ie a country where the interests of red and blue America overlap.

soccer mom/NASCAR dad – quintessential American voters. The soccer mom is a middle-to-upper-class, suburban or ex-urban mom with a cell phone, an SUV and kids to pick up after school. She's a moderate voter, and considered a major source of Bill Clinton's electoral victory. NASCAR dads are working class, uber-patriotic, averse to gay marriage and immigrants, and named for the racing association they love to watch. Considered a backbone of the Republican Party.

spin/flack – ways of throwing the press off politicians. Professional flacks, or spokespersons, 'spin' events and issues to their advantage. Take the abortion debate: 'pro-choice' activists become 'anti-life' to the 'pro-life' movement, whose opponents deem them 'anti-choice.'

stumping – bringing politics to the people; when candidates on the campaign trail speak at local town halls, schools and fairs to gain face recognition with voters. This most traditional of American campaign tactics has been subverted by internet campaigning via blogs, direct-mailing campaigns to homes and, of course, since the 1960s, TV.

teabaggers – a nickname for conservative protestors who held rallies – called 'tea parties' – across the country in 2009. The reference was to the Boston Tea Party that preceded the American Revolution, but it quickly evolved into double innuendo; 'teabagging' has long held another meaning in American sexual slang. Oh, just look it up. Anyways, both teabaggers and their critics co-opted the term; activists said they were 'teabagging government' and critics said activists were 'a bunch of teabaggers,' which raises questions over who is the bagger-er and bagger-ee in a teabagging scenario, as well as which position is inherently negative – questions that are, sadly, beyond the scope of this book.

SINCE THE OBAMA ELECTION

American public discourse is not at the height of decorum these days. On the conservative side, Ann Coulter's books about liberals are titled, *Slander, Treason* and *Godless* (the next one may as well be a randomly chosen four-letter expletive). Liberals answer back with books like *Rush Limbaugh is a Big, Fat Idiot*, written by then-comedian and now-senator Al Franken. Read the 'comments' section on any political blog. Go on; try it. We just did while researching this chapter, and the sheer bile, invective and hate coming from both sides of the aisle terrified us. Online anonymity plus a large audience brings out the worst in some people. If you chose to believe their rants, these days the country is either run by gay, socialist, illegal immigrants who are late for an abortion appointment, or seal-clubbing Wall Street executives who are too busy twirling their mustaches to turn off Fox News.

The thing is, while the extremists may dominate sound bytes, there is a large middle ground where Americans meet, every day, to compromise and move forward on the issues that affect their country. And in late 2008, Barack Obama, himself a synthesis – of nationalities, ideologies and race – came to personify this middle ground for many Americans. Of course liberals embraced him and hardcore conservatives rejected him, but pundits agree he could not have won without the support of some moderate Republicans and most independents.

Sometimes reaching a middle ground is about adhering to a gray moral calculus, but sometimes compromise is the seed of consensus, even community. Even critics concede Obama is a great orator, and like that other Great Communicator, Ronald Reagan, he has been able to redefine what America can be. Those who agree with this interpretation love Obama for the eloquence with which he expresses his vision, the departure he seems to represent from the past. Those who disagree see (perhaps ironically) the same qualities as Obama's supporters: a reshaping, revolutionizing force, one that is urban, international, removed from small towns and opposed to deregulation and self-interest. It must also be said, lest we be accused of ignoring the elephant in the room, that race influences all of the above, probably so deeply that many are unaware of its impact.

The point is, no politician has had so much impact on the American psyche in recent memory, and no single individual has had, by extension, such an impact on the Washington area. Obama has become the center of the nation's attention, and by proxy, so has his new home.

More and more talented types are being drawn into the District's four quadrants. Traditionally, cities like New York, San Francisco, Chicago, Houston and Los Angeles, along with DC, have been nodes of political power dotted on the American landscape. Today, at least, the work and battle for the America that could be – be that vision in line with or rebelling against Obama – is centered very strongly in Washington. This is a result of everything we have described above, plus government expansion, a loss of confidence in Wall Street following the 2008 financial crisis, and the general increase in quality of life in DC. The city's star has risen so much that major news services like Reuters are predicting the capital will eclipse Manhattan in importance and influence for the foreseeable future. Washington, DC is living, as the Chinese might say, in interesting times. That line is meant to be a curse, but to our ears it sounds like something to be hoped for as well. In any case, it sure is a great time to visit.

NEIGHBORHOODS

top picks

NEIGHBORHOODS

Washington, DC is evolving fast enough to make Darwin do a double take. For decades, this city, while officially divided into four quadrants (Northeast, Southeast, Southwest and Northwest), essentially consisted of three areas: the federal center, where the government ran itself; white DC, where 35% to 40% of the population lived in the ritziest corners

'The old identity of a two-toned city – rich white and poor black – has started shifting.'

of the Northwest quadrant; and majority black rest-of-DC. That other side of the city was often a hard place to come up. Crime, poverty and substance abuse were endemic, and sporadically, the nation's capital was also its murder capital.

Beginning in the 1990s, this situation began changing (although as recently as 2004, Washington had the highest per capita homicide rate in the country). Waves of Latino immigration, mainly from El Salvador, significantly altered Washington's ethnic make-up. Federal government expansion under Bill Clinton and both Bushes, the impact of the September 11 attacks and Barack Obama's election attracted large crops of young professionals, who in turn attracted developers. At around the same time, the city council wanted to revive the city's moribund Downtown and used gentrification to start carving out new shopping and eating districts. The plan was to attract citizens back who moved out of the District in the 1970s.

Thanks to all of the above, the old identity of a two-toned city – rich white and poor black – has started shifting. Don't get the wrong idea: DC's Northwest is still majority-white and wealthy, and it's where most of the sites, restaurants, shops and bars in this book are located. Outside of here, the National Mall and Capitol Hill, DC is often quietly residential, sometimes straight-up dangerous. We encourage you to see the city's harder side – a majority of its residents still live there, and they're the backbone of the District's identity – but go with, at the least, a local's advice, if not company.

In the rest of Washington, change is on the way. Young families have sidewalk coffees on U St, formerly crack alley. Capitol Hill, once off-limits past Eastern Market, has become pretty enough to double as the set of a Victorian novel. And some of the city's best bars and restaurants are popping up in stretches of Northwest that are adjacent to – a few are actually inside – the Northeast quadrant, long unexplored territory (unless you actually lived there).

To be frank, this gentrification has made DC less black, but the situation isn't as simple as 'more development = less diversity.' As lifelong Washingtonian Kenny Carroll puts it, a more livable DC doesn't have to mean a less African American one. In some areas an integration has occurred that no one would have predicted after the race riots of the mid-20th century.

This chapter begins within the National Mall, center of the city and symbology of a nation. We jaunt north to the White House and Foggy Bottom, Washington's version of a Central Business District ('business' being politics), then west into the brownstones and bucolic lanes of Georgetown. Back towards the Mall we head east to Capitol Hill, which uniquely blends the city's local and political qualities, then across the Anacostia to the streets of Southeast DC. Get your shop on under the neon lights of revitalized Downtown, enjoy a sidewalk beer and some gay nightlife in Dupont Circle, or hit Adams-Morgan to indulge your international palate and ethnic booty bounces. See the new, exciting and original directions of DC's development in Columbia Heights and Northeast, which includes the ever-popular U St Corridor, and take the kids to the residential prettiness of Upper Northwest. We wrap up in Northern Virginia, home of bedroom suburbs (that rarely sleep). For a great selection of DC tours on foot, bike, bus, even Segway (two-wheeled scooter), see p244.

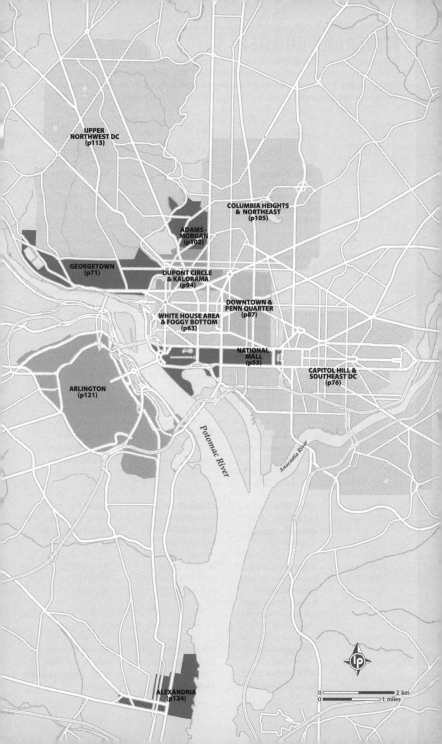

UPPER
NORTHWEST DC
(p113)

COLUMBIA HEIGHTS
& NORTHEAST
(p105)

ADAMS -
MORGAN
(p102)

GEORGETOWN
(p71)

DUPONT CIRCLE
& KALORAMA
(p94)

DOWNTOWN &
PENN QUARTER
(p87)

WHITE HOUSE AREA
& FOGGY BOTTOM
(p63)

NATIONAL
MALL
(p53)

CAPITOL HILL &
SOUTHEAST DC
(p76)

ARLINGTON
(p121)

Potomac River

Anacostia River

ALEXANDRIA
(p124)

0   2 km
0   1 miles

ITINERARY BUILDER

The table below allows you to plan a day's worth of activities in any area of the city. Simply select which area you wish to explore, and then mix and match from the corresponding listings to build your day. The first item in each cell represents a well-known highlight of the area, while the other items are more off-the-beaten-track gems.

ACTIVITIES	Sights & Activities	Eating	Shopping
National Mall	Lincoln Memorial (p55) Arthur M Sackler Gallery & Freer Gallery of Art (p60) Vietnam Veterans Memorial (p56)	Mitsitam Native Foods Cafe (p146) Source (p146)	National Museum of the American Indian (p130) National Air & Space Museum (p130) National Gallery of Art (p130)
White House Area & Foggy Bottom	White House (p65) Corcoran Gallery of Art (p66) Renwick Gallery (p66)	Equinox (p149) Georgia Brown's (p147) Kinkead's (p148)	White House Historical Association Gift Shop (p129) Indian Craft Shop (p128) ADC Map & Travel Center (p129)
Georgetown	C&O Canal & Towpath (p73) Dumbarton House (p74)	Citronelle (p152) Martin's Tavern (p150) Makoto (p151)	Big Planet Comics (p131) Relish (p133)
Capitol Hill & Southeast DC	Capitol (p77) Library of Congress (p80) Frederick Douglass National Historic Site (p83)	Eastern Market (p152) City Zen (p155) Argonaut (p154)	Remix (p134) Homebody (p133) Eastern Market (p133)
Downtown & Penn Quarter	National Archives (p89) Smithsonian American Art Museum (p90) National Museum of Women in the Arts (p91)	Rasika (p156) Acadiana (p158) Minibar at Café Atlantico (p158)	Apartment Zero (p134) Political Americana (p135) Coup de Foudre (p134)
Dupont Circle & Kalorama	Phillips Collection (p95) Embassy Row (p95) National Geographic Explorers Hall (p97)	Afterwords Café & Kramerbooks (p159) Bistrot du Coin (p159) Vidalia (p160)	Green & Blue (p137) Second Story Books (p136) Proper Topper (p136)
Columbia Heights & Northeast	Howard University (p108) United States National Arboretum (p109) Basilica of the National Shrine of the Immaculate Conception (p110)	Hitching Post (p166) Ben's Chili Bowl (p163) W Domku (p165)	Dekka (p139) Redeem (p139) Nana (p140)
Upper Northwest DC	Washington National Cathedral (p115) Rock Creek Park (p117) National Zoological Park (p116)	Comet Ping Pong (p166) Buck's Fishing & Camping (p167) Palena (p168)	Sullivan's Toy Store (p141) Wake Up Little Suzie (p141) Politics & Prose Bookstore (p140)

AREA

NATIONAL MALL

Eating p145; Shopping p130

A nation is many things: her people, her history, her politics and her amassed knowledge. Somehow, every item listed above is given architectural life on the National Mall, the center of iconography of the most iconic city in America. This is where the ideals of the most powerful nation in the world are expressed in stone, landscaping, educational institutions, monuments and memorials. It's the final destination of countless field trips, attic of the American psyche, situation point of the national symbology and…well, you're getting the idea.

It's also, for you first-timers, a big old lawn. Really, that's the gist of it – just about 3 miles of scrubby grass crisscrossed by sandy paths, sandwiched between Constitution and Independence Aves and the Capitol and Lincoln Memorial, pinned down by the Washington Monument, flanked by hot-dog vendors and T-shirt stands, and containing therein, somewhere amid everything we've described, the American experience.

OK, OK, don't get your hopes up: we're not saying some anthropomorphized red, white and blue creature hides in the Reflecting Pool (although that would be cool). But if you wander around enough out here you will get a sense of what makes this country tick. If your mind is set on it, it's impossible to come to the Mall and not absorb the momentum of the American experiment. Frontier pushing in the National Air and Space Museum; our military legacy inscribed in memorials; historical roots collected in the American History Museum; current events playing out in exhibits fronting the Newseum; creativity blooming in the National Gallery of Art; and the actual flora of the country flowering in the botanic gardens.

The experience is, unapologetically, pro-American. But that doesn't mean it shakes a flag in your face while blaring Toby Keith. When we say 'pro-American,' we're referring more to pro-America as an *ideal*, the highest possibility, the nation behaving best. To the immense credit of the Smithsonian curators and National Park staff who guide and interpret visitors through the Mall, there is a general recognition here that America hasn't always lived up to her promise. And yet the resulting dialogue doesn't come off as immature America-bashing either; rather the constant refrain heard 'round the Mall is there is always potential for change in this country, and always the possibility to push for something greater.

Perhaps this phenomenon is best realized in the Lincoln Memorial, which honors the president who helped expunge the country's original sin of slavery. On either side of the seated Lincoln are quotes that speak to the problems facing the USA and the confidence Lincoln had in our ability to overcome those obstacles. Faced with the enormity of this prospect, many visitors fall silent under Honest Abe's silent stare, worshippers at a secular temple to democracy…until some 15-year-old on a school trip from Florida shrieks with laughter or a pack of tourists affix zoom lenses to cameras or a protest breaks up the reverie.

That's the other thing about the Mall: it may be known as America's Front Yard, but perhaps 'Town Green,' in the original, New England sense of the word, is a better description. The green, after all, is both an informal community center and the place where citizens gathered to learn the news of the day, debate the issues generated by that news and put ideas forward to their elected officials. Here, instead of small public debate are the great rallies – I Have a Dream to a Million Moms to Bring Them Home Now – that have been the talk-pieces of the American conversation (and argument).

Here also, in the tradition of town greens, are people engaged in leisure: sunbathers, dog-walkers, Frisbee players and football games. All these folks are admittedly largely local, which should give you some insight into not just the American, but DC frame of mind. After all, in what other city are national icons so ubiquitous we don't let them get in the way of enjoying a good round of Ultimate?

ORIENTATION

The National Mall is a 400ft-wide green expanse stretching 3 miles from the Potomac in the west to Capitol Hill in the east. That said, if you count the Mall from the Lincoln Memorial to the Capitol building, where sights are primarily concentrated, it's 1.9 miles long. Lined with gravel paths and bordered by tree-shaded avenues (Constitution Ave to the north, Independence Ave to the south), the Mall is fringed by museums and dotted with monuments.

NATIONAL MALL

0 — 400 m
0 — 0.2 miles

(North Central Fwy) North

Watergate Complex
Kennedy Center
Rock Creek Parkway

White House
South Lawn
The Ellipse

See White House Area & Foggy Bottom Map (p64)

Rawlins Park
New York Ave NW
Virginia Ave NW
Federal Reserve

Georgetown Law School
Judiciary Square
Judiciary Square

Gallery Place Chinatown
Verizon Center
Chinatown

See Downtown & Penn Quarter Map (p88)

Metro Center

Department of Labor
John C St NW Marshall Park

Constitution Ave

Federal Triangle
Ronald Reagan Building/ International Trade Center
Interstate Commerce Commission

Archives/Navy Memorial
National Archives
Pennsylvania Ave NW
Indiana Ave NW

Constitution Ave NW

Constitution Gardens
Reflecting Pool
Rainbow Pool

National Mall

Madison Dr NW
National Mall

Smithsonian

Independence Ave SW
Forrestal Building
Department of Energy

FAA Building
Hancock Park

L'Enfant Plaza
L'Enfant Plaza
L'Enfant Plaza

Benjamin Banneker Park

Federal Center SW

Dwight D Eisenhower Fwy
Southwest DC

See Capitol Hill & Southeast DC Map (pp78–9)

Washington Ave SW

Maryland Ave SW
Jefferson Dr SW

West Potomac Park
Daniel French Dr SW
Independence Ave SW

Tidal Basin

East Potomac Park

W Basin Dr SW
Memorial Park

Washington Channel

Maine Ave SW
Water St SW

Ohio Dr SW
Potomac River

Raoul Wallenberg Pl / 15th St SW
14th St SW
Henry Bacon Dr NW

Constitution Ave NW
E St NW
F St NW
G St NW

1st St NW
2nd St NW
3rd St NW
4th St NW
6th St NW
7th St NW
8th St NW
9th St NW
10th St NW
11th St NW
12th St NW
13th St NW
14th St NW
15th St NW
17th St NW
18th St NW
19th St NW
20th St NW
22nd St NW
23rd St NW

D St NW
C St NW
E St NW

1st St SW
2nd St SW
3rd St SW
4th St SW
6th St SW
7th St SW
9th St SW
12th St SW
13th St SW
14th St SW

C St SW
D St SW
E St SW
G St SW
H St SW

School St SW
Virginia Ave SW

lonelyplanet.com

LINCOLN MEMORIAL Map p54

☎ 202-426-6841; www.nps.gov/linc; admission free; ☷ 9.30am-midnight; Ⓜ Foggy Bottom-GWU
In a city of icons, the inspiration for the back of the penny stands out in the crowd. It's the classicism evoked by the Greek temple design, or the way the memorial so perfectly anchors the Mall's west end, or maybe just the stony dignity of Lincoln's gaze and the power of his speeches engraved in the walls. Whatever; a visit here while gazing over the Reflecting Pool is a defining DC moment. These are the steps where lovers kiss and schoolchildren lounge, protestors gather and Martin Luther King Jr's dream seared itself into the national conscience. To add to the civil rights record, read the words of the Emancipation Proclamation and Lincoln's Second Inaugural speech, which flank the seated 'Papa Abraham.' Designed by Henry Bacon to resemble a Doric temple, the memorial's 36 columns represent the 36 states in Lincoln's union.

This is one of DC's cinematic scene stealers. Owen Wilson and Vince Vaughn discussed girls on the memorial steps in *Wedding Crashers;* Reese Witherspoon's Elle Woods sought Lincoln's advice in *Legally Blonde 2;* and Tom Hanks charged into the Reflecting Pool to kiss Jenny in *Forrest Gump.*

CIVIL RIGHTS RALLYING POINT

Since its completion in 1922 the Lincoln Memorial, built in honor of the Emancipation Proclamation's author, has also been a symbol of the Civil Rights movement. It hasn't always been a perfect one, though. Dr Robert Moten, president of historically black Tuskegee Institute, was invited to speak at the memorial's dedication, yet officials sat him in a segregated section of the audience. In 1939 black contralto Marian Anderson, barred from the Daughters of the American Revolution's Constitution Hall, sang from the memorial's steps. Most famously, the historic 1963 March on Washington reached its zenith here when Martin Luther King Jr gave his 'I Have a Dream' speech (an engraving of his words marks the spot where he stood).

We'd advise you not to follow his example. While the pool is a lovely addition to the face of the Mall, it's also – the mallards love this spot – a 2000ft vat of duck shit.

WASHINGTON MONUMENT Map p54

☎ 202-619-7222; www.nps.gov/wamo; cnr Constitution Ave & 15th St; admission free, reservations $2; ☷ 9am-5pm, to 10pm summer; Ⓜ Smithsonian
Oldest joke in DC: 'So, what part of Washington is his monument modeled on?' Yeah,

top picks

MONUMENTS & MEMORIALS

- Vietnam Veterans Memorial (below)
- Tomb of the Unknowns, Arlington National Cemetery (p121)
- Lincoln Memorial (p55)
- National WWII Memorial (opposite)
- Franklin Delano Roosevelt Memorial (opposite)

that's right, America has a bigger…obelisk than you. At 555ft the monument is not only the tallest building in DC (by federal law no structure can reach above it), it is also the tallest masonry structure in the world.

Construction began in 1848 but a lack of funds during the Civil War kept building in a quagmire and the 90,854-ton, brick-and-marble structure was not completed until 1888. The original marble was drawn from Maryland, but the source dried up about a third of the way through construction and contractors had to turn to Massachusetts for marble. If you look closely there is a visible delineation in color where the old and new marble meet.

Inside the monument, an elevator whisks you to an observation landing deck. In the days before September 11, 2001 it was possible to descend the 897 steps rather than take the elevator – the shaft's interior is decorated with inscribed stones. Believe it or not, when the monument first opened the elevator was not considered safe for women; men got to ride in style to the top, while women had to hoof it.

Same-day tickets for a timed entrance are available at the ticket kiosk on the monument grounds. Distribution starts at 8am; make sure you arrive early as tickets are limited. Alternatively, you can reserve your tickets for a small fee by calling in advance. Food, drink and large bags are prohibited.

VIETNAM VETERANS MEMORIAL
Map p54

☎ 202-426-6841; www.nps.gov/vive; admission free; ☻ 8am-midnight; Ⓜ Foggy Bottom-GWU
This simple memorial is the most powerful in the city, if not the nation. A black granite 'V' cuts into the Mall, just as the war it memorializes cut into the national psyche.

The memorial eschews mixing conflict with glory. Instead, it quietly records the names of service personnel KIA and MIA (killed in action and missing in action) in Vietnam, honoring those who gave their lives and explaining, in stark architectural language, the true price paid in war.

Originally planned to reconcile a divided nation, the memorial was conceived by Maya Lin, a 21-year-old Yale architecture student, following a nationwide call for proposed designs in 1982. The two walls of Indian granite meet in a 10ft apex; their polished, mirror surface invites visitors into the roll call of the dead. There are over 58,200 soldiers named on the wall (the number sporadically increases as names are added due to clerical errors in record keeping). Rank is not provided on the wall, and privates share space with majors. Unlike the soaring white Washington Monument and similar structures, the Vietnam Memorial is black, and burrows into the ground.

Paper indices at both ends help you locate individual names. Left mementos such as photos of babies and hand-scrawled notes bring tears to the most hardened hearts; these are collected by rangers and brought to the National Museum of American History (p59).

In 1984 opponents of Maya Lin's design insisted that a more traditional sculpture of soldiers be added to the monument. The Three Soldiers depicts a white, African American and Latino soldier who seem to be gazing upon the nearby sea of names. Also nearby is the tree-ringed Women in Vietnam Memorial depicting female soldiers aiding a fallen combatant.

TIDAL BASIN Map p54

☎ 202-484-0206; admission free; ☻ 8am-dusk; Ⓜ Smithsonian
Beloved for the magnificent Yoshino cherry trees that ring it, the Tidal Basin is an elegant aquatic interruption to the stone and grass of the Mall and its surrounding web of roads. The orchard was a gift from Japan in 1912; since then, every year in late March or early April the banks shimmer with pale pink blossoms. When said blossoms start to shed, the effect of soft pink snow against warm spring weather is intoxicating. The National Cherry Blossom Festival (p13) celebrates this event – late March and early April draw 750,000 visitors to DC for the festivities, which culminate in a big parade.

The amoeba-shaped Tidal Basin serves a practical purpose: flushing the adjacent Washington Channel. At high tide, river waters fill the basin through gates under the Inlet Bridge; at low tide, gates under the Outlet Bridge open and water streams into the channel.

Visit the Tidal Basin Boathouse (☎ 202-479-2426; 1501 Maine Ave SW; 4-/2-person boat rental $18/10; ◔ 10am-6pm daily Mar 15-Sep, 10am-6pm Wed-Sun Oct-Mar 14) and rent out a paddleboat. Make sure you bring the camera; there are great views, of the Jefferson Memorial in particular, from the water.

THOMAS JEFFERSON MEMORIAL
Map p54

☎ 202-426-6841; www.nps.gov/thje; admission free; ◔ 24hr; M Smithsonian

Set on the south bank of the Tidal Basin amid the cherry trees (check it out in late March or early April when the blossoms are blazing pink), this memorial honors the third US president, political philosopher, drafter of the Declaration of Independence and founder of the University of Virginia. Designed by John Russell Pope to resemble Jefferson's library at the university, the rounded monument was initially derided by critics as 'the Jefferson Muffin.' We think the circular shape is a nice contrast to the angles jutting out from so many other monuments. Inside is a 19ft bronze likeness, and excerpts from Jefferson's writings are etched into the walls.

FRANKLIN DELANO ROOSEVELT MEMORIAL
Map p54

☎ 202-426-6841; www.nps.gov/fdrm; Memorial Park; admission free; ◔ 24hr; M Smithsonian

Only good memorials manage to capture the essence of their subject, but the FDR Memorial takes it a step further, encapsulating the longest-serving president in US history and the era he governed.

On the Tidal Basin's west bank, this landscaped 7.5-acre space is composed of four red-granite 'rooms' that narrate FDR's presidency, from the Depression to the New Deal to WWII. The story of both the man and the 1930s and '40s is told through statuary and inscriptions, punctuated with cascades and peaceful alcoves.

The irony is, FDR didn't want a grand memorial. In fact, when asked about a more traditional memorial, he reportedly responded 'If any memorial is erected to me, I should like it to consist of a block about the size of this desk and placed in front of the Archives Building. I want it plain, without any ornamentation, with the simple carving 'In Memory Of.' This request was honored in 1965, with a small stone slab (Map p88; cnr 9th St & Pennsylvania Ave NW).

Come at night. There are few better evening views of the Mall than the sight of reflected marble shimmering in the glossy stillness of the Tidal Basin.

NATIONAL WWII MEMORIAL Map p54

☎ 202-619-7222; www.wwiimemorial.com; admission free; M Smithsonian

Dedicated on Memorial Day (May 29) 2004, the WWII memorial honors the unity that swept the nation during that conflict, plus the 16 million Americans who served in the armed forces during the war, 400,000 who died in it and millions more who helped the effort at home.

The memorial anchors the eastern end of the Reflecting Pool, serving as a balancing axis between the Washington Monument (p55) and Lincoln Memorial (p55). The centerpiece is a plaza dominated by dual arches symbolizing victory in the Atlantic and Pacific theaters, surrounded by 56 granite pillars, one for each state and territory plus the District of Columbia. The Freedom Wall is studded with 4000 hand-sculpted gold stars, one for every 100 Americans who lost their

KILROY IS THERE

During WWII, a popular bit of serviceman graffiti was of a bulbous-nosed man peeking over a wall under the words 'Kilroy Was Here.' Old Kilroy graced walls from London to Okinawa by war's end (rumor has it Hitler thought Kilroy was some kind of super spy), and he's snuck onto the WWII Memorial as well – but he's not easy to find.

From the Pacific Tower, walk out of the memorial (ie away from the main plaza). There's a path here; follow it past the wreath-bedecked state and territory columns. After the columns end, you'll see an alcove/niche with metal grating for flooring. Engraved into the surrounding walls is Kilroy, peeping away, safe in the knowledge that he may be the only official graffiti allowed on any monument in the District.

lives between 1941 and 1945 (the stars are replicas of those worn by mothers who lost their sons in the war). Today, you'll often see widows and families placing flowers or fading black-and-white photos of handsome young men at the foot of the wall. Bas-relief panels depict both combat and the mobilization of the home front, and quotes – some truly stirring – speckle the entire affair.

KOREAN WAR VETERANS MEMORIAL
Map p54

☎ 202-426-6841; www.nps.gov/kowa; admission free; ☾ 8am-11:45pm; Ⓜ Foggy Bottom-GWU
Nineteen steel soldiers wander through clumps of juniper past a wall bearing images of the 'Forgotten War' that assemble, in the distance, into a panorama of the Korean mountains. Best visited at night, when the sculpted patrol – representing all races and combat branches that served in the war – takes on a phantom cast. In winter, when snow folds over the infantry's field coats, the impact is especially powerful.

NATIONAL GALLERY OF ART Map p54

☎ 202-737-4215; www.nga.gov; cnr 4th St & Constitution Ave NW; admission free; ☾ 10am-5pm Mon-Sat, 11am-6pm Sun; Ⓜ Archives-Navy Memorial
Affiliated with but not a part of the Smithsonian, the National Gallery needs two buildings (connected by an underground tunnel) to house its massive collections (more than 110,000 objects) of painting, sculpture and decorative arts from the Middle Ages to the present. The gallery, being a generalist sort of spot, doesn't quite excel in any one area (the Hirshhorn has better modern art, and the American Art Museum keeps a better national retrospective), but it's still pretty impressive. Kids love the walking escalator that traverses the two buildings.

The original neoclassical building, known as the West Building, exhibits primarily European works, from the Middle Ages to the early 20th century, including pieces by El Greco, Monet and Cézanne. The National Gallery is also the only gallery in America displaying a da Vinci (Ginevra di' Benci). Interactive computers in the Micro Gallery allow visitors to design their own tour. Across 4th St NW, the angular East Building, designed by IM Pei, is where you'll find an incredible giant mobile designed by Alexander Calder, along with other abstract and modern works.

NATIONAL MUSEUM OF NATURAL HISTORY Map p54

☎ 202-633-1000; www.mnh.si.edu; cnr 10th St & Constitution Ave NW; admission free, IMAX adult $8.75; ☾ 10am-5:30pm Sep-May, to 7:30pm Jun-Aug, tours 10:30am & 1:30pm; Ⓜ Federal Triangle
Kids: bust out the dinosaur fangs and your best T-Rex shamble. It's time to drag mom and dad around till they drop.

Don't worry parents, you're only joining the several other million guests who annually enter the second-most-popular museum in the Smithsonian. Say hello to the famous African elephant dominating the entrance rotunda and the nearby rotting carcass of a giant squid and get ready to explore one of the most eclectic collections of, well, stuff, anywhere. The exhibits are a bit oddly mashed up – what exactly do Javanese shadow puppets have to do with birds of northern Europe?

Traipse past the Hall of Dinosaurs to the supposedly cursed Hope Diamond, Easter Island heads and a permanent insect exhibition sponsored, of course, by Orkin (a pest control company). New displays are constantly added, yet the museum manages to maintain the old-school charm that caused many a metro-area school kid (including this author) to fall in love with it back in the day.

Almost 200 scientists work here, which the museum claims is the largest concentration of experts in natural history and cultures in the world. In a somewhat political statement, which is uncommon for the Smithsonian, the museum has heavily promoted its Darwin and evolution exhibits as a counter to creationism proponents.

The Johnson IMAX Theater shows nature extravaganzas like Bugs! in 3D daily. Movies sell out so buy tickets as soon as you arrive, or online in advance. A fun Friday night adventure – for kids and adults – is to visit the IMAX Jazz Café.

NATIONAL AIR & SPACE MUSEUM
Map p54

☎ 202-633-1000; www.nasm.si.edu; cnr 4th St & Independence Ave SW; admission free, IMAX or planetarium adult $8.75; ☾ 10am-5:30pm, tours 10:15am & 1pm; Ⓜ L'Enfant Plaza

The most popular Smithsonian museum is one of the best for kids and kids at heart, full of interactivity and things that go fast/boom/swoosh/etc. When you visit, don't forget to touch the moon. No, really, there's an actual chunk of lunar love here, its well-worn surface pressed by millions of curious fingers over the years. Other must-sees include Chuck Yeager's sound-barrier-breaking Bell X-1, Lindbergh's Spirit of St Louis, the Lunar Lander and the Wright Brothers' original airplane. They all hang from wires off the enormous ceiling, directing your gaze ever upwards to the eternal vault of the endless sk – *ow* – watch it kid!

That's the drawback of this spot: eight million visitors traipse through the Air & Space museum annually, and they all seem to visit at the same time. But you gotta come anyways. C'mon – they've got real nuclear missiles! Plus astronaut ice cream (the stuff they actually eat in space; it tastes awful) in the gift shop and the Lockheed Martin IMAX Theater, which offers a rotating list of films shown throughout the day. Alternative shows at the Albert Einstein Planetarium send viewers hurtling through space on tours of the universe. Buy your tickets as soon as you arrive, or on the museum website before you visit.

The Air & Space is so awesome they made an attic for it: the Steven F Udvar-Hazy Center (off Map p122; www.nasm.si.edu/museum/udvarhazy; 14390 Air and Space Museum Parkway, Chantilly, VA). Highlights include the SR-71 Blackbird (the fastest jet in the world), space shuttle *Enterprise* and the Enola Gay (the B-29 that dropped the atomic bomb on Hiroshima). Visitors can hang out in the observation tower and watch the planes take off and land at Dulles airport, or catch shows at the on-site Airbus IMAX Theater. As of writing, a new wing called Phase 2, meant to showcase restoration efforts and archival material was under construction. To get out here, you'll need to either drive (take I-66 West to VA 267 West, then VA 28 South, then follow the signs) or take Metro bus 5A to Dulles. From there, it's an $8 to $12 taxi ride, or you can take a 50¢ Virginia Regional Transit (www.vatransit.org) bus to the museum.

Together these two sites comprise the world's largest collection of aviation and space artifacts, and folks, that's pretty damn cool.

NATIONAL MUSEUM OF AMERICAN HISTORY Map p54

☎ 202-633-1000; www.americanhistory.si.edu; cnr 14th St & Constitution Ave NW; admission free; 🕙 10am-5:30pm; Ⓜ Federal Triangle

After undergoing a long series of renovations, this institution has accented itself with the daily bric-a-brac of the American experience – synagogue shawls, protest signs and cotton gins – along with icons such as Dorothy's slippers and Kermit the Frog (yes, he is the cutest thing you'll find in Washington, DC. Even the pandas in the zoo can't compete). The centerpiece of the museum is a viewing space of the flag that flew over Fort McHenry in Baltimore during the War of 1812 – the same flag that inspired Francis Scott Key to pen *The Star-Spangled Banner*. In general, this is a better museum for children than adults; displays tend to be bright and interactive, perhaps a little too much so for those seeking a more serious engagement with the nation's history. There are still some old displays from pre-renovation days left over, which are great for their unintentional kitsch value.

HIRSHHORN MUSEUM & SCULPTURE GARDEN Map p54

☎ 202-633-4674; www.hirshhorn.si.edu; cnr 7th St & Independence Ave SW; admission free; 🕙 10am-5:30pm daily, to 8pm Thu Jul & Aug, sculpture garden 7:30am-dusk; Ⓜ L'Enfant Plaza

The Smithsonian's cylindrical modern art museum is the best of its kind in Washington. Sculptures and canvases are presented in chronological fashion, from modernism's early days to pop art to contemporary. Gallery spaces are usually airy and bright, infused with the right edge of cold showroom chic you expect in modern art museums. Highlights include sculptures by Rodin, Brancusi, Calder and Moore, along with canvases by Bacon, Miró, O'Keeffe, Warhol, Stella and Kiefer. On Fridays and Saturdays, the Improv Art Room invites children to create their own works of art.

Outside and across Jefferson Dr, the sunken Sculpture Garden feels, on the right day, like a bouncy jaunt through a Lewis Carroll Wonderland all prettified up. Young lovers, lost tourists and serene locals wander by sculptures such as Rodin's *The Burghers of Calais*.

UNITED STATES BOTANIC GARDEN
Map p54

☎ 202-225-8333; www.usbg.gov; 100 Maryland Ave SW; admission free; 🕙 10am-5pm; Ⓜ Capitol South

Resembling London's Crystal Palace, this iron-and-glass greenhouse provides a beautiful setting for displays of exotic and local plants. Make sure to check out the Titan Arum, also known as *Amorphophallus titanum* ('giant misshapen penis') and the 'corpse flower' (a Sumatran native that blooms rarely and randomly throughout the year, but when it does, it smells like rotten meat. Mmm!) Behind the conservatory, across Independence Ave, you'll find the grand Bartholdi Fountain.

NATIONAL MUSEUM OF ASIAN ART
Map p54

☎ 202-633-1000; www.asia.si.edu; admission free; 🕙 10am-5:30pm daily, to 8pm Thu Jul & Aug; Ⓜ Smithsonian

The dangling sculpture *Monkeys Grasping for the Moon*, an image of a dozen stylized primates fashioned into the word 'monkey' in a like number of languages (including Japanese, Hebrew, braille and Urdu) is perhaps the most impressive piece of introductory art to welcome you to a Smithsonian institution – and a reminder that you have just entered a very special museum. The Arthur M Sackler Gallery (1050 Independence Ave SW) and Freer Gallery of Art (cnr 12 St & Jefferson Dr SW) combine to form the National Museum of Asian Art, one of the most pleasant Smithsonian museums in the capital. Make sure to visit them in tandem.

This is simply a lovely spot in which to while away a Washington afternoon. Japanese silk scrolls, buddhas flashing *Mona Lisa* smiles, rare Islamic manuscripts and a treasure of Silk Road artifacts – many the gift of Dr Arthur M Sackler – are all housed in appealingly spare and well-executed galleries. When you finish in the Sackler, jaunt over to the Freer Gallery of Art, which offers its own incredible ensemble of ancient ceramics, Southeast Asian temple sculpture and centuries-old Chinese scrolls, a gift from Detroit industrialist Charles Lang Freer. The self-taught connoisseur was also a fan of James McNeill Whistler, whose works, somewhat incongruously, also appear here.

Like all Smithsonian institutions, free lectures, film screenings etc are hosted here; check www.si.edu for details.

NATIONAL MUSEUM OF AFRICAN ART Map p54

☎ 202-633-4600; www.nmafa.si.edu; 950 Independence Ave SW; admission free; 🕙 10am-5:30pm daily, to 8pm Thu Jul & Aug; Ⓜ Smithsonian

Enter the museum's ground-level pavilion through the Asian moon gates and geometric flower beds of the beautiful Enid A Haupt Memorial Garden, then descend into the dim underground exhibit space, connected by tunnel to the National Museum of Asian Art (left). Devoted to ancient and modern sub-Saharan African art, the quiet galleries display masks, textiles, ceramics, ritual objects and other examples of the visual traditions of a continent of over 900 distinct cultures. Intentionally or not, there's a definite West African focus here – this is the traditional art many people associate with Africa, including wooden masks, statues and fetish dolls, largely from Nigeria, Benin and Cameroon. That said, the museum is making admirable strides in showcasing more contemporary work from the continent. African dance troupes, theater companies and multimedia artists frequently stage shows here.

NATIONAL MUSEUM OF THE AMERICAN INDIAN Map p54

☎ 202-287-2020; www.americanindian.si.edu; cnr 4th St & Independence Ave SW; admission free; 🕙 10am-5:30pm Sep-May, to 7:30pm Jun-Aug; Ⓜ Smithsonian, Federal Center SW

The award for most impressive external architecture of any museum on the Mall (and perhaps in the city) goes to the Museum of the American Indian. The curving exterior blobs like an art-house amoeba on the eastern edge of the Mall; fashioned from rough Kasota limestone that blushes honey in the sunset, it manages to look rustic and strong yet liquid and organic all at once. In fact, there are no sharp edges to be found anywhere – the impression is one of nature flowing into the learning space, accentuated by an outside green area of wetlands and micro-biomes meant to simulate the ecosystem of the North American continent.

Inside, you'll find the story of Native Americans told in a format not often em-

THANK YOU, JAMES

Englishman James Smithson never set foot in the USA, let alone Washington, DC. Yet he was an inestimable boon to the District and the nation she governs thanks to the $508,318 he willed to America in 1826. The money was to be used to create an 'establishment for the increase and diffusion of knowledge,' and said gift horse was promptly looked in the mouth by the government.

'Every whippersnapper vagabond…might think it proper to have his name distinguished in the same way,' grumbled Senator William Preston, while Senator John C Calhoun argued it was 'beneath American dignity to accept presents from anyone.' Anti-British sentiment informed some of this debate: the 1814 British torching of Washington (see p21) remained fresh in many American minds. Finally, in 1846, Congress deigned to accept the gift and turned a cool half million into the final destination of countless elementary school field trips by constructing the Smithsonian.

So who was Smithson? A mineralogist by trade and shrewd investor by evidence (his gift was a fortune for its time), he was well-educated and wealthy by any measure. But his motivations for bequeathing so much money to the USA, as opposed to his native Britain (or anywhere else, for that matter), remain a mystery. Some say he was an antimonarchist who took a particular shine to the American Republic. He may have just loved learning; to quote Smithson, 'Every man is a valuable member of society who by his observations, researches, and experiments procures knowledge for men.' Today Smithson is entombed in the Smithsonian Castle (p62). His coffin incorrectly states he died at 75; he was 64.

He left behind quite a baby: the collected attic of the American psyche, as it were. Only 1% of the Smithsonian's approximately 140 million artworks, scientific specimens, artifacts and other objects is on display at any given point. Ten of its 18 DC museums are scattered across the National Mall, with the rest found around the city; the organization also operates the National Zoological Park and throws the annual Smithsonian Folklife Festival (p14) on the Mall every summer. The best part about the Smithsonian museums is that there's no entry fee, so you needn't feel guilty about not staying all day. Plus, if you're traveling with the tykes, free admission means you can come and go in accordance with your little ones' attention spans.

The Smithsonian needs (and is receiving) some expensive upkeep. It has been suggested the museums start charging for admission, but the powers that be won't hear of it, arguing fees would fly in the face of the Smithsonian's mission. The museums will stay free if it kills them, which is a sad possibility. Currently, the Arts & Industries Museum (www .si.edu/ai; 900 Jefferson Dr SW) is closed indefinitely.

---

ployed by mainstream museums, with mixed results. The idea, to use native communities' voices and their own interpretations, is imaginative. Unfortunately, by allowing each tribe to promote their own version of their culture, the exhibits can come off as marketing rather than learning material.

That said, the collection, which consists of nearly a million objects (sourced from Canada and Mexico as well as the United States) is impressive, and this museum is still worth a few hours of your time. The onsite Mitsitam Native Foods Cafe (p146) is the best dining option on the Mall.

NEWSEUM Map p54

☎ 888-639-7386; www.newseum.org; 555 Pennsylvania Ave; adult/child $20/13; 🕑 9am-5pm; Ⓜ Archives-Navy Memorial, Judiciary Square
Unaffiliated with the Smithsonian (ergo the cost of admission), the 'most interactive museum in the world' is dedicated to the craft of news gathering and dissemination. Unfortunately it offers a little too much flash and not quite enough substance –

lots of CNN-esque zippy graphics and booming montages of current events, but not a lot of insight into the day-to-day work of beat reporting. Still, it's great for the kids, and the memorial to journos killed in pursuit of the truth, plus exhibits on press freedoms and ethics, are worth the price of admission. It's also worth your time to wander in front of the Newseum, where the front pages of newspapers from around the world are displayed every day.

NATIONAL SCULPTURE GARDEN
Map p54

www.nga.gov/feature/sculpturegarden/general/index.shtm; cnr 9th St & Constitution Ave NW; admission free; 🕑 10am-6pm Mon-Thu & Sat, to 8:30pm Fri, 11am-6pm Sun; Ⓜ Archives-Navy Memorial
The National Gallery of Art's 6-acre garden is studded with whimsical sculptures such as Roy Lichtenstein's *House,* a giant Claes Oldenburg typewriter eraser and Louise Bourgeois' leggy *Spider.* They are scattered around a fountain – a great place to dip your feet in summer. From November to

March the garden's central fountain becomes an Ice Rink (adult/child $7/6; ☺ 10am-10pm). Skate rental is available. During summer the garden is open an hour later than the rest of the year and evening jazz concerts are held on Fridays starting around 5pm.

CONSTITUTION GARDENS Map p54
admission free; ☺ dawn-dusk; Ⓜ Smithsonian
Constitution Gardens is a bit of a locals' secret. Quiet, shady and serene, it's a reminder of the size of the Mall – how can such isolation exist amid so many tourists? Here's the simple layout: a copse of trees set off by a small kidney-shaped pool, punctuated by a tiny island holding the Signers' Memorial, a plaza honoring those who signed the Declaration of Independence. At the northeast corner is an elegantly aged stone cottage, a remnant of the days when the Washington City Canal flowed through this area. The 1835 C&O Canal Gatehouse was the lock-keepers' house for the lock that transferred boats from the City Canal onto the C&O Canal (p73), which begins in Georgetown. If you're in need of a romantic getaway, the 'kiss me' vibes don't get much better than this spot at sunset.

SMITHSONIAN CASTLE Map p54
☎ 202-633-1000; www.smithsonian.org; 1000 Jefferson Dr SW; admission free; ☺ 9am-4pm Mon-Sat; Ⓜ Smithsonian
James Renwick designed this turreted, red-sandstone fairy tale in 1855. Today the castle houses the Smithsonian Visitors Center (p247). This informative first stop on the Mall is a source for an orientation film, multilingual touch-screen displays and free guides and maps.

DISTRICT OF COLUMBIA WAR MEMORIAL Map p54
West Potomac Park off Independence Ave; admission free; ☺ 24hr
This small Greek-style temple commemorates local soldiers killed in WWI, making it the only local District memorial on the Mall. The circular structure is supported by 12 Doric 22ft-high marble columns; inside are the names of the 26,000 Washingtonians who served in the war and the 499 DC soldiers killed in action. In 2008, Representative Ted Poe of Texas put forward HR482, the Frank Buckles WWI Memorial Act (named for the last living US veteran of WWI). If passed, the law would expand the site into a national WWI memorial. As of writing the bill was referred to subcommittee; to follow its progress, see www.open congress.org/bill/111-h482/show.

GEORGE MASON MEMORIAL Map p54
☎ 202-426-6841; www.nps.gov/gemm; Ohio Dr SW; admission free; ☺ 8am-midnight; Ⓜ Smithsonian
This little oasis of flowers and fountains honors the famed statesman and author of the Commonwealth of Virginia Declaration of Rights (a forerunner to the US Bill of Rights). A bronze sculpture of Mason sits (literally; his legs are crossed and the man looks eminently relaxed) under a pretty covered arcade, amid wise words against slavery and in support of human rights.

WASHINGTON DC MARTIN LUTHER KING JR MEMORIAL Map p54
www.mlkmemorial.org; admission free; Ⓜ Smithsonian
The newest potential memorial on the Mall, and the first one to honor an African American, has been mired in funding difficulties for the past few years. Ground breaking started in the fall of 2006, with completion set for 2008, but as of this writing the memorial foundation was still trying to secure its final construction permits.

Once built, the MLK memorial will occupy space along the Tidal Basin, near the Jefferson and FDR Memorials, and will convey themes of democracy, justice and hope. The design includes a crescent-shaped wall with sermon inscriptions etched onto its stone surface. The centerpiece of the memorial will be a Stone of Hope, featuring a 30ft-tall likeness of Dr King.

WHITE HOUSE AREA & FOGGY BOTTOM

Eating p146; Shopping p128; Nightlife p173; Sleeping p203

The National Mall may be packed with the most symbols of the American experience, but for all its impressive sites it still may not take the stakes when you play image association with the words 'Washington, DC.' The one mental snapshot most people from outside the District have of the city is the White House, a pale flame slipped into a grid of dark, manicured grounds and stately architecture. Be-columned and bewitching, the president's residence is most impressive in the evening, when its backlighting takes on notes that are at once triumphant and dignified.

The neighborhood surrounding the White House isn't exactly residential – it's not like folks pop over to 1600 Pennsylvania Ave to borrow a cup of sugar. While the blocks adjacent to the White House *are* fronted by stately mansions of the sort you'd expect to see so close to the most important address in the country, these buildings aren't museum pieces. Instead they are, by and large, places of business, humming by day with the comings and goings of office workers, diplomats, lobbyists, tourists, bureaucrats and a largely immigrant serving staff who, quite literally, sweep the corridors of power.

Architecturally, you're walking around some of the city's prettiest gems, representing the height of American embellishment and decorative arts. All in all, there's a sense of regal importance on these streets blended with the bustle of a very alive and important nerve cluster of federal power. The resultant energy – dignified, self-important and ambitious – is key to the character of DC as a world capital.

This live-to-work neighborhood dies a sudden and severe death most nights, although there are a few overpriced, underwhelming nightclubs serving the whims of the elite, or those who want to feel elite. Beside that, a few excellent high-end restaurants and mediocre, largely chain-brand cafes and sandwich shops keep everyone in the area fed. Except the homeless. To the general surprise of many first-time visitors, and consternation of a fair few residents, green spaces such as McPherson and Farragut Sqs, mere blocks from the White House, are popular begging and sleeping spots for DC street people.

West of here is Foggy Bottom, a name you'll surely recognize from *The West Wing*, *The X Files*, *All the President's Men* and practically any other form of dramatic media that has taken the time to portray the District. The evocative name derives from both Foggy Bottom's low-lying geography, which serves as a catchment for Potomac mists, and the clouds of smoke that emanated from the heavy industry once concentrated here. Thanks to that industry this was once a blue-collar corner of town, a center for African American institutions and culture and a magnet for German and Irish immigrants, who found employment in local factories and foundries.

That's hardly the case today. Today Foggy Bottom is synonymous with the State Department, World Bank, IMF and other high-octane DC power-broker institutions. As a result there's a fairly sterile, corporate-y vibe here, broken by the buzz in some wheeler-dealer restaurants and one of the city's most famous institutes of higher education: George Washington University (GWU). The campus of 'G-dub,' as many call it, injects Foggy Bottom with a fair amount of frat boy-ish energy come evenings; the bar scene here may not be particularly big or varied, but it's raucous. Otherwise, the nearby Kennedy Center and GWU's own arts department both provide a nice dose of culture, a refreshing contrast to the seemingly endless office spaces.

While this is a 'hood many locals only visit from 9am to 5pm, there are good and valiant attempts at maintaining and reinvigorating the sense of community among Foggy Bottom's small but neighborly residential blocks.

ORIENTATION

Pennsylvania Ave cuts across Northwest DC on a diagonal from the Capitol to the White House, then continues on its northwestern trajectory into Georgetown, although not without a major detour (where there is no access for cars) around the president's home. The White House area and Foggy Bottom comprise a square (in shape as well as attitude) bounded by the Potomac River and the National Mall. For our purposes, the northern boundary of the neighborhood is M St NW, although K St NW – two blocks south – is a busier, more prominent thoroughfare. On the east, 14th St NW marks the line between the White House area and Downtown & Penn Quarter.

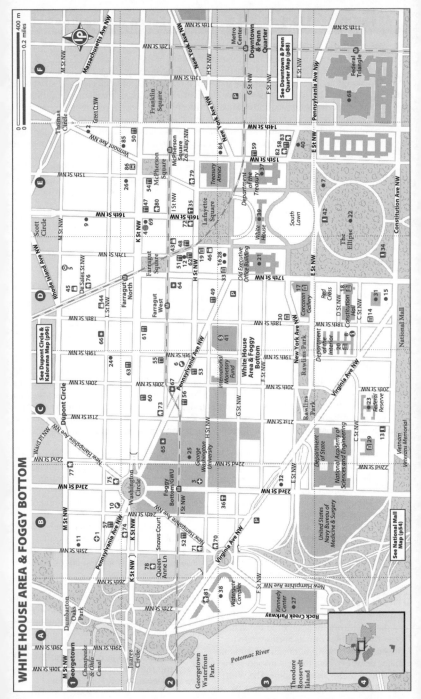

See Dupont Circle & Kalorama Map (p96)

See Downtown & Penn Quarter Map (p88)

See National Mall Map (p54)

Potomac River

0   400 m
0   0.2 miles

WHITE HOUSE AREA & FOGGY BOTTOM

Further west, the confluence of K St, 23rd St, Pennsylvania Ave and New Hampshire Ave forms Washington Circle, the top of Foggy Bottom. The campus of George Washington University (GWU) dominates the blocks south of Washington Circle. South of GWU, anchoring the west end of the neighborhood, the Kennedy Center and the Watergate rise over the Potomac.

NEIGHBORHOOD RESOURCES

- Foggy Bottom Association (www.savefoggy bottom.com)
- Golden Triangle Business Improvement District (www.goldentriangledc.com)

WHITE HOUSE AREA

WHITE HOUSE Map p64

☎ 202-456-7041; www.whitehouse.gov; 1600 Pennsylvania Ave NW; ☻ closed to public; Ⓜ Farragut West

Unlike many sites of similar caliber, the White House feels more uplifting than somber. Maybe that's because this is, at the end of the day, a home as well as a symbol. The White House stuns visitors with its sense of pomp and circumstance, yet it also charms with little left traces of those who have lived here before, which includes every US president since John Adams. Icon of the American presidency? Yeah. But it's also someone's front yard.

VISITING THE WHITE HOUSE

To get into the White House you either need to a) work there, b) be elected president, c) get invited or d) come on a public tour with a group of 10 or more. If you don't have enough heads, try anyway; sometimes groups are combined. Americans need to make a request through their Member of Congress up to six months in advance; tours are usually confirmed a month beforehand. Foreigners should contact their embassy in Washington, DC, which can submit a tour request on your behalf. The tour itself is self-guided and runs from 7:30am to 12:30pm Tuesday to Saturday; call ☎ 202-456-7041 for details.

The Presidential Palace – as it was once known – has changed a great deal over history. It was not originally white, for example. After the British burned the building in the War of 1812, it was restored and painted. Teddy Roosevelt gave official sanction to the executive mansion's popular name. Presidents have customized the property over time: Grant put in a personal zoo; FDR, a pool; Truman, a balcony; Bush, a horseshoe-throwing lane; and Clinton, a jogging track. Some residents never leave: it's said that Eleanor Roosevelt and Harry Truman both sighted Lincoln's ghost in Abe's old study.

An overhaul in 1950 gutted almost the entire interior, and Jacqueline Kennedy's extensive redecoration campaign in the 1960s replaced a previous hodgepodge of knickknacks with her immaculate style.

Getting inside the White House can be tough (see Visiting the White House, above), but the grounds are occasionally opened for special events such as Tee-ball on the South Lawn and the Easter Egg Roll, held every Easter Monday for kids aged three to six. In lieu of touring the actual White House, visitors can browse exhibits, watch historic reenactments and take a video tour of the White House at the Visitors Center (☎ 202-208-1631; www.nps.gov/whho; 1450 Pennsylvania Ave NW; admission free; 7:30am-4pm; M McPherson Sq) in the Malcolm Baldrige Hall in the Department of Commerce building. It's obviously not the same as seeing the real deal first-hand, but the center does do its job very well, giving good history sprinkled with great anecdotes on presidential spouses, kids and pets. Betcha didn't know each president designs their own Oval Office rug?

CORCORAN GALLERY OF ART Map p64
☎ 202-639-1700; www.corcoran.org; 500 17th St NW; adult/child under 6/student & senior $10/free/8; 10-5pm Wed & Fri-Sun, to 9pm Thu; M Farragut West

You'd think the largest private museum in the city couldn't compare to the Smithsonian – and you'd think wrong. The Corcoran's permanent gallery of American, European and contemporary art is grand enough, but special exhibitions, which focus on themes such as Lichtenstein's work, the art of the Harlem Renaissance and the theses projects culled from the Corcoran's own school of design, are the real standout. It's all located in a beautiful 1897 beaux-arts building overlooking the Ellipse. A major restoration of the facade is scheduled for completion in fall of 2010.

Behind the Corcoran, on E St NW between 18th and 20th Sts NW, pretty Rawlins Park is named for President US Grant's Secretary of War. With goldfish in its little pond and blooming magnolias in spring and summer, it's among downtown DC's more charming oases.

RENWICK GALLERY Map p64
☎ 202-633-7970; http://americanart.si.edu/renwick; cnr 17th St & Pennsylvania Ave NW; admission free; 10am-5:30pm; M Farragut West

Part of the Smithsonian American Art Museum, the Renwick highlights the American tradition of decorative arts and crafts. Housed in a regal 1859 mansion, there's a sense of eccentricity and loving whimsy; the 'crafts' here straddle a line between utilitarian and artistic expression. The many playful pieces make this a wonderful place to introduce kids to art. We love Kim Schmahmann's *Bureau of Bureaucracy*, a hilariously accurate expression of the futility of dealing with official ineptitude realized in a cabinet plucked from MC Escher's nightmares.

ST JOHN'S CHURCH Map p64
☎ 202-347-8766; 1525 H St NW; 9am-3pm, services 12.10pm Mon-Sat, 7:45am, 9am & 11am Sun, Spanish service 1pm Sun; M McPherson Sq

A small building, St John's isn't DC's most imposing church, but it is arguably its most important. That's because it's the 'Church of the Presidents' – every president since Madison has attended services here at least once, and pew 54 is reserved for the Big Guy (er, the president; not God).

LAFAYETTE SQUARE Map p64
Pennsylvania Ave btwn 15th & 17th Sts NW
The land north of 1600 Pennsylvania was originally deeded as part of the White House grounds. However, in 1804 President Thomas Jefferson decided to divide the plot and give half back to the public in the form of a park, now known as Lafayette Sq. A statue of Andrew Jackson astride a horse holds court in the center, while the statues anchoring the four corners are all of foreign-born revolutionary leaders, a nice reminder that non-American freedom fighters helped ensure American independence.

In the southeast corner check out the likeness of the Marquis de Lafayette, a revolutionary war general by the age of 19. Although Lafayette was branded a traitor in his native France following the war, he was consistently lauded in the young America. In the northeast corner is a memorial to Tadeusz Kosciusko, a Polish soldier and prominent engineer in Washington's army. The sculpture is one of the more in-your-face ones in town: Kosciusko towers over an angry imperial eagle killing a snake atop a globe, and an inscription at the base, taken from Scottish poet Thomas Campbell, reads: 'And Freedom shrieked as Kosciusko fell!'

ELLIPSE Map p64
Constitution Ave btwn 15th & 17th Sts NW
That elliptical road that circles the expansive park on the south side of the White House? It's imaginatively known as the Ellipse. The park is studded with a random collection of monuments, such as the Zero Milestone (the marker for highway distances all across the country) and the Second Division Memorial. But the more important function of the Ellipse is hosting sporting events, parades and festivals – from lighting the national Christmas tree, to military drill performances to Lance Armstrong's final ride.

DECATUR HOUSE Map p64
☎ 202-842-0920; www.decaturhouse.org; 748 Jackson Place NW, visitor entrance 1610 H St NW; admission by donation; ☷ 10am-5pm Tue, Wed, Fri & Sat, to 8pm Thu, noon-4pm Sun; Ⓜ Farragut West
Designed in 1818 by Benjamin Latrobe for the War of 1812 naval hero Stephen Decatur, Decatur House sits at Lafayette Sq's northwest corner. It holds the honor of being the first and last house on the square to be occupied as a private residence, and architecturally, it's an interesting mash-up of austere Federal and wedding cake Victorian influences. A tour details the lives of famous tenants – including Martin Van Buren and Henry Clay – and the slaves who waited upon them.

NATIONAL ACADEMY OF SCIENCES
Map p64
☎ 202-334-2000; www.nasonline.org; 2101 Constitution Ave NW; admission free; ☷ 9am-5pm Mon-Fri; Ⓜ Foggy Bottom-GWU
Made up of approximately 2100 members, including almost 200 Nobel Prize winners,

ARCHITECTURAL ACCENTS
There are a lot of interesting buildings in this part of town.

An office building by any other name, the designers of 800 Connecticut Ave knew it would be utilized by lobbyists and politicos. As a result it prickles with terraces and corner offices that provide excellent lines of site to the White House; TV news crews often use this space when they need footage of the president's pad. The Treasury Building (1500 Pennsylvania Ave) took 30 years and the work of some of America's most important 19th-century architects to build. It took a while to find a place to plop the building, and legend has it President Andrew Jackson, ticked off by foot-dragging, stood on the current spot and yelled, 'Build it here!' As a result, Pierre L'Enfant's planned clear line of sight between the White House and the Capitol was ruined.

The Eisenhower Building (cnr 17th St & Pennsylvania Ave) is done up with all the baroque flair of the late 19th-century, also known as the Gilded Age. The sloped mansard roof is European in origin, while its 900 columns are wonderfully ostentatious. Currently the building is used as an office wing of the executive branch.

The headquarters of the Daughters of the American Revolution (1776 D St NW), also known as Constitution Hall, is a great example of neoclassical architecture, and supposedly the largest complex of buildings in the world owned exclusively by women. In contrast to the above buildings, the Pan American Health Organization (525 23rd St NW) and the World Bank (1818 H St NW) headquarters are great examples of a muscular modernism; the latter in particular can seem brutal in places, while the former evokes a more friendly, futuristic feel.

these are the guys the government hits up for scientific advice (whether the government listens to them or not is, as you may have guessed, entirely up to the government). The NAS hosts scientific and art exhibitions and symposiums, and concerts are often held on Sunday afternoons.

The nicely landscaped grounds along Constitution Ave feature DC's most huggable monument (well, besides the Kitten and Puppy Memorial – kidding): the Albert Einstein statue. The larger-than-life, sandal-shod, chubby bronze reclines on a bench, while little kids crawl all over him and frolic on a 'star map,' which depicts the heavens that his theories reshaped for humanity.

ORGANIZATION OF AMERICAN STATES Map p64

☎ 202-458-3000; www.oas.org; 201 18th St NW; admission free; 🕑 10am-5pm Tue-Sun; Ⓜ Farragut West

A forerunner to the UN, the OAS was founded in 1890 to promote cooperation among North and South American nations. Its main building at 17th St and Constitution Ave is a marble palazzo surrounded by the sculpture-studded Aztec Gardens. In the small building behind it, the OAS operates the Art Museum of the Americas (www.museum.oas.org), featuring an incredible collection of art that spans the 20th century and the western hemisphere.

FEDERAL RESERVE Map p64

☎ 202-452-3324; www.federalreserve.gov; 20th St NW btwn C St & Constitution Ave; admission free; 🕑 tours by reservation; Ⓜ Farragut West

'The Fed,' which resembles a cross between a Greek temple and a Soviet-era bunker, is the Olympus of the Gods of the American Economy. Unfortunately, you won't see too much fiscal action on tours; these focus on the architecture of the Eccles Building, which houses the reserve. You do get to visit the board room, which looks like the place where the world's economy is batted about like a big ball of yarn between some very powerful cats. That said, the tour – which must be pre-arranged by calling at least two weeks in advance – is recommended for adults only (kids will likely get bored).

Visitors can also view the Fed's art collection, part of which is displayed in the atrium of the Eccles Building; the permanent collection is a survey of American art from the 1830s to the present. The board also presents rotating exhibitions of borrowed art on varied themes like currency design.

DEPARTMENT OF THE INTERIOR MUSEUM Map p64

☎ 202-208-4743; www.doi.gov/interiormuseum; 1849 C St NW; admission free; 🕑 8:30am-4:30pm Mon-Fri, 1-4pm 3rd Sat of month; Ⓜ Farragut West

Responsible for managing the nation's natural resources, the Department of the

PECULIAR PRESIDENTIAL PETS

Most of you have probably heard of Bo Obama (or as everyone calls him, 'Bobama'), the Portuguese water dog that is America's current first pet. He's cute, although this author thinks he kinda looks like something you scrub grotty pans with. We digress. Before Bo was Barney the terrier, preceded by Socks the cat, Buddy the Labrador and then…well, here are some suitably awesome pets you may never have known graced the presidential digs.

- Billy the pygmy hippo – rubber maker Harvey Firestone brought Billy all the way from Liberia for Calvin Coolidge in 1927, who, for the record, already owned a wallaby, a duiker (a kind of African antelope) and a raccoon. Billy ended up in the National Zoo when (contrary to his species name) he got too big for the White House.
- The Adams alligators – let's say you're the Marquis de Lafayette and you want to get a present for John Quincy Adams, the kind of guy who likes to go swimming, naked, in the Potomac every morning. How about: two alligators! In the 1820s, Adams, skinny-dipping badass that he was, happily housed the two reptiles in the White House bathtub.
- Pauline Wayne the cow – William Taft let Pauline, a Holstein gift from a Wisconsin Senator, graze the front lawn of the White House from 1909 to 1913, during his term. The trade-off? Pauline provided milk for the first family during Taft's last three years in office.
- Josiah the badger – all of the above animals were thoughtful presents to sitting presidents. Josiah, on the other hand, was apparently a furry assassination attempt. In 1903, a girl in Kansas threw ornery Josiah directly at Theodore Roosevelt. Roosevelt, the kind of guy who hunted lions and charged fortified positions like San Juan hill on foot, ended up taking the little guy back to Washington.

Interior operates this small but excellent museum to educate the public about its current goals and programs. It includes landscape art, Native American artifacts and some great historical photos of Native American life, as well as exhibits on wildlife and resource management. Reserve two weeks in advance for guided tours of the building itself, which contains 25 tremendous New Deal murals from the 1930s and 1940s. Adults need photo identification to enter.

BLAIR & LEE HOUSES Map p64
1653 Pennsylvania Ave NW; ⏷ **closed to public;** Ⓜ **Farragut West**
The 1824 Blair House has been the official presidential guesthouse since 1942, when Eleanor Roosevelt got sick of tripping over dignitaries in the White House. A plaque on the front fence commemorates the bodyguard killed here while protecting president Truman from a 1950 assassination attempt by pro-independence militants from Puerto Rico (Truman was living here while the White House was undergoing renovations).

The neighboring 1858 Lee House was built by Robert E Lee's family. This is where Lee declined command of the Union Army when the Civil War erupted.

FOGGY BOTTOM
GEORGE WASHINGTON UNIVERSITY
Map p64
☎ **202-994-1000; www.gwu.edu; 801 22nd St NW; admission free;** ⏷ **9am-5pm Mon-Fri, 10am-3pm Sat Aug-Apr;** Ⓜ **Foggy Bottom-GWU**
The university that shares the District's namesake spreads all throughout the streets of Foggy Bottom. Known as 'G-dub' or 'GW', this school has been a bedrock of Washington identity since its founding in 1821. Besides shaping much of the American political landscape, GW has shaped the capital itself, buying-up townhouses on such a scale that it is now the city's second-biggest landowner after the federal government. Plenty of famous alumni have studied here: Edgar Hoover, Jacqueline Kennedy Onassis, Colin Powell, Brian Williams, Haddaway (you know, the guy who sang 'What Is Love?').

The school is spread over several blocks between F, 20th and 24th Sts and Pennsyl-

vania Ave in Foggy Bottom. The best bit of the campus is University Yard, between G, H, 20th and 21st Sts, where Colonial-revival buildings flank a green park bedecked with roses and a statue of – who else? – Washington.

OCTAGON MUSEUM Map p64
☎ **202-638-3221; www.theoctagon.org; 1799 New York Ave NW;** ⏷ **tours by arrangement;** Ⓜ **Farragut West**
The apex of the Federal style of architecture pioneered in the USA also happens to be the oldest museum in America dedicated to architecture and design. Designed by William Thornton (the Capitol's first architect) in 1800, the building is a symmetrically winged structure designed to fit an odd triangular lot. Behind it, the American Institute of Architects' (AIA) large modern offices wrap around like a protective older brother. AIA operates Octagon House and the building was closed for renovation as of press time, but should be open by the time you read this; tours ($5 prerenovation) can be arranged by calling ahead.

K STREET Map p64
Ⓜ **Farragut North, McPherson Sq**
K St is the center of the Washington lobbying industry. This is where high-powered lawyers, consultants and, of course, lobbyists ('K St' and 'lobbyist' have practically become synonymous since the 1990s) bark into their Blackberries and enjoy expensive lunches. Come nightfall, the same power set comes back with hair considerably slicked and/or flattened to drink expensive cocktails while surrounded by the sort of people who swoon over everything we've just described.

In total contrast are some lovely nearby green spaces. Franklin Square (between 13th and 14th Sts) is a large stretch of green open space thick with trees, paths and benches. Check out the Victorian-era redbrick Franklin School keeping watch over the patch. The architecture around McPherson Square, named for Civil War general James B McPherson who once commanded the Army of Tennessee, is fabulous. Keep an eye out for the 1924 neoclassical, limestone Investment Building (cnr 15th & K Sts) and the lion's head plaques of the terracotta Southern Building (805 11th St), which are meticulously carved and date from 1910.

ST MARY'S EPISCOPAL CHURCH
Map p64

☎ 202-333-3985; http://stmarysfoggybottom
.org/smc; 730 23rd St NW; Ⓜ Foggy Bottom-GWU
Built in 1887, St Mary's was home to the
first black Episcopal congregation in DC.
James Renwick, designer of the Smithsonian Castle, created the beautiful redbrick
building especially for the congregation.
Above the altar are French-made painted-
glass windows that depict, among others,
the African bishop and martyr St Cyprian.

STATE DEPARTMENT Map p64

US Department of State; ☎ 202-647-3241; www
.state.gov, https://receptiontours.state.gov; cnr
22nd & C Sts NW; admission free; ⓨ tours by
reservation 9:30am, 10:30am & 2:45pm Mon-Fri;
Ⓜ Foggy Bottom-GWU
The headquarters of the American diplomatic corps is a forbidding, well-guarded
edifice, all modernist, blocky and un-
friendly. In stark contrast are the elegant
grand diplomatic reception rooms, where
Cabinet members and the Secretary of
State entertain visiting potentates amid
ornate 18th-century American antiques.
Call at least a month beforehand to reserve
a tour spot, and bring photo ID; no kids
under 12 are admitted.

WATERGATE COMPLEX Map p64

☎ 202-965-2300; www.watergatehotel.com; 2650
Virginia Ave NW; Ⓜ Foggy Bottom-GWU
The Watergate is an iconic bit of Washing-
tonia. The riverfront complex of private
apartments, designer boutiques and
deluxe hotel is an integral feature of the
city's facade. And then there's that little break-in that occurred here in 1972,
when the Democratic National Committee
headquarters was raided by Nixon's Committee to Re-elect the President – CREEP.
Monica Lewinsky, Ruth Bader Ginsburg
and Condoleezza Rice have all lived here.
As of writing, the interior of the complex
was closed to the public for renovations
through 2009.

GEORGETOWN

Eating p149; Shopping p129; Nightlife p173; Sleeping p206

As blue-blooded as the curves of the nearby Potomac River and the patrician pretensions of her inhabitants, Georgetown is Washington's house on the hill. To be more accurate, it's a series of beautiful houses, reflecting the best of American Federal and Victorian architecture, interspersed with velvet green gardens, high-end shopping arcades, hushed restaurants and a nightlife scene seemingly inhabited by H&M and J.Crew catalogues given preppie life. Lurking behind it all is the collegiate name behind the game: Georgetown University, the city's most prestigious school (sorry GWU, but it's true). Don't forget: just because she's pretty – and the university is very pretty – that doesn't mean she's dumb. Georgetown the school has cranked out a UN's worth of statesmen, many of whom eventually end up living in Georgetown the neighborhood.

Seeing as she's the poshest part of town, Georgetown doesn't tend to inspire ambiguity. Lovers rarely leave it, and haters rarely venture west of 26th St NW (for all intents, the 'hood's eastern border). We'll give you the lover's argument first: at all times of year this is an evocative place, combining the most elegant, wedding-cake exterior decor of Washington, DC with a genuine sense of lived-in bustle. In spring and summer it's green and gorgeous, the trees waving over filigreed brick romance, laughing co-eds and well-off families. In fall and winter Georgetown becomes dignified and reserved, her old-school atmosphere enhanced by the change of leaves or the flicker of gas lamps on snowy nights.

Historical buildings are thick on the ground, their gardens bursting with flowers and their gables dripping antebellum charm. Probably the most impressive piece of the neighborhood's historical heritage is the C&O Canal & Towpath, one of America's greatest hiking/biking trails, which starts here in cobbled, picturesque cutesy-ness.

The retail therapy in Georgetown is some of the best in the city; all the money lining local pockets translates into a lot of disposable income, and merchants are quick to seize on the opportunity to destroy that inner Buddhist screaming at you to forswear material goods. And since the wealthy like to live large, there are some great restaurants and bars tucked along these narrow streets; the former in particular have gotten more daring and interesting as American foodie culture has matured. In addition, some of the city's top old-line restaurants, the ones that don't have to advertise 'class' because enough presidents to start a new currency have dined at them, make their home here.

Truly, this is a land for the city's glitterati, but here comes the bad news: the upper crust has, in the past, been defensive about opening its neighborhood to just anyone. There's a subtle but palpable sense of exclusivity in many haunts, and to keep the commoners out, Georgetown residents killed any Metrorail extensions into their neighborhood in 1980. Bus connections have become regular over the years, but M St – the 'hood's main traffic and commercial artery – is notoriously one of DC's worst-clogged roads.

Plus, Georgetown is expensive. This is annoying on a simple budgetary level, but it also sucks some of the variety out of the neighborhood; shopping, for example, is almost uniformly top class and can be more concerned with brand name interests than original taste.

Despite these drawbacks, the students at Georgetown do a great job of keeping the energy in this neighborhood cranked to 11, and that combination of youthful buzz and aristocratic atmosphere is intoxicating. No matter how anti-elitist you may be, when Georgetown struts her best stuff – when the student bodies are all stumbling over each other from restaurant to pub to shop on a wine-warmed, hazy spring or summer evening – it's hard not to fall for the allure of the capital's equivalent of the prettiest, most popular girl in school. And for better or worse, Georgetown knows it.

ORIENTATION

Unless otherwise noted, all sites in this chapter are best accessed by bus; services are detailed in Getting to Gtown (p74).

Georgetown is wedged in between Rock Creek Park, Georgetown University and the Potomac River. The commercial heart is the intersection of M St NW and Wisconsin Ave; both streets are walled with shops, bars, restaurants and generally, traffic. Further south, the C&O Canal runs east to west between M St and the river. Georgetown University occupies the southwest corner of the neighborhood.

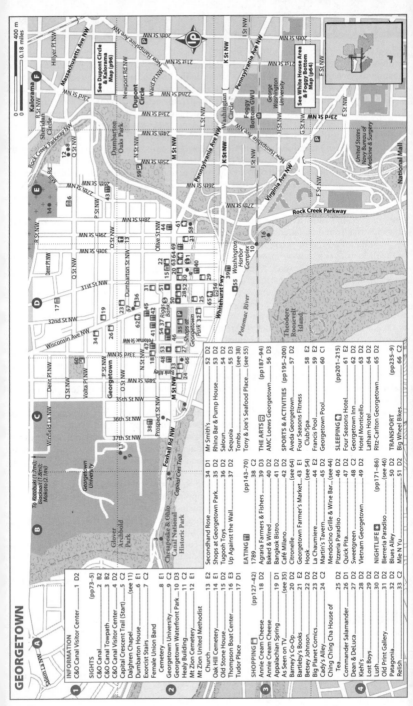

GEORGETOWN

INFORMATION
C&O Canal Visitor Center 1 D2

SIGHTS (pp73–5)
C&O Canal 2 B2
C&O Canal Towpath 3 B2
C&O Canal Visitor Center 4 D2
Capital Crescent Trail (Start) 5 C2
Dalgren Chapel .... (see 11)
Dumbarton House 6 E1
Exorcist Stairs 7 C2
Female Union Band
    Cemetery 8 E1
Georgetown University 9 C2
Georgetown Waterfront Park 10 D3
Healy Building 11 C2
Mt Zion Cemetery 12 E1
Mt Zion United Methodist
    Church 13 E2
Oak Hill Cemetery 14 E1
Old Stone House 15 D2
Thompson Boat Center 16 E3
Tudor Place 17 D1

SHOPPING (pp127–42)
1789 .... 18 D2
Agraria Farmers & Fishers 19 D1
Annie Cream Cheese 20 D2
Annie Cream Cheese 21 E2
Appalachian Spring .... (see 35)
Barney's Co-Op 20 D2
Bartleby's Books 21 E2
Betsey Johnson 22 D2
Big Planet Comics 23 D2
Cady's Alley 24 C2
Ching Ching Cha House of
    Tea 25 D2
Commander Salamander 26 D1
Dean & DeLuca 27 D2
Kiehl's 28 D2
Lost Boys 29 D2
Lush 30 D2
Old Print Gallery 31 D2
Patagonia 32 D2
Relish 33 C2

Secondhand Rose 34 D1
Shops at Georgetown Park 35 D2
Tugooh Toys 36 D2
Up Against the Wall 37 D2

EATING (pp143–70)
Bangkok Bistro 38 C2
Baked & Wired 39 D3
Bangkok Bistro 40 D2
Café Milano 41 D2
Citronelle 42 D2
Georgetown Farmer's Market .... (see 54)
Hook 43 E1
La Chaumiere 44 E2
Martin's Tavern 45 D2
Mendocino Grille & Wine Bar .... (see 44)
Pizzeria Paradiso 46 D2
Quick Pita 47 D2
Sweetgreen 48 C2
Vietnam Georgetown 49 D2

NIGHTLIFE (pp171–86)
Bierreria Paradiso .... (see 46)
Blues Alley 50 D2
Mie N Yu 51 D2

Mr Smith's 52 D2
Rhino Bar & Pump House 53 D2
Saloun 54 D2
Sequoia 55 D3
Tombs .... (see 38)
Tony & Joe's Seafood Place .... (see 55)

THE ARTS (pp187–94)
AMC Loews Georgetown 56 D3

SPORTS & ACTIVITIES (pp195–200)
Aveda Georgetown 57 D2
Four Seasons Fitness
    Club/Spa 58 E2
Francis Pool 59 E2
Georgetown Pool 60 C1

SLEEPING (pp201–215)
Four Seasons Hotel 61 E2
Georgetown Inn 62 D2
Hotel Monticello 63 D2
Latham Hotel 64 D2
Ritz-Carlton Georgetown 65 D2

TRANSPORT (pp235–9)
Big Wheel Bikes 66 C2

72

The grid is at its most effective here. M through T Sts NW run east–west, and numbered streets from 27th to 37th NW run north–south. Aside from a few streets, the grid is disrupted only by Wisconsin Ave, which cuts across the middle from north to south.

C&O CANAL & TOWPATH Map p72

☎ 202-653-5190; www.nps.gov/choh; ⊙ 24hr

There are all kinds of green escapes from Washington's urban jungle, but the C&O is one of the more pleasant, if only because of the unexpected way it leaps out at you. There you are, wandering through the Valley Girl paradise that is Georgetown on a sunny day, and all of a sudden: wooden water wheels, a green canal, shaggy horses, flat-bed barges and a cobbled path running alongside, all so bucolic you expect hobbits to emerge from the bushes with fiddles and ale.

The canal, one of the civil engineering feats of the 19th century, runs 185 miles from here to Cumberland, MD, and once brought goods and passengers from the capital to the then-beginning of the American West. Today the canal's towpath (boats were once hauled by horse) marks the start of a fabulous hiking-cycling trail. Rangers and costumed interpreters are on hand at the visitor center (1057 Thomas Jefferson St NW; ⊙ 10am-4pm), and rides in old-time boats are also available.

If you follow the path out of the city and into Maryland (heads up: this isn't a casual undertaking as you'll be heading several miles upstream before you cross the District line), there are many spots to get off the path and venture down to the river – some spots are all rocks and rapids, others calm and sandy holes perfect for a quick dip. With that said, beware: the Potomac has a very strong current.

GEORGETOWN UNIVERSITY Map p72

☎ 202-687-6538; www.georgetown.edu; cnr 37th & O Sts NW

The namesake of the neighborhood is the cornerstone of its identity, infusing the surrounding streets with its mixed patrician/party atmosphere. Founded in 1789, Georgetown was America's first Roman Catholic university, and was originally directed by the country's first black Jesuit, Father Patrick Healy. Notable Hoya (derived from the Latin *hoya saxa*, 'what rocks') alumni include both Clintons; notable lecturers include Madeleine Albright. The campus is handsome, if not overwhelmingly so. Near the east gate, the imposing, Flemish-style 1879 Healy Building is impressive with its tall clock tower. Lovely Dalghren Chapel and its quiet courtyard are hidden behind.

FUELED BY MULE

The C&O (Chesapeake & Ohio) Canal began in 1828 as a means of joining the Chesapeake Bay and the Ohio River, fulfilling a longtime dream to connect the Potomac River basin to the coastal plain. Unfortunately, while the project was a civil engineering feat, by the time it was complete in 1850, the C&O was already obsolete, rendered out of date by the railroad. Nonetheless, it remained in operation for 74 years until a series of floods closed it in 1924.

The canal almost became a highway but for the efforts of Supreme Court Justice William Douglas. Douglas was one of the most committed civil libertarians and environmentalists to sit the court (he once argued trees had legal standing and that 'the river as plaintiff speaks for the ecological unit of life that is part of it'). He felt the towpath should be set aside for future generations, and to prove his point he organized a creative publicity stunt. In March 1954, the judge led an eight-day hike from Cumberland to DC; of the 58 people who set out, only nine (including Douglas) made it to Georgetown. The ploy worked; press coverage of the hike was positive, as was the public reaction, and the tow path became a national park.

If you want to experience the canal the old-fashioned way, board the *Canal Clipper* or the *Georgetown*. Mules pull these barges full of passengers on one-hour journeys, rangers in period dress provide good commentary and a working lock raises and lowers the boat 8ft. Barges leave from the visitors center (above) two or three times a day, Wednesday through Sunday from May to October. Fares are adult/child/senior $8/5/6. This is a fabulous activity for children.

DUMBARTON HOUSE Map p72

☎ 202-337-2288; www.dumbartonhouse.org; 2715 Q St NW; adult/student incl tour $5/free; ⏰ 10am-2pm Tue-Sat, tours every hr 10:15am-1:15pm

Often confused with Dumbarton Oaks (p116), Dumbarton House is a modest Federal historic house, which was constructed by a wealthy family in 1798. Now it's run by the Colonial Dames of America, who take you on genteel but gently witty tours. The focus isn't just the house – chockablock with antique china, silver, furnishings, rugs, gowns and books – but quaint Federal customs, like passing round the chamber pot after formal dinners so gentlemen could have a group pee.

OLD STONE HOUSE Map p72

☎ 202-426-6851; www.nps.gov/olst; 3051 M St; admission free; ⏰ noon-5pm Wed-Sun

Built in 1765, the capital's oldest surviving building has been a tavern, brothel and boardinghouse (sometimes all at once) and today, despite sitting in the middle of M St, serves as a gardens and small museum on 18th-century American life. It was almost demolished in the 1950s, but a persistent (albeit false) rumor that L'Enfant used it as a workshop while designing DC saved it for posterity.

TUDOR PLACE Map p72

☎ 202-965-0400; www.tudorplace.org; 1644 31st St NW; house tour adult/child/student/senior $8/free/3/6, self-guided garden tour $3; ⏰ 10am-3pm Tue-Sat, from noon Sun

This 1816 neoclassical mansion was owned by Thomas Peter and Martha Custis Peter, granddaughter of Martha Washington. The urban estate stayed in the Peter family until it opened to the public in 1984, so it preserves pieces of the family's, as well as the country's, history. Today the mansion functions as a small museum, and features furnishings and artwork from Mount Vernon (p220), which give a nice insight into American decorative arts. The 5 acres of grounds are beautifully landscaped.

OAK HILL CEMETERY Map p72

☎ 202-337-2835; www.oakhillcemeterydc.org; cnr 30th & R Sts NW; ⏰ 9am-4:30pm Mon-Fri, 1-4pm Sun

This 24-acre, obelisk-studded cemetery contains winding walks and 19th-century gravestones set into the hillsides of Rock Creek. It's a fantastic spot for a quiet walk, especially in spring, when it seems like every wildflower in existence blooms on the grounds. James Renwick designed the lovely gatehouse and charming gneiss chapel.

GEORGETOWN WATERFRONT & WATERFRONT PARK Map p72

K St NW & Potomac River

The Waterfront is a favorite with couples on first dates, singles hoping to hook up, families on an evening stroll and yuppies showing off their big yachts. The heart of all this activity is the space between K St and the Potomac River. The riverside Washington Harbor (look for it east of 31st St) is a modern complex of towers set around a circular terraced plaza filled with fountains (they light up like rainbows at night).

GETTING TO GTOWN

The metro doesn't run out to Georgetown, but there's good bus service out here. You've got two good bets. Georgetown Metro Connection (www.georgetowndc.com/getting-here/shuttle) runs every 10 minutes from Rosslyn and Dupont Circle Metro, 7am to midnight Monday to Thursday, till 2am Friday, 8am to 2am Saturday and 8am to midnight Sunday. The fare is $1 each way, half off with a SmarTrip card (see p238). There are several stops along the way; check the website for details.

Or opt for the big red DC Circulator (www.dccirculator.com) bus, which runs from Union Station up Massachusetts Ave, west on K St onto Pennsylvania Ave, onto M St and finally, Wisconsin Ave. Again, plenty of stops are made on the way, and again, you can see them all listed at the Circulator website. Circulator buses run daily every 10 minutes from 7am to 9pm, with limited late-night service till midnight Sunday to Thursday and 2am Friday and Saturday. The fare is $1 each way.

If you want to be cheeky, you could try the free GUTS bus (Georgetown University Transportation Shuttle). This service runs from Rosslyn and Dupont Circle to the Georgetown University campus, but it's technically only open to Georgetown students, faculty and staff, plus staff and patients at Georgetown University Hospital. Drivers are supposed to check for school or hospital IDs, but they don't do so consistently. Seriously though – can't you shell out a buck?

AFRICAN AMERICAN GEORGETOWN

Three sites recall the history of Georgetown's 19th-century free black community, who lived in an area known as Herring Hill. Founded in 1816, Mt Zion United Methodist Church (Map p72; ☎ 202-234-0148; 1334 29th St NW) is DC's oldest black congregation. Its original site, on 27th St NW, was a stop on the Underground Railroad.

Nearby, at Mt Zion Cemetery (Map p72; 2700 Q St NW) and the adjacent Female Union Band Cemetery (Map p72; behind 2515-2531 Q St NW) are the overgrown headstones of many free black residents. The church hid escaping slaves in a vault here. You can reach the cemeteries from Wisconsin Ave by heading east on Q St NW and turning left at the path just before 2531 Q St NW.

Here you'll find loads of restaurants and alfresco bars. The waterfront on either side has been earmarked by the National Park Service to become Georgetown Waterfront Park (www.georgetownwaterfrontpark.org), a clot of pedestrian-friendly lanes, shady trees and general green sensibility. The grounds are a bit of a work in progress, but that progress seems to be coming along steadily.

EXORCIST STAIRS Map p72
3600 Prospect St NW

Across from the Key Bridge is a steep set of stairs that happens to be 1) a popular track for joggers and 2) the spot where demonically possessed Reagan of *The Exorcist* sent victims to their screaming deaths. Come on foggy nights, when the steps really are creepy as hell, and don't try and walk them drunk (trust us).

CAPITAL CRESCENT TRAIL Map p72
www.cctrail.org

Running between Bethesda and Georgetown, the constantly evolving Capital Crescent Trail is a fabulous (and very popular) jogging and biking route. Built on an abandoned railroad bed, the 11-mile trail is paved and is a great leisurely day trip through woody parkland – it links up with the C&O Canal & Towpath (p73) and paths through Rock Creek Park (p117). In Bethesda, MD, the trail begins at the Wisconsin Ave Tunnel, on Wisconsin Ave just south of Old Georgetown Rd (it is clearly marked and accessible from the Bethesda Metro station).

CAPITOL HILL & SOUTHEAST DC

Eating p152; Shopping p133; Nightlife p175; Sleeping p207

First-time visitors will be forgiven for assuming Capitol Hill, the geographic and legislative heart of the city, is all about power-broking, wheeling-dealing and smoky backroom bargains. But for residents, Capitol Hill is more about two 'co's – cozy and convivial – than cheap politician peekaboo. Heading east from the storied steps of the Capitol dome, the neighborhood happily disintegrates into an altogether lovely tangle of residential brownstone row houses, shaded by big, elderly trees that teem with what may be the most politically connected gray squirrel population on the planet. Bars and restaurants are sprinkled throughout, and they're mostly friendly neighborhood hangouts. Make no mistake: important people live out this way. But they don't proclaim it with as much self-importance as the nobility of Georgetown, or the dark-suited intimidation of G-men in Foggy Bottom.

Out this way journalists order pints of beer in dark pubs for Senate staffers who sit, forlorn, on the bottom of the congressional pecking order. Marines fresh from the local barracks slam shots and shout slogans, while community organizers trade jokes with their favorite bouncers, who, to a man, sport burgundy and gold in autumn. Come spring, the Nats caps come out, and in general this is a 'hood that, while sitting at the heart of the Federal power base, seems to challenge the DC-as-transient-city stereotype.

The true center of gravity on the Hill, for those who live here, is not the Capitol, but Eastern Market. This covered bazaar and the surrounding blocks showcase local food, outsider art, handmade crafts and a general bohemian vibe. It's the place to see and be seen on weekends with families and friends, proof again that Capitol Hill is more about neighborliness than nebbish power grubbing. Part of the reason for this community-centric vibe may be Capitol Hill's history. This used to be a run-down part of town, and as such it still possesses an enclave-ish sense of pride and self-respect. North of here is the Atlas District, situated along H St NE, an area that retains a lot of that old edginess. Today, that periphery is being funked up with a glut of some of the most interesting food and nightlife spots in the city.

Much of Capitol Hill is technically in the Southeast DC quadrant, but when folks say 'Southeast,' they're generally referring to the area named for and located across the Anacostia River, also known as River East or Far Southeast. This is the 'other DC,' often incorrectly referred to as 'Anacostia' (Anacostia is one neighborhood among many out here), primarily known to most of white DC as a place where crime occurs and poverty is rampant.

That perception isn't fair. Although there is still a lack of businesses in the area (including, as of writing, no sit-down restaurants except an IHOP chain restaurant), historical preservation grants are beautifying swathes of neighborhood. Most pertinently, the summer 2009 construction of the Department of Homeland Security (DHS) campus was the first Federal construction project to come east of the Anacostia River. The complex is the biggest Federal construction effort since the Pentagon was built, and while not without its controversies (some people argued the area should have become a mixed commercial-residential zone), it has generally been warmly received by local residents – in DC, money always follows Federal capital projects.

This isn't to say there aren't still problems here, but in many ways Far Southeast DC feels much more like a city of locals – who go to community meetings and wave at each other and act like *neighbors* – than other parts of town. There's admittedly little tourism infrastructure out this way, but if you tell a Washingtonian you're going across the river and they suck in their breath, tell them to calm down. This area isn't the war zone it's been made out to be – just a poorer, hardworking part of town that's seen its share of neglect and is trying to rise above it.

ORIENTATION

The Capitol building presides over its namesake neighborhood from its west end. House and Senate office buildings surround the building, while the Supreme Court, the three Library of Congress buildings and the Folger Shakespeare Library & Theatre are immediately east.

From this hub, E Capitol St runs east through residential Lincoln Park and terminates at the Armory and RFK Stadium. Constitution and Independence Aves do the same to the north and south, respectively, while Pennsylvania Ave juts out to the southeast on a diagonal and heads across the Anacostia River. In residential Capitol Hill, different streets in close proximity can have the same letter, depending on whether they are north or south of E Capitol St (ie A St NE is just two blocks north of A St SE). Pay attention to the directional (NE or SE) to avoid confusion.

Far Southeast refers to Washington, DC that is southeast of the Anacostia River. Hwy I-295 – known as the Anacostia Fwy in the south and Kenilworth Ave further north – cuts across the neighborhood and parallels the river.

Southwest DC – DC's smallest quadrant – is a triangle-shaped area south of Independence Ave (and the National Mall) and west of S Capitol St, home to several gigantic federal agencies, plus the Washington Channel. A finger of land known as East Potomac Park, or Hains Point, stretches south from the Tidal Basin and forms a peninsula between the Washington Channel and the Potomac River.

CAPITOL Map pp78-9

☎ 202-225-6827; www.aoc.gov; admission free; ⏱ 9am-5pm; Ⓜ Capitol South

The political center of the US government and geographic heart of the District, the Capitol sits atop a high hill overlooking the National Mall and the wide avenues flaring out to the city beyond. The towering 285ft cast-iron dome topped by the bronze Statue of Freedom, ornate fountains and marble Roman pillars set on sweeping lawns and flowering gardens scream: 'This is DC.'

Since 1800, this is where the legislative branch of American government – ie Congress – has met to write the country's laws. The lower House of Representatives (438 members) and upper Senate (100) meet respectively in the south and north wings of the building.

In 2008 work was finally completed on a visitor center (☎ 202-225-6827; www.aoc.gov; 1st St NE), which showcases the exhaustive background of a building that fairly sweats history. The center also provides free tours of the building – be on the lookout for statues of two famous residents per state, plus some of the most stunning, baroque/neoclassical architecture in the nation. The interior of the building is as daunting as the exterior, cluttered with busts, statues and personal mementos of generations of Congress members.

Pierre L'Enfant chose the site for the Capitol in his original 1791 city plans, describing it as 'a pedestal waiting for a moment.' Construction began in 1793, as George Washington laid the cornerstone, anointing it with wine and oil in Masonic style. In 1814, midway through construction, the British marched into DC and burnt the Capitol (and much of the city) to the ground. The dispiriting destruction tempted people to abandon Washington altogether, but the government finally rebuilt both city and structure. In 1855 the iron dome (weighing nine million pounds) was designed, replacing a smaller one; the House and Senate wings were added in 1857. The final touch, the 19ft *Freedom* sculpture, was placed atop the dome in 1863.

Inside the halls and ornate chambers you really get a feel for the power-playing side of DC. The centerpiece of the Capitol is the magnificent Rotunda (the area under the dome). A Constantino Brumidi frieze around the rim replays more than 400 years of American history. Look up into the eye of the dome for the *Apotheosis of Washington,* an allegorical fresco by the same artist. Other eye-catching creations include enormous oil paintings by John Trumbull, depicting scenes from the American Revolution.

When either the House of Representatives or the Senate is in session, a flag is raised above the appropriate south or north wing. Appropriately, the House office buildings – Rayburn, Longworth and Cannon – are on Independence Ave south of the Capitol; Senate buildings – Hart, Dirksen and Russell – are on Constitution Ave to the north.

NEIGHBORHOOD RESOURCES

- Anacostia Economic Development Corporation (www.anacostiacdc.com)
- And Now, Anacostia (http://anacostianow .blogspot.com)
- Barry Farm (Re)Mixed (http://barryfarm remixed.blogspot.com)
- Capitol Hill Association of Merchants and Professionals (www.champsdc.org)
- Capitol Hill Community Foundation (www .capitolhillcommunityfoundation.org)
- H Street Community Development Corporation (www.hstreetcdc.org)

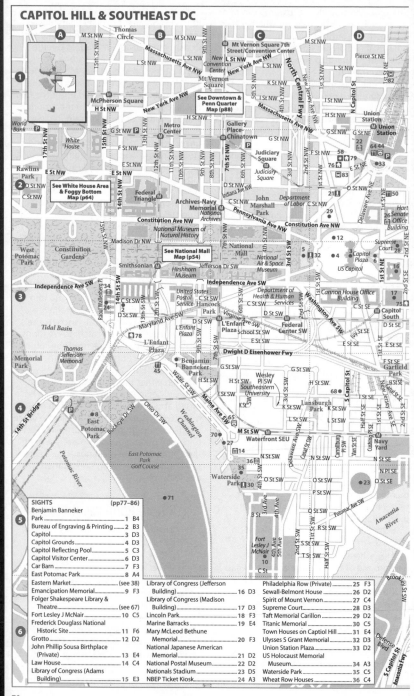

CAPITOL HILL & SOUTHEAST DC

SIGHTS	(pp77–86)
Benjamin Banneker Park	1 B4
Bureau of Engraving & Printing	2 B3
Capitol	3 D3
Capitol Grounds	4 D3
Capitol Reflecting Pool	5 C3
Capitol Visitor Center	6 D3
Car Barn	7 F3
East Potomac Park	8 A4
Eastern Market	(see 38)
Emancipation Memorial	9 F3
Folger Shakespeare Library & Theatre	(see 67)
Fort Lesley J McNair	10 C5
Frederick Douglass National Historic Site	11 F6
Grotto	12 D2
John Phillip Sousa Birthplace (Private)	13 E4
Law House	14 C4
Library of Congress (Adams Building)	15 E3

Library of Congress (Jefferson Building)	16 D3
Library of Congress (Madison Building)	17 D3
Lincoln Park	18 F3
Marine Barracks	19 E4
Mary McLeod Bethune Memorial	20 F3
National Japanese American Memorial	21 D2
National Postal Museum	22 D2
Nationals Stadium	23 D5
NBEP Ticket Kiosk	24 A3

Philadelphia Row (Private)	25 F3
Sewall-Belmont House	26 D2
Spirit of Mount Vernon	27 C4
Supreme Court	28 D3
Taft Memorial Carillon	29 D2
Titanic Memorial	30 C5
Town Houses on Captiol Hill	31 E4
Ulysses S Grant Memorial	32 D3
Union Station Plaza	33 D2
US Holocaust Memorial Museum	34 A3
Waterside Park	35 C5
Wheat Row Houses	36 C4

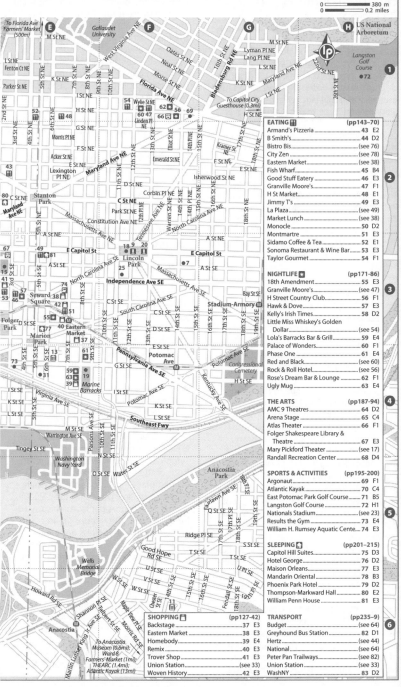

| 0 | 380 m |
| 0 | 0.2 miles |

EATING (pp143–70)
Armand's Pizzeria 43 E2
B Smith's 44 D2
Bistro Bis .... (see 76)
City Zen .... (see 78)
Eastern Market .... (see 38)
Fish Wharf 45 B4
Good Stuff Eatery 46 E3
Granville Moore's 47 F1
H St Market 48 E1
Jimmy T's 49 E3
La Plaza .... (see 49)
Market Lunch .... (see 38)
Monocle 50 D2
Montmartre 51 E3
Sidamo Coffee & Tea 52 E1
Sonoma Restaurant & Wine Bar 53 E3
Taylor Gourmet 54 F1

NIGHTLIFE (pp171–86)
18th Amendment 55 E3
Granville Moore's .... (see 47)
H Street Country Club 56 F1
Hawk & Dove 57 E3
Kelly's Irish Times 58 D2
Little Miss Whiskey's Golden
    Dollar .... (see 54)
Lola's Barracks Bar & Grill 59 E4
Palace of Wonders 60 F1
Phase One 61 E4
Red and Black .... (see 60)
Rock & Roll Hotel .... (see 56)
Rose's Dream Bar & Lounge 62 F1
Ugly Mug 63 E4

THE ARTS (pp187–94)
AMC 9 Theatres 64 D2
Arena Stage 65 C4
Atlas Theater 66 F1
Folger Shakespeare Library &
    Theatre 67 E3
Mary Pickford Theater .... (see 17)
Randall Recreation Center 68 D4

SPORTS & ACTIVITIES (pp195–200)
Argonaut 69 F1
Atlantic Kayak 70 C4
East Potomac Park Golf Course 71 B5
Langston Golf Course 72 H1
Nationals Stadium .... (see 23)
Results the Gym 73 E4
William H. Rumsey Aquatic Cente 74 E3

SLEEPING (pp201–215)
Capitol Hill Suites 75 D3
Hotel George 76 D2
Maison Orleans 77 E3
Mandarin Oriental 78 B3
Phoenix Park Hotel 79 D2
Thompson-Markward Hall 80 E2
William Penn House 81 E3

SHOPPING (pp127–42)
Backstage 37 E3
Eastern Market 38 E3
Homebody 39 E4
Remix 40 E3
Trover Shop 41 E3
Union Station .... (see 33)
Woven History 42 E3

TRANSPORT (pp235–9)
Budget .... (see 64)
Greyhound Bus Station 82 D1
Hertz .... (see 44)
National .... (see 64)
Peter Pan Trailways .... (see 82)
Union Station .... (see 33)
WashNY 83 D2

CAPITOL GROUNDS Map pp78-9

The Capitol's sweeping lawns owe their charm to famed landscape architect Frederick Law Olmsted, who also designed New York City's Central Park. During the Civil War, soldiers camped in Capitol halls and stomped around its lawns. In 1874, spring cleaning was in order: Olmsted added lush greenery and majestic terraces, creating an elegant landscape that gave rise to over 4000 trees from all 50 states and many countries: look for labels on the trunks. Northwest of the Capitol is the charming 1879 grotto, a redbrick hexagon with black-iron gates and an interior well.

At the base of Capitol Hill, the Capitol Reflecting Pool echoes the larger, rectangular Reflecting Pool at the other end of the Mall. This pool actually caps the I-395 freeway, which dips under the Mall here. The ornate Ulysses S Grant Monument dominates its eastern side, showing the general in horseback action.

LIBRARY OF CONGRESS Map pp78-9

☎ 202-707-5000; www.loc.gov; admission free; ☉ 10am-5pm Mon-Sat; Ⓜ Capitol South

The White House and the Capitol may be more iconic, but for our money (well, none, seeing as admission is free), the LOC, the world's largest library, is the most impressive structure in DC.

It's just the sheer *scope* of the thing: approximately 120 million items, including 22 million books, plus manuscripts, maps, photographs, films and prints shelved along over 500 miles of closed library stacks in the three main library buildings, Adams Building (cnr 2nd St & Independence Ave SE), Jefferson Building (cnr 1st & E Capitol Sts SE) and Madison Building (1st St SE btwn Independence Ave & C St SE). You don't get to see most of this material, unfortunately, but checking out where it's housed is still pretty damn impressive.

The centerpiece of the LOC tourist experience is the historic 1897 Jefferson Building, where you can wander around the spectacular Great Hall, ornate with stained glass and marble. The LOC's purpose is simple – to collect all the knowledge in the world. The artwork of the Great Hall reflects the beauty that emerges from such amassed wisdom, and the arduous task of cataloguing it. Goddesses and cherubs represent different fields of knowledge, scraps of the human experience that are realized in the form of some of the world's rarest books. Multimedia kiosks provide the minutest details of the library's awe-inspiring collection.

Anyone over the age of 18 carrying photo ID can use the library, and more than a million people do so each year. The Main Reading Room, which resembles nothing less than an ant colony harvesting books, is in the Jefferson Building, but it's just one of 22 reading rooms. The Library of Congress is a research library, meaning you can't check the books out, but you can read them inside its confines.

The Madison Building also hosts concerts, and screens classic films in the Mary Pickford Theater (p194).

SUPREME COURT Map pp78-9

☎ 202-479-3030; www.supremecourtus.gov; 1 1st St NE; admission free; ☉ 9am-4:30pm Mon-Fri; Ⓜ Capitol South

The highest court in the land is also the head of the least prominent branch of government: the United States judiciary. As such, the actual Supreme Court building, one of the last Greek classical structures built in DC, isn't as iconic as the Capitol or the White House (the respective centers of the legislative and executive branches). This suited a few folks just fine in the past. When the building came up in 1935, some justices felt it was too large, and didn't properly reflect the subdued influence of the nine justices within.

The design scheme was to create, in typically Federal government style, a Greek Temple of Justice. The seated figures in front of the building represent the female Contemplation of Justice and the male Guardian of Law; panels on the 13,000lb bronze front doors depict the history of jurisprudence. The interior grand corridor and Great Hall are no less impressive. Downstairs is an exhibit on the history of the court and a striking statue of John Marshall, fourth chief justice. Friezes within the courtroom also depict legal history and heroes, which has caused no little debate among Americans (see One Thousand Arguments over the Ten Commandments, opposite).

On days when court's not in session you can hear lectures about the Supreme Court in the courtroom. When court is in session, try to hear an oral argument. Lines form out front starting at 8am: choose the ap-

ONE THOUSAND ARGUMENTS OVER THE TEN COMMANDMENTS

The issue of separating church and state is one of the main battlefronts in the American culture wars, and Supreme Court architecture has often been in the middle of the cross fire.

The sculpture *Justice the Guardian of Liberty*, on the east (ie back) pediment of the court's exterior, prominently displays Moses bearing two tablets. In addition, an interior frieze in the main courtroom also depicts Moses, again with tablets in hand. This is proof, according to some, that the Ten Commandments should be displayed inside American courthouses and schools, a traditional aim of the antiseparation of church and state movement.

The problem is, these claims take Moses out of artistic context. In the exterior sculpture he is presented with Solon of Athens and Confucius; the figures are meant to represent great lawgivers of 'the East' and Moses' tablets are deliberately left blank. In the interior frieze, Moses' tablets are numbed, Roman-style, I to X, but Adolph Weinman, who designed the frieze, told the court (his letter is kept in court archives) the numbers represent the Bill of Rights, not the Ten Commandments.

Moses is also represented with 17 other lawgivers in a frieze that runs along the north and south walls of the main courtroom. Included among these lawgivers are Hammurabi, Napoleon and the Islamic Prophet Muhammad. The Council on American Islamic Relations has asked for the Muhammad depiction to be removed as Islamic law forbids depictions of the prophet, but that request was turned down by Justice William Rehnquist, who argued the depiction is a respectful one meant to honor Muhammad's jurisprudence.

propriate one depending on whether you wish to sit through the entire argument or observe the court in session for a few minutes. Justices hear arguments at 10am Monday to Wednesday for two weeks every month from October to April. The release of orders and opinions, open to the public, takes place in May and June. Check the *Washington Post*'s Supreme Court calendar listing or the Supreme Court website for case details.

UNION STATION Map pp78-9

☎ 202-289-1908; www.unionstationdc.com; 50 Massachusetts Ave NE; ◷ 10am-9pm Mon-Sat, noon-6pm Sun; Ⓜ Union Station

How beautiful is Union Station? Well, even commuters who use it to get to work – people who should loathe the sight of it – say the grand entrance hall, meant to resemble a Roman triumphal arch, never fails to impress. This was the first structure built in accordance with the McMillan plan, the 1901 campaign to revitalize DC's then dead urban core. Union is one of the pinnacles of the beaux arts and city beautiful movements that transformed the American urban landscape in the 20th century. Besides being an architectural gem, Union is also a semi-minimall and serves as Washington's main rail hub.

The main hall, known as the Grand Concourse, is patterned after the Roman Baths of Diocletian (although shields are strategically placed across the waists of the legionnaire statues – for the record, they're supposed to be anatomically correct, but rumor holds only one was built that way). In the station's east wing is the old Presidential Waiting Room (now B Smith's), where dignitaries and celebrities once alighted when they traveled to DC.

The station's exterior offers vistas of the Capitol and avenues radiating south toward the Mall. Just south along Louisiana Ave NW you'll find Union Station Plaza, a grassy park with a large fountain cascade, and the Taft Memorial Carillon, whose bells ring every quarter-hour.

EASTERN MARKET Map pp78-9

☎ 202-546-2698; www.easternmarket.net; cnr 7th St & N Carolina Ave SE; ◷ 10am-6pm Tue-Fri, 8am-4pm Sat & Sun; Ⓜ Eastern Market

The Capitol dome might win the word-image association game with visitors, but 'the' Market probably sweeps the title among locals when it comes to Capitol Hill. That's because Eastern Market makes the Hill a neighborhood as opposed to…well, a hill. Packed with good food, crafts and every ethnicity in the area, this roofed bazaar is a must-visit on weekends. Built in 1873, it is the last of the 19th-century covered markets that once supplied most of DC's food. South Hall has food stands, bakeries, flower stands and delis. North Hall is an arts center where craftspeople sell handmade wares. Come Christmas, this is the best place in town to buy a tree. See also the entries in the Eating (p152) and Shopping (p133) chapters.

DEVELOPMENT DONE RIGHT

At I St and Ellen Wilson Pl, between 6th and 7th Sts SE, lies an excellent example of skillfully executed urban renewal. Once the site of a neglected low-rise housing project (the Ellen Wilson dwellings, named for the first wife of Woodrow Wilson, who pushed her husband to pass the first public federal housing legislation), this area now hosts the Town Houses on Capitol Hill (Map pp78–9), designed by Weinstein Associates in 2000. While the complex may not look like a high-volume residence area, it actually houses more people than the old Wilson dwellings, and units are still priced within the affordable housing bracket. Best of all, the townhouses fit into the handsome surrounding neighborhood. These skinny row houses may look a little flimsy, but their facades organically mesh into the adjacent brownstones, facilitating a much-needed sense of community and aesthetic continuity.

FOLGER SHAKESPEARE LIBRARY & THEATRE Map pp78-9

☎ 202-544-4600; www.folger.edu; 201 E Capitol St; admission free; ⏰ 10am-4pm Mon-Sat, tours 11am; Ⓜ Capitol South

The world's largest collection of the bard's works, including seven First Folios, is housed at the Folger Library: its Great Hall exhibits Shakespearean artifacts and other rare Renaissance manuscripts. Most of the rarities are housed in the library's reading rooms, closed to all but scholars, except on Shakespeare's birthday (April 23), but you can peek electronically via the multimedia computers in the Shakespeare Gallery. The gorgeous Elizabethan Theatre replicates a theater of Shakespeare's time; with its woodcarvings and sky canopy, the castle is an intimate setting for plays, readings and performances, including the stellar annual PEN/Faulkner readings. East of the building is the Elizabethan Garden, full of flowers and herbs that were cultivated during Shakespeare's time.

The Folger building itself is notable for being the most prominent example of the modernist-classical hybrid movement that swept Washington, DC during the Great Depression. Jokingly referred to as 'Stark Deco,' it tends to inspire strong feelings; lovers say it elegantly pays homage to Greek classicism and 20th-century modernism, while haters say it ruins both styles.

SEWALL-BELMONT HOUSE Map pp78-9

☎ 202-546-1210; www.sewallbelmont.org; 144 Constitution Ave NE; admission by donation; ⏰ noon-4pm Wed-Sun; Ⓜ Union Station, Capitol South

The District – sadly – lacks a specific monument and museum to the women's rights movement, but it does have this historic house, home base of the

National Woman's Party since 1929, and 43-year residence of the party's legendary founder, suffragette Alice Paul. Paul spearheaded efforts to gain the vote for women (enshrined in the 19th Amendment) and wrote the Equal Rights Amendment. Docents show off historical exhibits, portraits, sculpture and a library that celebrates feminist heroes.

LINCOLN PARK Map pp78-9
E Capitol St btwn 11th & 13th Sts SE

Lincoln Park is the lively center of Capitol Hill's east end. Freed black slaves raised the funds to erect the 1876 Emancipation Memorial, which portrays the snapping of slavery's chains as Lincoln proffers the Emancipation Proclamation. The Mary McLeod Bethune Memorial, DC's first statue of a black woman, honors the educator and founder of the National Council of Negro Women. Near the park, the Car Barn (cnr 14th & E Capitol Sts), now private housing, was DC's 19th-century trolley turnaround. South of here on 11th St SE, an 1860s builder constructed the lovely Philadelphia Row (124-54 11th St SE) for his homesick Philly-born wife.

NATIONAL POSTAL MUSEUM
Map pp78-9

☎ 202-633-1000; www.postalmuseum.si.edu; 2 Massachusetts Ave NE; admission free; ⏰ 10am-5:30pm; Ⓜ Union Station

Philatelists, rejoice. In the National Capitol Post Office Building, just west of Union Station, the kid-friendly Postal Museum has exhibits on postal history from the Pony Express to modern times. Gawk at mail planes, beautiful old stamps, Cliff Clavin's postal carrier uniform (from the TV sitcom *Cheers*) and special exhibits of old letters (from soldiers, pioneers and others).

SOUTHEAST DC

ANACOSTIA MUSEUM off Map pp78-9

☎ 202-287-3306; www.si.edu/anacostia; 1901 Fort Pl SE; admission free; ⏱ 10am-5pm; 🚍 W1, W2 from Anacostia Metro

This museum wears several hats: as community hall and museum for the surrounding black neighborhood of Anacostia, and as a place for rotating exhibits from the nomadic Smithsonian Museum of African American culture (to have a home in 2010). The latter in particular is worth the trip here, but be aware that you can't really walk to the museum; you'll either need a taxi, your own wheels or the bus.

FREDERICK DOUGLASS NATIONAL HISTORIC SITE Map pp78-9

☎ 202-426-5961; www.nps.gov/frdo; 1411 W St SE; admission free; ⏱ 9am-4pm Sep-May, to 5pm Jun-Aug; 🚍 B2, B4 from Anacostia Metro

The hilltop home – Cedar Hill – of the escaped slave, abolitionist, man of letters and icon of the American Civil Rights movement is maintained as a nice museum that overlooks, in a figurative and literal way, the city and neighborhood that represents his nation's highest hopes and harshest realities. Douglass lived from 1877 until his death in 1895. The house still contains most of his original furnishings, down to his wire-rim eyeglasses on his roll-top desk.

Start your visit with the corny intro movie in the visitor center, then proceed to one of the excellent hourly tours.

NATIONALS STADIUM Map pp78-9

☎ 888-632-6287; 1500 S Capitol St SE; admission free; Ⓜ Navy Yard

Everyone, even skeptics of baseball's neighborhood-rejuvenating powers, at least hoped the home of the Washington Nationals, DC's Major League Baseball franchise, could serve as a cornerstone for regeneration in tough Southeast. Unfortunately, while the skin surrounding the stadium is scrubbed, past that the 'hood is hard. Catch a game if you can; the Nats, playing dozens of home games a season, are a strong social glue among DC's transients and natives.

THEARC off Map pp78-9

☎ 202-889-5901; www.thearcdc.org; 1901 Mississippi Ave SE; Ⓜ Southern Avenue, 🚍 94 (Stanton Rd Line), 30, 32, 34, 35, 36 (Pennsylvania Ave Line) & W2, 3 (Southeast Community Hospital-Anacostia Line)

The Town Hall Education, Arts & Recreation Campus (THEARC) has been a cornerstone for community redevelopment in River East/Far Southeast. A multipurpose community center, arts education campus and performance space, the building was the first one of its kind in what was then a

THE RISE OF RIVER EAST

Are you from DC? I was born in Southeast Washington, DC. The first few years of my life I attended Stanton Elementary until our family purchased a home in nearby Prince Georges County.

Why do you live in your current location? After a person has obtained DC residency for one year they qualify for DC's terrific first-time home-buyers' program. After a year here I was able to purchase a condo unit in Congress Heights (in River East) at an awesome rate. Department of Homeland Security (DHS) has just broken ground on a new headquarters less than a mile away from my home. This is the biggest project of its kind in DC since the construction of the Pentagon. I think the River East community has so much to offer and it is good to already have a home in a place that is in the midst of a transformation.

How has the area changed since you grew up here? So much has changed in River East in the last three years. We have gotten a brand-new grocery store, $500,000 single family homes are under construction and many of the city's last remaining projects are slated to be demolished. The Town Hall Education, Arts & Recreation Campus (THEARC; above) has also made an enormous impact on the area. We have the Honfleur Art Gallery, which hosts fashion shows, neighborhood mixers and small shows. We expect a lot of interest once DHS brings 14,000 federal employees to River East. Of course, those government employees will need places to eat, shop and have a drink before heading home if they haven't moved into the neighborhood already. There are many town home and condo communities under construction, and historic Anacostia is getting its first coffee shop. We're experiencing a facelift to say the least.

LaShaun N Smith is an employee of the Treasury Department and author of neighborhood blog South East Socialite *(http://southeastsocialite.blogspot.com).*

neglected area of town, and its impact has really brought some of the surrounding blocks back to life. If you want a sense of the pulse of contemporary African American DC, catch a show or see one of the frequent special exhibitions held here, or ask about volunteering through the center.

MARINE BARRACKS Map pp78-9
☎ 202-433-4073/4/5; www.mbw.usmc.mil; cnr 8th & I Sts SE; ☾ parade 8:45pm Fri; Ⓜ Eastern Market
The 'Eighth and Eye Marines' are on largely ceremonial duty at the nation's oldest Marine Corps post. Most famously, this is home barracks of the Marine Corps Band, once headed by John Philip Sousa, king of the military march, who was born nearby at 636 G St SE. On summer Friday evenings, the two-hour ceremonial drill parade featuring the band, drum and bugle corps and silent drill team is a must-see. Call weeks in advance for reservations or show up for general admission (not guaranteed) at 8:15pm.

SOUTHWEST DC

Washington's smallest quadrant consists of Smithsonian spillover from the Mall, the federal center, which includes several executive branch department buildings, and the two residential neighborhoods of Southwest Waterfront and Bellevue. See www.swdc.org for more information.

UNITED STATES HOLOCAUST MEMORIAL MUSEUM Map pp78-9
☎ 202-488-0400; www.ushmm.org; 100 Raoul Wallenberg Pl SW; admission free; ☾ 10am-5:20pm Jul-Mar, to 6:30pm Apr-Jun; Ⓜ Smithsonian
Both grim summation of human nature and fierce confirmation of basic goodness, the Holocaust Museum is unlike any other museum in Washington, DC. In remembering the millions murdered by the Nazis, it is brutal, direct and impassioned. Visitors are given the identity card of a single Holocaust victim, narrowing the scope of suffering to the individual level while paying thorough, overarching tribute to its powerful subject. Many visitors leave in tears, and few are unmoved. James Ingo Freed designed the extraordinary building in 1993 and its stark facade and steel-and-glass interior echo the death camps themselves.

Apart from the permanent exhibits, the candlelit Hall of Remembrance is a sanctuary for quiet reflection; the Wexner Learning Center offers text archives, photographs, films and oral testimony available on touch-screen computers. The museum is also a major advocate against, and information clearing house on, ongoing genocides. If you have young children, there is a gentler kids' installation, Remember the Children, on the 1st floor.

Same-day passes to view the permanent exhibit are required March to August, available at the pass desk on the 1st floor. The passes allow entrance at a designated time (arrive early because they do run out). Alternatively, for a small surcharge, tickets are available in advance at www.tickets.com or by phoning ☎ 800-400-9373.

Tragically, an African American guard was murdered here by a white supremacist in 2009. Security has been tightened and the staff of the museum seem, if anything, more dedicated to their mission as a result of the attack.

BUREAU OF ENGRAVING & PRINTING Map pp78-9
☎ 202-874-2330; www.bep.treas.gov; cnr 14th & C Sts SW; admission free; ☾ visitors center 8am-3:30pm, to 7:30pm summer, tours 9am-10:45am & 12:30-2pm Mon-Fri, 8am-3:45pm & 5-7pm summer; Ⓜ Smithsonian
Cha-ching! Like a Pink Floyd single given stony form, this is where the most important currency in the world (well, for now…damn you euro!) gets churned out – something like $700 million a day. Forty-minute guided tours demonstrate how money is designed, printed and cut, from wads of green ink to the stuff that is sadly lacking in a travel writer's wallet. During the summer season (April to August here), line up at the NBEP ticket kiosk (Raoul Wallenberg Pl) for tickets; arrive early (it opens at 8am), as only a limited number are distributed. For the rest of the year you can come in through the main entrance.

EAST POTOMAC PARK Map pp78-9
Ohio Dr SW
Physically a stone's throw from the National Mall, as tourists go, East Potomac Park may as well be in Siberia. A very pleasant, green, cherry-blossom-lined Siberia that is a lovely spot for walking, fishing and general gamboling (not that you can't do any

of that stuff in the real Siberia). A 5-mile paved trail, great for cycling or in-line skating, runs around the park's circumference, paralleling Ohio Dr. The center of the park is the East Potomac Park golf course (p199).

The park sits on a finger of land that extends southward from the Tidal Basin into the Potomac River. On foot, you can access it by following trails that lead from the Thomas Jefferson Memorial (p57) under the bridges. If you drive out this way, you can park on the shoulder of Ohio Dr.

WATERSIDE PARK Map pp78-9
Ⓜ Waterfront-SEU

A few historic homes – curiosities in this neighborhood – survived the 1950s urban clearance. The Law House (1252 6th St SW) is a Federal-style row house that was built by one of the first DC land speculators in 1796. From the same period, the Wheat Row houses (1313-1321 4th St SW), south of N St SW, have human-scale brick facades that add warmth to the neighborhood.

TITANIC MEMORIAL Map pp78-9
Waterside Park; Ⓜ Waterfront-SEU

Near the Waterfront's south end, Waterside Park contains this memorial to honor the men who sacrificed their lives to save the women and children aboard the sinking ship. Just south is Fort Lesley J McNair, an army post established in 1791 and burned by the British in 1814. The Lincoln-assassination conspirators were hung at McNair in 1865; it now houses the National Defense University and National War College (closed to the public).

BENJAMIN BANNEKER PARK
Map pp78-9
cnr 10th & G Sts SW

This park honors Benjamin Banneker, a free black, self-taught astronomer, mathematician and one of the original surveyors of the 10-sq-mile plot that would define the District. It's a grassy little circle near the Waterfront. You'll need to drive here.

NATIONAL JAPANESE AMERICAN MEMORIAL Map pp78-9
http://njamf.com; Louisiana Ave btwn New Jersey Ave & D St; 🕑 24hr

During WWII, thousands of West Coast Japanese American citizens were held in internment camps as suspected 'enemy aliens.' Even as this discrimination occurred under government mandate, hundreds of their relatives enrolled in the all Japanese American 442nd Infantry Regiment, which would go on to become the most decorated American combat unit of the war. Both soldiers and interred civilians are honored in this plaza, centered on a statue depicting two cranes bound with barbed wire.

CAP HILL CRAWL
Walking Tour

This is a bit of an expedition into American identity, following the course of Capitol Hill's elevation. We'll juke between neighborhood markets, mass-transit commuter nexuses, some lovely museums and the seats of two branches of government. In under 3 miles. Lace up your booties, and let's roll…

1 Eastern Market Get out of Eastern Market Metro and walk about 20m north to Eastern Market (p81) itself. This is the true heart of Capitol Hill: a neighborhood hangout, covered bazaar and just generally great place to soak up some local flavor. Literally. Get something to grub on and some coffee while you're at it, as you've got a long day of DC exploration ahead of you.

2 Library of Congress Walk west on Independence Ave SE toward the Capitol Dome, which is sort of hard to miss. First, we're going to pop into the Library of Congress (p80) for an excellent guided tour of a building that's almost as impressive as its mission: gathering all of the knowledge in the world under one roof.

3 Capitol Visitor Center Now go underground into the Capitol Visitor Center (p77). You can easily spend two or more hours here learning about the seat of the legislative branch of government (ie Congress).

4 The Supreme Court Just across the street is the Supreme Court (p80). If you happen to stumble upon the day of an interesting case, you may find that your tour has come to an abrupt, albeit serendipitous end – watching oral arguments conducted in front of the nine justices is an opportunity that shouldn't be passed up.

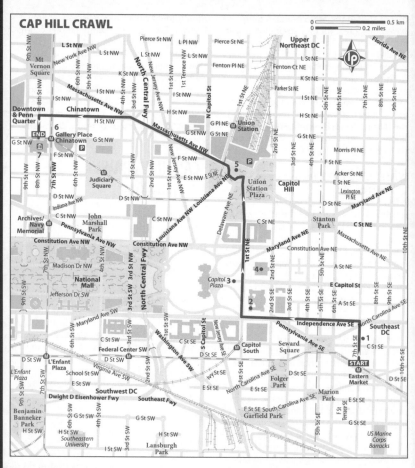

CAP HILL CRAWL

5 Union Station Head north (right if you're facing the National Mall from the Supreme Court) along 1st St NE until you get to Union Station (p81). This is one of the masterpieces of the early-20th-century beaux-arts movement, a veritable Greek temple of a train station. There's a food court in the basement if you need some fuel.

6 Chinatown From Union Station, follow Massachusetts Ave NW on a diagonal northwest, then head left on H St. Once you get to 7th St NW, you're in DC's tiny Chinatown. There are a few signs in Chinese script and a lot of Asian restaurants, but in general the vibe is one of a glitzy area that surrounds the local super stadium (which, in this case happens to be the nearby Verizon Center).

WALK FACTS

Start Eastern Market Metro
End Smithsonian American Art Museum
Distance 2.7 miles
Duration 3-4 hours
Fuel stops Eastern Market and Union Station

7 Smithsonian American Art Museum We'll finish in one of our favorite museums (p90) in town. Split between the National Portrait Gallery and Museum of American Art, this is one of the best collections of domestic creativity in the country. You've now seen where the most powerful nation in the world governs itself, where that government eats and commutes and a repository of its homegrown aesthetics. Not bad for a day's traveling.

DOWNTOWN & PENN QUARTER

Eating p155; Shopping p134; Nightlife p177; Sleeping p208

Most cities are anchored by a central business district that blends shopping, eating and office blocks: in other words, a traditional 'downtown.' But Washington has traditionally revolved around the National Mall – a fascinating city center to be sure, but not really one that lends itself to the commercial heartbeat you generally find in the middle of the urban anatomy. For years, the immediate space north of the Mall was a gray transition area between the monuments and the city's neighborhoods, avoided by tourists and shunned by businesses. To be frank, it was pretty forgettable.

So give credit where credit is due: the revitalization of this area into a genuine DC Downtown over the course of the 1990s has been nothing short of an urban planning coup. The neighborhood both emerges from and is attached to Penn Quarter, a corridor formed by the line Pennsylvania Ave creates between the White House and the Capitol (and hence the legislative and the executive branches of government). As downtowns go, Washington's is both very similar to every other one you've experienced and possessed of genuine distinctness. There are the usual chain stores and bright lights, but the orbit of the area revolves around the enormous, gaudy Verizon Center, home of DC's professional basketball and hockey teams, and some of the biggest and best museums in the city – from international spies to the heart of American art, this is a district that feeds your mind as well as your stomach.

Not that your stomach – or liver – gets ignored. The cachet of Downtown has unsurprisingly improved in direct proportion to a flowering of eating, nightlife, grand hotels and shopping. While this good life tends to come with a not so lovely price tag, there are a few cheap surprises to be discovered here as well. On the down side, the immediate area around the Verizon Center gets almost unbearably crowded on evenings; forgive us for tapping into our inner grumpy old coot, but for some reason this has become one of *the* spots in the District to be an obnoxious teenage loiterer.

Downtown was previously known as Chinatown, and DC's tiny Chinatown is still here… where? No, just there. Ah, you already missed it dude. But seriously, Chinatown officially still begins around 7th and H Sts NW, although these days it's just a few blocks of businesses fronted by a huge Heavenly Arch. Once this was a somewhat more authentic Chinatown; your author remembers being a kid in the 1980s, gawking at old women sitting in typical rice farmer squats, selling fresh produce from the side of the street. Fat chance of spotting such sights now. Today Chinatown's businesses still front their marquees in Mandarin and Cantonese, but the old, grungy cafeterias and their perfect Peking duck are largely a thing of the past (in case you're wondering, they've mostly moved to the Maryland and Virginia 'burbs). Most Chinese restaurants aren't even that – they've evolved, become more fusion-y and willing to serve Japanese sushi and Thai curry and (gasp) even tapas. We suppose that's life in the big city, but we also bemoan the loss of an area that once felt like a big, smelly mah-jongg parlor.

Of course there are all kinds of distinctly 'DC' buildings down here. If you're just dying to make your eyes bleed, why not take a gander at the headquarters of the Federal Bureau of Investigation (10th St and Pennsylvania Ave). This concrete, brutalist affront to all that is good and holy should be seen, if only to say you have laid eyes on, and we're not kidding, the single ugliest building in the entire damn District. Or make friends with a journalist (you need to be a working member of the press or a guest of one to get in) and have them show you around the National Press Club (14th and F Sts), where some of the most interesting lectures in the city are held on a daily basis.

ORIENTATION

Downtown roughly applies to the area north of the National Mall and east of the White House (for our purposes, between 4th and 14th Sts NW and Constitution Ave and P St NW).

Downtown's main drag – 7th St NW – runs from the National Archives and Navy Me- morial in the south, north to Mt Vernon Sq and beyond to the Washington Convention Center complex. Chinatown and the Verizon Center sit at the very center. East of China- town is Judiciary Sq.

Immediately north of the Mall, Pennsyl- vania Ave and Penn Quarter stretch from the Capitol northwest toward the White House.

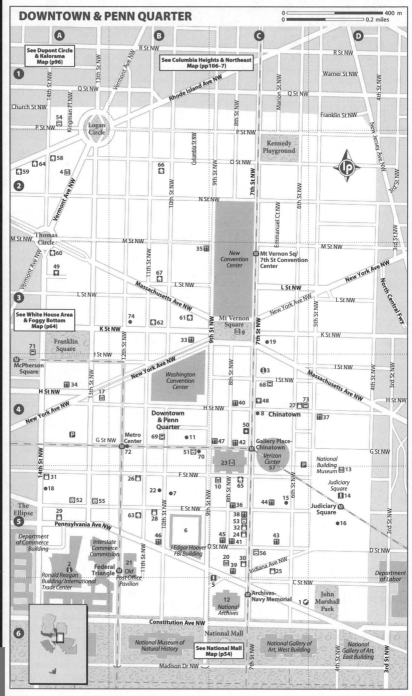

DOWNTOWN & PENN QUARTER

See Dupont Circle & Kalorama Map (p96)

See Columbia Heights & Northeast Map (pp106–7)

See White House Area & Foggy Bottom Map (p64)

The Ronald Reagan Building occupies two entire blocks, from 12th St to 14 St NW, along Pennsylvania Ave. This southwestern corner of the neighborhood is sometimes called Federal Triangle. Metro Center, the hub and main interchange point of the Metro rail system, is a few blocks north.

PENN QUARTER

NATIONAL ARCHIVES Map p88

☎ 866-272-6272; www.archives.gov; 700 Pennsylvania Ave NW; admission free; ☉ 10am-5:30pm Sep-Mar, to 7pm Apr-Aug; Ⓜ Archives-Navy Memorial

The importance of the archives, or more specifically what is contained within them, cannot be overstated; herein lays the Constitution, the Declaration of Independ-

NEIGHBORHOOD RESOURCES

- Chinatown Chamber of Commerce (www .chinatownchamber.us)
- Downtown Business Improvement District (www.downtowndc.org)
- Penn Quarter Living (http://pqliving.com)
- Penn Quarter Neighborhood Association (www.pennquarter.org)

ence and the Bill of Rights. If the USA has a mission statement, it's here. Seeing these documents in person is one of those DC experiences that gets even hard-bitten locals to whisper 'wow.'

The documents are contained in a dimly lit rotunda within a grand neoclassical building. Just before you reach the main

top picks

ROMANTIC DC

- Constitution Gardens (p62)
- Lafayette Square (p67)
- East Potomac Park (p84)
- United States National Arboretum (p109)
- Lincoln Memorial steps (p55)

event, you'll see a 1297 version of the Magna Carta, courtesy of Texas billionaire (and former presidential candidate) Ross Perot. Don't expect to linger over the Big Three (guards make you keep moving) but you can study the Magna Carta and other documents at your leisure. If you use the flash on your camera, you will get yelled at. Also, you're destroying irreplaceable artifacts of the American experience, which kinda kills the party for the rest of us.

The archives themselves preserve reams of essential government documents, from the Louisiana Purchase Treaty to the Emancipation Proclamation. Researchers can access documents from 8:45am to 5pm Monday to Saturday; enter from Pennsylvania Ave.

SMITHSONIAN AMERICAN ART MUSEUM Map p88

☎ 202-275-1500; www.americanart.si.edu; cnr 9th & F Sts NW; admission free; Ⓜ Gallery Pl-Chinatown

If you only visit one art museum in Washington, DC, make it this one, technically composed of two institutions. There is, simply put, no better collection of American art in the world. Collectively, these museums are known as the Smithsonian American Art Museum.

The National Portrait Gallery is, in its way, a portrait of America, seizing and interpreting the nation's visage by displaying her multiple faces throughout the ages. The Museum of American Art, on the other hand, exhibits the beauty and vision of those figures, the external aesthetic of the humanity so eloquently captured in the Portrait Gallery. Both occupy three floors in the 19th-century US Patent Office building, a neoclassical quadrangle that hosted Lincoln's second inaugural ball and a Civil War hospital. Walt Whitman based *The Wound-*

Dresser upon his experiences as a volunteer nurse here ('The hurt and wounded I pacify with soothing hand/I sit by the restless all the dark night…'). The top floor, which connects the two museums via the Gilded Age Patent Hall, is one of the most impressive spaces in the city. Above this massive collection are annex spaces and electronic archives for those wishing to delve deeper into the experience.

INTERNATIONAL SPY MUSEUM

Map p88

☎ 202-393-7798; www.spymuseum.org; 800 F St NW; adult/child $18/15; Ⓨ 10am-8pm Apr-Oct, to 6pm Nov-Mar; Ⓜ Gallery Pl-Chinatown

One of DC's most popular museums is flashy, over the top, and probably guilty of overtly glamming up a life of intelligence gathering. But who cares? You basically want to see Q's lab, and that's what a trip to the International Spy Museum feels like. Kids go crazy for this spot, but be warned: lines form long and early.

There are all kinds of artifacts, anecdotes and interactive displays on the inside, and guests are invited to play the role of a secret agent by adopting a cover at the start of their visit. Throughout the museum, you can try to identify disguises, listen to bugs and spot hidden cameras. A lot of the exhibit is historical in nature, focusing on the Cold War in particular (a re-creation of the tunnel under the Berlin Wall is an eerie winner).

The museum sponsors a huge range of activities outside of its permanent exhibition. KidSpy Overnight, held once a year, is basically a spy-themed slumber party held within the museum; participants get to wear disguises, break codes, discover a mole and basically blow the top off an elaborate clandestine mystery. It's only open to kids aged nine to 13, although an adult is required for every two minispies; the cost is $115 per person.

Spy at Night ($22) is a similarly themed hour-long role-play/puzzle challenge for adults held in the evening; the main difference is alcohol is served and you don't get to sleep over (although who knows? You might just meet that special undercover someone, as it were). Spy in the City ($14) is a sort of GPS-driven scavenger hunt across DC with an attached plotline that Jack Bauer from *24* would appreciate. The two-hour Spy City Tour ($75) takes in 25 skullduggery-associated sites across the city; there's an interactive mission component to this tour as well. All of the above are great fun, and can be booked through the museum's website.

FORD'S THEATRE & PETERSEN HOUSE Map p88

☎ 202-426-6924; www.nps.gov/foth; 511 10th St NW; admission free; ⏰ 9am-5pm; Ⓜ Metro Center
On April 14, 1865, John Wilkes Booth, actor and Confederate sympathizer, assassinated Abraham Lincoln, as president and Mrs Lincoln watched *Our American Cousin* in the Presidential Box of Ford's Theatre. The box remains draped with a period flag to this day. The theater is open during the day to visitors (except during rehearsals or matinee performances), but you'll need to get a (free) ticket with timed entry from the theater box office; you can also reserve a pass from Ticketmaster (☎ 202-397-7328; www .ticketmaster.com) – a surcharge may apply. For details on performances, see the Arts chapter (p190).

Check out the Lincoln Museum in the basement, which maps out the assassination's details and displays related artifacts. After being shot, the unconscious president was carried across the street to die at Petersen House (516 10th St NW), which is also open to the public; its tiny, unassuming rooms create a moving personal portrait of the president's slow and tragic death. Another assassination-related site is nearby: Surratt House, now the restaurant Wok & Roll (604 H St NW), is where the Lincoln-assassination conspirators met in 1865. Its owner, Confederate spy Mary Surratt, was eventually hanged at Fort McNair.

NATIONAL MUSEUM OF WOMEN IN THE ARTS Map p88

☎ 202-783-5000; www.nmwa.org; 1250 New York Ave NW; adult/child/student & senior $10/free/8; ⏰ 10am-5pm Mon-Sat, from noon Sun; Ⓜ Metro Center
The only American museum exclusively devoted to women's artwork resides in this Renaissance-Revival mansion. Its collection – 2600 works by almost 700 female artists from 28 countries – moves from Renaissance artists such as Lavinia Fontana to 20th-century works by Kahlo, O'Keeffe and Frankenthaler. The permanent collection is largely paintings, and

mostly portraits – not as rich a range as one might hope. But special collections are incredibly varied, ranging from Maria Sibylla Merian's natural history engravings to Native American pottery.

NAVY MEMORIAL & NAVAL HERITAGE CENTER Map p88

☎ 202-737-2300; www.navymemorial.org; 701 Pennsylvania Ave NW, Market Sq; admission free; ⏰ 9:30am-5pm Mon-Sat; Ⓜ Archives-Navy Memorial
The hunched figure of the *Lone Sailor*, warding off the wind with his flipped-up pea coat, waiting quietly by his duffel, is our favorite service (rather than war) memorial in the city. No other work of art quite captures the quiet strength that drives enlisted personnel on and brings them home after years away. The sailor waits in a circular plaza bordered by masts sporting semaphore flags; the space is meant to evoke both the vastness and ubiquity of the sea. The Naval Heritage Center, on the same grounds, displays artifacts and ship models, and has a meditation room and Navy Memorial Log.

MARTIN LUTHER KING JR MEMORIAL LIBRARY Map p88

☎ 202-727-0321; www.dclibrary.org; 901 G St NW; admission free; ⏰ 9:30am-9pm Mon & Tue, to 5:30pm Wed-Sat; Ⓜ Metro Center
Designed by Mies van der Rohe, this low-slung, sleek central branch of the DC public library system is as warm and fuzzy as a goodnight story on the inside, especially the colorful mural portraying the Civil Rights movement. This is an important community and cultural center, sponsoring readings, concerts, films and children's activities. You can also access the internet here.

OLD POST OFFICE PAVILION Map p88

☎ 202-289-4224; www.oldpostofficedc.com; cnr 12th St & Pennsylvania Ave NW; admission free; ⏰ 10am-8pm Mon-Sat, to 7pm Sun Mar-Aug, 10am-7pm Mon-Sat, to 6pm Sun Sep-Feb; Ⓜ Federal Triangle
The landmark 1899 Old Post Office Pavilion – nicknamed 'Old Tooth' for its spiky clock tower – is a downtown success story. Threatened with demolition during much of the 20th century, the Romanesque building was restored in 1978 and

became a key Penn Quarter attraction. Its beautiful, bunting-draped, 10-story central atrium holds shops, a large (and pretty good, as these things go) food court, a discount-ticket counter and government agencies. The Park Service operates a glass elevator that takes visitors to the 270ft-high observation deck for a broad view of downtown and close-up look at the carillon bells.

JUDICIARY SQUARE

HISTORICAL SOCIETY OF WASHINGTON, DC Map p88

☎ 202-383-1850; www.historydc.org; 800 Mt Vernon Sq; admission free; ☉ 10am-5pm Tue-Sat; Ⓜ Mt Vernon Sq/7th St-Convention Center, Gallery Pl-Chinatown

Sadly, the City Museum of Washington DC has closed its doors, but the District's Historical Society still occupies the museum's old digs in the Carnegie Library at Mt Vernon Sq. If you have any interest in DC as a living, breathing city of neighborhoods, immigrants and working lives outside of the Federal scene, come here – the extensive library of books, photographs, maps and other archives is a treasure. Staff are a trove of knowledge and opinions on the current state of DC.

NATIONAL BUILDING MUSEUM

Map p88

☎ 202-272-2448; www.nbm.org; Judiciary Sq, 401 F St NW; suggested donation $5; ☉ 10am-5pm Mon-Sat, from 11am Sun; Ⓜ Judiciary Sq

Devoted to the architectural arts, this museum is appropriately housed in an architectural jewel: the 1887 Old Pension Building. Four stories of ornamented balconies flank the dramatic 316ft-wide atrium, and the Corinthian columns are among the largest in the world, rising 75ft high. An inventive system of windows and archways keeps the so-called Great Hall constantly glimmering in natural light, and this space has hosted 17 inaugural balls – from Grover Cleveland's in 1885 to Barack Obama's in 2009.

The showy space easily overshadows the exhibits, but they're worthwhile nonetheless – 'Washington: City and Symbol' examines the deeper symbolism of DC architecture; and 'Tools as Art' features highlights from a collection donated by John Hechinger, hardware industry pioneer.

Check the website for a schedule of rotating exhibits, concerts and family programs.

NATIONAL LAW ENFORCEMENT OFFICERS MEMORIAL Map p88

☎ 202-737-3400; www.nleomf.com; 605 E St NW; admission free; ☉ memorial 24hr, visitors center 9am-5pm Mon-Fri, from 10am Sat, from noon Sun; Ⓜ Judiciary Sq

The memorial on Judiciary Sq commemorates US police officers killed on duty since 1794. In the style of the Vietnam Veterans Memorial, names of the dead are carved on two marble walls curving around a plaza; new names are added during a moving candlelight vigil each year in May. Peeking over the walls, bronze lion statues protect their sleeping cubs (presumably as law enforcement officers protect us).

The nearby visitor center houses several exhibits about the history of the memorial and the law enforcement officers it honors. Plans are underway for a National Law Enforcement Museum, which will open across from the memorial on an as-yet-to-be-determined date.

CHINATOWN & THE CONVENTION CENTER

CHINATOWN Map p88

7th & H Sts NW; Ⓜ Gallery Pl-Chinatown

Most visitors to DC's dinky Chinatown are surprised they didn't trip over it. Anchored on H and 7th Sts NW, this was once a major Asian entrepôt, but today most Asians in the Washington area live in the Maryland/Virginia 'burbs. However small she may be, Chinatown is still entered through Friendship Arch, the largest single-span arch in the world – local wags say the structure should be renamed the 'Starbucks-Fuddruckers Gateway' seeing as both chains now flank Chinatown's entrance. This used to be an infamous boozer strip, now scrubbed and shiny thanks to the nearby Verizon Center, but if you miss the old 'hood you can still buy a bottle of Mad Dog for under $3 at Chinatown Market (cnr H St & 6th St NW).

VERIZON CENTER Map p88

☎ 202-628-3200; www.mcicenter.com; 601 F St; Ⓜ Gallery Pl-Chinatown

When the sparkling $200 million, 20,000ft-high MCI Center opened in 1997 (the name change occurred in 2006 after Verizon bought MCI), the streets surrounding it were, to put it lightly, a bit gritty. Families definitely didn't wander out this way. All that changed within a few months of the stadium opening – sports bars, shops and restaurants bloomed like neon flowers, luxury condominiums replaced old tenements and all of a sudden, the most dangerous thing on the block was bad traffic and rude teenagers. The NBA's Washington Wizards and NHL's Capitals both call the center their home turf, the spot hosts major concerts, and even when there are no events, it functions as a ghastly shopping mall.

NATIONAL PUBLIC RADIO Map p88

☎ 202-513-3232; www.npr.org; 635 Massachusetts Ave NW; admission free; ☾ tours 11am Thu; Ⓜ Mt Vernon Sq/7th St-Convention Center

If, like us, you cannot complete the day without *Morning Edition*, *All Things Considered* and *This American Life*, may we direct you to the wedge-like headquarters of NPR,

the best thing to happen to radio since… nah, pretty much ever. Tours include strolls past the foreign and national desks and a peek into the organization's satellite control room.

BETHUNE COUNCIL HOUSE Map p88

☎ 202-673-2402; www.nps.gov/mamc; 1318 Vermont Ave NW; ☾ 9am-5pm Mon-Sat; Ⓜ McPherson Sq

Mary McLeod Bethune, founder of the Daytona Educational and Industrial School for Negro Girls, served as President Franklin Roosevelt's special advisor on minority affairs. In Washington, DC, she rose through the political ranks to become the first African American woman to head a federal office. Her Vermont Ave home, where she lived for seven years, has been transformed into an archive, research center and small museum administered by the National Park Service. Rangers lead tours and show videotapes about Bethune's life, and exhibits, lectures and workshops on black history are held here as well.

Eating p158; Shopping p135; Nightlife p177; Sleeping p210

Dupont Circle – 'the' Circle, or much more commonly, Dupont – has long served as the joint between the differing enclaves of DC's urban identity. It's upper class, but not so aristocratic as Georgetown and Upper Northwest; a workspace for a large white-collar population, but not as businesslike as the employment nexuses of Foggy Bottom and Penn Quarter; residential, but livelier than the row houses in Northeast DC and Capitol Hill.

In fact, if Dupont held onto any one identity in the mid- to late-20th century, it was filling the shoes of the Downtown that had yet to be built. This was where the city's middle and upper class shopped, dined out, sat at cafes, perused art and generally engaged in the sort of dilettantism that is the soul of a city experience.

Perhaps it's a mark of the weakness of DC's official Downtown that people still seek that urban *je ne sais quoi* amid Dupont's striking brick buildings and leafy green overgrowth. Or maybe this area's popularity simply speaks to Dupont's many inherent strengths. This is such a *handsome* neighborhood. Every street is anchored by fine dining, good bars, cute shops and a few elements that are uniquely Washington and universally admired by residents and tourists.

The first quality is embassies. While fine slices of foreign soil are sprinkled throughout the District (seriously; embassy grounds are technically another nation's territory), Dupont possesses Washington's highest concentration of overseas outposts. This was once millionaire country, and the brick mansions of the old elite are still very thick on the ground here. Throughout the 20th century, these gorgeous homes were rented out to the ambassadorial staff of myriad nations. While there are some impressive, ubermodern architectural wonders posted as embassies in other parts of town, we still appreciate the old-school dignity and elegance of those consulates and missions strutting their Victorian stuff around the Circle.

The other facet of Dupont's identity that sets it apart is its gay population. Indeed, for many DC residents the word 'Dupont' and the image of a rainbow flag are practically synonymous. Far and away, this is the center of Washington's LGBT community, although with that said, gay men are far more in evidence than their lesbian counterparts. The scene is more racially diverse than most and cuts across a wide variety of ages as well. It's also overwhelmingly well-educated and well-off, and as a result, Dupont's combination gay and international pulse tends to beat out the social rhythm for young professionals of all stripes and persuasions.

That well-to-do, educated elite stands in stark contrast to a large homeless population that congregates in the actual Dupont Circle, a traffic rotunda that surrounds a statue of Samuel Francis Dupont, rear admiral of the Union Navy during the Civil War. And the sophistication of the local intelligentsia vanishes in the screams emanating from some of the city's thumpiest nightclubs and bars. While quiet dinners and bottles of wine are laughed over at one end of Connecticut Ave, on the other side of the Circle, Congressional interns and an under-30 crowd tap into their inner banshees, shrieking the rounds long into the night. This dichotomy can be seen as just an example of variety if you're in a good mood, but if you're not it can feel as jarring as plopping a frat kegger next to a rave next to a wine tasting next to a poetry reading.

Kalorama adjoins Dupont Circle to the northwest. Greek for 'beautiful view,' it was named for an estate built by Jefferson confidante Joel Barlow that dominated this hilly area in the 19th century. Today its grand embassies and mansions are being drawn into the multiethnic, party-people corridor of the U St area, bringing this patrician's perch down to earth by a few steps. That said, it's still a very fine and stately part of town, a sort of Dupont with an extra helping of regal reserve; this is still one of the most concentrated loci of DC's storied 'cave dwellers' (old-money residents).

ORIENTATION

Dupont Circle really is a traffic circle where major Massachusetts Ave and Connecticut Ave intersect with New Hampshire Ave and 19th and P Sts NW. The surrounding number and letter streets (roughly 16th through 22nd Sts NW running north to south, and M through T Sts NW running east to west) are mixed residential and commercial areas. Buzzing pockets of activity pop up at 18th St between P and Q Sts NW, and 20th and M Sts NW.

Northwest of Dupont Circle, foreign embassies pepper Massachusetts Ave. Sheridan Circle, at its intersection with 22nd and R Sts

NW, is the center of Washington's diplomatic community.

For our purposes, the neighborhood is bounded by Rock Creek Park in the west, T St in the north, 16th St in the east and M St in the south. In the northwest corner (bounded by Massachusetts, Connecticut and Florida Aves, and Rock Creek Park) is quieter but no less elegant Kalorama. The fashionable West End is in the southwest corner between New Hampshire Ave and Rock Creek Park.

EMBASSY ROW Map p96 & Map p114
Massachusetts Ave btwn Observatory & Dupont Circles NW; Ⓜ Dupont Circle

How quickly can you leave the country? It takes about five minutes; just stroll north along Mass Ave from Dupont Circle (the traffic circle the neighborhood is named for) and you pass roughly 50 embassies housed in mansions that range from the elegant to the imposing to the out there, plus the foreign soil they technically rest on. FYI, the 'electronic embassy' (www.embassy.org) is a good resource on all things diplomatic in town.

Many consider the 4-acre British Embassy (Map p114) the queen of the row. Look for a fantastic 1928 redbrick mansion with a statue of Winston Churchill out the front, with one foot placed on British soil, the other outside the embassy property line, planted in the USA (it's a symbol of his Anglo-American descent and solidarity between the two allies). The building mixes up several architectural styles that reflect an idealized image of a bygone America, from colonial facades to a garden that could have been a set piece in *Gone With the Wind*.

PHILLIPS COLLECTION Map p96
☎ 387-2151; www.phillipscollection.org; 1600 21st St NW; admission Mon-Fri free, Sat & Sun $10; ☷ 10am-5pm Tue, Wed, Fri & Sat, to 8:30pm Thu, 11am-6pm Sun

NEIGHBORHOOD RESOURCES
- Dupont Circle Advisory Neighborhood Commission (www.dupontcircleanc.net)
- Dupont Circle Citizens Association (www.dupont-circle.org)
- Kalorama Citizens Association (www.kalorama citizens.org)

top picks

MUSEUMS

- Smithsonian American Art Museum (p90)
- Corcoran Gallery of Art (p66)
- Hirshhorn Museum (p59)
- United States Holocaust Memorial Museum (p84)
- National Museum of Asian Art (p60)

Don't think of the oldest modern art museum in the country as a gallery; it's more like a house, immaculately designed and dappled with some of the best creativity you'll ever see for free. Van Gogh, Rothko and O'Keeffe grace the permanent collection, while special exhibits pull in conceptual talent like Christo. Over 22,000 sq ft of a 2006-added wing is underground, out of respect for the surrounding Georgian neighborhood. On Thursdays the gallery hosts Artful Evenings, featuring live jazz and free appetizers. Extra admission fees apply to special exhibits on weekends.

TEXTILE MUSEUM Map p96
☎ 202-667-0441; www.textilemuseum.org; 2320 S St NW; suggested donation $5; ☷ 10am-5pm Tue-Sat, from 1pm Sun; Ⓜ Dupont Circle

This gem is the country's only textile museum, and is as unappreciated as the art itself. In two historic mansions, its cool, dimly lit galleries hold exquisite fabrics and carpets dating from 3000 BC to the present. Accompanying wall commentary explains how the textiles mirror the social, spiritual, economic and aesthetic values of the societies that made them. Founded in 1925, its collection includes rare kimonos, pre-Columbian weaving, American quilts and Ottoman embroidery. (Find the flaw: traditional textile artists, from Islamic carpet makers to Appalachian quilters, weave intentional flaws into their work to avoid mimicking God's perfection.)

Upstairs, the learning center will keep older kids entertained – and learning – for hours. Hands-on (literally) exhibits demonstrate weaving patterns, dying techniques and lots more. Group tours are available by reservation from 10:15am to 3pm Monday to Saturday (from 1:30pm Thursday).

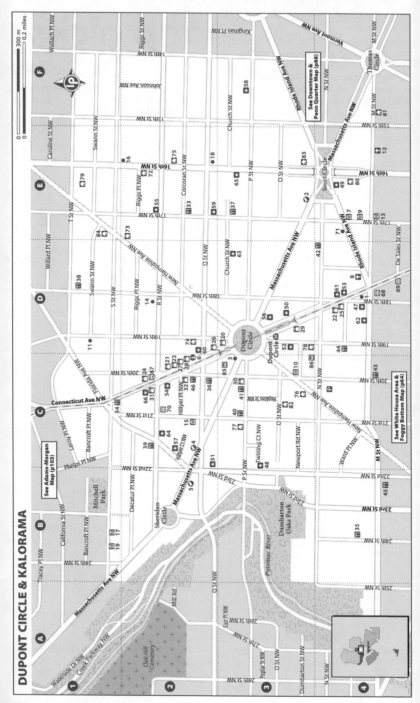

DUPONT CIRCLE & KALORAMA

See Adams-Morgan Map (p103)

See Downtown & Penn Quarter Map (p88)

See White House Area & Foggy Bottom Map (p64)

0   300 m
0   0.2 miles

Oak Hill Cemetery

Mitchell Park

Sheridan Circle

Dupont Circle

Scott Circle

Thomas Circle

Dumbarton Oaks Park

Potomac River

Rock Creek Parkway NW

Connecticut Ave NW

Massachusetts Ave NW

New Hampshire Ave NW

Rhode Island Ave NW

Vermont Ave NW

NATIONAL GEOGRAPHIC EXPLORERS HALL Map p96

☎ 202-857-7588; www.nationalgeographic.com; cnr 17th & M Sts NW; admission free; 🕐 9am-5pm Mon-Sat, from 10am Sun; Ⓜ Farragut North

The museum at National Geographic Society headquarters can't compete with the Smithsonian's more extensive offerings downtown, but it's worth a stop if you have kids in tow. They'll enjoy the rotating, hands-on exhibits on exploration, adventure and earth sciences, drawn from the society's well-documented exhibitions to the far corners of the Earth (and beyond).

The society's year-round series, Live… from National Geographic, at the Gilbert Grosvenor Auditorium (☎ 202-857-7700), located in the National Geographic Society Headquarters next to the Explorers Hall, includes films, concerts and lectures by famed researchers and explorers.

HEURICH HOUSE Map p96

☎ 202-429-1894; 1307 New Hampshire Ave NW; admission by donation $5; 🕐 tours 11:30am & 1pm Wed-Fri, 11:30am, 1pm & 2:30pm Sat; Ⓜ Dupont Circle

We like to call this place 'the castle that beer built.' Heurich House is immediately recognizable, a medieval manor in the midst of modern America. While there are a lot of baroque and Renaissance swishes, this was also the first District building to appreciably rely on reinforced concrete. The 31-room mansion was designed by John Granville Myers for German-born brewer Christian Heurich, a man who loved beer with a passion we can appreciate. One quote along the walls states: *'Raum ist in der kleinsten Kammer fur den grossten Katzenjammer'* ('There is room in the smallest chamber for the biggest hangover'), a sentiment you may blearily agree with after a night out in Dupont.

DUPONT CIRCLE & KALORAMA

METROPOLITAN AME CHURCH
Map p96

Metropolitan African Methodist Episcopal Church; ☎ 202-331-1426; www.metropolitanamec. org; 1518 M St NW; ☻ 10am-6pm Mon-Sat; Ⓜ McPherson Sq

Built and paid for in 1886 by former slaves (quite a feat considering its impressive size), the Metropolitan AME Church occupies an imposing redbrick Gothic structure and is one of the city's most handsome, yet striking, churches. Statesman and orator Frederick Douglass often preached here, and his state funeral was held here in February 1895. On the day of his burial, black schools closed, crowds packed the exterior to pay respect and flags flew at half-mast.

CATHEDRAL OF ST MATTHEW THE APOSTLE Map p96

☎ 202-347-3215; www.stmatthewscathedral .org; 1725 Rhode Island Ave NW; ☻ tours 2:30pm Sun, mass 5:30pm Sat, 7am, 8:30am, 10am (Latin), 11:30am, 1pm (Spanish) & 5:30pm Sun; Ⓜ Dupont Circle

The sturdy redbrick exterior doesn't hint at the marvelous mosaics and gilding within this 1889 Catholic cathedral, where JFK was laid in state and his funeral mass was held. Its vast central dome, altars and chapels depict biblical saints and eminent New World personages – from Simón Bolívar to Elizabeth Ann Seton – in stained glass, murals and scintillating Italianate mosaics; almost no surface is left undecorated. Evening's the best time to visit, when flickering candles illuminate the sanctuary, but you can attend mass on Sunday morning or slip in almost any time to look around.

SCOTTISH RITE TEMPLE Map p96

☎ 202-232-3579; www.scottishrite.org; 1733 16th St NW; admission free; ☻ 10am-4pm Mon-Thu; Ⓜ Dupont Circle

The regional headquarters of the Scottish Rite Freemasons, also known as the House of the Temple, is one of the most eye-catching buildings in the District. That's because it looks like a magic temple lifted out of a comic book, all the more incredible for basically sitting amid a tangle of residential row houses. It's as if someone plopped the Parthenon in the middle of Shady Acres suburbia.

There's a lot of heavy Masonic symbolism and ritual associated with the building. Thirty-three columns surround the building, representing the 33rd Degree, an honorary distinction conferred on outstanding Masons. Two sphinxes, Wisdom and Power, guard the entrance, and past the gates of bronze that front the building (really), the grand atrium looks like a collision zone between the Egyptian and Greek antiquities departments of a major museum. Note the pharaonic statues and chairs modeled to resemble thrones from the Temple of Dionysus. For a secret society, the Masons ain't exactly subtle interior decorators.

You can tour all of this fascinating minutia for free by calling ahead, which is great fun in and of itself. We love it when the receptionist answers with a chirpy, 'Supreme Council?'

WOODROW WILSON HOUSE Map p96

☎ 202-387-4062; www.woodrowwilsonhouse.org; 2340 S St NW; adult/student/senior $7.50/3/6.50; ☻ 10am-4pm Tue-Sun; Ⓜ Dupont Circle

This Georgian-revival mansion offers guided hour-long tours focusing on the 28th president's life and legacy. Genteel elderly docents discuss highlights of Wilson's career (WWI, the League of Nations) and home, which has been restored to the period of his residence (1921–24). The tour features a garden, a stairwell conservatory, European bronzes, 1920s-era china and Mrs Wilson's elegant dresses, all of which offer a glamorous portrait of Roaring '20s DC society.

CHARLES SUMNER SCHOOL & ARCHIVES Map p96

☎ 202-442-6060; www.k12.dc.us/dcps/home.html; 1201 17th St NW; admission free; ☻ 10am-5pm Mon-Sat; Ⓜ Dupont Circle

The stately, dignified Sumner building is a great example of solidly beautiful redbrick 19th-century urban design, but it is an even better testament to civil rights and education. Back in 1877, this was where the first high-school class of African Americans was graduated out of the school system. Today you can find the DC Public School archives here, as well as a museum that displays local public school memorabilia along with exhibits on Frederick Douglass.

CAPITALLY KOSHER

Two of Washington's most prominent Judaica sights can be found amid the brown-red bricks of Dupont Circle. The Washington DC Jewish Community Center (☎ 202-518-9400; www.washingtondcjcc.org; 1529 16th St NW) hosts plenty of arts activities, interfaith dialogues, community action programs and the like. The community center's sleek, box-y headquarters is a treat in itself, resembling the exterior of a modern art museum.

The National Museum of American Jewish Military History (☎ 202-265-6280; www.nmajmh.org; 1811 R St NW; admission free; ☉ 9am-5pm Mon-Fri) is a small but fascinating peak into the wartime exploits of American Jews. It's currently renovating its permanent exhibition into a more modern, interactive multimedia experience. In the meantime, displays on Jewish Medal of Honor recipients and the history of death camp liberation – among others – are a cool enough reason to pop in.

The above locations are best accessed from Dupont Circle Metro station.

L RON HUBBARD HOUSE Map p96
☎ 202-234-7490; www.lronhubbard.org/houses/dc; 1812 19th St NW; admission free; ☉ 10am-8pm; Ⓜ Dupont Circle

For three years (1957–60) the father of the Church of Scientology occupied this rather handsome Dupont house, working on developing his own religion for the masses. Today, Hubbard's old house is something of a shrine for scientologists from around the world. OK, OK: we know Scientology has become a bit of a straw man in recent years, an easy word association with 'kooky,' but it's also a religion with millions of adherents, and said worshippers take this place pretty seriously. We're not saying you have to, but if the spirit moves you (as it were), this is the Scientology equivalent of Bethlehem, or something close to it. This is also where the Founding Church of Scientology, which still holds services, was established.

B'NAI B'RITH KLUTZNICK MUSEUM
Map p96
☎ 202-857-6583; http://bnaibrith.org; 2020 K St NW; Ⓜ Dupont Circle

This museum is currently closed to the public, but may be open by the time you read this. If you can get inside, you'll find one of the country's largest Judaica collections, which is currently displayed online at www.bnaibrith.org/prog_serv/museum_virtual-gallery.cfm.

EMBASSY ROW RAMBLE
Walking Tour

Architecture, internationalism and where these two abstracts intersect are the objective of this tour. We'll be ambling past the stately mansions along Massachusetts Ave,

also known as Embassy Row, where the streets are packed with diplomats and the parking spaces are all reserved for their shiny black Benzes. Most embassies were once private residences dating from the turn of the century – a time when industrialists and financiers dealt with insecurity complexes by turning their homes into brick wedding cakes.

1 Blaine Mansion The ominous Blaine Mansion (2000 Massachusetts Ave) was built in 1881 by Republican party founder 'Slippery Jim' Blaine. It *looks* like it was built by Snidley Whiplash and his dark magic Haunted House construction company. It isn't actually a diplomatic building, but it ranks as the oldest surviving mansion in the Dupont Circle area.

2 Indonesian Embassy The Walsh-McLean House (2020 Massachusetts Ave) houses the Indonesian embassy. Gold-mining magnate Thomas Walsh commissioned the home in 1903, when it was said to be the costliest house in the city (not surprising, considering the gold-flecked marble pillars). To honor his fortune, Walsh embedded in the foundation a gold nugget, which has never been found. See also Ambassadorial Architecture & Anecdotes, p39.

3 Anderson House Continue up Massachusetts Ave to the grand Anderson House (☎ 202-785-2040; 2118 Massachusetts Ave; ☉ 1-4pm Tue-Sat), base of the Society of Cincinnati. This historical society is dedicated to educating the public about the Revolutionary War, and offers free tours of the impressive interior of its headquarters.

4 Mahatma Gandhi Across the street from Anderson House, a simple statue of Mahatma Gandhi – a gift from the people of India – sits in front of the Indian embassy.

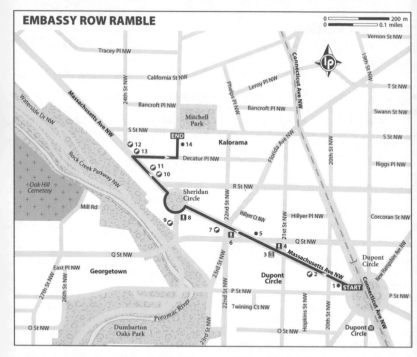

EMBASSY ROW RAMBLE

Tracey Pl NW
California St NW
Bancroft Pl NW
S St NW
END
Decatur Pl NW
Kalorama
Mitchell Park
Sheridan Circle
R St NW
Hillyer Ct NW
Hillyer Pl NW
Q St NW
Massachusetts Ave NW
Dupont Circle
P St NW
Twining Ct NW
O St NW
Vernon St NW
Connecticut Ave NW
Leroy Pl NW
Phelps Pl NW
Bancroft Pl NW
Florida Ave NW
T St NW
Swann St NW
S St NW
Riggs Pl NW
Corcoran St NW
START
Dupont Circle
New Hampshire Ave NW
Waterside Dr NW
Massachusetts Ave NW
Rock Creek Parkway NW
Oak Hill Cemetery
Mill Rd
Q St NW
Georgetown
East Pl NW
Potomac River
Dumbarton Oaks Park
Mitchell Park

0 — 200 m
0 — 0.1 miles

5 Cosmos Club The rich mansion designed to resemble Petit Trianon at Versailles has been the headquarters for the Cosmos Club (2121 Massachusetts Ave) since 1952. The building is a befitting home for the most prominent social club of DC's intellectual elite: from the rich, wood-paneled library to the sculpted lion overlooking the blooming gardens, it oozes culture, class, and why-don't-you-just-keep-on-walking-you 'tude.

6 Tomas Masaryk On the south side of Massachusetts Ave, a bronze statue honors Tomas Masaryk, a leading advocate for Czech independence after WWI and the first president of the new state of Czechoslovakia (1918–35).

7 Luxembourg Embassy Nearby is the Luxembourg embassy (2200 Massachusetts Ave). Built in the grand court style of Louis XIV for congressman Alexander Stewart, the property was later sold to the Grand Duchess of Luxembourg, who lived here in exile during WWII.

8 Philip Sheridan Now you are approaching Sheridan Circle, wreathed in lavish embassies and centered on Gutzon Borglum's equestrian

statue of Civil War General Philip Sheridan. (Borglum later sculpted Mt Rushmore.) The nearby plaque memorializes the 1976 car-bomb assassination of pro-Salvador Allende Chilean exile Orlando Letelier; agents of the Pinochet dictatorship were later connected to the murder.

9 Turkish Ambassador's Residence What does one do after making millions and millions of dollars off patenting the grooved bottle cap? If you're Edward Everett, you move into digs that will one day become the Turkish embassy, and later the ambassador's residence (cnr Sheridan Circle & 23rd St). The building, which has some Ottoman influences, was designed by George Oakley Totten, who was the official architect of the Ottoman Sultan Abdul Hamid II.

10 Embassy of Haiti There's not much to say about the beaux-arts jewel that is the Haitian embassy (2311 Massachusetts Ave). It's a compact, beautiful example of the best of DC-style old-line mansions.

11 Moran House Next door, the 1908 Moran House is now the Pakistani embassy (2315 Massachusetts Ave). A masterpiece courtesy of George Totten, the building is decked out with stucco beaux-arts embellishments.

12 Embassy of Cameroon The Cameroon embassy (2349 Massachusetts Ave) is yet another work by Totten. He designed this castle-like mansion for Norwegian diplomat Christian Hauge, who died in a snowshoe accident before its completion.

13 Embassy of Croatia At No 2343, a cross-legged sculpture of St Jerome dreams over his book. This masterpiece was the work of renowned Croatian sculptor Ivan Meštrović; appropriately, it fronts the embassy of his homeland.

14 Spanish Steps Take a detour east on Decatur Pl to 23rd St. The rise up to S St NW here was deemed too steep for the road, so city planners constructed a delightful pedestrian staircase, which has been dubbed the 'Spanish Steps' for its resemblance to Rome's Piazza di Spagna. Climb the steps, have a stare over the vista, and rest assured you've probably just been tracked by the security cameras of roughly a dozen foreign intelligence services. And you thought the day was wasted!

ADAMS-MORGAN

Eating p161; Shopping p137; Nightlife p179; Sleeping p212

Adams-Morgan has traditionally been Washington's fun, nightlife-driven incarnation of the global village phenomenon, the place to get Ethiopian food for dinner and try your luck at picking up an Egyptian date for drinks. But it has changed a bit over the years. Oh, the Latino and African cafes and restaurants remain the same, and most nights 'the Morgan' (or in DC text message-ese, 'Admo') still feels like it was playfully scooped out of the southern Atlantic Ocean, plucked from an island that occupies some perfect fault line between *lingala* and the *lambada*.

Still, over the years both the famous nightlife scene and the neighborhood's residential character have become a bit more middle class. It's a young, cosmopolitan middle class, the sort of people who appreciate immigrant cooking and ethnic music. But the actual immigrants themselves have largely moved to the 'burbs of Northern Virginia and Maryland, or distant DC neighborhoods such as Fort Totten. An international masala of characters still comes here to smoke *shisha,* rent the latest Nigerian DVDs and run their businesses. But they rest their heads elsewhere.

That's life in the big city folks. And we still believe this may be the only place in the world where you can get Ethiopian, Mexican, Italian, Salvadoran and New Orleans Creole food (plus, yeah, there's a McDonald's) on one street – the famed 18th St NW. At night, that same street, whether you love it or hate it – and everyone in DC seems to experience both emotions at some point – is one of the great bar crawls in town. Bored kids from the 'burbs, the aforementioned international crowd, Hill rats, Dupont cats, Georgetown brats, a multi-racial crew of young professionals and even a fair amount of party people from the rough side of town all throw aside their differences for a while to shake a tail feather and scream in your face. The next morning, a small Latino market may post on a corner, while folks toting laptops head for local cafes.

ORIENTATION

Adams-Morgan is just south of the intersection of Columbia Rd and 18th St NW. East of the hub is Meridian Hill, which marks the geological fall line between the rocky piedmont plateau and the softer coastal plain. Malcolm X Park, which runs along 16th St NW, marks the eastern boundary of the neighborhood. The western boundary is Rock Creek Park and the zoo. Just north is Mt Pleasant, DC's most Latino neighborhood.

18TH STREET NW AND COLUMBIA ROAD Map p103

If you're looking for DC's most easily accessed international side with a fair heaping helping of food and nightlife thrown in, wander up 18th St NW and nearby Columbia Rd. As of writing, there were close to 40 restaurants and nightspots lining 18th St between Florida Ave and Columbia Rd, a stretch of blocks also packed with stores selling African, Asian and Latin American bric-a-brac. During the day the area can feel a little listless, but as soon as that sun starts

to set the strip starts to come alive. Nearby Columbia Rd has become one of the main thoroughfares for DC's Latino community, and the spot where these two streets intersect is the launching point of many a capital night out.

DISTRICT OF COLUMBIA ARTS CENTER Map p103

☎ 202-462-7833; www.dcartscenter.org; 2438 18th St NW; ⓧ gallery 2-7pm Wed-Sun; Ⓜ Woodley Park Zoo/Adams Morgan
This grassroots center offers emerging artists a space to showcase their work, from theater to multimedia creations. The 750-sq-ft gallery features rotating

NEIGHBORHOOD RESOURCES

- Adams Morgan Main Street (www.ammain street.org)
- Adams Morgan Online (www.adamsmorgan .net)
- Meridian Hill Neighborhood Association (www.meridianhilldc.org)

visual arts exhibits, while plays and other theatrical productions take place in the 50-seat black-box theater. Have a look at the website to see if anything interesting is going on.

MALCOLM X PARK Map p103
btwn W & 16th St & Euclid & 16th St NW; Ⓜ U Street-Cardozo/African American Civil War Memorial
This is an incredible bit of green space that gets short shrift in the list of America's great urban parks. What makes it special is the way the park emphasizes its distinctive geography. Lying on the fall line between the upland Piedmont Plateau and flat Atlantic Coastal Plain, the grounds are terraced like a hanging garden replete

with waterfalls, sandstone terraces and assorted embellishments that feel almost Tuscan. Out-of-towners call this Meridian Hill Park.

MERIDIAN INTERNATIONAL CENTER Map p103
☎ 202-667-6800; www.meridian.org; 1630 Crescent Pl; admission free; ⏰ 2-5pm Wed-Sun; Ⓜ U Street-Cardozo/African American Civil War Memorial
Many people who have lived in Washington for years haven't even heard of Meridian House, which isn't surprising – this impressive mansion does spring out of nowhere, looking like the headquarters for some world-dominating secret society. In fact, it's an education and hospitality

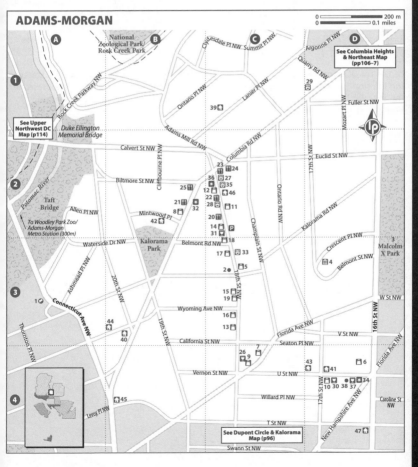

ADAMS-MORGAN

ADAMS-MORGAN

center for DC's international community; the interior grounds are as impressive as the exterior facade. John Russell Pope built the structure to resemble a French country chateau, complete with a stately walled entrance, a charming cobblestone courtyard and a decorated limestone facade.

Probably no Washington neighborhood has changed more in the past few years than the U St Corridor and Columbia Heights. The former has become DC's 'it' area, and the latter is fast approaching that status. For now, these 'hoods mark the shifting line of Washington's latest growth spurt of new development.

A little history, first, for a very historic district. Back at the end of the 19th century this was one of the most vibrant black neighborhoods in the country. Civil Rights leaders Archibald and Francis Grimké lived here, as did Calvin Chase, editor of the crusading *Washington Bee*. Black lawyers, doctors and tradespeople opened offices along U St, which blossomed into a separate downtown for those excluded by racism from DC's other shop. The 12th St YMCA – now known as the Thurgood Marshall Center (1816 12th St NW) – was the informal headquarters of local Civil Rights activists for 70 years.

The 'hood was, if anything, even more active on the arts front. Duke Ellington grew up on T St; Pearl Bailey waited tables and danced at U St's Republic Gardens (p184); Ella Fitzgerald sang at Bohemian Caverns (p183); Louis Armstrong played the Dance Hall at V and 9th Sts; and the Lincoln Theatre (p191) and Howard Theatre presented Harlem's and DC's finest to black audiences. Shaw was a high point on the renowned 'chitlin circuit' of black entertainment districts.

But with integration came black and white flight to the suburbs, especially in the 1970s. In the introduction of this book (p2), we explained to you that U St was one of the epicenters of the 1968 race riots that gutted the center of the city. For decades afterwards this area remained a ghetto. There were blocks on U St that were, essentially, open-air drug markets.

Then, in 1991, the U Street-Cardozo Metro station (now U Street-Cardozo/African American Civil War Memorial) opened. At the same time, a series of new condo developments was planned. People started flooding back to the area, particularly young professionals and blacks (often both), excited by the opportunity of an affordable, up-and-coming neighborhood.

Which is exactly what this became: a laughing madhouse of good eats, good drinks and eccentric indie boutiques. People jog here now, and it's not to get away from anything besides an art gallery as they proceed to a vintage jewelry sale.

North of here, Columbia Heights and neighboring Mt Pleasant have a reputation as being an enclave for Latino immigrants and hipsters – two of the seemingly fastest growing demographics in the city. As the apartment complexes in U St fill up and neighborhood bars and restaurants spread out like very hip acne across the face of Columbia Heights, the condo brigade has followed in their footsteps. The construction of a huge Target-anchored mall complex in 2008 sent Latinos west to Mt Pleasant and the hipster types east, and on their heels came hundreds more young professionals. Today you see many MacBooks getting toted into wi-fi spots, prompting one local reader to comment: 'These hipsters are just yuppies with tattoos.'

Nearby Shaw's history was intimately tied to U St's – in fact, Shaw was arguably more important to DC's black history. Today it's not nearly as gentrified as U St or Columbia Heights, but it doesn't have to be: this is where Howard University, the country's oldest black college, is located. Intellectual, activism-oriented Howard is as much a determinant of Shaw's character as Georgetown University is of her namesake neighborhood.

Northeast of here is (duh) Northeast DC, a largely quiet stretch of lovely residential blocks sitting over what may be DC's next hottest real estate wave. Catholic University is here, as well as some pretty impressive churches, and every now and then a new delicious restaurant or funky bar unexpectedly pops up on everyone's radar.

ORIENTATION

This is a big sprawling area consisting of several neighborhoods. Shaw is a rectangular block that sits above Downtown, stretching from Logan Circle in the south, to Harvard St in the north, and, for our purposes, from 14th St NW in the west to N Capitol St in the east. The district is bisected by north–south Georgia Ave, which becomes 7th St south of Florida Ave. Much of Shaw's northeastern corner is consumed by the Howard University campus. East of here, between 2nd

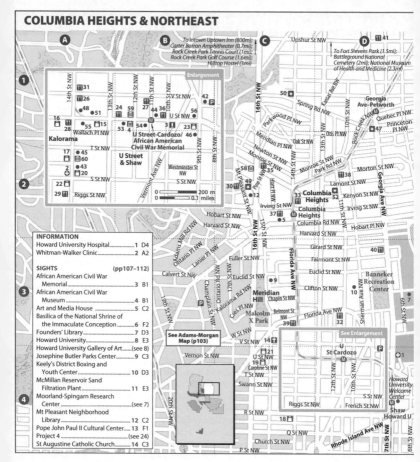

COLUMBIA HEIGHTS & NORTHEAST

INFORMATION
Howard University Hospital...............1 D4
Whitman-Walker Clinic........................2 A2

SIGHTS (pp107–112)
African American Civil War
  Memorial...3 B1
African American Civil War
  Museum..4 B1
Art and Media House........................5 C2
Basilica of the National Shrine of
  the Immaculate Conception 6 F2
Founders' Library...............................7 D3
Howard University..............................8 E3
Howard University Gallery of Art......(see 8)
Josephine Butler Parks Center............9 C3
Keely's District Boxing and
  Youth Center................................10 D3
McMillan Reservoir Sand
  Filtration Plant.............................11 E3
Moorland-Spingarn Research
  Center..(see 7)
Mt Pleasant Neighborhood
  Library...12 C2
Pope John Paul II Cultural Center.....13 F1
Project 4...(see 24)
St Augustine Catholic Church...........14 C3

and 7th Sts NW, is LeDroit Park, a small subdivision of Victorian homes. Originally a segregated white enclave, the subdivision later attracted Howard's faculty and other black elite.

The U St Corridor runs from roughly 13th & U St to 17th and U St NW. South of here, at the intersection of Rhode Island and Vermont Aves with 13th and P Sts NW, is Logan Circle.

For our purposes, Columbia Heights runs from Mt Pleasant St in the west to roughly 11th St NW in the east, and from Euclid St NW in the south to the Georgia Ave/Petworth Metro station up top. Two roads, 14th and 16th Sts NW, make up the main north–south thoroughfares.

DC's Northeast quadrant is huge. Bladensburg Rd and Rhode Island Ave (Rte 1) cut across from southeast to northwest, while New York Ave (Rte 50) roars by east to west. The eastern boundary is the Anacostia River, and the Maryland line is the north border. Northwest of Rhode Island Ave, the Brookland neighborhood emerges around Catholic University and Trinity College. There is a little downtown Brookland center along 12th St NE between Monroe and Perry Sts.

Further south, Gallaudet University is squeezed in between New York Ave and Bladensburg Rd, flanked on either side by Brentwood Park and Mt Olivet Cemetery. Tucked into the southeast corner of the quadrant, the pristine US National Arboretum occupies almost all the space between Bladensburg Rd, New York Ave and the Anacostia River.

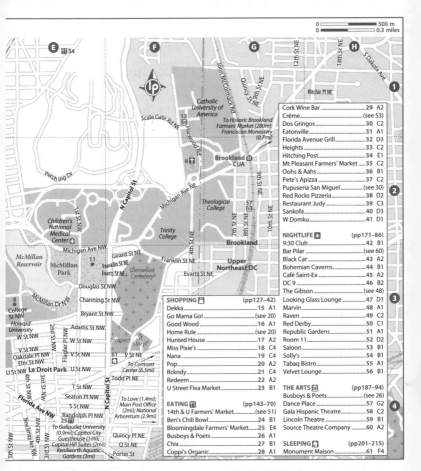

| 0 | | 500 m |
| 0 | | 0.3 miles |

Cork Wine Bar 29 A2
Crème .... (see 53)
Dos Gringos 30 C2
Eatonville 31 A1
Florida Avenue Grill 32 D3
Heights 33 C2
Hitching Post 34 E1
Mt Pleasant Farmers' Market 35 C2
Oohs & Aahs 36 B1
Pete's Apizza 37 C2
Pupuseria San Miguel .... (see 30)
Red Rocks Pizzeria 38 D2
Restaurant Judy 39 C3
Sankofa 40 D3
W Domku 41 D1

NIGHTLIFE ☐   (pp171–86)
9:30 Club 42 B1
Bar Pilar .... (see 60)
Black Cat 43 B1
Bohemian Caverns 44 B1
Café Saint-Ex 45 A2
DC 9 .... 46 B2
The Gibson .... (see 48)
Looking Glass Lounge 47 D1
Marvin 48 A2
Raven 49 C2
Red Derby 50 C1
Republic Gardens 51 A1
Room 11 .... 52 D2
Saloon 53 B1
Solly's 54 B1
Tabaq Bistro 55 B1
Velvet Lounge 56 B1

THE ARTS ☐   (pp187–94)
Busboys & Poets .... (see 26)
Dance Place 57 G2
Gala Hispanic Theatre 58 C2
Lincoln Theatre 59 B1
Source Theatre Company 60 A2

SLEEPING ☐   (pp201–215)
Monument Maison 61 F4

SHOPPING ☐   (pp127–42)
Dekka 15 A1
Go Mama Go! .... (see 20)
Good Wood 16 A1
Home Rule .... (see 20)
Hunted House 17 A2
Miss Pixie's 18 C4
Nana 19 C4
Pop 20 A2
Rckndy 21 C4
Redeem 22 A2
U Street Flea Market 23 B1

EATING ☐   (pp143–70)
14th & U Farmers' Market .... (see 51)
Ben's Chili Bowl 24 B1
Bloomingdale Farmers' Market ... 25 E4
Busboys & Poets 26 A1
Chix 27 B1
Coppi's Organic 28 A1

Map labels: 34, Catholic University of America, To Historic Brookland Farmers' Market (280m); Franciscan Monastery (0.7mi), Scale Gate Rd NE, Brookland CUA, Theological College, Trinity College, Brookland, Upper Northeast DC, Children's National Medical Center, McMillan Reservoir, McMillan Park, Michigan Ave NW, Girard St NE, Franklin St NE, Evarts St NE, Glenwood Cemetery, Douglas St NW, Channing St NW, Bryant St NW, Adams St NW, Prospect St Marys, College St NW, Howard University, V St NW, Oakdale Pl NW, Elm St NW, Le Droit Park, U St NW, T St NW, Seaton Pl NW, S St NW, Randolph Pl NW, To Love (1.4mi); Main Post Office (2mi); National Arboretum (2.9mi), To Gallaudet University (0.9mi); Capitol City Guesthouse (1mi); Capital Hill Suites (2mi); Kenilworth Aquatic Gardens (3mi), Quincy Pl NE, Q St NE, Porter St, Todd Pl NE, To Comcast Center (6.5mi), N Capitol St, Florida Ave NW, Pershing Dr, 16th St McCormack Rd, Quincy St NE, Ritchie Pl NE, 12th St NE, 14th St NE, S Dakota Ave

U STREET & SHAW

AFRICAN AMERICAN CIVIL WAR MEMORIAL Map pp106–7

☎ 202-667-2667; www.afroamcivilwar.org; cnr U St & Vermont Ave NW; Ⓜ U Street-Cardozo/African American Civil War Memorial

Standing at the center of a granite plaza, this bronze statue depicting rifle-bearing troops is DC's first major art piece by black sculptor Ed Hamilton. The sculpture is surrounded on three sides by the Wall of Honor, listing the names of 209,145 black troops who fought in the Union Army, as well as the 7000 white soldiers who served alongside them. You can use the directory to locate individual names within each of the regiments.

AFRICAN AMERICAN CIVIL WAR MUSEUM Map pp106–7

☎ 202-667-2667; www.afroamcivilwar.org; 1200 U St NW; admission free; ⏱ 10am-5pm Mon-Fri, to 2pm Sat; Ⓜ U Street-Cardozo/African American Civil War Memorial

Every museum has a mission; this one makes the point that for some, the Civil War was about secession versus union, but for others, it was a matter of breaking human bondage. The permanent exhibit includes photographs, documents and some audiovisual programs following African American history from the Civil War through the Civil Rights movement. The Civil War Soldiers and Sailors Project allows visitors to search for ancestors in databases of black troops, regiments and battles. In 2010 the museum will begin moving into the nearby

NEIGHBORHOOD RESOURCES

- Brookland Area Writers and Artists (www .bawadc.com)
- Edgewood Neighborhood Association (www .edgewooddc.org)
- In Shaw (http://inshaw.com/blog)
- Mt Pleasant Organizations (www.mtpleas antdc.org/organizations)
- PetworthDC (www.petworthdc.net)
- Prince of Petworth (http://princeofpetworth .blogspot.com)
- Trinidad Neighborhood Association (http:// trinidad-dc.org)
- U Street Neighborhood Association (www .csnadc.org)

Grimke building (corner Vermont Ave and U St), just next to the memorial (p107), which will allow for an expansion of its exhibits.

HOWARD UNIVERSITY Map pp106-7
☎ 202-806-6100; www.howard.edu; 2400 6th St NW; Ⓜ Shaw-Howard U
The Shaw neighborhood is as defined by Howard University as Georgetown is by her titular school. Founded in 1867, this remains the nation's most prestigious traditionally African American institute of higher education. Distinguished alumni include the late Supreme Court Justice Thurgood Marshall (who enrolled after he was turned away from the University of Maryland's then all-white law school), Ralph Bunche, Nobel laureate Toni Morrison and former New York City mayor David Dinkins. Today Howard enrolls around 12,000 students in 18 schools. There are campus tours (☎ 202-806-2755) and a friendly Welcome Center (1739 7th St NW). The surrounding streets are largely filled with vegan cafes serving ital (Rastafari-approved) food, bookstores selling Pan-African and black nationalist lit, and record stores stocked with funk, jazz, blues and hip-hop.

Founders' Library, a handsome Georgian building with a gold spire and giant clock, is the campus' architectural centerpiece. It houses the Moorland-Spingarn Research Center (☎ 202-806-7239; Ⓨ 9am-4:45pm Mon & Wed, to 4:30pm Fri), which boasts the nation's largest collection of African American literature. Nearby the Howard University Gallery of Art (☎ 202-806-7070; Childers Hall; Ⓨ 9:30am-5pm Mon-

Fri, noon-4pm Sun) has an impressive collection of work, largely dominated by African and African American artists.

ST AUGUSTINE CATHOLIC CHURCH
Map pp106-7
☎ 202-265-1470; www.saintaugustine-dc.org; cnr 15th & V Sts NW; Ⓨ mass 12:30pm Sun; Ⓜ U Street-Cardozo/African American Civil War Memorial
Let the spirit move you at DC's oldest black Catholic congregation. Clad in Kenti cloth and sporting soloists just waiting to bust their lungs, the 165 members of the St Augustine gospel choir rock the house every Sunday at 12:30pm. The mass is long, but it's a hell of a lot of fun and spiritually nourishing to boot. For calmer but equally beautiful music, come for 10am mass, when the church chorale sings traditional Catholic hymns.

Founded in 1858, St Augustine's congregation moved to the Gothic-revival building at 15th and V Sts NW in 1961. It was a bold move, and marked a merger with an all-white congregation; the joined churches became known as Sts Paul & Augustine. The name reverted to St Augustine in 1982, but the congregation continues to welcome members of all races and ethnic groups. If you go, wear your Sunday best.

COLUMBIA HEIGHTS & MOUNT PLEASANT

MOUNT PLEASANT STREET Map pp106-7
Mt Pleasant St NW; Ⓜ Columbia Heights
There's no consensus as to why so many immigrants in the metro area are Central American as opposed to Mexican, but what can be confirmed is Mt Pleasant St is the corazon of DC's Latino, largely Salvadoran community. Every few businesses advertise money-transfer services to San Salvador or surrounds, or sell cheap, delicious pupusas (Salvadoran baked turnovers stuffed with cheese and pork), or both. Look out for the 7-Eleven, popularly known as El Seven (cnr Kenyon St & Mt Pleasant St NW); the storefront is a popular informal hangout (inside, it's just a 7-Eleven).

NORTHEAST DC

On Michigan Ave and North Capitol St, you'll notice a string of cylindrical concrete structures that look like the entrance to the

Kingdom of the Mole People sticking out of a grassy field. This is the McMillan Reservoir Sand Filtration Plant; the buildings are ruins of old water reservoirs. This is a huge, open and basically unused area. The District hasn't been able to decide what to do with it since 1987 – suggestions range from new park to more housing and on. In the meantime, those old reservoir towers look pretty cool from the road.

UNITED STATES NATIONAL ARBORETUM off Map pp106-7
☎ 202-245-2726; www.usna.usda.gov; 3501 New York Ave NE; admission free, tram tour adult/child/student $4/2/3; ☉ 8am-5pm, tram tours Sat, Sun & holidays Apr-Oct

The best things in life – or this city – require a little effort. In this case, you need wheels to reach the greatest green space in Washington, almost 450 acres of meadowland, sylvan theatres and a pastoral setting that feels somewhere between bucolic Americana countryside and a Romantic artist's conception of classical Greek ruralscapes.

Stop at the Administration Building near the R St gate for a map and information. Highlights include the Bonsai & Penjing Museum (☉ 10am-4pm), east of the Administration Building, and the Capitol Columns Garden, south along Ellipse Rd. The latter is studded with Corinthian pillars removed from the Capitol in the 1950s.

The best times to visit are spring (March to May, when the azaleas bloom) and fall

(September to November, for colorful autumn leaves). No direct buses serve the gardens and they're hard to negotiate on foot, so drive or cycle.

KENILWORTH AQUATIC GARDENS off Map pp106-7
☎ 202-426-6905; www.nps.gov/keaq; 1550 Anacostia Ave NE; admission free; ☉ 7am-4pm; Ⓜ Deanwood

DC was built on a marsh, a beautiful, brackish, low-lying ripple of sawgrass and steel-blue water, wind-coaxed and tide touched by the inflow of the Potomac from the Chesapeake Bay. You'd never know all that now, of course, unless you come to the only national park in the USA devoted to water plants. The aquatic gardens were begun as the hobby of a Civil War veteran and operated for 56 years as a commercial water garden, until the federal government purchased them in 1938. Today this is the only place in the city to see the natural wetlands the District sprang from; look out for beaver dams, clouds of birds and the more traditional manicured grounds, quilted in water lilies and lotus.

NATIONAL MUSEUM OF HEALTH AND MEDICINE off Map pp106-7
NMHM; ☎ 202-782-2200; www.nmhm.washingtondc.museum; 6900 Georgia Ave NW; admission free; ☉ 10am-5:30pm; Ⓜ Takoma

Located in the Walter Reed Army Medical center, the NMHM is one of the older

ARTISTS, ATHLETES AND DC YOUTH IN COLUMBIA HEIGHTS

Two of our favorite community organizations in the city are based in Columbia Heights. They both do a great job of training DC kids to be both creative and disciplined, albeit using very different methods. Both of these sites are easily accessed from the Columbia Heights Metro station.

The Art and Media House (☎ 202-319-2225; www.artmediahouse.org; 1419 Columbia Rd NW) is based in two Skittles-bright renovated homes that also house its parent organization, the DC Latin American Youth Center (www .layc-dc.org). Art and Media House provides all of the arts and humanities programs for the center, offering music and visual arts classes, media training in audio and digital recording, and a spot to showcase all of the above work. The classes are consistently popular within the Latino community, and the work that comes out of the house is always excellent.

Keely's District Boxing and Youth Center (☎ 202-232-0193/4; http://keelysyouthcenter.com; 2501 11th St NW) was set up by former lightweight world champion boxer Keely Thompson. The gym mixes up literacy and nutrition programs with its physical training regimen, and teaches kids not just how to fight, but more importantly, when to. Keely's fundraising galas are a thing of local legend, and the gym has become a cornerstone of the neighborhood.

Both of the above sites welcome visitors and volunteers, but call ahead to see what their staffing situation is like, or to make donations.

Also nearby is the headquarters of a group lauded as one of the best community-urban partnerships working in the country: the Josephine Butler Parks Center (☎ 202-462-7275; www.washingtonparks.net/parks_center; 2437 15th St NW), which coordinates many of the District's neighborhood, arts and environmental organizations.

museums in the city (opened in 1862) and one of the few partially operated by the military. That's because the focus of the museum's eclectic collection is military medicine – the displays on Civil War combat 'nursing' are gruesome and fascinating in equal measure. This is hands-on stuff (well, not literally) and not for the faint hearted – visitors will see the effects of diseases, the tools used to battle them and all the messy side and after effects. Probably the most popular exhibit remains the paraphernalia connected to Abraham Lincoln's assassination, including the bullet that killed him and bits of bone and hair from Lincoln's skull.

BASILICA OF THE NATIONAL SHRINE OF THE IMMACULATE CONCEPTION
Map pp106-7

☎ 202-526-8300; www.nationalshrine.com; 400 Michigan Ave NE; ☻ 7am-7pm Apr-Oct, to 6pm Nov-Mar; Ⓜ Brookland-CUA

The largest Catholic house of worship in North America can host 6000 worshippers (Some might say that's when the building is at critical *mass*. Get it? Sorry.) This is an enormous, impressive, but somehow unimposing edifice, more Byzantine than Vatican in its aesthetic. Outlaid with some 75,000 sq ft of mosaic work and a crypt modeled after early Christian catacombs, the (literal) crowning glory is a dome that could have been lifted off the Hagia Sophia in Istanbul. The Marian shrine sports an eclectic mix of Romanesque and Byzantine motifs, all anchored by a 329ft minaret-shaped campanile. Downstairs, the original eastern-style crypt church has low, mosaic-covered vaulted ceilings lit by votives and chandeliers. Upstairs, the main sanctuary is lined with elaborate saints' chapels, lit by rose windows and fronted by a dazzling mosaic of a stern Christ.

FRANCISCAN MONASTERY
off Map pp106-7

☎ 202-526-6800; www.myfranciscan.com; 1400 Quincy St NE; admission by donation; ☻ hourly tours 9am-4pm Mon-Sat, 1-4pm Sun

This honey-colored compound leaps out like an unexpected religious slap from the surrounding parkland and residential row houses. Also known as Mt St Sepulchre, the building is pretty but not particularly unique; more interesting are the care-fully maintained grounds, threaded with walkways that lead past 44 acres of tulips, dogwoods, cherry trees and roses – and some unintentionally tacky re-creations of the Middle East. See, the Order of St Francis is charged with the guardianship of the Holy Land's sacred sites, and it has interpreted that task in a unique way here, constructing replicas for the faithful on its grounds. There are life-size fake-granite reproductions of the Tomb of Mary and the Grotto at Lourdes, and within Mt St Sepulchre itself are reproductions of the Roman Catacombs under the sanctuary floor. These dark, narrow passages wind past some fake tombs and the very real remains of Sts Innocent and Benignus; claustrophobes need not apply. It's all creepy and fascinating, like a holy Disneyland.

GALLAUDET UNIVERSITY off Map pp106-7

☎ 202-651-5000; www.gallaudet.edu; 800 Florida Ave NE

The first university for deaf and hard-of-hearing students in the world occupies a lovely manicured campus of bucolic green and Gothic accents north of Capitol Hill. Notable buildings include College Hall, an antique vision in brownstone, and Chapel Hall, a gorgeous Gothic structure that screams academia. Fun fact: the American football huddle was invented here when the Bisons (the school team) noticed other teams were trying to interpret their sign language while they plotted their plays. If you speak sign language, note that Gallaudet is a bilingual institution where English sign language and ASL are both practiced. Union Station is the closest Metro station, but it's a little over a mile walk (25 minutes) from the Metro; you may want to cab or drive out here.

POPE JOHN PAUL II CULTURAL CENTER Map pp106-7

☎ 202-635-5400; www.jp2cc.org; 3900 Harwood Rd NE; admission by suggested donation adult $5, senior & student $4; ☻ 10am-5pm Tue & Thu-Sat, noon-5pm Sun; Ⓜ Brookland-CUA

This impressive modernist-style structure is an unexpected setting for an interactive museum of the Catholic Church. Five galleries explore the history of the church, personal faith, and its relation to science, community and social service. The excellent Gallery of Imagination allows visitors to participate in a carillon-ringing ensemble or design an electronic stained-glass window.

FORT STEVENS PARK off Map pp106-7
☎ 202-895-6070; cnr 13th & Quackenbos Sts NW; 🚌 E2, E3, E4 from Friendship Heights, 71, 72 from Gallery Pl-Chinatown

In a raid on July 11, 1864, Confederate General Jubal Early attacked Fort Stevens, the northernmost of the defensive ramparts ringing the city. A small but fierce battle raged – the only time the Civil War touched District soil – until Early's men withdrew across the Potomac. Abraham Lincoln himself was drawn into the shooting: the president, observing the battle from Fort Stevens' parapet, popped his head up so many times that Oliver Wendell Holmes, Jr, then a Union captain, yelled 'Get down, you damn fool, before you get shot!' The fort has been partially restored, and 41 Union men who died in its defense are buried at tiny Battleground National Cemetery (6625 Georgia Ave), a half-mile north. Information on the battle can be found at http://americancivil war.com/statepic/dc/dc001.html.

U STREET STROLLING
Walking Tour

The U St Corridor is one of the most fashionable, walkable neighborhoods in the city, and offers some good insight into the direction the city is taking as an eating, shopping and arts destination. The area is also rich in the city's African American heritage.

1 Africa American Civil War Memorial

Exit the U Street-Cardozo/African American Civil War Memorial Metro station at the 10th St exit and wander around the memorial (p107) plaza. Why is this sculpture here? As early as 1999, U St was a dangerous, mainly African American ghetto. The Metro stop, which opened in 1991, was one of the first heralds of new development; the nearby memorial reminds black residents that the rebuilding of their community has been accomplished before, by ancestors who fought for their people's freedom.

2 Duke Ellington Mural

Now walk west along U St – the numbered cross streets should be going up. At 1200 U St is a mural of Duke Ellington, perhaps DC's most renowned musical native son, who grew up just around the way

on Bates St. The mural was commissioned by Eugenia Lucas, who owned a business, 'Mood Indigo' (named for an Ellington song), that once occupied these premises. Lucas worked with white muralist G Byron Peck, community leaders and corporate sponsors to get the art up. It was completed in 1997.

3 Lincoln Theatre

Nearby, at 1215 U St is the Lincoln Theatre (p191), the heart of what was once termed 'Black Broadway' – Billie Holiday, Ella Fitzgerald, Louis Armstrong and Cab Calloway all graced this stage. When desegregation opened all city theaters to black audience members, the Lincoln suffered losses; the '68 riots shut it down. Revitalization projects in the early '90s reopened the theatre, and today it's another crucial link in the U St chain of being.

4 Ben's Chili Bowl

Just next door, pop into Ben's Chili Bowl (p163), one of the city's most iconic restaurants and a keystone U St business. Ben's is one of the only businesses to have lasted since the 1950s, and besides, it's one of the best spots for late-night munchies in town. If you're hungry, we highly recommend scarfing a chili half-smoke.

5 Dekka

One of the newer signs of U St's arrival is Dekka (p139), a fantastic indie shopping boutique that sort of doubles as an arts and designer collective. Souvenirs should be sought herein.

6 Hunted House

Roll down 14th St (turn left, and head toward T St) until you get to Hunted House (p140), which kinda resembles the house from Shel Silverstein's *A Light in the Attic*. Inside is all sorts of quirky vintage furniture, should you want to ship a deco dinette set back home.

7 Black Cat

Across the way is the Black Cat (p183), one of the original white music clubs in the area. Well, 'white' isn't fair; there's a mixed crowd here, but the music scene is more rock-oriented. The club was started by Foo Fighter's Dave Grohl and hosts ripping sets most nights.

8 Malcolm X Park

Take a walk west on Swann St NW, then a long detour north to Malcolm X Park (p103). Officially, this is Meridian Hill, but no one ever calls it that. This is a beautifully landscaped space that drapes over the land in several pretty green steps,

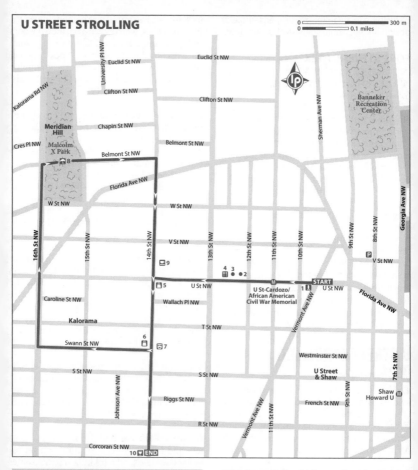

U STREET STROLLING

0 ——————— 300 m
0 ——————— 0.1 miles

9 Busboys & Poets Go east from Malcolm X Park, then south (right) onto 14th St NW until you reach Busboys & Poets (p164). If you're hungry, grab an excellent sandwich or pizza here, or at least a coffee, and make sure you peruse the attached progressive bookstore. There are often readings and performances – Busboys is one of the artistic linchpins of the U St revival.

10 HR57 If it's evening, head south on 14th St to just past the intersection of Corcoran and 14th Sts. This is HR57 (1610 14th St NW; ❍ from 8:30pm Wed-Sat). The city's jazz and blues archives are contained herein, and great live performances recall the heyday of U St jazz.

WALK FACTS

Start African American Civil War Memorial
End HR57
Distance 2.8 miles
Duration 2-2½ hours
Fuel stops Ben's Chili Bowl and Busboys & Poets

decked out with Tuscan-style pavilions and cascading water fountains. This used to be a dangerous area, but community-watch patrols and grassroots security have turned it into one of the most family friendly outdoor destinations in the city.

The long, leafy lanes of Upper Northwest have long been *the* place for upper-income Washingtonians to settle their families. While Georgetown houses more of the city's elite, the presence of its university and the traffic snarls along M St have made it less appealing to folks seeking a quiet place to raise their children. In comparison, Upper Northwest caters much more to those seeking the quiet pleasures of strictly enforced slow driving, large houses with bigger yards and the general sense of space you'd likely associate with the suburbs of commuter Maryland and Northern Virginia.

Still, at the end of the day Upper Northwest *isn't* the 'burbs. People live here so they can still technically be within the city while accessing all the advantages that lay therein. This makes for an interesting social dynamic – the population here appreciates the good life that comes from green space and bucolic lanes, but they're still appreciative of the arts scene, cultural diversity and the general vibe that makes city living so special. They just generally desire all of the above while also, understandably, wanting safe streets and good schools. The point is, while Upper Northwest may initially come off as an oasis from the city, it actually contains many of the best qualities of the Washington experience. It helps that many of the neighborhood's inhabitants are members of Washington's wonky elite – the established journalists, professors, diplomats, think-tank staffers and politicos who not only contribute to, but lay the groundwork for the fascinating DC dialogues and debates that make this town a unique place to live.

This is a big neighborhood, and as such it's divided into several distinct districts. Woodley Park and Cleveland Park lay just across Rock St Parkway from Adams-Morgan and Dupont Circle. This proximity to two loci of urban cool has rubbed off on these 'hoods, and as such they make a good transition space between the quieter stretches of far Upper Northwest and the rest of the city. There's lots of ethnic eating and a few quirky cafes in this area, not quite possessed of the nightlife-friendly edge on the other side of the Parkway, but hardly boring either. Indeed, some of the city's most exciting restaurants have posted up this way, attracted by a population that has disposable income to spend and an increasingly savvy attitude toward food. This is also a great area for the kids, as evidenced by the nearby National Zoo. That said, be warned: opportunistic muggers do occasionally prowl these streets late at night.

Upper Northwest stretches on a left-leaning diagonal following Connecticut Ave all the way out to Friendship Heights, which borders Chevy Chase, MD. Along the way it passes through North Cleveland Park and Forest Hills, all very quiet and supremely pleasant clumps of residential bliss. Here and there small shopping strips break up the picket fences, but seeing as the local population is both well-off and discerning, you're hard-pressed to find chain-brand stores out this way. Even in its stillest reaches, the dining and retail options here tend to be distinctive and innovative.

To the east of Connecticut is Rock Creek Park. Sure, it's a forest in a city, so it's only relatively large, but Rock Creek is vast enough to conceal a population of coyotes, and on hot summer days the cooling effect of all those trees is palpable; you can seriously feel the thermometer drop as you approach the green. West of Connecticut is Tenleytown and the area surrounding American University. With the exception of a few big-box stores and their accompanying traffic jams, this is still awfully nice residential country, where the architecture runs the gamut from late-19th-century brownstones to modernist mansions. One thing these homes share is hefty price tags: in 2009 the average listing in Spring Valley, which surrounds the American University campus, was $2.3 million.

ORIENTATION

Upper Northwest stretches from W St – just north of Georgetown and Shaw – all the way to the Maryland line, which is marked by the diagonal southwest–northeast Western Ave. Rock Creek Park runs north–south down the center of the quadrant. For our purposes, the northern boundary of this area is Military Rd NW, while Rock Creek Park forms its eastern edge.

West of the park is mostly affluent residential neighborhoods, with major pockets of development along Connecticut and Wisconsin Aves. Heading up Wisconsin Ave, just

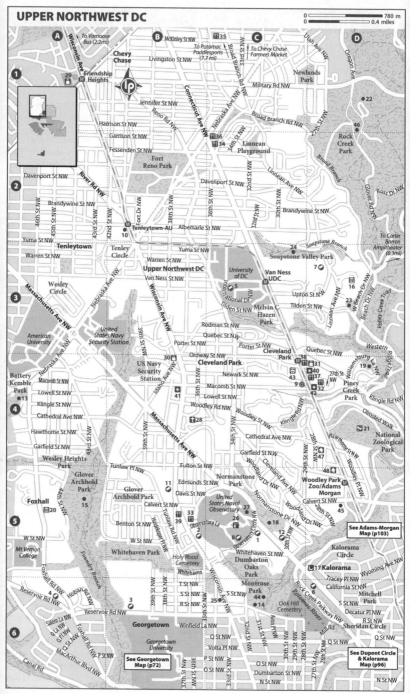

UPPER NORTHWEST DC

To Vamoose Bus (2.2mi)

McKinley St NW 🚾35

To Potomac Paddlesports (7.1mi)

To Chevy Chase Farmers Market

Utah Ave NW

Oregon Ave

Wisconsin Ave NW

Chevy Chase

Livingston St NW

Newlands Park

🏛29 Friendship Heights Ⓜ

Jennifer St NW

Reno Rd NW

Nebraska Ave NW

Military Rd NW

Connecticut Ave NW

Broad Branch Rd NW

●22

Harrison St NW

46●

Garrison St NW

Broad Branch Rd NW

Rock Creek Park

Fessenden St NW

🚾36
🚾34

Linnean Playground

38th St NW

Linnean Ave NW

Broad Branch

Fort Reno Park

Davenport St NW

River Rd NW

32nd St NW

Davenport St NW

Ross Dr NW

36th St NW

Brandywine St NW

Glover Rd NW

Brandywine St NW

46th St NW
45th St NW
43rd St NW
42nd St NW
Fort Dr NW

30th St NW

🚇10 Tenleytown-AU Ⓜ

Albemarle St NW

Tenleytown

Yuma St NW

Yuma St NW

Warren St NW

To Carter Barron Amphitheater (0.3mi)

Soapstone Branch

Warren St NW

Tenley Circle

24●

Soapstone Valley Park

Upper Northwest DC

Van Ness St NW

Van Ness St NW

University of DC

Van Ness UDC

7 Ⓞ

Wesley Circle

Nebraska Ave NW

Wisconsin Ave NW

39th St NW

5 Ⓞ

International Dr NW

Melvin C Hazen Park

Upton St NW

W Beach Dr NW

Valley Creek Trail

Western

🏛16

Massachusetts Ave NW

American University

Tilden St NW

Tilden St NW

23●

Rodman St NW

Quebec St NW

Porter St NW

United States Navy Security Station

Quebec St NW

Cleveland Park

38th St NW

Ordway St NW

🚾38

🚾31

🚾40

Western

🏛19

Battery Kemble Park

Nebraska Ave NW

Macomb St NW

30 🏛

US Navy Security Station

Cleveland Park

Newark St NW

43 🚾
9 Ⓞ

🚾37
🚾32

27th St NW

Williamsburg La NW

●13

Lowell St NW

Idaho Ave NW

Macomb St NW

42 🚾

Piney Creek Park

Klingle St NW

Klingle Rd NW

Klingle St NW

Cathedral Ave NW

41 🚾

Lowell St NW

Woodley Rd NW

34th St NW

Woodley St NW

Olmsted Walk

Hawthorne St NW

Garfield St NW

Massachusetts Ave NW

🚾28

Cathedral Ave NW

🚾21

National Zoological Park

Wesley Heights Park

35th St NW

Garfield St NW

Woodland Dr NW

Cleveland Ave NW

28th St NW

Hawthorne St NW

🚾47

Glover Archbold Park

11 Ⓞ

Edmunds St NW

Tunlaw Pl NW

Normanstone Park

Davis St NW

Woodland Dr NW

48 🏛

Woodley Park Zoo/Adams Morgan

Foxhall

🏛20

Calvert St NW

United States Naval Observatory

Normanstone Dr NW

45●

Glover Archbold Park

Tunlaw Rd NW

33 🚾
39 🚾

27 ●

Calvert St NW

29th St NW

●15

Benton St NW

Observatory La

26 ●

See Adams-Morgan Map (p103)

W St NW

2 Ⓞ

18 ●

30th St NW

W St NW

8 Ⓞ

12 ●

Mt Vernon College

Foxhall Rd NW

Foundry Branch

Whitehaven Park

Holy Rood Cemetery

Whitehaven St NW

Kalorama Circle

Ⓒ17 **Kalorama**

Tracey Pl NW

Wyoming Ave NW

Reservoir Rd NW

Hoban Rd NW

Whitehaven

Dumbarton Oaks Park

California St NW

6●

Mitchell Park

Salem La NW

T St NW

T St NW

S St NW

Montrose Park

Rock Creek Parkway

S St NW

Decatur Pl NW

Q La NW

Cl Pl NW

S St NW

3 Ⓞ

R St NW

25 ●

44 ●
●14

Oak Hill Cemetery

Sheridan Circle

Reservoir Rd NW

Reservoir Rd NW

Georgetown

Winfield La NW

Q St NW

31st St NW

Potomac River

Mill Rd

Q St NW

Canal Rd

MacArthur Blvd NW

Georgetown University

See Georgetown Map (p72)

Volta Pl NW

P St NW

37th St NW
36th St NW
35th St NW
34th St NW

33rd St NW

32nd St NW
31st St NW

30th St NW
29th St NW

28th St NW
27th St NW

See Dupont Circle & Kalorama Map (p96)

O St NW

Dumbarton St NW

N St NW

N St NW

north of Georgetown, is Glover Park (named for the park that dominates the neighborhood), a quaint community housing graduate students and young families. Further north is Tenleytown and American University.

Woodley Park and Cleveland Park occupy the streets between Connecticut and Wisconsin Aves. The Washington National Cathedral is tucked off Wisconsin Ave. The zoo is nestled in between Connecticut Ave and Rock Creek Park.

WASHINGTON NATIONAL CATHEDRAL Map p114

☎ 202-537-6200; www.nationalcathedral.org; cnr **Massachusetts & Wisconsin Aves NW; suggested donation adult/student & senior $5/3, tours $5-10;** ⏰ **10am-5:30pm Mon-Fri, to 8pm May-Sep, 10am-4:30pm Sat, 8am-5pm Sun;** Ⓜ **Tenleytown**
Open to all faiths and creeds, this house of worship, while run by the Episcopal diocese, has conducted services for Protestants, Catholics, Muslims, Jews, Buddhists and Baha'is. Presidents attend multifaith services following their inauguration, state funerals are hosted inside and this was where Martin Luther King Jr gave his last Sunday sermon. Technically, it took 82 years to build this edifice – Teddy Roo-

NEIGHBORHOOD RESOURCES

- Brightwood Community Association (www .brightwooddc.com)
- Cleveland Park (www.clevelandpark.com)
- Glover Park Citizens' Association (www .gpcadc.org)
- Tenleytown (http://tenleytown.com)
- Ward 3 DC (http://ward3dc.blogspot.com)
- Woodley Park (www.dcnet.com/woodley)

sevelt laid the cornerstone in 1908, and construction didn't technically stop until 1990.

The National Cathedral has become such an iconic feature of the city skyline it is hard to imagine a time when its construction was a controversial issue, but there was some strong opposition to this building back in the day. Critics argued that cathedrals were more European than American, and that their proportions were a symbol of religious power that didn't jive in a nation partly founded on the premise of freedom of religion and separation of church and state. However, the multifaith character of worship here helped mollify these arguments.

UPPER NORTHWEST DC

INFORMATION		
British Embassy	1	C5
Chinese Embassy Visa Office	2	B5
Embassy of France	3	B6
Embassy of Germany	4	A6
Embassy of Israel	5	C3
Embassy of Japan	6	D6
Embassy of the Netherlands	7	D3
La Maison Française	(see 3)	
New Zealand Embassy	8	C5
Public Library - Cleveland Park Branch	9	C4
Public Library Tenley-Friendship Branch	10	B2
Russian Embassy	11	B5
South African Embassy	12	C5

SIGHTS	(pp115–19)	
Battery Kemble Park	13	A4
Dumbarton Oaks	14	C6
Glover Archbold Park	15	A5
Hillwood Museum	16	D3
Islamic Center	17	D5
Joaquin Miller Cabin	(see 22)	
Kahlil Gibran Memorial Garden	18	C5
Klingle Mansion	19	D4

Kreeger Museum	20	A5
La Maison Française	(see 3)	
National Zoological Park	21	D4
Nature Center & Planetarium	22	D1
Rock Creek Gallery	23	D3
Soapstone Valley Park	24	C3
Spiral Flight	25	C6
US Naval Observatory	26	C5
Vice-President's Residence (Admiral's House)	27	C5
Washington National Cathedral	28	B4

SHOPPING 🛍	(pp127–42)	
Krön Chocolatier	(see 29)	
Mazza Gallerie	29	A1
National Zoological Park	(see 21)	
Politics & Prose Bookstore	(see 34)	
Sullivan's Toy Store	30	B4
Wake Up Little Suzie	31	D4

EATING 🍴	(pp143–70)	
Ardeo's	32	D4
Blue Ridge	33	B5
Buck's Fishing and Camping	34	C2
Chevy Chase Farmers' Market	35	C1

Comet Ping Pong	36	C2
Nam Viet	37	D4
Palena	38	C4
Rocklands Barbecue	39	B5
Vace Deli	(see 37)	

NIGHTLIFE 🌟	(pp171–86)	
Aroma	40	D4
Enology	41	B4
Nanny O'Brien's Irish Pub	42	D4

THE ARTS 🎭	(pp187–94)	
AMC Loews Uptown 1	43	C4
Politics & Prose Bookstore	(see 34)	

SPORTS & ACTIVITIES	(pp195–200)	
Montrose Park Tennis Court	44	C6
Omni Shoreham	45	D5
Rock Creek Horse Center	46	D1

SLEEPING 🛏	(pp201–215)	
Kalorama Guest House at Woodley Park	47	D4
Woodley Park Guesthouse	48	D5

top picks

The building is elegant, but also powerfully neo-Gothic. While it wouldn't look out of place in many European cities, it's embellished by some American accents. In a nod to US geography, the column capitals on the north side of the building include igloo motifs. One of the interior stained-glass windows is studded with a moon rock, and Darth Vader's head shares spaces with the gargoyles arranged around the parapets. A diverse range of themed tours takes in all of the above; check the website for details and to make advance bookings.

Take the elevator to the tower overlook for expansive city views. In the main sanctuary, chapels honor the Apollo astronauts, Martin Luther King, Abe Lincoln, and abstract ideas such as peace and justice; in the crypt, you can find the bodies of Helen Keller and Woodrow Wilson, among others. Outside, the charming Bishop's Garden is graced with winding paths that lend a mood of solitude.

The 11am Sunday service features lovely choral music and a 10-bell peal of the carillon afterwards. Cathedral choristers sing Evensong at 5:30pm Tuesday to Thursday during the school year.

NATIONAL ZOOLOGICAL PARK
Map p114

☎ 202-673-4800; http://nationalzoo.si.edu; 3001 Connecticut Ave NW; admission free; ☾ 6am-8pm Apr-Oct, to 6pm Nov-Mar; Ⓜ Cleveland Park, Woodley Park Zoo/Adams Morgan

As the National Zoo enters its 120th year of existence, it celebrates a birthday attended by some controversy (several animals'

deaths in the last decade and the resignation of a director), hope (two words: giant pandas) and cautious optimism exemplified by the birth of a lowland gorilla. Still one of the best zoos around, the National gently sprawls over 163 acres cut through by a mini-Amazon, the interactive Think Tank, which examines animal intelligence, and the excellent Asia Trail, which winds around aforementioned pandas, clouded leopards and red pandas.

The Smithsonian Institution zoo was founded in 1889 and planned by Frederick Law Olmsted, designer of New York's Central Park. The zoo's grounds follow the natural contours of a woodland-canyon, and the exhibits are noted for their natural-habitat settings. The zoo is intensively involved in worldwide ecological study and species-preservation work.

It's hard to pick one favorite part of the zoo. The Great Ape House is always popular; on-site orangutans prance around on external cable crossings across the rest of the zoo. The dark Bat Cave is always a hit with the kids, and big-cat fans will love the cheetahs' display, What's for Dinner?, where overly honest scales inform you who would like to feast on you ('100lb to 150lb – you're a female warthog. A pack of lions could finish you off in an hour.') Currently, the zoo is expanding the existing elephant house. In December, local businesses compete with each other to showcase elaborate Christmas-light displays fashioned to resemble animals; it's a great holiday treat to wander amid the brightness on sharp winter evenings.

DUMBARTON OAKS Map p114

☎ 202-339-6401; www.doaks.org; 1703 32nd St NW; museum admission free, gardens adult/senior & child $8/5; ☾ gardens 2-6pm, to 5pm Tue-Sun winter, museum 2-5pm Tue-Sun

One of the finest mansions in DC is set on some of its finest gardens, a multi-terraced study in pruned elegance. Nineteen ponds and pools are dolloped over 16 acres of landscaped goodness. In the mansion itself is a collection of fine Byzantine and pre-Columbian art, an intricately painted beamed ceiling and El Greco's *The Visitation*. As a bonus, this is where folks decided to found the UN in 1944. The house is operated by the trustees of Harvard University, so Harvard students, faculty and staff get in for free.

ROCK CREEK PARK Map p114

☎ 202-895-6070; www.nps.gov/rocr; M Cleveland Park, Woodley Park Zoo/Adams Morgan

At 1700 acres, Rock Creek is twice the size of New York's Central Park and feels a hell of a lot more wild. You can be out here and feel utterly removed from the city. Even coyotes have settled into the wilderness (they're not dangerous, by the way). Rock Creek Park begins at the Potomac's east bank near Georgetown and extends to and beyond the northern city boundaries. Narrow in its southern stretches, where it hews to the winding course of the waterway it's named for, it broadens into wide, peaceful parklands in Upper Northwest DC. Terrific trails extend the entire length, and the boundaries enclose Civil War forts, dense forest and wildflower-strewn fields.

Cell phone 'tours' are stationed around the park; when you see a dial-and-discover sign, just enter the listed number. A good first stop for visitors is the Nature Center & Planetarium (☎ 202-426-6829; off Military Rd; ☽ 9am-5pm Wed-Sun). Besides exhibits on park flora, fauna and history, it has two small nature trails, tons of information and maps and field guides to the city. A 'touch table' is set up for kids, and rangers lead child-oriented nature walks.

A bit further north of here, on the west side of Beach Dr, is the Joaquin Miller Cabin, a log house that once sheltered the famed nature poet. Further south, the Soapstone Valley Park extension, off Connecticut Ave at Albemarle St NW, preserves quarries where the area's original Algonquin residents dug soapstone for shaping their cookware.

Alongside the creek, the 1820 Pierce Mill (☎ 202-426-6908; Tilden St; ☽ 9am-5pm Wed-Sun Sep-May, daily Jun-Aug) is a beautiful fieldstone building that was once a water-driven gristmill. Next door, local artists display work in a 19th-century carriage house known as the Rock Creek Gallery (☎ 202-244-2482; 2401 Tilden St; ☽ 11am-4:30pm Thu-Sun).

In summer, pick up an events calendar at the Carter Barron Amphitheater (☎ 202-426-0486; www.nps.gov/rocr/cbarron; cnr 16th & Kennedy Sts NW), a 4000-seat outdoor theater where concerts and plays, many of which are free, are held on summer evenings.

The remains of Civil War forts are among the park's most fascinating sites. During the war, Washington was, essentially, a massive urban armory and supply house for the Union Army. Its position near the Confederate lines made it vulnerable to attack, so forts were hastily erected on the city's high points. By spring 1865, 68 forts and 93 batteries bristled on hilltops around DC.

Overlooking Rock Creek in Cleveland Park is the Klingle Mansion (☎ 202-282-1063; 3545 Williamsburg Lane; ☽ 7:45am-4:15pm Mon-Fri). Built in 1823 by Joshua Pierce, the 10-room Pennsylvania Dutch fieldstone house is now park headquarters, open for information and permits for special events.

GLOVER ARCHBOLD PARK & BATTERY KEMBLE PARK Map p114

☒ D1 from Dupont Circle to Glover Park, D3, D6 from Dupont Circle to Battery Kemble Park

Glover is a sinuous, winding park, extending from Van Ness St NW in Tenleytown down to the western border of Georgetown University. Its 180 tree-covered acres follow the course of little Foundry Branch Creek, along which runs a pretty nature trail. Further west, skinny Battery Kemble Park, about a mile long but less than a quarter-mile wide, separates the wealthy Foxhall and Palisades neighborhoods of far northwestern DC. Managed by the National Park Service, the park preserves the site of a little two-gun battery that helped defend western DC against Confederate troops during the Civil War.

HILLWOOD MUSEUM & GARDENS Map p114

☎ 202-686-5807; www.hillwoodmuseum.org; 4155 Linnean Ave NW; suggested donation adult/child/student/senior $12/5/7/10; ☽ 10am-5pm Tue-Sat Feb-Dec; M Van Ness-UDC, Cleveland Park

Hillwood, the former estate of Marjorie Merriweather Post (of Post cereal fame) and her third husband, the ambassador to the USSR, contains the biggest collection of Russian imperial art to be found outside of Russia. Post convinced Stalin and the Soviets to sell her loads of Czarist swag, and her impressive collection includes furniture, paintings and a shockingly gorgeous collection of Fabergé eggs and jewelry. As a bonus, the 25-acre estate incorporates some lovely gardens (which include Post's dog cemetery), a greenhouse and a

top picks

museum shop. The on-site cafe serves up Russian treats (borscht, blintzes and the like) and afternoon tea.

KREEGER MUSEUM Map p114

☎ 202-338-3552; www.kreegermuseum.org; 2401 Foxhall Rd NW; adult/senior & student $10/7; ☉ tours by reservation 10:30am & 1:30pm Tue-Fri, without reservation 10am-4pm Sat

One of DC's more obscure attractions, this little-known museum is tucked away in the hills northwest of Georgetown and houses a fantastic collection of 20th-century modernist art. The art – by Renoir, Picasso and Mark Rothko, among many others – represents the amassed collection of David and Carem Kreeger, and their individual taste adds a charming degree of intimacy to the experience; you feel more like you're popping into a home than visiting a museum. Speaking of visiting, you must do so on 90-minute, reservation-only tours unless you come for Saturday open houses. Exhibits are constantly rotated, so you're just as likely to see Monet's dappled impressionism as Edvard Munch's dark expressionism.

LA MAISON FRANÇAISE Map p114

☎ 202-944-6091; www.la-maison-francaise.org; 4101 Reservoir Rd NW; ☉ 10am-4pm Mon-Fri

French for 'The Maison Francaise' (heh), La Maison is otherwise known as the French Embassy. The beating heart of Gallic DC occupies eight elegantly landscaped acres, anchored by the marble, modern-esque embassy itself. Countless cultural activities

pop off here every week; check the website for listings. Not to stereotype, but if you'd like to sip some good wine and gaze at interesting art, theater, dance and the like, this is the place to visit.

KAHLIL GIBRAN MEMORIAL GARDEN
Map p114

3100 Massachusetts Ave NW; Ⓜ Dupont Circle

In the midst of the wooded ravine known as Normanstone Park, the Kahlil Gibran garden memorializes the arch-deity of soupy spiritual poetry. Its centerpieces are a moody bust of the Lebanese mystic and a star-shaped fountain surrounded by flowers, hedges and limestone benches engraved with various Gibranisms: 'We live only to discover beauty. All else is a form of waiting.' From a trailhead just north of the garden, you can hop onto trails that link to Rock Creek and Glover Archbold Parks.

ISLAMIC CENTER Map p114

☎ 202-332-8343; www.theislamiccenter.com; 2551 Massachusetts Ave NW; admission free; ☉ 10am-5pm; Ⓜ Dupont Circle

Topped with a 160ft minaret, this pale limestone structure is the national mosque for American Muslims. It is delicately inscribed with Quranic verse, so it appears to float above Massachusetts Ave. Inside, the mosque glows with bright floral tiling, thick Persian rugs and gilt-trimmed ceilings detailed with more Quranic verse. You can enter to look around; remove your shoes, and women must bring scarves to cover their hair.

US NAVAL OBSERVATORY Map p114

☎ 202-762-1438; www.usno.navy.mil; 3450 Massachusetts Ave NW; admission free; ☉ tours by reservation 8:30pm Mon

If you're ever late to an appointment after visiting this place, you've got no excuse, buddy: the Naval Observatory is the official source of time for the US military and by extension, the country, so you know the clocks are set right here. Framed by a pair of stately, white ship's anchors, the observatory, created in the 1800s, is here 'to determine the positions and motions of celestial objects, provide astronomical data, measure the Earth's rotation, and maintain the Master Clock for the US.' Modern DC's light pollution prevents important observational work these days, but that cesium-beam atomic clock is still tickin'. Tours let you peek through telescopes and yak with astronomers, but they fill up weeks in advance, may be cancelled at any time and are only offered on select Mondays at 8:30pm, so reserve early – check the website or phone. On observatory grounds above Massachusetts Ave is the official Vice President's Residence (Admiral's House), which is closed to the public. Driving is the best way to reach the observatory.

Eating p168; Shopping p141; Nightlife p185; Sleeping p215

To slightly paraphrase a famous track: been spendin' most our lives, livin' in a yuppie's paradise. Welcome to Northern Virginia, one of the capital's major bedroom 'burbs (for the purposes of this book, we concentrate on the towns of Arlington and Alexandria). People here have a smirking relationship with their home: aware it's a bit slick and suburban and loving it despite – or because of – all that.

Northern Virginia combines some crucial capital sites – the imposing federal muscle of the Pentagon and the elegiac rows of cemeteries in Arlington, the twee charm of Old Town Alexandria and the stately elegance of Mt Vernon – with cozy pubs, kickin' pool halls and most of the trappings of suburban bliss. Make no mistake, the dozens of incorporated communities out this way, such as Ballston, Clarendon, Rosslyn, Chantilly, and Reston (to name a few) are very much commuter country, even though plenty of folks who live here never make their way into the city outside of office hours.

Why? they ask, pointing out that in Northern Virginia, they've got all the restaurants, shopping and nightlife of DC concentrated in an area that's much safer, often cheaper and several scrubs cleaner (although even the most dedicated Virginian will admit the traffic isn't much better than city driving). Safe, green-conscious, well-trimmed, smells nice. NoVa is the perfect neighbor just across from the picket fence of the Potomac.

The thing is, sometimes being too clean makes you antiseptic, while lack of an edge makes the most seemingly attractive dish bland. Washington the city overcomes these issues with its diversity. But to be fair to Virginia lovers, it's not like NoVa is entirely white-bread territory, even if it occasionally feels as such. Look a little deeper: out on Wilson Blvd the area's largest Vietnamese community clusters around the Eden Center, a Saigon market churned through a chain-brand-looking strip mall, while Annandale may possess the best Korean barbecue on the eastern seaboard. Ex-Ethiopian army officers whip up raw beef and homemade cheese in spicy-scented cafes in Falls Church, while Salvadorans and Nicaraguans mix it up while waiting in line for roast Peruvian chicken.

So how does this differ from Washington, DC? Well, out here there's not quite the close proximity that leads to daily interaction and comfort between communities you get within the city. That's one reason why many people move to the 'burbs, after all – to have a bit more space from each other. As a result, at the end of the day Northern Virginia can look very much like a million other mall-dominated American towns. Fortunately, proximity to DC gives the communities here a sense of political awareness that's lacking in the rest of the country. This is partly why, during every election cycle, Virginia politicians have to play to a completely different demographic in NoVa – the towns out this way may look like Anywhere America, but their residents have the cosmopolitan savvy that comes from living near one of the most dynamic cities in the world.

ORIENTATION

Arlington's neighborhoods are clustered around Metro stops just across the Potomac River from Northwest DC. Rosslyn is a steel-and-glass district in the north of town, directly across the Francis Scott Key Bridge from Georgetown. From here, Metro's Orange Line heads west, with stops at neighborhoods such as Courthouse, Clarendon, Virginia Sq and Ballston.

Metro's Blue Line turns south from Rosslyn and follows the Potomac River. In addition to Arlington Cemetery and Pentagon, Blue Line stops at Pentagon City and Crystal City: both corporate areas with hotels, high-rises and shopping malls. Ronald Reagan Washington National Airport is in the southern corner of Arlington on the Potomac River.

Alexandria is located south of Arlington along the Potomac River. The main streets are north–south Washington St (George Washington Memorial Parkway) and east–west King St. Addresses are numbered by the 100s (eg Cameron to Queen is the 200 block north).

The historic area, Old Town, is a square bounded by the King St Metro to the west, Slaters Lane to the north, the Potomac River to the east and Duke St, for our purposes, to the south. Most historic sights lie between Washington St and the river.

ARLINGTON

PENTAGON Map p122

☎ 703-695-1776; www.pentagon.gov, http://pen
tagon.afis.osd.mil; memorial admission free;
☷ closed to public; Ⓜ Pentagon

The US Department of Defense is housed
in what may be the world's biggest office
building, which took just 16 months to
build back in WWII. About 25,000 people
work in the massive polygon, which has
more than a dozen miles of corridors and
five sides surrounding a 5-acre courtyard.
But while the formidable edifice appears
impenetrable, 184 people were killed here
on September 11, 2001, when American
Airlines flight 77 crashed into the side of
the building. Just outside of the Pentagon
is a tranquil memorial to these victims
(including passengers of flight 77); the
grounds consist of 184 benches engraved
with a victim's name, shaded by 85 pa-
perback maple trees. Since the attacks

NEIGHBORHOOD RESOURCES

- City of Arlington (www.arlingtonva.us)
- City of Falls Church (www.fallschurchva.gov)
- Rosslyn (www.rosslynva.org)
- Visit Alexandria (http://visitalexandriava.com)

the Pentagon building is open only for
pre-arranged group tours (be sure to call
at least several weeks in advance or visit
http://pentagon.afis.osd.mil). Virtual tours
are online at www.defenselink.mil/pubs/
pentagon.

NATIONAL AIR FORCE MEMORIAL
Map p122

www.airforcememorial.org; ☷ 24hr; Ⓜ Arlington
Cemetery

Overlooking the Pentagon and adjacent
to Arlington National Cemetery, this new
memorial is (somewhat oddly) especially

REMEMBERING AMERICA'S HEROES – VISITING ARLINGTON NATIONAL CEMETERY

Washington's marble often celebrates America's victories and achievements, but Arlington National Cemetery (Map p122; ☎ 703-607-8000, tourmobile 888-868-7707; www.arlingtoncemetery.net; admission free, tourmobile adult/child $7.50/3.75; ☷ 8am-5pm Oct-Mar, to 7pm Apr-Sep; Ⓜ Arlington Cemetery) makes an elegiac counterpoint: commemorating her losses. Specifically, the sacrifice of over 290,000 service members (and dependents) marked by simple white headstones and the left mementos of over four million annual visitors. These 612 acres contain the dead of every war the US has fought since the Revolution, as well as American leaders such as JFK, Oliver Wendell Holmes and Medgar Evers.

At the end of Memorial Dr, the first site you'll see is the Women in Military Service for America Memorial, honoring women who have served in the armed forces in times of war and peace, from the Revolution onward. The memorial includes an education center and theater.

On the slopes above are the Kennedy gravesites. Near the eternal flame that marks the grave of John F Kennedy lie gravestones for Jacqueline Kennedy Onassis and their two children who died in infancy, and Robert Kennedy. Just as this book was being written, Ted Kennedy, the youngest brother of John and Robert, was laid alongside his siblings.

The Tomb of the Unknowns holds unidentified bodies from WWI, WWII and the Korean War. Soldiers march before it 24 hours a day, performing an impressive ceremonial changing of the guard every hour (every half-hour mid-March to September). For several years after the Vietnam War, the US government had no 'unknown' Vietnam War soldier to inter here. All recovered remains were identified, albeit slowly, via new forensic techniques. Finally, in 1984, an appropriately anonymous set of remains was located, and Defense Secretary Caspar Weinberger approved their burial in the tomb.

But in 1998, the family of Michael J Blassie, an air force lieutenant shot down near An Loc in 1972, discovered via DNA testing that the corpse was that of their lost relative. Blassie was removed in the first-ever Unknowns disinterment and reburied in Missouri. The Vietnam crypt at Arlington, meanwhile, stands permanently empty. The word 'Vietnam' and the dates of the conflict have been replaced with the inscription, 'Honoring and Keeping Faith with America's Missing Servicemen.'

Other memorials include the Confederate Monument, the tomb of Pierre L'Enfant, the mast of the battleship USS Maine, the Challenger memorial and the Nurses' Memorial. The Iwo Jima Memorial, displaying the famous raising of the flag over Mt Suribachi, is on the cemetery's northern fringes. You can also check out the graves of boxer Joe Louis, explorer Rear-Admiral Richard Byrd Jr and President William Taft. Please note funerals are held at the cemetery daily; if you see a ceremony, act with proper respect.

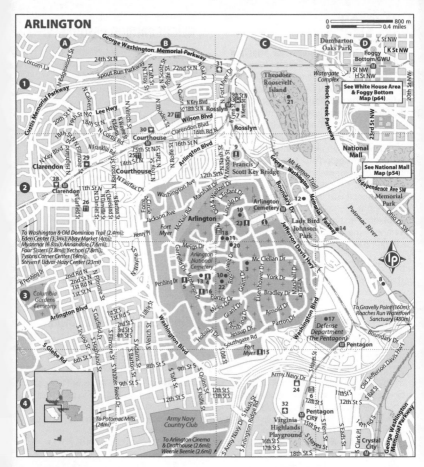

ARLINGTON

0 — 800 m
0 — 0.4 miles

attractive from the highway. It pays tribute to the millions of men and women who served in the air force and its predecessor organizations via a series of twisting metal arcs, meant to represent flight in motion.

GEORGE WASHINGTON MEMORIAL PARKWAY Map p122

☎ 703-289-2500; www.nps.gov/gwmp; Ⓜ Rosslyn

The 25-mile Virginia portion of this highway honors its namesake with recreation areas and memorials all the way south to his old estate at Mt Vernon. It's lined with remnants of George Washington's life and works, such as his old Patowmack Company canal (in Great Falls National Park) and parks that were once part of his farmlands

(Riverside Park, Fort Hunt Park). The road is a pleasant alternative to the traffic-choked highway arteries further away from the river, but you need to pull off to really appreciate the sites.

The 18.5-mile-long Mt Vernon Trail parallels the parkway from Francis Scott Key Bridge to Mt Vernon – it's paved and perfect for cycling. Along the way, Lady Bird Johnson Park commemorates the First Lady who tried to beautify the capital via greenery-planting campaigns and includes a memorial grove dedicated to her husband. Just north of Ronald Reagan Washington National Airport, Gravelly Point provides a vantage point for watching the planes take off and land; or you can check out the naturally airborne creatures at the Roaches Run Waterfowl Sanctuary.

ARLINGTON

THEODORE ROOSEVELT ISLAND
Map p122

☎ 703-289-2500; www.nps.gov/this; admission free; ☽ dawn-dusk; Ⓜ Rosslyn
This 91-acre wooded island, in the Potomac off Rosslyn, is a wilderness preserve honoring the conservation-minded 26th US president. A large memorial plaza and statue of Teddy dominate the island's center, and trails and boardwalks snake around the shorelines. The island's swampy fringes shelter birds, raccoons and other small animals, and there are great views of the Kennedy Center and Georgetown University across the river. The island is accessible from the Mt Vernon Trail (opposite) and is a convenient stop on a long bike ride or jog, but note bikes aren't permitted on the island itself; lock them up in the parking lot.

WASHINGTON & OLD DOMINION
TRAIL off Map p122

W&OD; ☎ 703-729-0596; www.wodfriends.org; admission free; ☽ dawn-dusk; Ⓜ East Falls Church
Despite its dense suburbs, northern Virginia is laced with hiking and biking trails. The 45-mile paved Washington & Old Dominion Trail follows an old railway bed from Shirlington, in southern Arlington, to Purcellville, in Virginia's Allegheny foothills. (For the truly ambitious, it's a short jump from here to the 2000 miles of Appalachian Trail, p227, going south to Georgia and north to Maine.) The scenic, well-maintained trail allows horseback riding between Vienna and Purcellville. Exit right from the East Falls Church Metro station.

FREEDOM PARK Map p122
1101 Wilson Blvd; Ⓜ Rosslyn
Paying tribute to a free press, Freedom Park features a memorial honoring journalists killed on the job. You'll also find icons from political struggles around the world on display, including chunks of the Berlin Wall. It's a nice spot to sit for a while and contemplate.

DEA MUSEUM Map p122
United States Drug Enforcement Agency Museum; ☎ 202-307-3463; www.deamuseum.org; 7200 Army Navy Dr; admission free; ☽ 10am-4pm Mon-Fri; Ⓜ Pentagon City
If you've got issues with the US War on Drugs, you may want to give the Drug Enforcement Agency (DEA) Museum a pass. If, on the other hand, you think all drug users and pushers should go to jail for a very long time and drugs and terrorism go hand in hand – or if you just have a thing for heavy-handed propaganda – well, stop on by. We're not trying to be flip, by the way – most Washington museums do a good job of presenting all sides of controversial issues such as the Vietnam War versus the antiwar movement, but there's no such nuance here. Then again, this is the only place in official Washington that displays bongs.

ARLINGTON HOUSE Map p122
☎ 703-557-0613; www.arlingtoncemetery .net/arlhouse; admission free; ☽ 9:30am-4:30pm; Ⓜ Arlington Cemetery
In one of the great spite moves of American history, thousands of Union war dead

THE GARDEN OF EDEN

One of Washington's most fascinating ethnic enclaves isn't technically in Washington. Instead, drive west past Arlington to Seven Sisters, VA and the Eden Center, which is, basically, a bit of Saigon that got lost in America. And we mean 'Saigon' – this is a shopping center/strip mall entirely occupied and operated by South Vietnamese refugees and their descendants. You can gamble (well, not officially), buy unusual Vietnamese medicines and, of course, eat. Anywhere. It's all as fresh as a Southeast Asian street stall. FYI – those needing *bee bim bap* should hit up nearby Annandale, VA for the region's best Korean chow. There's been talk about officially renaming the center of Annandale 'Koreatown' – there's something close to 1000 businesses here catering to the Korean community – and the local shops, bad pun approaching, are certainly full of Seoul.

were buried in the 1100-acre grounds of Confederate General Robert E Lee's home. After the war, the Lee family sued the federal government for reimbursement: the government paid them off, and Arlington Cemetery was born. The historic house is open for public tours, and is a lovely example of Virginia grand manor architecture.

ALEXANDRIA

TORPEDO FACTORY ART CENTER
Map p125

☎ 703-838-4565; www.torpedofactory.org; 105 N Union St; admission free; ☼ 10am-5pm; 🚌 Old Town shuttle from King St Metro

What do you do with a former munitions dump and arms factory? How about turn it into one of the best art spaces in the region? Three floors of artists studios and free creativity are on offer in Old Town Alexandria, as well as the opportunity to buy paintings and sculptures direct from their creators.

The Alexandria Archaeology Museum is also housed here. This is the laboratory where archaeologists clean up and catalog the artifacts they have unearthed at local digs. First-hand observation of the work, excavation exhibits and hands-on discovery kits allow visitors to witness and participate in the reconstruction of Alexandria's history.

GEORGE WASHINGTON MASONIC NATIONAL MEMORIAL Map p125

☎ 703-683-2007; www.gwmemorial.org; 101 Callahan Dr at King St; admission free; ☼ 9am-4pm Apr-Oct, from 10am Nov-Mar, tours on the hr; Ⓜ King St Metro

Alexandria's most prominent landmark features a fine view from its 333ft tower, where you can see the Capitol, Mount

Vernon and the Potomac River. It is modeled after the lighthouse in Alexandria, and honors the first president (who was initiated into the Masons in Fredericksburg in 1752 and later became Worshipful Master of Alexandria Lodge No 22). Artifacts of Washington's life and a striking bronze statue do the job.

ALEXANDRIA BLACK HISTORY RESOURCE CENTER Map p125

☎ 703-838-4356; www.alexblackhistory.org; 638 N Alfred St; admission free; ☼ 10am-4pm Tue-Sat, 1-5pm Sun; Ⓜ Braddock Rd

Paintings, photographs, books and other memorabilia documenting the black experience in Alexandria, one of America's major slave ports, are on display at this small resource center (enter from Wythe St). Pick up a brochure for self-guided walking tours of important Alexandria black-history sites. In the next-door annex, the Watson Reading Room has a wealth of books and documents on African American topics. Operated by the museum, the African American Heritage Park (Holland Lane) is worth a stop to see headstones from a 19th-century black cemetery.

FORT WARD MUSEUM & HISTORIC SITE off Map p125

☎ 703-838-4848; www.fortward.org; 4301 W Braddock Rd; admission free; ☼ 9am-dusk, museum 9am-4pm Tue-Sat, noon-5pm Sun; 🚌 Old Town shuttle from King St Metro

Fort Ward, northwest of Old Town along Braddock Rd, is the best-restored of the 162 Civil War forts known as the Defenses of Washington. The Northwest Bastion of the fort has been completely restored, and the remaining earthwork walls give a good sense of the defenses' original appearance. The on-site museum features exhibits on Civil War topics.

FRIENDSHIP FIREHOUSE MUSEUM
Map p125

☎ 703-838-3891; http://oha.alexandriava .gov/friendship; 107 S Alfred St; admission free; ⏱ 10am-4pm Fri & Sat, 1-4pm Sun; 🚌 Old Town shuttle from King St Metro

This 1855 Italianate firehouse displays historic firefighting gear – a great draw for kids. Local legend has it that George Washington helped found this volunteer fire company, served as its captain and even paid for a new fire engine.

CHRIST CHURCH Map p125

☎ 703-549-1450; www.historicchristchurch .org; 118 N Washington St; admission by donation; ⏱ 9am-4pm Mon-Sat, 2-4pm Sun; 🚌 Old Town shuttle from King St Metro

Since 1773, this redbrick Georgian-style church has welcomed worshipers from George Washington to Robert E Lee. The cemetery contains the mass grave of Confederate soldiers.

GADSBY'S TAVERN MUSEUM Map p125

☎ 703-838-4242; http://oha.alexandriava.gov/ gadsby; 134 N Royal St; adult/child $4/2; ⏱ 10am-5pm Tue-Sat, 1-5pm Sun & Mon Apr-Oct, 11am-4pm Wed-Sat, 1-4pm Sun Nov-Mar; 🚌 Old Town shuttle from King St Metro

Once a real tavern (operated by John Gadsby from 1796 to 1808), this building now houses a museum demonstrating the prominent role of the tavern in Alexandria during the 18th century. As the center of local political, business and social life, the tavern was frequented by anybody who

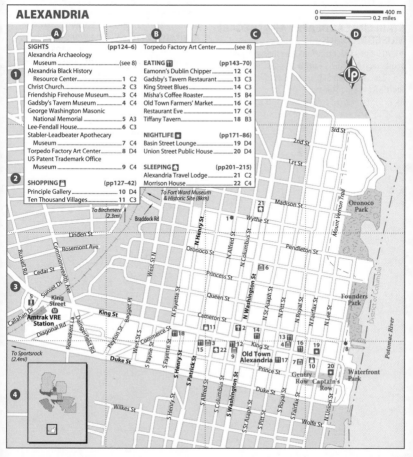

ALEXANDRIA

SIGHTS	(pp124–6)
Alexandria Archaeology Museum	(see 8)
Alexandria Black History Resource Center	1 C2
Christ Church	2 C3
Friendship Firehouse Museum	3 C4
Gadsby's Tavern Museum	4 C4
George Washington Masonic National Memorial	5 A3
Lee-Fendall House	6 C3
Stabler-Leadbeater Apothecary Museum	7 C4
Torpedo Factory Art Center	8 D4
US Patent Trademark Office Museum	9 C4

SHOPPING	(pp127–42)
Principle Gallery	10 D4
Ten Thousand Villages	11 C3

| Torpedo Factory Art Center | (see 8) |

EATING	(pp143–70)
Eamonn's Dublin Chipper	12 C4
Gadsby's Tavern Restaurant	13 C3
King Street Blues	14 C3
Misha's Coffee Roaster	15 B4
Old Town Farmers' Market	16 C4
Restaurant Eve	17 C4
Tiffany Tavern	18 B3

NIGHTLIFE	(pp171–86)
Basin Street Lounge	19 D4
Union Street Public House	20 D4

SLEEPING	(pp201–215)
Alexandria Travel Lodge	21 C2
Morrison House	22 C4

To Fort Ward Museum & Historic Site (8km)

To Birchmere (2.3mi)

To Sportsrock (2.4mi)

Braddock Rd

Linden St

Rosemont Ave

Cedar St

King Street

Amtrak VRE Station

Callahan Dr

Diagonal Rd

Russell Rd

Commonwealth Ave

Sunset Dr

King St

Rolfe St

Bagget Pl

West St N

Oronoco St

Princess St

Queen St

Cameron St

Madison St

Wythe St

Pendleton St

N Henry St

N Alfred St

N Columbus St

N Washington St

N Fayette St

N St Asaph St

N Pitt St

N Royal St

N Fairfax St

N Lee St

Old Town Alexandria

Duke St

Prince St

Gentry Row

Captain's Row

Wilkes St

S Henry St

S Patrick St

S Alfred St

S Columbus St

S Washington St

S St Asaph St

S Royal St

S Fairfax St

N Union St

Wolfe St

1st St

2nd St

3rd St

Mount Vernon Trail

Oronoco Park

Founders Park

District of Columbia

Potomac River

Waterfront Park

0 — 400 m
0 — 0.2 miles

was anybody, including George Washington, Thomas Jefferson and the Marquis de Lafayette. The rooms are restored to their 18th-century appearance, and the tavern occasionally still hosts pricey balls.

LEE-FENDALL HOUSE Map p125

☎ 703-548-1789; www.leefendallhouse.org; 614 Oronoco St; adult/child $5/3; ☟ 10am-4pm Tue-Sat, 1-4pm Sun, tours on the hr; Ⓜ Braddock Rd
Between 1785 and 1903 generations of the storied Lee family lived in this architecturally impressive house. Guided tours show the restored house as it probably was in the 1850s and 1860s, showcasing Lee family heirlooms and personal effects, and period furniture. The Georgian-style town house (607 Oronoco St; ☟ closed to public) across the street was Robert E Lee's childhood home from 1810.

STABLER-LEADBEATER APOTHECARY MUSEUM Map p125

☎ 703-838-3852; http://oha.alexandriava.gov/apothecary; 105-107 S Fairfax St; adult/child $4/2; ☟ 10am-4pm Mon-Sat, 1-5pm Sun; ☒ Old Town shuttle from King St Metro
In 1792 Edward Stabler opened up his apothecary – a family business that would operate for the next 141 years, until the Depression forced the shop to close. Quite a bit of history was shut inside at that time, including over 8000 medical objects. Now the shop is a museum; its shelves are lined with 900 beautiful hand-blown apothecary bottles and strange old items such as Martha Washington's Scouring Compound.

US PATENT & TRADEMARK OFFICE MUSEUM Map p125

☎ 571-272-8400; 600 Dulany St, Madison Bldg; admission free; ☟ 9am-5pm Mon-Fri, noon-5pm Sat; ☒ Old Town shuttle from King St Metro
This nearly new museum tells the history of the United States patent. Step inside to see where the story started in 1917 in Memphis, TN, when a wholesale grocer named Clarence Saunders invented and patented what he called 'self-servicing' stores, now commonly known as supermarkets. Incidentally, he went from rags to riches and almost back to rags again, but you'll have to visit the museum to get the rest of the story, along with displays depicting other famous and influential patents.

SHOPPING

top picks

What's your recommendation? www.lonelyplanet.com/washington-dc

SHOPPING

Shopping in DC can mean many things, from browsing atmospheric antique shops to perusing rare titles at secondhand booksellers; there are temptations for lovers of vinyl, kitschy home furnishings, one-of-a-kind jewelry and art, and handicrafts imported from all corners of the globe.

To the outsider, the DC fashion scene may seem like all blue suits and khakis, with government insiders and corporate types defining the reigning aesthetic. This stereotype – not inaccurate in some quarters of the city – misses by a wide margin Washington in all her multicultural beauty. This is a city where you'll find an assortment of funky vintage shops, fashion-forward boutiques, couture-loving consignment stores and specialty shops dealing in African robes, hats, lingerie, urban gear and stylish footwear.

DC also has the nation's best collection of politically oriented souvenirs, from rhinestone-studded Obama hats to stars-and-stripes boxer shorts, rubber Nixon masks and White House snow globes, placemats and ties. Museum shops are also good places to browse, containing iconic gifts like stuffed pandas from the National Zoological Park and balsa-wood airplanes from the National Air & Space Museum, as well as more unusual finds like Kenyan handicrafts from the National Museum of African Art, weavings from indigenous tribes at the National Museum of the American Indian and hand-painted and decorative East-Asian pieces in the Freer Gallery of Art.

If you can't find it on the streets of Washington, or time is limited, you can also visit one of the vast shopping centers in the suburbs (see p141).

Shopping Areas

Georgetown is DC's number-one shopping district, with stores lining M St and Wisconsin Ave. Adams-Morgan, along 18th St, has a handful of shops selling African handicrafts, books, records and vintage clothes. Nearby Columbia Heights has a growing number of boutiques and one-of-a-kind stores along U St and 14th St. Dupont Circle is another major shopping area, with stores on Connecticut Ave and the streets running off the circle. The Smithsonian museums each have their own souvenir stores – some better than others (see p130 for recommendations). Downtown you'll find plenty of stores selling whimsical DC souvenirs, T-shirts and political schlock. Further out, Alexandria's Old Town has an impressive variety of antiques, art galleries and craft shops.

Opening Hours

Generally, stores in DC are open 10am to 7pm Monday to Saturday and noon to 5pm Sunday, although some close on Sunday (some boutiques close on Monday instead). Smaller shops may close at 5pm daily, or stay open until 7pm one night a week, eg Thursday. Museum shops open according to museum hours.

Sales Taxes & Refunds

Sales tax is 6% in DC and 5% in Virginia. For more info, see p246.

WHITE HOUSE AREA & FOGGY BOTTOM

You'll find many tourist-aimed souvenir shops throughout these neighborhoods. There are some gems here, however, including a small travel store, a Native American craft shop and the AIA bookstore for architectural junkies.

INDIAN CRAFT SHOP Map p64   Art
☎ 202-208-4056; 1849 C St NW, No 1023 Dept of Interior; ⊗ 8:30am-4:30pm Mon-Fri; Ⓜ Farragut West
Representing over 45 tribal groups in the US, this crowded one-room shop sells gorgeous but costly basketry, weavings, pottery, beadwork and carvings made by Native Americans. It's hidden inside the Department of the Interior; show photo ID to enter the building.

AMERICAN INSTITUTE OF ARCHITECTS BOOKSTORE Map p64   Books
☎ 800-242-3837; 1735 New York Ave NW; ⊗ 9am-5pm Mon-Fri; Ⓜ Foggy Bottom
Architecture buffs are in good company in this small specialty shop, which stocks the latest architecture and design titles and periodicals. For the classic overview on the city's iconic buildings, pick up the AIA *Guide to the Architecture of Washington, DC.*

FILENE'S BASEMENT

Map p64   Discount Clothing

☎ 202-872-8430; 1133 Connecticut Ave NW; ⏰ 9:30am-8pm Mon-Sat, noon-5pm Sun; Ⓜ Farragut North

If you aren't from the east coast, you probably haven't ever had the privilege of shopping at Boston-based Filene's Basement. This discount store is a bargain-hunter's paradise, devoted to men's and women's clothing, shoes and accessories. You'll have to dig, but you can score pieces by the likes of Dolce & Gabbana, Marc Jacobs, Prada, Ralph Lauren, BCBG, DKNY and Missoni. Filene's has a second location inside the Shops at National Place (p135).

CHOCOLATE MOOSE

Map p64   Housewares, Toys & Accessories

☎ 202-463-0992; 1743 L St NW; ⏰ 10am-6pm Mon-Sat; Ⓜ Farragut North

In an otherwise staid stretch of L Street, Chocolate Moose lures in shoppers with its campy window displays and smiling brown moose. Among the array of temptations are leopard-printed wine glasses, candy-colored jewelry and wallets, dog-faced cake servers, wind-up toys and the famous punching nun puppet.

ADC MAP & TRAVEL CENTER

Map p64   Maps

☎ 202-628-2608; 1636 I St NW; ⏰ 9am-6:30pm Mon-Thu, 9am-5:30pm Fri, 9am-5pm Sat; Ⓜ Farragut West

This wee downtown storefront is packed with everything from road atlases to language guides, with huge foldout sheet maps of the district, children's activity guides and a small selection of globes.

RENWICK GALLERY Map p64   Museum Shop

☎ 202-357-2700; cnr 17th St & Pennsylvania Ave NW; Ⓜ Farragut West

In one of DC's best museum shops handmade textiles and hand-dyed silks are available, as is glasswork, woodwork and unique jewelry, much of it rather affordable. Its excellent choice of books includes how-to manuals on jewelry- and fabric-making, ceramics, glassblowing and cabinetry, many appropriate for kids.

WHITE HOUSE HISTORICAL ASSOCIATION GIFT SHOP

Map p64   Souvenirs

☎ 202-737-8292; 740 Jackson Pl NW, Lafayette Sq; ⏰ 9am-4pm Mon-Fri; Ⓜ Farragut West

Peruse a wide selection of books, videos, gifts, posters, Christmas ornaments, jewelry, postcards and educational materials, all on the theme of the big house across the square. This is the place to buy your dad a White House necktie. There is a similarly stocked store in the White House Visitors Center.

GEORGETOWN

Washington's best and most popular shopping area, Georgetown satisfies nearly every purchasing need in glittering storefronts lining its historic streets. You can spend big at galleries and well-known designer boutiques or penny-pinch at secondhand clothing shops and used bookstores. In between, the options are wide, with specialty shops dealing in gourmet food and wine, exotic teas, comic books, handmade soaps and much more. The main

CLOTHING SIZES

Women's clothing

Aus/UK	8	10	12	14	16	18
Europe	36	38	40	42	44	46
Japan	5	7	9	11	13	15
USA	6	8	10	12	14	16

Women's shoes

Aus/USA	5	6	7	8	9	10
Europe	35	36	37	38	39	40
France only	35	36	38	39	40	42
Japan	22	23	24	25	26	27
UK	3½	4½	5½	6½	7½	8½

Men's clothing

Aus	92	96	100	104	108	112
Europe	46	48	50	52	54	56
Japan	S		M	M		L
UK/USA	35	36	37	38	39	40

Men's shirts (collar sizes)

Aus/Japan	38	39	40	41	42	43
Europe	38	39	40	41	42	43
UK/USA	15	15½	16	16½	17	17½

Men's shoes

Aus/UK	7	8	9	10	11	12
Europe	41	42	43	44½	46	47
Japan	26	27	27½	28	29	30
USA	7½	8½	9½	10½	11½	12½

Measurements approximate only; try before you buy

SHOPPING GEORGETOWN

SHOPPING THE NATIONAL MALL

Scattered along the National Mall are Washington's most famous sights, which for the inveterate shopper means unearthing rare finds among the many museum stores. Amazonian artwork, West African handicrafts and surreal space food are just a few things not to miss when cruising 'the Mall.'

- **Arthur M Sackler Gallery** (Map p54; ☎ 202-633-1000; www.asia.si.edu; 1050 Independence Ave SW; ⏲ 10am-5:30pm, to 8pm Thu Jul & Aug; Ⓜ Smithsonian) Featuring Asian art posters and limited-edition prints, jewelry and world crafts.
- **Freer Gallery of Art** (Map p54; ☎ 202-633-1000; www.asia.si.edu; 1050 Independence Ave SW; ⏲ 10am-5:30pm, to 8pm Thu Jul & Aug; Ⓜ Smithsonian) Browse the antique ceramics from Asia, plus unique prints, scarves, bags and Eastern music. Knowledgeable staff.
- **National Air & Space Museum** (Map p54; ☎ 202-357-2700; cnr 6th St & Independence Ave SW; ⏲ 10am-5:30pm; Ⓜ Smithsonian) A three-floor emporium offering books, toys, kites, posters, model aircraft and such iconic DC souvenirs as freeze-dried astronaut ice cream.
- **National Gallery of Art** (Map p54; ☎ 202-737-4215; www.nga.gov; cnr 4th St & Constitution Ave NW; ⏲ 10am-5pm Mon-Sat, 11am-6pm Sun; Ⓜ Archives-Navy Memorial) Boasts several museum shops, including one lining the underground corridor linking the East and West Buildings. You'll find framed and unframed reproductions of the museum's best-known works, greeting cards, jewelry, creative games and activities for kids and loads of books.
- **National Museum of African Art** (Map p54; ☎ 202-357-2700; 950 Independence Ave SW; ⏲ 10am-5:30pm; Ⓜ Smithsonian) A great gift-buying spot with African textiles, baskets, musical instruments and dolls. Don't overlook the exquisite Tuareg jewelry.
- **National Museum of American History** (Map p54; ☎ 202-357-2700; cnr 14th St & Constitution Ave NW; ⏲ 10am-5:30pm; Ⓜ Smithsonian) Features replica souvenirs (brass binoculars, lanterns, wooden model ships), plus books and DVDs on all aspects of American culture and history.
- **National Museum of Natural History** (Map p54; ☎ 202-357-2700; cnr 10th St & Constitution Ave NW; ⏲ 10am-5:30pm; Ⓜ Smithsonian) This museum has four different specialty shops, including a bottom-floor store devoted to toys, stuffed dinosaurs and East Asian–themed items (origami sets, silk purses, kimonos). Outside the Geology Hall, the gem store sells fine and costume jewelry, vases, bowls, candleholders and a variety of unpolished stones.
- **National Museum of the American Indian** (Map p54; ☎ 202-287-2020; www.americanindian.si.edu; cnr 4th St & Independence Ave SW; ⏲ 10am-5:30pm, to 7:30pm Jun-Aug; Ⓜ Smithsonian) The smaller first-floor shop sells pottery, artwork and jewelry made by tribes from across the Americas. The busier store upstairs has books, crafts and native-themed souvenirs (dream catchers, Mola purses, replica arrowheads).

shopping strip is M St between 27th and 35th Sts. Wisconsin Ave has a mix of both chain stores and more unusual shops selling antique prints, old-fashioned toys and urban wear. Another place to check out is the Shops at Georgetown Park (M St), a surprisingly elegant mall. Do stroll down the side streets – as this is where you'll find the more imaginative stores.

PATAGONIA Map p72   Active Apparel

☎ 202-333-1776; 1048 Wisconsin Ave NW; ⏲ 11am-7pm Mon-Fri, 10am-7pm Sat, 11am-5pm Sun; 🚌 Georgetown shuttle, DC Circulator

Staffed with knowledgeable sales clerks and stocked with everything you need for a trip to the great outdoors, this tri-level shop has a giant collection of Patagonia's trusted gear, including trendy garb for women and men along with camping supplies, down jackets, and hiking shoes and shorts.

APPALACHIAN SPRING Map p72   Art

☎ 202-337-5780; 1415 Wisconsin Ave NW; 🚌 Georgetown shuttle, DC Circulator

Touting its motto, 'celebrating American craft,' this local chain features handmade pottery, woodcarvings, quilts and jewelry. The carved wooden boxes and hand-blown glass bowls make nice gifts.

BARTLEBY'S BOOKS Map p72   Books

☎ 202-298-0486; 1132 29th St NW; 🚌 Georgetown shuttle, DC Circulator

A neighborhood classic, Bartleby's Books has packed shelves lined with used and rare editions covering all manner of subjects. The selection is particularly strong in American lore – presidential biographies, political history and works by American writers and poets – with first editions and antiquarian books kept in the front cabinets.

ANNIE CREAM CHEESE Map p72   Clothing

☎ 202-298-5555; 3279 M St NW; 🚌 Georgetown shuttle, DC Circulator

One of several vintage shops in Georgetown, Annie's has some of the best selections, at least for women. You'll find tennis skirts, oversized sunglasses, sexy skirts and tops, glammy high heels – with a bevy of top designers represented. The men's selection is poor, unless monochrome polyester shirts and pleather jackets strike your fancy.

BARNEY'S CO-OP

Map p72   Clothing & Accessories

☎ 202-350-5382; 3040 M St NW; 🚌 Georgetown shuttle, DC Circulator

The well-known New York outfitter brings a dash of cutting-edge style to the DC fashion scene in this large two-level store in the heart of M St. Among the well-edited collection are Alexander Wang dresses, APC jackets for men, Jack Spade messenger bags and Vera Cuero footwear. Prices are high, but look for Barney's own Co-op label to find the deals.

COMMANDER SALAMANDER

Map p72   Clothing & Accessories

☎ 202-337-2265; 1420 Wisconsin Ave NW; ⏱ 10am-9pm Mon-Thu, 10am-10pm Fri & Sat, 11am-7pm Sun; 🚌 Georgetown shuttle, DC Circulator

This rock-and-roll store sells urban clothes and gear to give you that edgy look of the streets – if that's what you're after. Look for Blac Label shirts and jackets, chrome-plated belts, roaring tiger trucker hats, candy-colored Nike hi-tops and oversized Flüd watches.

BIG PLANET COMICS Map p72   Comics

☎ 202-342-1961; 3145 Dumbarton St NW; ⏱ 11am-7pm, to 8pm Wed, to 6pm Sat, noon-5pm Sun; 🚌 Georgetown shuttle, DC Circulator

Not just for comic-book-loving geeks, Big Planet appeals to a surprisingly diverse audience, with an excellent collection of limited editions and graphic novels, plus posters, t-shirts, manga material and collectible stuff.

BETSEY JOHNSON Map p72   Designer Boutique

☎ 202-338-4090; 3029 M St NW; 🚌 Georgetown shuttle, DC Circulator

Perennially trendy designer Betsey Johnson serves up her latest creations, always

top picks

SHOPPING STRIPS

- **M Street NW, Georgetown** (Map p72) The city's densest selection of stores with galleries, bookshops, gourmet grocers, vintage shops and dozens of indie and name-brand clothing retailers.
- **Connecticut Avenue, Dupont Circle** (Map p96) On the blocks leading north and south of Dupont Circle, you'll find good browsing for books, wine, music and men's and women's fashion.
- **18th Street NW, Adams-Morgan** (Map p103) This bar-and-restaurant strip also has funky shops selling records, used books, African handicrafts, vintage clothes, fancy door knobs and more.
- **U Street NW, Columbia Heights** (Map pp106–7) A newly gentrified street with stores selling second-hand clothing, antiques, kitschy home furnishings and art.
- **14th Street NW, Columbia Heights** (Map pp106–7) Leading south of U St, you'll find a scattered assortment of shops selling everything from stylish urban apparel to kitsch to 1960s furniture.
- **King Street, Alexandria** (Map p125) Hit the brick sidewalks of pretty King St for an array of galleries, jewelers, antique stores and craft shops.

featuring lots of gauze, velvet and lace, in her dishy pink boutique. The designer has girly yet punk flair, using many vibrant pinks against black lace. Check the sale rack: Betsey Johnson on sale is very affordable.

KIEHL'S Map p72   Face, Hair & Body

☎ 202-333-5101; 3110 M St NW; 🚌 Georgetown shuttle, DC Circulator

Kiehl's products are well known for their exceptional quality. This neat brick shop with friendly and helpful salespeople is filled with all the Kiehl's goodies you could ever want – shampoos and conditioners, rich and creamy body lotions and energizing facial scrubs.

DEAN & DELUCA Map p72   Gourmet Food

☎ 202-342-2500; 3276 M St NW; ⏱ 10am-8pm Sun-Thu, 10am-9pm Fri & Sat; 🚌 Georgetown shuttle, DC Circulator

The New York gourmet chain has an overwhelming and mouthwatering selection of produce, meat and baked goods in this revamped brick warehouse. Outside is a lovely canopied dining area for noshing on ready-made sandwiches, soups and pastries.

UP AGAINST THE WALL
Map p72   Hip-Hop Clothing
☎ 202-337-9316; 3219 M St NW; 🚍 Georgetown shuttle, DC Circulator
This music-blaring boutique is one of DC's top funky fashion spots for the hip-hop set. It sells baggy jeans, sports jerseys and all the other bling you need to dress like a rapper.

LOST BOYS Map p72   Men's Clothing
☎ 202-333-0093; 1033 31st St NW; 🚍 Georgetown shuttle, DC Circulator
A recent addition to DC's fashion scene, Lost Boys sells stylish but staid men's clothing for that well-tailored, slightly preppy Georgetown look. Super soft James Perse polos, Ernest & Sewn jeans, candy-striped Steve Alan button-downs and skinny ties by Band of Outsiders are a few recent hits.

OLD PRINT GALLERY Map p72   Prints
☎ 202-965-1818; 1220 31st St NW; ⏱ 10am-5:30pm Mon-Sat; 🚍 Georgetown shuttle, DC Circulator
This small store sells a fine array of vintage maps and prints, from the botanical to the architectural, with American portraits, gardens, locomotives, birds and New England scenes all on view. Prints are arranged by category and you can pay extra to have them framed. It's a great place to browse and hold a bit of history in your hands.

CADY'S ALLEY Map p72   Shopping Lane
www.cadysalley.com; 3318 M St NW; 🚍 Georgetown shuttle, DC Circulator
Not a store per se, Cady's Alley is exactly that, a small street lined with ubercool (and often expensive) interior-design boutiques selling everything from concept furniture to faucets of the future.

SHOPS AT GEORGETOWN PARK
Map p72   Shopping Mall
☎ 202-342-8190; 3222 M St NW; ⏱ 9am-9pm Mon-Sat, noon-6pm Sun; 🚍 Georgetown shuttle, DC Circulator
Set in a 19th-century cast-iron building that once sheltered horse-drawn omnibuses,

this elegant mall (with skylights and hanging plants) contains more than 100 shops. On the bottom level, you'll find a meager food court, trickling fountains and a few shops, while the other levels contain well known stores like H&M, Anthropologie, Intermix and Victoria's Secret.

LUSH Map p72   Soap
☎ 202-333-6950; 3066 M St NW; 🚍 Georgetown shuttle, DC Circulator
A cleaner world awaits inside sweet-smelling Lush. A purveyor of handmade, all-natural soaps, Lush brings high art to the common bath experience. Top selections include honey- and toffee-scented lump soap, rosebud-filled bath bombs (which fizz in the tub) and bergamot-and-lemon bubble bars (for the bubble-bath experience).

CHING CHING CHA HOUSE OF TEA
Map p72   Tea
☎ 202-333-8288; 1063 Wisconsin Ave NW; ⏱ 11am-9pm Tue-Sat, to 7pm Sun; 🚍 Georgetown shuttle, DC Circulator
This atmospheric wood-paneled teahouse feels a world away from the shopping mayhem on M St. Stop in for a light meal or a refreshing pot of rare tea; the shop stocks an amazing variety of exquisite teas, along with books, ceramic tea sets and teapots.

TUGOOH TOYS Map p72   Toys
☎ 202-338-9476; 1319 Wisconsin Ave NW; 🚍 Georgetown shuttle, DC Circulator
This splendid store is a great place to browse, even if you're not packing a rug rat on your hip. You'll find eco-friendly toys and games, including racecars made of bamboo and lots of cuddly animals made with high-quality organic cotton. Lots of items made of wood and other natural substances give an old-fashioned charm to the place.

AS SEEN ON TV Map p72   TV Merchandise
☎ 202-333-4595; bottom level, Shops at Georgetown Park, 3222 M St NW; 🚍 Georgetown shuttle, DC Circulator
The objects for sale here don't exactly represent the zenith of American culture, but they make for a good laugh nonetheless; and it's true, many items are sold on TV (or at least they were before the 1980s came screeching to a halt). You'll find Tae-Bo videos (not DVDs), supercharged potato peelers, ab-

dominal rockers, battery-operated scissors, snuggies (that most beloved of wearable blankets), electric hair clipper-brush combos and all manner of products endorsed by George Foreman. ASOT also sells poorly dubbed kung-fu movies to complete the walk down memory lane.

RELISH Map p72 — Women's Clothing
☎ 202-333-5343; 3312 Cady's Alley NW; ☙ 10am-6pm Mon-Sat; ▣ Georgetown shuttle, DC Circulator

Set on peaceful Cady's Alley (opposite), Relish sells high-end fashion for the girls. The two-level store boasts top-name labels and indie designers alike, including pieces by Marni, Jilsander and Nicole Fahri. Shoes, bags and accessories all make nice eye candy.

SECONDHAND ROSE
Map p72 — Women's Clothing
☎ 202-337-3378; 1516 Wisconsin Ave NW; ☙ 11:30am-6pm Mon-Sat, 1-6pm Sun; ▣ Georgetown shuttle, DC Circulator

This small, cramped secondhand shop sells consignment clothing, usually well-known labels and nothing more than two years old. This isn't a place for bargain hunters – no $10 dresses here – but Secondhand Rose has a speedy turnover and all items are in good condition.

CAPITOL HILL & SOUTHEAST DC

The big draw in the neighborhood is the Eastern Market, a splendid place to pick up fresh fruits, vegetables and other edible items. The time to go is on the weekends, when a lively craft market and adjoining flea market surround the area. The grand Union Station houses a few craft sellers as well as a shopping mall. The Hill is also home to a decent vintage-clothing shop, a campy home furnishings store and plenty of places selling Obama T-shirts and other political mementos.

BACKSTAGE Map pp78-9 — Costumes
☎ 202-544-5744; 545 8th St SE; ☙ 11am-7pm Mon-Sat; Ⓜ Eastern Market

This costume store caters to both the drag crowd and government types in search of unusual attire for masquerade parties. It rents outfits, and you can buy funky face paints, wigs and masks – including those creepy presidential masks (covering every president from Nixon to Obama).

WOVEN HISTORY
Map pp78-9 — Crafts & Textiles
☎ 202-543-1705; 315 7th St SE; ☙ 10am-6pm; Ⓜ Eastern Market

It's like a Silk Road caravan got lost and pitched up near the Eastern Market. This lovely emporium is stuffed with crafts, carpets and tapestries from across Central Asia, Tibet and Mongolia, and unlike a lot of stores of this genre, feels more like an authentic tented bazaar than a hippie hangout.

HOMEBODY Map pp78-9 — Home Furnishings
☎ 202-544-8445; 715 8th St SE; ☙ 11am-7pm Tue-Sat, noon-6pm Sun; Ⓜ Eastern Market

A good stop on your way to or from Eastern Market is the fun and colorful Homebody. Here you'll encounter a range of eye-catching gift ideas, including painted candelabras, decorative wall clocks, painted drinking glasses, graphic dinner plates and windup robot insects.

UNION STATION Map pp78-9 — Mall
☎ 202-289-1908; www.unionstationdc.com; 50 Massachusetts Ave NE; ☙ 10am-9pm Mon-Sat, noon-6pm Sun; Ⓜ Union Station

Not only an architectural landmark and a train depot, Union Station is also a good-sized mall, complete with multiscreen cinema, food court, restaurants and dozens of shops. The options are fairly run-of-the-mill, though the East Hall has unique vendors, including Lost City Art (with its eclectic global collection of clothing and accessories) and Appalachian Spring, with its arts and crafts. For more on Union Station, see p81.

EASTERN MARKET Map pp78-9 — Market
☎ 202-698-5253; www.easternmarketdc.com; 225 7th St SE; ☙ 7am-7pm Tue-Fri, 7am-6pm Sat, 9am-5pm Sun; Ⓜ Eastern Market

Eastern Market's South Hall is the closest DC gets to foodie heaven: in its friendly confines sit a bakery, dairy, fish counter, poultry counter, butcher, flower stalls, and a beautiful selection of fruits and vegetables (including organic items). You can put together a real Southern feast here – the Southern Maryland Seafood Company serves up the blue crabs and shrimp, and there's also a stand selling cooked food.

On weekends, both the artists and the farmers markets spill out onto the sidewalks. Besides fresh produce, you can pick up scarves, prints, handmade soaps and candles, colorful pottery, painted ceramics, art prints and unusual jewelry. Across the street at the weekend flea market (www.eastern market.net; ☿ 9am-5pm Sat & Sun), you'll find yet more crafty items, plus a handful of antique vendors. See also the entries in Neighborhoods (p81) and Eating (p152).

REMIX Map pp78-9   Secondhand Clothing
☎ 202-547-0211; 645 Pennsylvania Ave SE; Ⓜ Eastern Market

One of the few vintage shops in the area, the Remix has a good selection of men's and women's attire from decades past. You'll find soft leather gloves, fuzzy pink boas, slender strapless dresses, mirrored sunglasses, and satin smoking jackets and western shirts for the gents. There's a private room with couture pieces – Oscar de la Renta and Pucci as well as delicate dresses and gowns dating back to the 1910s.

DOWNTOWN & PENN QUARTER

Downtown and the Penn Quarter has a number of intriguing shops and specialty stores, though the concentration is thinner here than elsewhere. Revitalized 7th St is the liveliest strip in the neighborhood with a handful of galleries and trendy shops sprinkled among the restaurants and bars.

TOUCHSTONE GALLERY Map p88   Art
☎ 202-347-2787; www.touchstonegallery.com; 406 7th St NW; ☿ 11am-5pm Wed-Fri, noon-5pm Sat & Sun; Ⓜ Archives-Navy Memorial

One location encompasses several galleries, including the spacious, artist-owned Touchstone Gallery, which exhibits contemporary works created by some of its 30 to 35 member artists. Works cover multiple media, including sculpture, painting and the occasional esoteric installation.

CELADON Map p88   Beauty Products
202-347-3333; 1180 F St NW; ☿ 9am-7pm Mon-Fri, 8am-4pm Sat; Ⓜ Metro Center

Washingtonians come to this rather luxurious spa for a day's pampering – from perfect pedicures to Swedish massages – but check out the store in front for an impressive array of beauty products by such upscale designers as Peter Thomas Roth and Jack Black.

PUA NATURALLY Map p88   Clothing
☎ 202-347-4543; 701 Pennsylvania Ave NW; Ⓜ Archives-Navy Memorial

Pua Naturally provides a refreshing retreat from museum-hopping. Women head here to splurge on high-end ethnic clothing, like long flowing skirts and hand-woven jackets from southern Asia.

ARTIFACTORY Map p88   Gifts & Home Furnishings
☎ 202-393-2727; 641 Indiana Ave NW; Ⓜ Archives-Navy Memorial

Some of the pieces at this African and Asian gallery-store are worthy of museum displays – and priced to match. Others are less precious and reasonably marked. Inside one of the city's oldest buildings, Artifactory procures sculptures, masks and clothing from both continents.

APARTMENT ZERO Map p88   Home Furnishings
☎ 202-628-4067; www.apartmentzero.com; 407 7th St NW; ☿ 11am-6pm Wed-Sat, noon-5pm Sun; Ⓜ Archives-Navy Memorial

Apartment Zero is not 'just' a design and homewares store. Framed by some of America's best art museums, it's more like a small special exhibition itself, displaying the cutting edge of American form and functionality – except the pieces here are for sale.

COUP DE FOUDRE Map p88   Lingerie
☎ 202-393-0878; www.coupdefoudrelingerie.com; 1008 E St NW; ☿ 11am-6pm Mon-Sat; Ⓜ Metro Center

Local men dream of the day their girlfriends take them here and say, 'What should I get, honey?' Women also love Coup; the lingerie makes Victoria's Secret look gauche, and the mom-and-daughter owners have a passion for prettying up your bottom drawer.

OLD POST OFFICE PAVILION
Map p88   Mall
☎ 202-289-4224; cnr 12th St & Pennsylvania Ave NW; Ⓜ Federal Triangle

It's not exactly a shopping center, but it does have a tourist-crowded food court, as well as souvenir shops, newsstands and stores. It's worth a visit just for a look around the gorgeous central atrium. For more details, see p91.

SHOPS AT NATIONAL PLACE
Map p88   Mall

☎ 202-662-1250; 529 W 14th St NW; ⏲ 10am-7pm Mon-Sat, noon-5pm Sun; Ⓜ Metro Center

This little mall has a handful of stores and a food court. Aside from the designer discount emporium, Filene's Basement (p129), it's not worth a special trip.

INTERNATIONAL SPY MUSEUM
Map p88   Museum Shop

☎ 202-393-7798; www.spymuseumstore.org; 800 F St NW; ⏲ 10am-6pm; Ⓜ Gallery Pl-Chinatown

Let's face it, every so often everyone needs a pair of reverse-mirrored sunglasses, whether you are being followed or you just want to check out the hottie behind you in the elevator. Now you know where to get them, and piles of other nifty spy gadgets you may need some day. Other Bond-gear that might come in handy includes concealed video and listening devices, disguise kits, micro cameras and recorder pens.

NATIONAL BUILDING MUSEUM
Map p88   Museum Shop

☎ 202-272-2448; www.nbm.org; 401 F St NW; ⏲ 10am-5pm Mon-Sat, 11am-5pm Sun; Ⓜ Judiciary Sq

This museum shop is an amateur architect's dream, with small pieces of furniture, rich coffee-table books, paper models of famed buildings, and a collection of books on American and international architecture.

NATIONAL MUSEUM OF WOMEN IN THE ARTS
Map p88   Museum Shop

☎ 202-222-7270; www.nmwa.org; 1250 New York Ave NW; ⏲ 10am-5pm Mon-Sat, noon-5pm Sun; Ⓜ Metro Center

This unique institution dedicated to women artists has an equally unique shop. A small room left of the museum entrance, it holds books, prints, posters, jewelry and handicrafts – all created by women.

POLITICAL AMERICANA
Map p88   Souvenirs

☎ 800-333-4555; 1331 Pennsylvania Ave NW; Ⓜ Federal Triangle

You'll have to dig a bit, but hidden amid the bland heaps of token Americana trinkets are one-of-a-kind political souvenirs –

signed documents by famous statesmen, single-print historical photos and DVDs of important moments in American history.

TEAISM
Map p88   Teas

☎ 202-638-6010; 400 8th St NW; ⏲ 10am-6pm Mon-Fri, 11am-6pm Sat, noon-6pm Sun; Ⓜ Archives-Navy Memorial

Next to the inviting cafe of the same name (p156), Teaism sells dozens of loose-leaf teas, from smoky lapsang souchong to organic jasmine and rich green teas – all concealed in artful boxes behind the counter. You can also buy teapots, mugs, strainers and ornate display boxes (covered with handmade paper).

DUPONT CIRCLE & KALORAMA

The shopping action in Dupont Circle is along Connecticut Ave north and south of the roundabout, where you'll find books, wine, stylish clothing for men and women, CDs, gay literature and even guitars. There are good restaurants and bars in the area – fine destinations when you tire of emptying the wallet.

CLAUDE TAYLOR PHOTOGRAPHY
Map p96   Art Gallery

☎ 202-518-4000; www.travelphotography.net; 1627 Connecticut Ave NW; Ⓜ Dupont Circle

Claude Taylor's glossy travel photographs feature people and landscapes from around the world. The photographer has a keen eye for color and composition, and the prints (which come in all shapes and sizes) run from $35 to $100, for small to large format. You can also purchase them framed.

KRAMERBOOKS
Map p96   Books

☎ 202-387-1400; 1517 Connecticut Ave NW; ⏲ 8:30am-1:30am Sun-Thu, 24hr Fri & Sat; Ⓜ Dupont Circle

With the Afterwords Café (p159) and bar behind the shop, this round-the-clock bookstore is as much a spot for schmoozing as for shopping. You can grab a meal, have a pint and flirt with comely strangers (the store is a fabled pick-up spot for straights and gays). This flagship independent – which leapt into First Amendment history when it firmly refused to release Lewinsky's book-buying list to Starr's snoops – features fine current literature, travel and politics sections.

LAMBDA RISING Map p96 Books
☎ 202-462-6969; 1625 Connecticut Ave NW;
🕐 10am-10pm Sun-Thu, 10am-midnight Fri & Sat;
Ⓜ Dupont Circle
This landmark in gay and lesbian DC sells CDs and videos, as well as books covering a range of provocative topics. Check out the flyers and free giveaways near the door to find out what's happening in gay DC.

SECOND STORY BOOKS
Map p96 Books & Music
☎ 202-659-8884; 2000 P St NW; 🕐 10am-10pm;
Ⓜ Dupont Circle
Packed with dusty secondhand tomes, this atmospheric Dupont Circle bookshop also sells secondhand CDs (mostly jazz and classical). The prices are decent, and the choices are broad (particularly in the realm of history and Americana).

PROPER TOPPER Map p96 Hats & Accessories
☎ 202-842-3055; 1350 Connecticut Ave NW;
🕐 10am-8pm Mon-Fri, 10am-7pm Sat, noon-6pm Sun; Ⓜ Dupont Circle
Fedoras, panama hats, short- and wide-brimmed straw hats – they're all for sale at the Proper Topper, along with children's books, wallets, jewelry, scarves and a few snazzy black dresses.

TABLETOP Map p96 Home Furnishings
☎ 202-387-7117; 1608 20th St NW; 🕐 noon-8pm Mon-Sat, to 6pm Sun; Ⓜ Dupont Circle
Also known as the best little design store in Dupont, Tabletop is evidence that DC is a lot more chic than some give it credit for. With the kooky candles, postmodern purses and postindustrial housewares taken together, your living space will be pampered.

GINZA Map p96 Homewares
☎ 202-331-7991; 1721 Connecticut Ave NW;
Ⓜ Dupont Circle
Japan is the theme at Ginza. There is a nice selection of beautiful (looking and sounding) indoor fountains, scented candles and other interesting elements of Asian decor.

BEADAZZLED Map p96 Jewelry
☎ 202-265-2323; 1507 Connecticut Ave NW;
Ⓜ Dupont Circle
Crafty types and jewelry lovers should not miss this specialty shop, which carries all things small and stringable. The selection from around the world ranges from 5¢ clay doohickeys to expensive pearls. Helpful staff will tell you how to put them together, and classes are offered on weekends.

MELODY RECORD SHOP Map p96 Music
☎ 202-232-4002; 1623 Connecticut Ave NW;
🕐 10am-10pm Sun-Thu, 10am-11pm Fri & Sat;
Ⓜ Dupont Circle
This well-stocked shop was recently voted DC's best music store by readers of the *Washington City Paper*. It's not surprising given the huge inventory of CDs and DVDs – over 300,000 at last count. World music, jazz, blues, indie and classic rock are well represented. The digitized collection allows browsers to listen to anything in the store.

GUITAR SHOP Map p96 Musical Instruments
☎ 202-331-7333; 1216 Connecticut Ave NW;
🕐 noon-7pm Mon-Fri, 11am-6pm Sat; Ⓜ Dupont Circle
Although it's the size of a phone booth, this is DC's most impressive instrument retailer and repairer. Around since 1922, this store has serviced Springsteen and Dylan. The dedicated staff are quite helpful in assisting musicians to find what they really need. The 2000-plus inventory ranges from top-of-the-line Martins to inexpensive beginner guitars, plus banjos, mandolins, harmonicas and more.

PHILLIPS COLLECTION Map p96 Museum Shop
☎ 202-387-2151; 1600 21st St NW; 🕐 10am-5pm Tue-Sat, noon-7pm Sun; Ⓜ Dupont Circle
The museum shop has a good collection of posters, pop and scholarly art books, and knickknacks imprinted with famous paintings, such as umbrellas sporting Renoir's *Luncheon of the Boating Party* and Monet water-lily mugs.

SECONDI Map p96 Secondhand Clothing
☎ 202-667-1122; 1702 Connecticut Ave NW;
Ⓜ Dupont Circle
Up a narrow row of stairs, Secondi is filled with beautiful top labels like Marc Jacobs jackets and slightly loved Manolo Blahniks. It's not the cheapest shop in the city, but it has a good collection of big-name designers.

BEST CELLARS Map p96   Wine
☎ 202-387-3146; 1643 Connecticut Ave NW;
🕑 10am-9pm Mon-Thu, 10am-10pm Fri & Sat;
Ⓜ Dupont Circle
Arranged by taste categories (juicy, luscious, smooth) rather than by grape or region, Best Cellars reinvents the traditional wine-shopping experience. The prices are affordable (from $9 to $15) and wine and liqueur tastings add to the appeal. In addition to wine, Best Cellars carries spirits – including the artisanal products of Leopold Brothers (try the Absinthe Verte).

BETSY FISHER Map p96   Women's Clothing
☎ 202-785-1975; 1224 Connecticut Ave NW;
Ⓜ Dupont Circle
The sales team at this classy women's boutique makes you feel like a queen while trying on fantastic pieces by designers like Diane von Furstenberg and Nicole Miller. The styles run the gamut from funky and fashion forward to elegant but a touch on the conservative side.

GREEN & BLUE Map p96   Women's Clothing
☎ 223-6644; 1350 Connecticut Ave NW; 🕑 10am-8pm Mon-Fri, 11am-7pm Sat, noon-6pm Sun;
Ⓜ Dupont Circle
The boutique may be named for soothing colors, but its cool tones aren't just swatches of the palette; there are plenty of smart blouses, clutches and assorted accessories here that run the rainbow in terms of presentation, and all suggest style.

ADAMS-MORGAN
Although better known for its nightlife than its shops, Adams-Morgan has some funky boutiques, antique shops and stores selling ethnic knickknacks.

BRASS KNOB Map p103   Antiques & Doorknobs
☎ 202-332-3370; 2311 18th St NW; 🕑 10:30am-6pm Mon-Sat, noon-5pm Sun; Ⓜ Woodley Park Zoo/Adams Morgan
This unique two-floor shop sells 'rescues' from old buildings: fixtures, lamps, tiles, mantelpieces and mirrors. The store's *raison d'être* though is the doorknob – brass, wooden, glass, elaborate, polished and antique. The Brass Knob is an absolute fantasyland for anybody renovating (or even just living in) an old house or apartment. Staff can help you find whatever you need,

and the classical music overhead adds to the charm.

OYA MINI BAZAAR Map p103   Art
☎ 202-667-9853; 2420 18th St NW; 🕑 noon-11pm; Ⓜ Woodley Park Zoo/Adams Morgan
One of several West African handicraft shops in the neighborhood, Oya Mini Bazaar stocks an impressive selection of wooden masks, tapestries, small sculptures, batik prints, woven baskets and other curios. The prices are quite reasonable.

TORO MATA Map p103   Art
☎ 202-232-3890; 2410 18th St NW; Ⓜ Woodley Park Zoo/Adams Morgan
If your Andean trip fell through this year, Toro Mata provides a good backup plan. Inside this handsomely laid-out store, you'll find a well-curated selection of Peruvian objects, including fluffy Alpaca rugs and cuddly stuffed animals, hand-carved chess sets and folk-art tableau, colorful tapestries, furniture and woven hats and sweaters. The friendly owners have a wealth of knowledge on Peru.

IDLE TIME BOOKS Map p103   Books
☎ 202-232-4774; 2467 18th St NW; 🕑 11am-10pm; Ⓜ Woodley Park Zoo/Adams Morgan
Three creaky wooden floors are stuffed with secondhand literature and nonfiction, including one of the best secondhand political and history collections in the city. Its sci-fi, sports and humor sections are top-notch, and there's a good newsstand in its front window.

YAWA BOOKS & GIFTS Map p103   Books
☎ 202-483-6805; 2206 18th St NW; 🕑 11am-7pm Mon-Fri, 11am-9pm Sat; Ⓜ Woodley Park Zoo/Adams Morgan
The focus here is on the books – lots of 'em – addressing African American political, social and cultural issues. Sports, spirituality, sex…nothing is overlooked. There is also a good selection of fiction by African American writers.

CARAMEL Map pp106-7   Clothing
☎ 202-265-1930; 1603 U St NW; Ⓜ U Street-Cardozo
This dapper little boutique on U St sells a well-edited selection of men's and women's clothing and accessories that aim for

INSIDE SCOOP ON THE DC FASHION SCENE

How would you characterize the DC fashion scene? The DC fashion scene is what others may describe as schizophrenic at best. What I mean is that it has different personalities. The same woman who works on the Hill will change to her *Sex and the City* outfit for happy hour, or her casual chic at the gym with her trainer and then her traditional corporate casual for the PTA meeting. The average Washingtonian woman's closet is a myriad of fashion.

In your own collection, where do you get inspiration? I am a huge fan of award shows and red-carpet events. I mostly look to old Hollywood glamour for inspiration. I think if a garment is well made and stylish, it will work in any market.

How did DC Fashion Week come about? I had produced fashion shows for other designers for a number of years and realized there was a void when it came to attracting buyers and media. When I discovered that DC did not have an official trade show for fashion, I had DC Fashion Week registered as a trademark and produced the first event – which was a huge hit. We soon discovered that there was a huge international interest in the fashion scene here. We are definitely establishing DC as a major fashion capital.

Do you see any relationship between the fashion on the streets and the political party in power? Has fashion changed since Obama came to the White House? There is a huge interest in the fashion scene here now, even more so since the arrival of the Obamas. I don't see a relationship between the two. The world is finding out that women who wear evening gowns also wear shorts. I don't think the world knows that Washingtonians dress for the occasion and not for the press. It was totally acceptable for Michelle to wear shorts on vacation in 100°F weather.

Speaking of the First Lady, how has Michelle Obama impacted the fashion scene? Historically, politicians are not known for their fashion sense. Their ensembles are the equivalent of a work uniform. However when you have a new star that can attract the attention of the masses, it has an effect. Michelle brought more attention to some styles that true fashion insiders were already aware of. She is not necessarily setting trends, but she is showing that she has great style.

What do you see as the future of fashion in DC? I think DC will remain a tale of two cities in regard to fashion. You will always have your traditional corporate Capitol Hill types as well as your young hip fashionistas. I sincerely hope that one day you will not see men in Timberland boots and shorts in the summer. I can hope, can't I?

An interview with Ean Williams, fashion designer and founder of DC Fashion Week (p13).

a stylish effortlessness. Look for comely I-Shandi dresses, eye-catching Leather Island belts and incredibly soft denim apparel. The artwork on the walls is also for sale – all created by local artists.

KOBOS Map p103 Clothing
☎ 202-332-9580; 2444 18th St NW; ⏲ Mon-Sat; Ⓜ Woodley Park Zoo/Adams Morgan

Not at all your average clothing shop, Kobos is an African clothier. The Afro boutique carries a good selection of kente cloth, as well as cool tapestries and African music.

MEEPS VINTAGE FASHIONETTE
Map p103 Clothing
☎ 202-265-6546; 2104 18th St NW; ⏲ noon-7pm Mon-Sat, to 5pm Sun; Ⓜ Woodley Park Zoo/Adams Morgan

This vintage clothier is a fun place to browse with its racks of mod dresses, cowboy shirts, suede jackets, beaded purses, leather boots, Jackie O sunglasses and denim jumpsuits. Meeps also carries a small

selection of local designers – mostly clever and eye-catching T-shirts.

SKYNEAR & CO Map p103 Home Furnishings
☎ 202-797-7160; 2122 Wyoming Ave NW; Ⓜ Woodley Park Zoo/Adams Morgan

Explore four levels of rooms crowded with 'stressed' armoires, funky sofas and kitschy coffee tables. The furnishings are unique and prices are reasonable.

GREATER GOODS
Map pp106-7 Home Products & Toys
☎ 202-449-6070; 1626 U St NW; ⏲ 3-8pm Mon, 11am-8pm Tue-Sat, to 6pm Sun; Ⓜ U Street-Cardozo

Inside this earth-friendly shop you'll find green cleaning products, Sigg water bottles, organic toys, bamboo cookware, solar products (including a Japanese-style lamp and a rather imaginative solar cooking pot) and much more. There are books on living sustainably, and free seminars on solar energy, living off the grid and the like.

FOR THE GREATER GOOD
Map p103   Men's Clothing
☎ 202-387-0177; 1781 Florida Ave NW; Ⓜ Woodley Park Zoo/Adams Morgan

Portraits of Mao, Malcolm X, Che Guevara and other cult figures adorn the walls of this exquisite little shop. The clothes here – fine denim, high-end sweaters, button-downs and handsome jackets – are trim and nicely cut, creating a stylish well-tailored look. If the fashion here seems a little too staid, head two doors down to its sister shop, Commonwealth (☎ 202-265-1830; 1781 Florida Ave). With a purely hip-hop aesthetic, this shop sells one-of-a-kind sneakers and graphic T-shirts.

SMASH!
Map p103   Music & Clothing
☎ 202-387-6274; 2314 18th St NW; ☽ noon-9pm Mon-Thu, to 10pm Fri & Sat, to 7pm Sun; Ⓜ Woodley Park Zoo/Adams Morgan

There's a slightly punk-rock vibe to this small upstairs shop. In addition to a solid selection of vinyl (covering mostly classic and indie rock and soul), Smash! sells used and new CDs and youthful streetwear (punky T-shirts, Doc Martens and secondhand clothing).

FLEET FEET
Map p103   Shoes
☎ 202-387-3888; 1841 Columbia Rd NW; Ⓜ Woodley Park Zoo/Adams Morgan

Shoes for every sporting activity are on sale here; service is personalized and the staff try to match customers' feet with their activity of choice.

SHAKE YOUR BOOTY
Map p103   Women's Shoes
☎ 202-518-8205; 2324 18th St NW; Ⓜ Woodley Park Zoo/Adams Morgan

'Booty' here means boots…and pumps and sandals and any accessories you might need to hit the town (and then shake your other booty). The footwear here is trendy and fun.

COLUMBIA HEIGHTS & NORTHEAST

Once a shopping wasteland, this still-edgy 'hood is growing hipper by the day. On both 14th St and U St, where streetwalkers once roamed, you'll find upscale boutiques, quirky design and furniture shops, and a growing number of art galleries and secondhand clothing stores.

GOOD WOOD
Map pp106-7   Antiques
☎ 202-986-3640; 1428 U St NW; ☽ 11am-7pm Wed, Fri & Sat, 5-9pm Thu, 11am-5pm Sun; Ⓜ U Street-Cardozo

Even if you're not in the market for a mid-century armoire, Good Wood is well worth a visit. This warm, atmospheric store has a fine selection of antiques, including hand-crafted chairs and tables, elegant lamps and wall hangings, plus other decorative items.

MISS PIXIE'S
Map pp106-7   Antiques
☎ 202-232-8171; 1626 14th St NW; ☽ noon-7pm Wed-Sun; Ⓜ U Street-Cardozo

One of the best places to browse in the neighborhood, Miss Pixie's is piled high with relics from the past, from stuffed leather armchairs to 1960s lawn ornaments. You'll find dishes, ashtrays, rocking chairs, black-and-white photos and plenty of other curiosities. There's a cafe upstairs.

GO MAMA GO!
Map pp106-7   Art
☎ 202-299-0850; www.gomamago.com; 1809 14th St NW; Ⓜ U Street-Cardozo

These 'moms with an attitude' offer pottery and art handcrafted by Asian and African artisans. The unique dinnerware is green, blue, cobalt – all clear, strong colors with very simple shapes.

DEKKA
Map pp106-7   Art & Clothing
☎ 202-986-1370; www.dekkafam.com; 1338 U St NW; ☽ 1:30-7:30pm Tue-Fri, 10am-7pm Sat & Sun; Ⓜ U Street-Cardozo

Overlooking a lively stretch of U St, Dekka is a youthful and creative space where you pick up locally made fashion, jewelry and artwork. Stylish T-shirts, whimsical dresses and framed black-and-white photographs are just a small part of the eclectic merchandise, which includes the work of over 30 local artists and designers. Stop in on the first Saturday of the month (from 6:30pm to 10:30pm) for cocktails, video, music and designer specials.

REDEEM
Map pp106-7   Clothing
☎ 202-332-7447; 1734 14th St NW Ⓜ U Street-Cardozo

'It's never too late to change', is the motto of this enticing little clothier on 14th St. Redeem carries indie labels and a small selection of local designers, and targets urban and hip but cashed-up customers. Look for Ernest & Sewn denim, Colcci ankle boots, Corpus sweaters and other unique labels.

POP Map pp106-7 Clothing & Accessories
☎ 202-332-3312; 1803 14th St NW; ☺ 11am-7pm Mon-Sat, noon-6pm Sun; Ⓜ U Street-Cardozo
This boutique for women and men features designers like Ben Sherman and Tipton Charles. Prices can be high, so check the sale rack.

PULP Map pp106-7 Gifts
☎ 202-462-7857; 1803 14th St NW; Ⓜ U Street-Cardozo
This quirky, kitschy gift shop has all kinds of things you were not looking for – funky frames, funny cards, silly toys, smelly candles, retro art and tons of political gag gifts. It's a good place to come looking for a gift (as long as you don't know what you are looking for).

HUNTED HOUSE
Map pp106-7 Home Furnishings
☎ 202-549-7493; www.huntedhousedc.com; 1830 14th St NW; ☺ 1-7pm Thu, noon-6pm Fri, from 11am Sat & Sun; Ⓜ U Street-Cardozo
Every piece of vintage furniture stuffing this walk-up, laid out to resemble a functioning (quite attractive) apartment, is a gem of the deco or modernism design movement. We could spend hours staring at the Jetsons-esque TV in the sitting room, which is sadly never for sale. Open Tuesday by appointment.

RCKNDY Map pp106-7 Home Furnishings
☎ 202-332-5639; 1515 U St NW; ☺ 11am-8pm Mon & Wed-Sat, noon-6pm Sun; Ⓜ U Street-Cardozo
Colorful, kitschy and pleasing to the eye, Rckndy makes a great stop on the U St shopping circuit. Here you'll find candy-colored ceramics (sushi sets, mugs, planters), curious silkscreen wall hangings, modular furniture and those fascinating conversation pieces – the lifelike Harry Allen piggy banks.

HOME RULE Map pp106-7 Homewares
☎ 202-797-5544; 1807 14th St NW; Ⓜ U Street-Cardozo
Tired of Pottery Barn homogeneity around your house? Check out Home Rule's amus-

ingly original stock: frog-shaped toothbrush holders, brightly colored martini glasses, animal-shaped salt-and-pepper sets, and rugs and linens, too. The mosaic decorating the front counter symbolizes the U St district's revitalization – it's made with smashed glass from the 1968 riots.

U STREET FLEA MARKET
Map pp106-7 Market
cnr U & 9th St NW; ☺ noon-8pm Sat & Sun Ⓜ U Street-Cardozo
You won't (likely) find a cute vintage frock here – this is a real flea market, patronized by folks who consider secondhand shopping a necessity rather than just a diversion. That said, there are usually awesome albums for sale, a few local crafts and a sense of U St's vibe circa 1980s BG (Before Gentrification).

NANA Map pp106-7 Women's Clothing
☎ 202-667-6955; 1528 U St NW; ☺ noon-7pm Mon-Fri, to 6pm Sat, to 5pm Sun; Ⓜ U Street-Cardozo
Nana is a sweet little boutique selling a mix of funky and classic fashions. Look for Holly Aiken bags, Dagg & Stacey coats and blouses, dresses and skirts by Classic Girl, Uppsee Daisies and Elaine Perlov. Nana throws in a few well placed vintage pieces to complete the look.

UPPER NORTHWEST DC

Shops are strung out across this corner of the city, although you'll find major clusters near Metro stations on both Wisconsin and Connecticut Aves. The area around the Cineplex Odeon Uptown movie theater is a good starting point. Further north, near the Maryland line, Friendship Heights is home to Mazza Gallerie (opposite), a trendy shopping mall with lots of designer labels.

POLITICS & PROSE BOOKSTORE
Off map p114 Books
☎ 202-364-1919; 5015 Connecticut Ave NW; ☺ 9am-10pm Mon-Thu, to 11pm Fri & Sat, 10am-8pm Sun; 🚌 L1, L2
Way up in Northwest DC is a key literary nexus and coffeehouse. This active independent has an excellent selection of literary fiction and nonfiction – it's fiercely supportive of local authors – plus it has

dedicated staff, high-profile readings and 15 active book clubs.

KRÖN CHOCOLATIER
Off map p114   Gourmet Food

☎ 202-966-4946; Mazza Gallerie, 5300 Wisconsin Ave NW; Ⓜ Friendship Heights

This shop is known for hand-dipped truffles and amusing novelties, like edible chocolate baskets, milk-chocolate telephones and cars.

WAKE UP LITTLE SUZIE Map p114   Gifts

☎ 202-244-0700; 3409 Connecticut Ave NW; Ⓜ Cleveland Park

This funny and original gift shop sells stuff like neon clocks, bright metal-and-ceramic jewelry, polka-dotted pottery, cards and T-shirts. If you have a need for an *Invasion of the Monster Women* lunch box or boxing-rabbi windup doll, Suzie's your woman.

NATIONAL ZOOLOGICAL PARK
Map p114   Museum Shop

☎ 202-673-4800; 3001 Connecticut Ave NW; Ⓜ Woodley Park Zoo/Adams Morgan

The National Zoological Park has several shops on its grounds that sell toys and products featuring all manner of charismatic fauna: ostriches, seals, tigers, wolves, elephants and the inevitable pandas. (Bring home a plastic hyena for less-beloved relatives.) It also has the Zoo Bookstore, in the Education Building on the Connecticut Ave NW side, which has a decent natural-history and field-guide section.

SULLIVAN'S TOY STORE Map p114   Toys

☎ 202-362-1343; 3412 Wisconsin Ave NW; 🚌 30, 32, 34, 36

This independent toy store specializes in European and educational toys that are a nice antidote to the video-game fare of many children's toy stores.

NORTHERN VIRGINIA

The most charming shopping here is in Alexandria, along cobbled King St in Old Town. Here you'll find craft stores and antique shops, art galleries, used booksellers and more.

PRINCIPLE GALLERY Map p125   Art

☎ 703-739-9326; 208 King St; 🚌 Old Town shuttle from King Street Metro

One of a growing number of galleries along King St, this approachable place often assembles some of the best collections. Principle represents artists from across the globe, and even if you're not in the art market, it's worth a peek inside.

SHOPPING IN THE SUBURBS: THE OTHER MALL EXPERIENCE

For a complete break from the DC shopping experience, head to the 'burbs. Here you'll find big shopping malls that appeal to both fashionistas and bargain hunters alike.

Fashion Centre at Pentagon City (Map p122; ☎ 703-415-2400; 1100 S Hayes St, Arlington; ☽ 10am-9:30pm Mon-Sat, 11am-6pm Sun; Ⓜ Pentagon City) Houses 170 shops, including Macy's, Nordstrom, a cinema and a food court beneath skylights. This was where Monica Lewinsky got busted by Ken Starr's troopers back in '98.

Mazza Gallerie (off Map p114; ☎ 202-966-6114; 5300 Wisconsin Ave NW; ☽ 10am-8pm Mon-Fri, to 7pm Sat, noon-5pm Sun; Ⓜ Friendship Heights) This upscale mall is on the Red Line near the Maryland border. Anchored by Neiman-Marcus, Mazza has a variety of upscale boutiques, plus a Williams-Sonoma. Downstairs is a seven-screen movie theater.

Potomac Mills (off Map p122; 703-496-9300; 2700 Potomac Mills Circle, Woodbridge, VA; ☽ 10am-9pm Mon-Sat, 11am-6pm Sun) A fire-breathing monster of mid-Atlantic outlet malls, just a half-hour drive south of DC, it features about 250 discount shops, including Ikea, Saks, Marshall's and Spiegel. This place now draws more tourists (about 24 million per year) and tour buses than Williamsburg or Virginia's other historic sites, which might say something about Americans' priorities. Take Exit 158-B off I-95.

Tysons Corner Center (off Map p122; ☎ 703-847-7300; 1961 Chain Bridge Rd, McLean; ☽ 10am-9:30pm Mon-Sat, 11am-7pm Sun) Further north in Virginia and just west of the Beltway is this gigantic shopping complex that has, over the years, metastasized into its own strange, sidewalkless suburban Edge City. It has about 250 stores from big department stores like Bloomie's to Nordstrom, and smaller shops from Abercrombie & Fitch to Georgetown Tobacco. The adjacent complex carries haute-couture: Louis Vuitton, Gucci, Fendi, Chanel and Hermés. You'll need to drive here.

TORPEDO FACTORY ART CENTER

Map p125   Gallery Shop

☎ 703-838-4565; www.torpedofactory.org; 105 N Union St; ⊒ Old Town shuttle from King Street Metro

Built during WWI to manufacture torpedoes, this complex today manufactures art. At the center of a revamped waterfront with a marina, shops, parks, walkways, residences, offices and restaurants, it houses nearly 200 artists and craftspeople who sell their creations directly from their studios.

TEN THOUSAND VILLAGES

Map p125   Imported Goods

☎ 703-684-1435; 915 King St; ☺ 11am-7pm Mon-Sat, noon-6pm Sun; ⊒ Old Town shuttle from King Street Metro

A store with a conscience, Ten Thousand Villages imports handicrafts from all across the globe, and is one of the founding members of the International Fair Trade Association. You'll find high-quality pottery, home furnishings and textiles here, plus children's books, jewelry, coffee and chocolate.

EATING

top picks

- Minibar at Café Atlantico (p158)
- Hitching Post (p166)
- Four Sisters (p168)
- Ben's Chili Bowl (p163)
- Vidalia (p160)
- W Domku (p165)
- Fish Wharf (p155)
- Eatonville (p164)
- Meskerem (p162)
- Eastern Market (p152)

What's your recommendation? www.lonelyplanet.com/washington-dc

EATING

Washington has been blowing up as an eating destination lately. New restaurants seem to open on a monthly basis, and they're generating a lot of buzz among the city's increasingly food-conscious population and the international foodie scene as a whole. There are a few factors we get to thank for all this increased culinary exposure.

First: DC, once a city that was fairly stridently divided between rich and poor, has become more middle class since the 1990s. Accompanying waves of gentrification and a Manhattan-worthy influx of young professionals in the 1990s and 'noughties' (the first decade of the new century) all underlined this demographic transformation. Combined with the general growth of the American foodie movement in the same period, the impact on going-out culture has been, gastronomically speaking, fantastic. The demand for restaurants increased at around the same rate as taste discernment. Quantity and quality are two things that rarely seem to grow in tandem, but that's essentially been the case, food-wise, in the nation's capital for the past two decades.

The scrubbing of DC's Downtown district has helped in this regard as well. Conventioneers and politicos are simply more comfortable exploring what has become a safer city, and the restaurant industry has responded accordingly on the supply side. This has, after all, long been a city of power lunches and impress-the-ambassador banquets. The capital's occasionally self-important attitude in this regard – all the pomp, wheedling and snake oil that goes into wowing potential political allies and enemies – has occasionally been a boon to local chefs. They've been allowed free reign to show off and impress; as long as they made clients happy, they could indulge their creativity.

But let's get down to the basics of what really makes DC dining so fine. Basically, it's the blend of two seemingly disparate ingredients: globalization and localism. This is one of the most diverse, international cities of its size in America, heavily populated by immigrants, expats and diplomats from every inhabited continent in the world. People from far away crave the food of home, and as such there's a glut of good ethnic eating and ethnic influences around here. Salvadoran, Ethiopian, Vietnamese, French, Spanish, West African – they've all become Washingtonian.

This overseas influence has upped the cosmopolitan tastes of the town as a whole. Washingtonians tend to be an educated, worldly bunch, and they know what they're talking about when they say the salmon at Teaism isn't up to scratch to the stuff they had as a JET-program teacher in Fukuoka. If they're down on the *wat* (stew) in one Ethiopian place, that's only because they've had better at a little strip mall shack in Falls Church. On that note, many of the city's best *cheap* ethnic eats are now outside of the city, sprinkled through the suburbs.

We don't want to leave out the localism angle. The locally sourced food movement has been a huge boon to the Washington eating scene. Many visitors to the District don't have an understanding of its unique geography, the way it's situated between two of the best food production areas in America: the Chesapeake Bay and the Virginia Piedmont. From the former comes crabs, oysters and rockfish; the latter provides game, pork, wine and peanuts. Keep in mind DC also occupies the fault line between two of America's greatest culinary regions: the Northeast and the South. We got soul food and its high-class incarnations balancing out one end of our palate, street dogs known as half-smokes anchoring the other end of the eating geography. Throw in an increasing population of celebrity chefs, ambitious young cooks, immigrant talent and savvy on the part of the consumer when it comes to selecting between all of the above, and you get a capital that knows how to keep itself happily fed.

Opening Hours

Most restaurants are open for lunch and dinner daily, although there are exceptions. Restaurants that depend on weekday business-lunch trade (such as in the White House Area) may be open for dinner only on weekends, or not at all. Other restaurants – especially family-owned joints – may close on Sunday or Monday. DC also has its share of breakfast joints (most top-end hotel restaurants serve breakfast) and 24-hour diners.

Unless noted otherwise, in this book consider breakfast to be from 7am or 8am to 11am; lunch from 11am or 11:30am to 2:30pm or 3pm and dinner to be from 5:30pm to 10:30pm, later (until 11pm or midnight) on Friday and Saturday. Many DC restaurants are also open for Saturday and Sunday brunch, which generally lasts from around 10am or 11am till 2pm or 3pm.

How Much?

Travelers in Washington can expect to spend a fair amount of their budgets on eating out. For travelers on a budget, food courts and takeout, where large portions are inexpensive, are handy options, and self-catering isn't too difficult. Otherwise, a restaurant dinner with a drink usually starts at $30 to $35 and the price goes up as high as you are willing. Lunch is usually half to two-thirds the cost of dinner; the prices given in our reviews are off the dinner menu.

Booking Tables

While most restaurants do not require bookings, it is recommended on weekends, especially at upscale restaurants. Normally, a phone call that afternoon or the day before is sufficient, although some of the hottest, new restaurants require reservations several days or even weeks in advance.

Takeout & To Go

Having a picnic on the National Mall or the banks of the Potomac is among the most pleasant dining experiences in DC. Grabbing a 'takeout' meal is common in the States; many fancier restaurants offer this service, which can be a good way to save money and eat well – phone in your order, pick it up and you're good to go. You won't have to tip or pay for over-priced drinks (the local liquor store sells the same bottle of Italian red for a fraction of the restaurant price), which can cut your bill nearly in half. DC's farmers markets (p167) and gourmet stores offer a wonderful selection of fresh produce

PRICE GUIDE

$	under $18
$$	$18-32
$$$	more than $32

to pack in your picnic basket or chow in front of the TV.

If you really can't be bothered to get up, Takeout Taxi Washington (☎ in Virginia 703-578-3663, in DC 202-986-0111; www.takeouttaxi.com) delivers food from numerous DC restaurants straight to your room for a service fee of between $5 and $10 (you'll also be expected to tip the delivery person around 15% on top of this).

Tipping

Not tipping in restaurants is unacceptable. US servers make less than minimum wage and rely on tips to earn their living. Tipping 15% of the total bill is the accepted minimum. If service is good, 20% is a decent average tip, while it is appropriate to tip more if service is exceptional.

NATIONAL MALL

The Mall has always been a bit of a food desert. There's hot-dog and half-smoke vendors stationed around, while most museums have overpriced restaurants with mediocre menus. There are a few exceptions, which we have listed below. Don't forget to get astronaut ice cream from the Air & Space Museum (p58) – it's nasty, but novel.

PAVILION CAFÉ Map p54   Cafe $
☎ 289-3361; www.pavilioncafe.com; cnr Constitution Ave & 7th S SW; ◷ lunch & dinner; Ⓜ Archives-Navy Memorial
Set amid the rambling sylvan serenity of the Sculpture Garden (p61) of the National Gallery of Art, this pasta- and panini-style place makes for a green dream on spring days; from late May to October, free jazz concerts enrich the evening every Friday.

CASCADE CAFÉ Map p54   Cafe $
☎ 202-216-2480; East Bldg, National Gallery of Art, cnr 4th St & Constitution Ave NW; mains from $10; ◷ 10am-3pm Mon-Sat, 11am-4pm Sun; Ⓜ Archives-Navy Memorial
Oh what a lovely place for a bowl of tortellini or a croissant sandwich. Located at the juncture of the wings of the National Gallery of Art, the Cascade offers views of just that: a shimmering, IM Pei–designed artificial waterfall. It's one of the best coffee stops in any Washington museum. Food is of the soup and sandwich sort, and is available for picnic wrap if you'd like to eat outdoors.

UP IN HALF SMOKE

DC's claim to native culinary fame is the half-smoke, a bigger, coarser, spicier and better version of your hot dog. There's little agreement on where the name comes from – half beef/half pork? (But some are all beef!) Because the sausage is usually split down the middle? Because they can be grilled or steamed? Who knows? But there is general consensus as to what goes on a half-smoke. New Yorkers like their mustard and relish, Chicagoans dress their dogs with a freakin' garden, and in DC? Chili and chopped onions, baby.

Ben's Chili Bowl (p163), possibly the most famous restaurant in the city, sets the half-smoke standard, but to be honest – don't kill us, Ben's patrons – the best sausage in the area isn't in DC. It's (gasp) in Arlington. Weenie Beenie (p168), idiotic name aside, simply serves a very mean half-smoke. You can try the generally passable versions available in the hot-dog stands around town, but go to Ben's or Beanie's at least once for the real thing.

MITSITAM NATIVE FOODS CAFE

Map p54   Native American $$

☎ 202-633-1000; National Museum of the American Indian, cnr 4th St & Independence Ave SW; mains $8-18; 🕑 10am-5pm; Ⓜ Smithsonian
Without a doubt the best museum food on the Mall, the Mitsitam introduces visitors to the palette of five regional Native American cuisines, from the blue corn tortillas and slow-smoked barbeque of the southwest to wild rice and cranberry-stuffed turkey in the eastern woodlands. Menus rotate daily, and mixed among the tourists are a fair few regular local office workers seeking an indulgent lunch.

SOURCE Map p54   Fusion $$$

☎ 202-673-6100; Newseum, 555 Pennsylvania Ave NW; mains $25; 🕑 lunch & dinner Mon-Fri, dinner only Sat; Ⓜ Archives-Navy Memorial, Judiciary Square
Wolfgang Puck makes your visit to the Newseum a tasty, stylish one, with an icily modern two-story restaurant that feels like the canteen of a spaceship. The food is typical of Puck's fusion repertoire, which favors Asian flavors – tuna tartar tipped with shaved bonito and sesame-miso cones. The most interesting palette experiments involve Puck-ish (heh) variations on local standards; pairing a Maryland crab cake with a tempura-fried soft crab could be insulting to native cuisine, but ends up creating an intriguing dichotomy of taste experiences.

WHITE HOUSE AREA & FOGGY BOTTOM

As you might guess, this is high-end eating territory, the pinnacle of the power lunch and show-off dinner school of sartorial activity. With all that said, you usually get what you pay for – there's too much competition around for local chefs to rest too lazily on their laurels.

BREADLINE Map p64   Bakery/Deli $

☎ 202-822-8900; http://thebreadlinedc.blogspot .com; 1751 Pennsylvania Ave NW; sandwiches from $6; 🕑 7:30am-3:30pm; Ⓜ Farragut West
'Food is ammunition – don't waste it!' commands a WWII-era poster on the wall of this polished bakery and sandwich shop. Come here for a good, cheap lunch, but don't be surprised if you end up waiting in lines stretching out the door; office workers love the line, and with reason. The fresh and filling sandwiches are gorgeous, as are the to-die-for sweet treats.

SICHUAN PAVILION Map p64   Chinese $

☎ 202-466-7790; sichuanpavilion.googlepages .com; 1814 K St NW; mains $9-16; 🕑 noon-9pm; Ⓜ Farragut North
Why do we think this unassuming spot may be the best Chinese in the city? Because so many Chinese come here, far from any ethnic enclaves out in the 'burbs, to dine on fiery, oily classics of the old school. Piquant Sichaun (or Szechaun) cuisine is often blanded-up for Western customers around the world, but these guys keep it real for all their clientele, Asian or otherwise. The *mapa tofu* is particularly stinky and sublime.

KAZ SUSHI BISTRO Map p64   Japanese $$

☎ 202-530-5500; http://kazsushibistro.com; 1915 I St NW; lunch specials $10, mains $10-20; 🕑 lunch & dinner Mon-Fri, dinner Sat; Ⓜ Farragut West
Fusing East and West, chef Kaz Okochi presents his own invention, 'free-style Japanese cuisine.' The sushi on its own is fresh and flavorful and good enough. Many clever combinations, however, add a certain *je ne sais quoi* to the traditional tastes.

FOUNDING FARMERS Map p64 American $$

☎ 202-822-8783; www.wearefoundingfarmers
.com; 1924 Pennsylvania Ave NW; mains $12-24;
☺ breakfast, lunch & dinner Mon-Fri, brunch,
lunch & dinner Sat & Sun; Ⓜ Foggy Bottom-GWU,
Farragut West

They serve 'bacon cocktails' here. No, really.
And they're awesome, as is the frosty decor
of pickled goods in jars overlooking an
art gallery of a dining space, a combination of made-from-scratch and modern art
that reflects the nature of the food: locally
sourced, New American – figs, prosciutto,
fried chicken and ricotta ravioli with
creamed corn. Our one complaint is the
location – the rustic Americana thing isn't
well served by essentially occupying the
ground floor of an office building.

CAFÉ DU PARC Map p64 French $$

☎ 202-942-7000; www.cafeduparc.com; 1401
Pennsylvania Ave NW; mains $14-22; ☺ breakfast,
lunch & dinner; Ⓜ Metro Center, Federal Triangle

Du Parc is one of the best bistros in town,
a place for French fare devoid of embellishment but ripping in honest, strong flavors
and deceptively simple preparation. The
mussels and beef tartar may be the best in
the city, which would be reason enough
to visit, but the calf liver, kissed perfectly
by the pan and a drizzle of shallots, olive-
crusted local rockfish and crisp shavings
of pork belly make us want to pitch a tent
on the terrace. Which is a good spot for
outdoor dining, by the way. Breakfast here
is lovely – a nice blend of American and
Continental dishes – and presents the opportunity for politico spotting.

BOMBAY CLUB Map p64 Indian $$

☎ 202-659-3727; www.bombayclubdc.com; 815
Connecticut Ave NW; mains $15-25; ☺ lunch &
dinner; Ⓜ Farragut West

No bad sitar music and clunky curry here;
this is India done up by several notches. The
seafood curries like the Goan fish or lobster
cooked in fenugreek and garam masala are
solidly wonderful, and plates like wild boar
vindaloo are as tasty as they are novel. Action stars agree; Bombay Club is popular with
the likes of Harrison Ford and Bruce Willis.

OLD EBBITT GRILL Map p64 American $$

☎ 202-347-4800; www.ebbitt.com; 675 15th St
NW; mains $15-25; ☺ 7:30am-1am, from 8:30am
Sat & Sun; Ⓜ Metro Center

The Grill is something of an institution,
having occupied its prime, adjacent-to-
just-about-everything (the White House,
the Mall, Penn Quarter) real estate since
1846. This is as down to earth as fine DC
dining gets. Political players (and lots of
tourists) pack into the brass and wood
interior, the sound of their conversation
rumbling across a dining room where good
burgers, oysters and fish-and-chip type fare
are rotated out almost as quickly as the
clientele.

GEORGIA BROWN'S Map p64 Southern $$

☎ 202-393-4499; www.gbrowns.com; 950 15th St
NW; mains $16-32; ☺ lunch & dinner Mon-Fri, din-
ner Sat, brunch & dinner Sun; Ⓜ McPherson Sq

Georgia Brown's treats the humble ingredients of the American South (shrimp,
okra, red rice, grits and sausage) with
the respect great French chefs give their
provincial dishes. The result is consistently
excellent regional American cuisine: high-
class Southern food from the Carolina
Lowcountry served in a warm, autumnal
interior. This was a favorite spot for the
Clintons during their presidency (we're
not sure if it still is during Hillary's Secretary of State-ship) and remains very much
in vogue with the city's black elite and
professionals.

OVAL ROOM Map p64 American $$

☎ 202-463-8700; www.ovalroom.com; 800 Connecticut Ave NW; mains $20-36; ☺ lunch & dinner
Mon-Fri, dinner Sat; Ⓜ Farragut West

The Oval Room occupies some pretty
prime real estate, sitting in the equidistant
center of a Polygon of Power formed by
the Hay-Adams Hotel, Army & Navy Club,
Eisenhower Building and Decatur House.
(We can imagine a Dan Brown character
drawing marker lines between all of the
above to the Oval, whispering, 'It all *fits*!'
But we digress.) You could plop the Oval in
bloody Bethesda and it'd still serve stand-
out food, generally of the American-hint-
of-Mediterranean genre. This author loves
butter and cream, yet he'll admit the Oval's
eschewing of the above in favor of allowing ingredients to hold their own intensity,
such as foie gras with lemon and lavender,
or bass laced with a delicate mix of anise
and toasted almonds, works wonders.
Condoleezza Rice agrees; this is her favorite
restaurant in town.

DC COAST Map p64 — Seafood $$

☎ 202-216-5988; www.dccoast.com; 1401 K St NW; mains $22-30; ☽ lunch & dinner Mon-Fri, dinner Sat; Ⓜ McPherson Sq

If Poseidon hired an art deco revivalist to redo his temple, the final result would probably end up looking something like DC Coast's interior. It's a beautiful space, more chaotic for the constant hum of lobbyist lunchers. Join the crowd; who can pass up a 'Tower of Crab' with spicy, citrusy Tabasco butter?

CIRCLE BISTRO Map p64 — French $$

☎ 202-293-5390; www.thecirclehotel.com; 1 Washington Circle NW; mains $23-28; ☽ lunch & dinner Mon-Fri, dinner Sat; Ⓜ Farragut West

When it comes to intimate French dining, the Circle ups the romance level, brings the price point down a notch and presents a menu that's solid if not particularly inspiring. This is fine dining with American ingredients, and while you may not be surprised by dishes such as trout with artichoke hearts or a squid-ink pasta (such things seem *de rigeur* of late), that doesn't mean you won't be delighted by them – the food is, simply, quite good. The service is generally even better, which adds to the appeal of using this spot for a date night.

PRIME RIB Map p64 — Steakhouse $$$

☎ 202-466-8811; www.theprimerib.com; 2020 K St NW; mains $25-43; ☽ lunch & dinner Mon-Fri, dinner Sat; Ⓜ Farragut North

There are lots of K St restaurants that serve up fusiony, modernist, wasabi-crusted-panko-seaweed-octopus-brioche kinda fare. Not the Prime Rib. Excuse a bit of chauvinism, but power, friends, is still best exemplified by sitting in a dark-wood dining room cutting deals over hunks of seared cow the size of a midget, then stepping outside for a cigar (damned smoking ban) and coming back in for a cognac. With a side of testosterone. The wait staff, clad in tuxedos, dress the part, and you'd better too – that means ties and jackets, men. Actually, you don't need the jacket at lunch, at which time the Rib delivers a $25 set menu that is quite a good deal. The food lives up to the atmosphere; while this place may not be cutting edge, that doesn't mean it isn't good at what it does.

KINKEAD'S Map p64 — Seafood $$$

☎ 202-296-7700; www.kinkead.com; 2000 Pennsylvania Ave NW; mains $26-34; Ⓜ Foggy Bottom-GWU

Robert Kinkead's restaurant is one of the most revered of DC's old-line establishments; where others have let quality slip and slide as their name has grown, or vanished altogether, this place endures and improves. Long before being a foodie or localvore was popular – in fact, back when a sign of status was having your Japanese tuna flown in from across the ocean – this seafood powerhouse was concentrating on artfully teasing the best flavors it could find from nearby fisheries and farms. For this commitment to the region and good food in general, we give our enthusiastic endorsement. Try the flounder with tasso ham and thank us later.

OCCIDENTAL GRILL Map p64 — Steakhouse $$$

☎ 202-783-1475; www.occidentaldc.com; 1475 Pennsylvania Ave NW; mains $28-37; Ⓜ Metro Center

This DC institution is practically wall-papered with mug shots of congressmen and other political celebs who have dined here throughout the years. Although the Occidental isn't the nerve center it once was, plenty of bigwigs still roll up their pinstripes to dive into hamburgers, chops, steaks and seafood.

TEATRO GOLDONI Map p64 — Italian $$$

☎ 202-955-9494; www.teatrogoldoni.com; 1909 K St NW; mains from $30; ☽ lunch & dinner Mon-Fri, dinner Sat; Ⓜ Farragut West

Teatro used to be just that – a sort of crazy clown carnival of very colorful, eye-catching, yet fairly 'meh' Italian dining. We loved (and still love) the *Commedia del Arte* ambience, a refreshing change from the starched-shirt formality so common in Foggy Bottom, but the food wasn't worth the price. No longer, though. Chef Enzo Fargione has brought discipline and style to the menu without sacrificing the madcap flair that is Goldoni's signature. Pasta stuffed with sweetbreads and sausage, all sweating a thick walnut sauce, should be too much (it almost is), but Fargione's kitchen manages to restrain the richness just enough so the flavors don't muddle. On the other hand, the veal, dressed in rosemary and mushrooms, stands on its simple, succulent self. *Bravissimo*.

EQUINOX Map p64 American $$$

☎ 202-331-8118; www.equinoxrestaurant.com; 818 Connecticut Ave NW; mains $31-34; ⏲ dinner daily & lunch Mon-Fri; Ⓜ Farragut West

Equinox is as mom-and-pop as high-end White House–adjacent dining gets – Todd Gray and wife Ellen Kassoff are the respective chef and manager. The intimacy of the restaurant's executive staff extends into the menu, which has long eschewed pricey export ingredients in favor of meat, fish, fowl and fruit sourced from the Shenandoah and Chesapeake Bay. That said, while Gray's ingredients are rooted in the mid-Atlantic, he can cross the pond for cooking inspiration; the duck breast served over black Indian rice is juicy and comforting, the rice pillow soft, and the accompaniment of roasted cherries plucked from the best rural French traditions.

ADOUR Map p64 French $$$

☎ 202-509-8000; www.adour-washingtondc.com; 923 16th St NW; ⏲ breakfast daily, dinner Tue-Sat; mains $31-46; Ⓜ Farragut West, MacPherson Sq

Alain Ducasse is one of those celebrity chef names whispered in hushed tones of reverence (or screamed through a gold bullhorn of marketing exuberance, if you do PR for Adour). People talk about Adour, Ducasse's first Washington, DC outpost, based in the St Regis Washington (p204) hotel, in more down-to-earth terms: good. Very good. Really good. Great? That's getting there. Admittedly, this restaurant has a big name to live up to, and our experience is limited by its newness – but we expect great things. The menu changes with the season, but in general it pays homage to the richest traditions of French cuisine and the universal palette of a discerning foodie (a summer dish of buttered lobster speckled with light seasonal fruits is a good example). Bonus: the wine list here is phenomenal.

MARCEL'S Map p64 French $$$

☎ 202-296-1166; www.marcelsdc.com; 2401 Pennsylvania Ave NW; fix menu from $52; ⏲ dinner; Ⓜ Foggy Bottom-GWU

The trick with French cuisine is keeping true to the classics while adding the right edge of modern embellishment. Marcel's has this tricky formula down. Old school, fill-you-up-by-a-fire fare like pork belly and turbot with peas is hearty and thick,

inducing pleasant drowsiness and a satisfied sense of stuffed. But the sprucing on the side – quail egg and cornichons, or the miso that accompanies the Alaskan cod – is just understated enough to ratchet the dining experience into a level approaching, and even dipping into, greatness. A classy touch: Marcel's offers a complimentary limousine service to the Kennedy Center, so this is an ideal spot for pre-theater dining.

GEORGETOWN

The Georgetown dining scene was staid for a while. The competition out here was thick with well-established classics like 1789 and folks didn't seem interested in trying new options, but this situation changed as DC's star became ascendant with young urbanites. Now some of the city's best new restaurants occupy DC's far-left patrician pocket.

Unless otherwise noted, all of the following are public-transport accessible via DC Circulator or the Georgetown shuttle (see p74).

BAKED & WIRED Map p72 Bakery $

☎ 202-333-2500; www.bakedandwired.com; 1052 Thomas Jefferson St NW; baked goods $3-5; ⏲ 6am-7pm Mon-Fri, 9am-7pm Sat, 11am-5pm Sun

With one of the nation's great universities a spilled cappuccino away, you'd think Georgetown would have more hip coffee shops, but alas, there's a lack. B&W makes up for this lost ground with a studio-chic interior and, more importantly, great coffee and some of the best cupcakes in DC. It's a supremely cheerful, smile-at-the-world sort of place, just the right kind of sunny disposition this occasionally stuffy neighborhood needs.

QUICK PITA Map p72 Middle Eastern $

☎ 202-338-7482; 1210 Potomac St NW; sandwiches from $5; ⏲ 11am-3am Sun-Thu, to 4am Fri & Sat

There's a million late-night joints in Georgetown selling falafel to drunk kids. This is the one we go to. Why? The yogurt is a little saltier, the stools a little more stable so we don't fall on our faces, the schwarma a little greasier and the guys behind the counter curse at each other in Arabic with just a little more vehemence. It's cozy like that.

KOTOBUKI off Map p72 — Japanese $

☎ 202-625-9080; www.kotobukiusa.com; 4822 MacArthur Blvd NW; sushi $6.25-15; ✆ lunch daily, dinner Mon-Sat

Kotobuki is one of the better spots for sushi in the city, both by dint of its excellent sushi and sashimi platters (at around $12 for a lunch and $18 for a dinner platter, a good deal), its tucked-away location, which adds a feeling of random discovery, and its oh-so-Japanese interior, all stripped-down aesthetic overlaid by running cursive kanji script on the walls. It's upstairs above a more expensive sushi joint.

SWEETGREEN Map p72 — Salads $

☎ 202-337-9338; www.sweetgreen.com; 3333 M St NW; dishes $10; ✆ 11am-9pm Mon-Wed, from 9am Thu & Fri, noon-8pm Sat & Sun

One day, we'll catch the guys at Sweetgreen selling polar-bear-cub tacos to lumberjacks in the back room. We're sure that's the dark secret to this place – no business can be so cutely macrobiotic! Until then, we admit these are some of the freshest, cheapest salads in the city. Just leave room for the nonfat Sweetflow frozen yogurt – every time you buy one, an acre of the Amazon Rainforest grows back. No, not really, but you get the sense it could happen – everyone here is such a damn do-gooder. Try and catch Sweetgreen's mobile incarnation, Sweetflow Mobile (p159), as it trundles around town.

VIETNAM GEORGETOWN

Map p72 — Vietnamese $

☎ 202-337-4536; 2928 M St NW; mains from $10

We have to admit: if we plunked Vietnam Georgetown next to some other Vietnamese places we've been to, it might not warrant too much praise. But in this neck of the woods, when we want *pho* (beef noodle soup), we come here. The lunch buffet is particularly good value, the setting and the staff are charming, if somewhat frazzled, and the garden out back is especially attractive on a summer evening. Part of the appeal of this place is the history; this was the first Vietnamese restaurant in the DC area. The owners were staff at the old South Vietnamese embassy, and this was a favorite spot for Reagan, Bush Sr and Clinton staffers during the '80s and '90s.

PIZZERIA PARADISO Map p72 — Italian $

☎ 202-337-1245; www.eatyourpizza.com; 3282 M St NW; mains from $11

This casual restaurant serves wood-oven Neapolitan-style pizzas with scrumptious toppings to crowds of starving patrons with rave results. The pizza crust is perfect – light, crisp and a little flaky. Great people-watching from the big plate-glass windows, popular happy hours, and a hand-picked beer and ale selection heighten the appeal. There's a second location in Dupont Circle.

BANGKOK BISTRO Map p72 — Thai $$

☎ 202-337-2424; www.bangkokbistrodc.com; 3251 Prospect St NW; mains $10-20; ✆ lunch & dinner

Don't expect a cute little hole-in-the-wall plucked straight outta Thailand; Bangkok Bistro is big and brash and usually packed. To be honest, it's not so much Thai as Thai-American, influenced by Asia but distinctly Yankee in its huge, arm-waving 'look-at-me' approach, modern decor, slick waitstaff and somewhat watered-down Thai. But it's also popular as hell, so they're doing something right. We always like the drunken noodles and curry mains, plus the inevitable people parade that marches by.

MARTIN'S TAVERN Map p72 — American $$

☎ 202-333-7370; www.martins-tavern.com; 1264 Wisconsin Ave NW; mains $10-25

John F Kennedy proposed to Jackie in booth three at Georgetown's oldest saloon, and if you're thinking of popping the question there today, the attentive waitstaff keep the champagne chilled for that very reason. With an old-English country scene, including the requisite fox-and-hound hunting prints on the wall, this DC institution serves a mean cheeseburger and icy cold pints of beer to college students and senators alike.

AGRARIA FARMERS & FISHERS

Map p72 — American $$

☎ 202-298-0003; www.farmersandfishers.com; 3000 K St NW; mains $10-25; ✆ lunch & dinner

Location, location, location, mission. Huh? Well, you know the importance of the first three, and Agraria's setting is as good as it gets: overlooking the Georgetown waterfront, a prime people-watching perch. But we love this place more for her mission: serving high-quality food sourced through sustainable partnerships with local small agricultural operators. Admittedly, sometimes this commitment to doing right induces eye rolls; having the soft tacos described as an 'homage to the field workers who plant, tend and harvest our food' is a bit tacky. But that's a minor complaint. We're not going to come down too hard on a restaurant that does its part for local communities, especially when the food is so on; try the 'baked potato pizza,' fresh fish dusted with Old Bay, butter and lemon, or any of the burgers (some swear this is the best beef in town).

MAKOTO Off map p72 *Japanese $$*
☎ 202-298-6866; 4844 MacArthur Blvd NW; mains $15-25; ❒ lunch Tue-Sat, dinner Tue-Sun

When we want sushi in the city we often opt for Makoto, simply by dint of it being so classically…*Japanese*. We probably need to clarify that comment. See, we don't just mean the staff are Japanese or there's flute and funny-one-string-guitar music playing in the back (although they are, and there is). It's that special Japanese attention to detail. The napkins look like origami. The wasabi is fresh grated. You leave your shoes at the door. The *geisha* – ok, waitresses, but they're so attentive you'd be forgiven for mixing up the terms – might as well wipe your mouth and hold your hand in the toilet. And the food, needless to say, is excellent. There's no mucking about; this is old-school stuff prepared with the height of focus and technique. For a splurge (around $60), try the *kaiseki,* a 10-course seasonal tasting menu.

BLACKSALT off map p72 *Seafood $$*
☎ 202-342-9101; 4883 MacArthur Blvd NW; mains $15-25; ❒ lunch Tue-Sat, dinner Tue-Sun

There are many who claim BlackSalt serves both the best seafood and operates the best fish market in the city. We won't lay those laurels down yet, but we're also acknowledging that we hate having to drive or bus out here. As fish markets go, this one is very Georgetown-oriented, which is to say fresh, artesian, organic – and expensive. As restaurants go…well, we give it to chef Danny Wells: the man loves fish. He loves cooking fish, finding new flavors, delving into whatever culinary pleasure one can ratchet out of a sole, or skate or soft-shell crab. We'd say he's spot-on with his shifting, innovative menu about 80% of the time, which is a fine ratio by our math.

MENDOCINO GRILLE & WINE BAR
Map p72 *American $$*
☎ 202-333-2912; www.mendocinodc.com; 2917 M St NW; mains $18-30; ❒ dinner

The fusion here is done with just the right light touch, giving Mendocino's menu the sort of refreshing kick you get out of a cool West Coast breeze. Fish comes floating on nutty jasmine rice, framed by meaty mushrooms, while a chard salad has twists of citric bite and chili heat. For all that, we especially love having wine and cheese nights here; whoever picks the stuff out really knows their *fromage,* which is as modern and refreshing as the interior decor. To sum Mendocino up: this is very fine contemporary California cuisine, which compliments all the contemporary California SUVs driven by all the nearby contemporary California Georgetown undergrads.

HOOK Map p72 *Seafood $$$*
☎ 202-625-4488; www.hookdc.com; 3241 M St NW; mains $25-30; ❒ lunch Tue-Fri, brunch Sat & Sun, dinner daily

Simple and sexy, with a frosty white Zen interior, Hook is the fish bar of the future: locally sourced seafood prepped artful and uncomplicated, so the flesh of your flounder or rockfish is allowed to play with just the right nudge in the direction of deliciousness. Yellowfin swims delectably out of a cloud of white bean puree, while bass floats atop polenta, its creamy flesh complimented by smoky pork belly.

1789 Map p72 *American $$$*
☎ 202-965-1789; www.1789restaurant.com; 1226 36th St; mains $20-40; ❒ dinner

If one restaurant were to exemplify not only Georgetown, but all that Georgetown represents – the brownstone political aristocracy of Washington, DC – it would be 1789. Located in a smart Federal row house, the setting is colonial, cozy and distinguished all at once. As a bonus, the food is excellent. This kitchen was one of the first high-end geniuses of the 'rustic New American' genre, so if you're going to try local ingredients sexed up with provincial flare, such as roasted Virginia rabbit with country ham and English peas, this is the spot to indulge your taste buds. Formal wear (jacket) is not only expected, but required for dinner.

CAFÉ MILANO Map p72 — Italian $$$

☎ 202-333-6183; www.cafemilano.net; 3251 Prospect St; mains $20-45; ⊙ 11:30am-midnight Sun-Wed, to 2am Thu-Sat

Widely regarded as one of the best bring-your-date-out-for-some-upscale-Italian eateries in the city, Milano has been racking up political bigwigs and besotted Georgetown couples for years with its executions of northern Italian favorites. It is ridiculously pricey, though; while we accept you're paying for atmosphere along with food, self-importance and the (admittedly good) chance of some DC celebrity-spotting don't warrant some of the price tags on this menu. For a good deal that still translates into some pretty good eating, order one of the pastas.

LA CHAUMIERE Map p72 — French $$$

☎ 202-338-1784; www.lachaumieredc.com; 2813 M St NW; mains from $25; ⊙ lunch Mon-Fri, dinner Mon-Sat

There's artists and there's craftsmen, and La Chaumiere's kitchen seems to fall into the second category. This isn't a bad thing; there's no fooling around with funny envelope pushing here, just very good classical French food prepared in an intimate dining room that screams 'expensive date.' This is hearty, stick-to-your-bones stuff straight from the *terroir* – duck breast, saddle of rabbit, calf brains – things that are long- and slow-braised with love. Screw art. We'll take the loving work of these craftsmen any day.

CITRONELLE Map p72 — French $$$

☎ 202-625-2150; www.citronelledc.com; Latham Hotel, 3000 M St NW; dinner from $105; ⊙ dinner

Citronelle regularly lurks near the very top of every Washington best restaurant list ever compiled. Big name Michel Richard started this show, a split-level study in the most creative twists tweakable on the American palate, yet grounded in French classicism. Part of what makes dining here so special is the emphasis on fun over formality. The cooks seem to laugh through their creations, such as salmon in a chicken (?!) jus, or the famous short ribs, braised for three days, then pan-seared (?!?) into something…well, medium-rare and amazing. This is the silly envelope's edge of what can be done in DC cuisine; if you're a visiting foodie, this should go on your 'can't-miss' list.

CAPITOL HILL & SOUTHEAST DC

Capitol Hill has long been an outpost for the DC burger bar, the sort of unpretentious spot where you roll up your sleeves and slather on some ketchup and – 'Sorry, yes Senator? I'll be back on the Hill right away! Damn, there goes my lunch.' Hipper upscale spots are popping up, and there's a big friendly farmers market in the middle of it all.

H St NE is a formerly grotty section of town being transformed by a glut of new restaurants and bars; the scene seems to shift every few months, but we've included here what was great as of press time.

EASTERN MARKET

Map pp78-9 — Self-catering $

www.easternmarket.net; cnr 7th St & North Carolina Ave SE; ⊙ 10am-6pm Tue-Fri, 8am-4pm Sat & Sun; Ⓜ Eastern Market

Fresh produce, from-the-farm meat, stinky cheese and great seafood – these are all good and served in Eastern Market, but we like coming here because it becomes, more or less, the nerve center of Capitol Hill on weekends. Families shop, browsers browse, friends laugh – look, it's just fun. There are several regular food stalls inside; our favorite is Market Lunch, right across from Southern Maryland seafoods. The food is obviously local and fresh, with the fried oyster sandwich and lemonade leading the pack of our favorite DC weekend lunches. You'd be hard pressed to spend more than $10. See also the entries in Neighborhoods (p81) and Shopping (p133).

SIDAMO COFFEE & TEA

Map pp78-9 — Cafe $

☎ 202-548-0081; www.sidamocoffeeandtea.com; 417 H St NE; snacks around $3; ⊙ 7am-7pm Mon-Fri, 8am-6pm Sat, 8am-5pm Sun; 🚍 X3, X2, 90/92 from Union Station

DC is lacking in the cafe department. Yeah, we've got Starbucks and some other chains out the wazoo, but indies where you can pound away on wi-fi and smell beans roasting and write books while blustery days go by? Not so much. Sidamo, thankfully, makes up for us in this regard. Owned by an Ethiopian family, this is excellent, organic African coffee, tasty and strong as hell. There's wi-fi, friendly staff and that right bohemian atmosphere, which, while overplayed in other parts of the world, doesn't get enough play in the capital. On Sundays at 2pm, the family puts on an Ethiopian coffee ceremony; all customers are invited to participate.

JIMMY T'S Map pp78-9 American $

☎ 202-546-3646; 501 E Capitol St; breakfast & lunch from $6; ☺ 7am-3pm Tue-Sun; Ⓜ Eastern Market

Jimmy's is a neighborhood joint of the old school, where folks come in with their dogs, cram in to read the *Post,* have a burger or a coffee or an omelet (breakfast all day, by the way) and basically be themselves. If you're hungover on Sunday and in Cap Hill, come here for a greasy cure. Cash only.

TAYLOR GOURMET Map pp78-9 Deli $

☎ 202-684-7001; www.taylorgourmet.com; 1116 H St NE; sandwiches from $7; ☺ lunch & dinner; 🚌 X3, X2, 90/92 from Union Station

When you just need a good sandwich, stat, Taylor's got you covered. For about (or a little over) $10 you can walk out of here with a foot of excellent anything between two pieces of bread, dressed with nicely shredded lettuce and brilliant oil and vinegar. We race here for the Race Street – turkey, prosciutto, pesto and mozzarella. There's a good Italian deli in the back.

GOOD STUFF EATERY

Map pp78-9 American $

☎ 202-543-8222; www.goodstuffeatery.com; 303 Pennsylvania Ave SE; mains $7; ☺ lunch & dinner, Mon-Sat; Ⓜ Eastern Market

Good Stuff chef Spike Mendelsohn is one of the most buzzed-about young chefs in the District, and he's cut out a controversial reputation for himself. Pros? He wants to bring good food at a good price to the masses, his sliders (mini-burgers) swept the South Beach Food & Wine Festival in 2009 and he works his kitchen – this is a celebrity chef who actually cooks your meal. Cons? He does reality shows like *Top Chef,* wears a dumb hat and his name is 'Spike.' Screw it; how about the food? Well, Good Stuff is good stuff: burgers, salads, shakes and fries, done with nice attention to detail and fresh ingredients. Plus, the salad comes with cornbread (nice). Still, if you're going to spend over $10 a head (which you likely will, fries and drink included), you want a bit more ambience than a fast-food joint, which is what Good Stuff feels like. Ah well – keep the fantastic food fresh, Spike, and we'll love you, hat and all.

LA PLAZA Map pp78-9 Latin American $

☎ 202-546-9512; 501 E Capitol St; mains from $8; ☺ lunch & dinner; Ⓜ Eastern Market

There are two prime times to go to La Plaza: for lunch, when it's occupied by Hill types seeking some cheap, filling (and very tasty)

CATERING TO THE MASSES

For thousands of DC residents, especially those in poorer parts of the city, the closest places to buy groceries are convenience stores packed with fatty, high-sugar junk food. To combat this nutrition nightmare, several food banks are working with local produce providers to bring healthy, locally sourced food into the city – a nice intersection of entrepreneurship and activism.

The largest food bank in the region is Capital Area Food Bank (☎ 202-526-5344; www.capitalareafoodbank .org), which distributes some 20 million lbs to over 700 partner agencies annually. If you're interested in volunteering with the program, get in touch via the website and phone number; the food bank is always in need of chefs, nutrition class teachers, distributors, etc. This can be a great way to learn about the capital's local produce and providers while helping said capital keep itself well-fed all at once. The Food Bank also helps operate farmers markets in some of the poorer parts of town, including the Ward 8 Farmers Market (off Map pp78–9; Martin Luther King Jr & Alabama Ave SE; ☺ 9am-2pm Sat Jun-Nov).

If you're self-catering, consider contacting the folks at DC Produce Cooperative (☎ 888-415-2667; www.produce coop.com). They sell wholesale 'Freggie' boxes of locally sourced fruits and veg for much cheaper than you get at the grocery store. Call them to arrange a pick-up location, and keep in mind they operate on the first and third weeks of the month. This is wholesale stuff, so you'll have to give your produce a good wash.

Finally, if you're interested in truly local food – stuff grown in the capital's backyards – get in touch with the folks at DC Urban Gardeners (www.dc-urban-gardener-news.com) and Rooting DC (www.rootingdc.org). The webmasters and contributors at both of these blogs are in thick with the dozens of urban garden projects that are sprouting (pun intended) all across the city, often in areas that need a vegetable patch's aesthetic and nutritional compliments.

Tex-Mex and Salvadorian fare, and at night, when they serve margaritas that will *kick your ass*. The staff are crazy friendly; if you shoot the breeze with them enough, the tequila starts pouring so quick you don't even know when you shtart shlurrin' yer speesh…uh oh.

ARMAND'S PIZZERIA Map pp78-9 Pizza $
☎ 202-547-6600; www.armandspizza.com; 226 Massachusetts Ave NE; pizza from $12 ⏰ 11am-9:30pm, to 10pm Sat, 4-9pm Sun; Ⓜ Union Station
The best pizza on the hill is served Chicago-style (deep crust) and pleasantly greasy. It's almost next door to the right-wing Heritage Foundation, so depending on your politics, you can share some pie with Newt Gingrich or throw it at him.

GRANVILLE MOORE'S
Map pp78-9 Belgian $
☎ 202-399-2546; www.granvillemoores.com; 1238 H St NE; mains $12-16; ⏰ 5pm-midnight Sun-Thu, to 3am Fri & Sat; 🚌 X3, X2, 90/92 from Union Station
Walking into Granville's is like walking into a medieval pub where the hobbits have tattoos and a bit of attitude. It's sweetly dark, redolent with the pure smells of beer and slow-cooking meat (oh yeah). The whole place screams cozy, and the food is fantastic: big meaty burgers, sandwiches, smoky bacon, runny cheese and bowls of shellfish, all accompanied by mountains of perfectly prepared *frites*. The fireside setting is perfect on a winter's eve, and locals have been known to fall on their faces over the bison cheesesteak.

ARGONAUT Map pp78-9 American $$
☎ 202-397-1416; http://argonaut.typepad.com; 1430 Maryland Ave NE; mains $9-21; ⏰ 5pm-2am Mon-Thu, 4pm-3am Fri, 1pm-3am Sat, 11am-2am Sun; 🚌 X3, X2, 90/92 from Union Station
You can get locally sourced organic goodness all around this town, but the setting is often some intimidating chic-spot straight from the Matrix, and the price is usually hovering near the ozone layer. Not at the 'Naut. It looks and feels like a corner spot where folks repair for a beer after work, and in truth, people still do so here. You should too, but don't miss the mouthwatering pumpkin ravioli or fries doused in Old Bay seasoning. Hipster enough to be different, but not so much that locals have fled the premises, this is a great date spot for someone who's a little off-kilter.

SONOMA RESTAURANT & WINE BAR
Map pp78-9 American $$
☎ 202-544-8088; www.sonomadc.com; 223 Pennsylvania Ave SE; mains $12-28 ⏰ lunch & dinner; Ⓜ Eastern Market
Wine bars became all the buzz in DC for a few years in the mid-noughties (ie 2000s), and Sonoma has long stood out from the pack. The decor is sleek-chic but warm, like a fireplace den decorated by a *coutre* Scandinavian designer's grandmother, and the food is fantastic, a nice sampling of Mid-Atlantic delicacies like bluebay mussels with chorizo and rainbow trout laid out with summer pumpkins. You can rely on the staff to pick good wine pairings, but if you're an oenophile the extensive grape menu shouldn't disappoint.

B SMITH'S Map pp78-9 Southern $$
☎ 202-289-6188; www.bsmith.com/restaurant_dc_home.php; Union Station, 50 Massachusetts Ave; mains $19-31; ⏰ lunch & dinner; Ⓜ Union Station
With its spectacular vaulted ceilings, marble floors and ionic columns, you can't beat this place's location in the former Presidential Waiting Hall at Union Station. It is a remarkable contrast to the down-home Southern fare served here by former model Barbara Smith (whose unclouded complexion once graced Oil of Olay ads). Which is not to say the food is not delicious: it is. She upgrades Southern classics to sophisticated oeuvres in ways fun and unexpected, eg vegetarian ribs and the 'Swamp Thang,' a mess of crawfish, scallops and shrimp on collard greens swimming in Dijon cream. The restaurant attracts an affluent African American crowd and is as popular for après-work drinks as it is for dinner. The ambiance is soul soothing, with mellow lights and music, muted colors and mod art on the walls.

MONOCLE Map pp78-9 American $$$
☎ 202-546-4488; http://themonocle.com; 107 D St NE; mains $18-36; ⏰ lunch & dinner Mon-Fri; Ⓜ Union Station
The Monocle's food – very American surf-and-turf type stuff – is 3.5 stars out of 5. Generally good, occasionally great, sometimes disappointing. But people don't come here to eat so much as to celebrity spot, and seeing as this good ol' boys' club is just behind the Capitol, your chances of seeing Senator Smith aren't bad. The dark

bar and the walls help hit home the fact that this is a politicians' place first and foremost; note the quotes ('If you want a friend in Washington, get a dog').

BISTRO BIS Map pp78-9 French $$$
☎ 202-661-2700; www.bistrobis.com; Hotel George, 15 E St NW; mains $25-32; ⏰ breakfast, lunch & dinner; Ⓜ Union Station
Jeff Buben is the chef behind the nouveau Southern fare in Vidalia (p160), and he takes a Southern approach – big portions and rich flavors – to the menu at Bis. The combination works; there's a rustic affability between classical Southern American and French cuisine, and the two seemingly disparate cultures find delicious common ground in this warm dining room. Concrete examples? Try the crisp frisee salad accompanied by big, sweet sides of applewood bacon, or a smoky duck confit offset by tarty sweet kisses from big cherries. Bistro Bis opens for breakfast, one of the few restaurants in its class to do so, making it the perfect spot to squeeze in a gourmet omelet and glass of freshly squeezed juice before dashing off to explore the city.

MONTMARTRE Map pp78-9 French $$$
☎ 202-544-1244; 327 7th St SE; mains $25-40; ⏰ lunch & dinner, Tue-Sun; Ⓜ Eastern Market
One of the better pure French spots in town, Montmartre is ensconced in a warm, neighborly location cluttered in a *mam-man's* dining room kinda way, complimented by great wines and some very fine steak, served bloody and yummy. This is more of a neighborhood spot than a political dinner date, which adds to the feeling of cozy authenticity. The homemade pâté is silky and rich, deserts are delightful, and all in all this is a place French expats take their friends to give them a taste of home – the praise doesn't come much higher than that.

SOUTHWEST DC
There are two places worth checking out down here: one very, very working man, blue collar, the other totally upscale chi chi-tastic.

FISH WHARF Map pp78-9 Seafood $
Waterfront, Washington Channel; meals from $6; ⏰ 7:30am-8:30pm Sun-Thu, to 9:30pm Jun-Aug, 7:30am-9pm Fri & Sat, to 10pm Jun-Aug; Ⓜ L'Enfant Plaza

In case you didn't know, Washington, DC is basically in Maryland, and Maryland does the best seafood in America. You get it fresh as hell – still flopping – here, where locals will kill, strip, shell, gut, fry, broil or whatever your fish, crabs, oysters etc in front of your eyes. Have a seat and a beer on the nearby benches and bliss out. If you haven't had steamed hard crabs with Old Bay, or a fried soft-shell crab sandwich, have some, now, *now* for God's sake. The wharf is also known as the Main Ave Fish Market.

CITY ZEN Map pp78-9 American $$$
☎ 202-544-1244; www.mandarinoriental.com/washington/dining/cityzen; Mandarin Oriental Hotel, 1330 Maryland Ave SW; fix menu $75-110; ⏰ dinner Tue-Sat; Ⓜ Smithsonian
James Beard–award-winning chef Eric Zeibold heads the kitchen at one of DC's most acclaimed restaurants. Zeibold is something of a legend in US culinary circles; he came up in California's French Laundry (arguably the best restaurant in America, some say the world) and approaches food with what we'd call *fierce* innovation; this is the kind of guy who mixes red snapper skin with lentils and can make you think a monkfish liver was a slice of perfect foie gras. The tasting menu of most foodies' sweatiest fantasies is served in a dining room that's almost blinding in its ritzy opulence. To cut a very fine deal, treat yourself to the $50 bar tasting menu.

DOWNTOWN & PENN QUARTER
During the boom years of the 1990s, the neighborhoods north of the Mall transformed themselves. Once this area was a ghost town after dark, but now you can find established restaurant districts in Chinatown, along 7th and 8th Sts NW and close to the White House. For cheap eats try the food court at Old Post Office Pavilion (p91) at lunch.

RED VELVET CUPCAKERY
Map p88 Cupcakes $
☎ 202-347-7895; http://redvelvetcupcakery.com; 675 E St NW; cupcakes from $3; ⏰ 11am-11pm; Ⓜ Gallery Pl-Chinatown, Metro Center
A lot of locals go ape-poo for this place, and we feel the need to say: calm down.

It's just a cupcake. Yes, yes, a very good cupcake, but sheesh...anyways, you can't convince the converted. The titular pastry is well described by its name: soft, rich and all around decadent.

FULL KEE Map p88   Chinese $
☎ 202-371-2233; 509 H St NW; mains from $6; 🕑 11am-1am Sun-Thu, to 3am Fri & Sat; Ⓜ Gallery Pl-Chinatown
Although you may find more atmosphere on the moon, you won't find a better Chinese dive in the city limits. Fill yourself for next to nothing with a simple noodle dish or stir-fry, but make sure you leave some room for the duck, which is divine stuff. Try it with some mambo sauce (DC's almost citrus-y version of sweet and sour). Cash only.

TEAISM Map p88   Teahouse $
☎ 202-638-6010; 400 8th St NW; mains from $8; 🕑 breakfast, lunch & dinner; Ⓜ Archives-Navy Memorial
This teahouse is unique in the area for its very affordable lunch options – hot noodle dishes and fresh bento boxes – and its pleasantly relaxing atmosphere. It's a grand spot for a bento box after a day of Mall sightseeing. The salty oat cookies are gorgeous. Has locations in Dupont Circle and Foggy Bottom as well.

JALEO Map p88   Spanish $$
☎ 202-628-7949; www.jaleo.com; 480 7th St NW; tapas $4-8, mains $15; Ⓜ Archives-Navy Memorial
The whole tapas thing has been done to death, but Jaleo helped start the trend in DC and it still serves some of the best Spanish cuisine in town. The interior is an Iberian pastiche of explosive color and vintage mural-dom, which all underlines, rather than overpowers, the quality of the excellent food. Opt for the tapas over the main dishes, which are a bit overpriced, and why not wash down those little plates with a heavy *rioja* to get that Flamenco edge on.

MATCHBOX PIZZA Map p88   Pizza $$
☎ 202-289-4441; www.matchboxdc.com; 713 H St NW; pizza $12-22; 🕑 lunch & dinner; Ⓜ Gallery Pl-Chinatown
Lines stretch round the block, the buzz is deafening and happy, the smells lead you in like a lost, cheesy lover: welcome to one of the most popular pizzerias in town. The pie here has rocketed into the DC gastronomic universe, and you can't come here now without finding Matchbox packed with the curious and the satisfied. What's so good about it? Fresh ingredients, a thin, blistered crust baked by angels and more fresh ingredients.

ZAYTINYA Map p88   Mediterranean $$
☎ 202-638-0800; www.zaytinya.com; 701 9th St NW; meze $6-12, lunch mains $12, dinner mains $20; 🕑 lunch & dinner Ⓜ Gallery Pl-Chinatown
Ninja-clad waitstaff prowl the high clean walls in this elegant bi-level, one of the culinary crown jewels of chef Jose Andres. In Zaytinya – still sexy, in an area where the competition to be hip is furious – the extensive menu of hot and cold meze ('little dishes') reflects the rich, regional diversity of Greek, Turkish and Lebanese cuisine.

LOCANDA Map p88   Italian $$
☎ 202-547-0002; www.locandadc.com 633 Pennsylvania Ave SE; mains $14-24; 🕑 lunch Mon-Fri, dinner daily; Ⓜ Eastern Market
Old-school Italian with just the right touches of modern embellishment, Locanda is lush. The menu isn't particularly challenging – if you've ever had a nice Italian night out, you know what to expect – but that doesn't mean it isn't good. These may be small pasta plates (more Italian than Italian-American, which always tries to suffocate you in penne), but there's an inverse quality–quantity equation at play. The menu shifts with the seasons; we remember a wild-mushroom gemelli from spring 2009 that seemed to sum up the season on our taste buds.

RASIKA Map p88   Indian $$
☎ 202-637-1222; www.rasikarestaurant.com; 633 D St NW; mains $16-23, mains; 🕑 lunch Mon-Fri, dinner daily; Ⓜ Archives-Navy Memorial
We may have to disagree with the *Washingtonian* magazine here for describing Rasika ('flavors,' in Sanskrit) as a 'gateway drug' to those who may be nervous about Indian food. Rasika is incredible, likely the best Indian food in town, but take a first timer to sub-continental grub and they'll be ruined. This ain't your average McMasala's. Rather, it's as cutting edge as Indian food gets, both in terms of menu and

presentation. The latter resembles a Jaipur palace decorated by a flock of modernist art gallery curators; the former…well, it's *good*. Narangi duck is juicy, almost softly unctuous, but pleasantly nutty thanks to the addition of cashews; the deceptively simple dal (lentils) have the right kiss of sharp fenugreek. Vegans and vegetarians will feel a lot of love here.

CAFÉ MOZART Map p88 German $$
☎ 202-347-5732; www.cafemozartonline.com; 1331 H St NW; mains $18-27; ⊗ breakfast, lunch & dinner Ⓜ Metro Center

Germans don't get enough credit for their food. Sure, a lot of it is meat and potatoes, but let's not forget: it's often very good meat and potatoes. This rather excellent German grocery store has a nice restaurant in the back that serves great sauerkraut, spaetzle and schnitzel; hell, they'll probably do you up a *currywurst* if you ask nice. Best of all, they host (wait for it) accordion concerts on Tuesdays and Sundays, and opera nights on Wednesdays. *Das ist* awesome!

ZOLA Map p88 American $$
☎ 202-654-0999; www.zoladc.com; International Spy Museum, 800 F St; mains $18-30; ⊗ lunch Mon-Fri, dinner daily; Ⓜ Gallery Pl-Chinatown

A subtle but playful theme of espionage runs through this hip restaurant, named for French author Emile Zola, who championed the case of Alfred Dreyfus when he was falsely accused of being a spy. Located inside the International Spy Museum (p90), it's only appropriate that guests should be able to monitor the kitchen through discreet one-way mirrors in the booths, or slip off to the restroom through a hidden door. Black-and-white photographs and projections of coded text further add to the mysterious air in the restaurant. In the midst of this secrecy, Zola's cuisine is pretty straight up. Bleu cheese pasta on local veal is nicely over the top, and a pretty gazpacho is enlivened by watermelon and olive oil.

PROOF Map p88 Wine Bar $$
☎ 202-737-7663; www.proofdc.com; 775 G St NW; small plates $9-14, mains $21-29; ⊗ lunch Mon-Fri, dinner daily; Ⓜ Gallery Pl-Chinatown

One of the most acclaimed new wine bar/ small plates restaurants in the city, Proof

has become one of the poshest culinary stars in the Downtown firmament of late. Everything is excellent – the duck and pork confit in cassoulet is a smoky marriage made in heaven – but if you want to keep costs down and still eat well, opt for the excellent cheese and charcuterie dishes, which are likely the best compliments to the epic wine menu. The four-course $56 tasting menu is also a winner that gives you a good idea of what the kitchen is capable of, but if you're in a group, try to mix and match off sexy small plates like cozy flatbread under creamy ricotta and lightly fried soft-shell crab complimented by a dandelion salad that makes your heart grin.

TENPENH Map p88 Asian $$
☎ 202-393-4500; www.tenpenh.com; 1001 Pennsylvania Ave; mains $23-27; ⊗ lunch Mon-Fri, dinner daily; Ⓜ Federal Triangle, Metro Center

Jewel-toned walls and shimmering lights, an abstract painting of an Asian warrior, a 17th-century black Buddha statue: such stylistic touches set the tone for this ultra-hip Asian-fusion masterpiece. The food is by no means secondary, however. Jeff Tunks – of DC Coast fame – adds ingredients and spices from China, Thailand and Vietnam to his well-honed traditional techniques, resulting in eclectic but exceptional culinary experiences for his guests.

POSTE Map p88 American $$$
☎ 202-783-6060; www.postebrasserie.com; Hotel Monaco, 555 8th St NW; mains $25-30; ⊗ breakfast, lunch & dinner; Ⓜ Gallery Pl-Chinatown

Named for its previous incarnation as the mail sorting room for the city post office, Poste has been busted out it's A game these days. The menu is playfully attractive, divided between 'pasta,' 'pasture' and 'garden' sections; the outdoor courtyard is one of the best alfresco dining spaces in the city; and the food lives up to this high bar. Chicken and corn? Sounds boring; executed flawlessly. Wreckfish with a wine-poached egg? Silly, sexy, beautifully presented and prepared. And give them credit for lightening up the fearsome *tête de veau* (head of cow) by rolling quail eggs, black truffles and frisee into a lovely terrine of veal cheeks. Come evenings, this is one of the better cocktail bars in town (p177).

ACADIANA Map p88   Southern $$$

☎ 202-408-8848; www.acadianarestaurant.com; 901 New York Ave NW; mains $23-33; ❤ lunch & dinner Mon-Fri, brunch Sun; Ⓜ Gallery Pl-Chinatown, Metro Center

Louisiana probably has the best homegrown culinary tradition in the USA, and all over the country different chefs try to capture the richness of our greatest gift to regional cooking. Acadiana is the DC effort, and it's a good one. This is rich, heart-attack stuff, so come prepared for duck glazed in pepper jelly, sweet watermelon salad set off by spicy pecans, and veal dunked in mushroom gravy set atop a hot bed of jalapeno grits. The interior is a bit sterile – not nearly colorful enough for a Louisiana restaurant – but the food makes up for this decor deficit.

CORDUROY Map p88   American $$$

☎ 202-589-0699; www.corduroydc.com; 1122 9th St NW; mains $24-37; ❤ lunch & dinner Mon-Fri, dinner Sat; Ⓜ Mt Vernon Sq/7th St-Convention Center

Corduroy is a study in understated excellence. From its appearance – so subtle you can miss it while walking past – to a postmodern menu of cleverly deconstructed dishes, this is a restaurant that challenges you to love your food for what it is. We'll happily oblige, so long as they give us another crack at that lamb loin with the sugar snaps, or the intriguing, surprisingly rich sea-urchin linguine. Chef Tom Power (awesome name, by the way) respects his food, bringing out its best without bending it to any preconceived notions of what tastes right.

MINIBAR AT CAFÉ ATLANTICO
Map p88   American $$$

☎ 202-393-0821; www.cafeatlantico.com/miniBar/miniBar.htm; 405 8th St NW; tasting menu $120; Ⓜ Archives-Navy Memorial

Atlantico's minibar is foodie nirvana, where the curious get wowed by animal bits spun into cotton candy and cocktails frothed into clouds and all the conceptualization of food that says we, as a society, have a lot of time on our hands. The tasting menu is often delicious, and at least original; even if every dish isn't a winner, it's hard not to appreciate the innovation involved. There's a sense of madcap experimentation here, as you expect from the best efforts of head chef Jose Andres, and we'll happily embrace that delicious lunacy.

DUPONT CIRCLE & KALORAMA

Dupont Circle contains therein the best of DC's dining scene. Classy nouveau cuisine and upscale ethnic eateries cater to the flocks of diplomats and businesspeople, and casual cafes cater to the more bohemian.

WELL-DRESSED BURRITO
Map p96   Tex-Mex $

☎ 202-293-0515; www.cffolks.com; 1220 19th St NW; mains $8; ❤ 11:45am-2:15pm; Ⓜ Dupont Circle

Brought to you by CF Folks, a local catering firm, well-dressed burrito deals in…well, do we need to spell it out? These burritos are a good antidote to overly hungry stomachs. Enter through the alley.

ZORBA'S CAFÉ Map p96   Greek $

☎ 202-387-8555; 1612 20th St NW; mains $8-12; Ⓜ Dupont Circle

Generous portions of moussaka and souvlaki, as well as pitchers of Rolling Rock, make this Greek diner one of DC's best bargain haunts. Contrary to the menu's promise, you will probably not confuse yourself for being in the Greek Isles (despite the bouzouki music). But the fresh food and quick service make this family-run place a good option.

MALAYSIA KOPITIAM Map p96   Malaysian $

☎ 202-833-6232; www.malaysiakopitiam.com; 1827 M St NW; mains $10 ❤ lunch & dinner; Ⓜ Farragut North, Dupont Circle

If you are familiar with Malaysian food, this is as close as you get to a Penang street stall in Washington. If you're not, may we introduce you to: laksa, bowls of noodle soup cut with coconut milk and pillowy chunks of chicken, and spiced dry fish, and anything cooked in a banana leaf. It's all next door to Camelot, DC's most (in)famous stripper bar.

LAURIOL PLAZA Map p96   Tex-Mex $

☎ 202-387-0035; www.lauriolplaza.com; 1835 18th St NW; mains $9.25-15; ❤ lunch & dinner; Ⓜ Dupont Circle

The Mexican food here is so-so – it's decent Tex-Mex with some flash, nothing too surprising, served with efficiency if not

EATING ON THE FOODWAGON

In case you feel like you haven't experienced enough interesting travel destinations in DC, may we direct your attention to the strange land of Merlindia.

There's not too many Merlindians in DC. To the best of our knowledge, it's just the four Fojol Brothers – Ababa-Du, Gewpee, Kipoto and Dingo. But the influence of this famous foursome is felt far and wide in our fair capital thanks to the culinary joy they bring to city streets. Clad in turbans and framed by their droopy mustaches, the brothers Fojol patrol city streets in their colorful van, blaring circus music, screaming 'It's a traveling culinary carnival,' and attracting all kinds of hungry followers.

That's because the Fojols (http://fojol.com) – real names: Will Carroll, Peter Korbel and Justin and Adam Vitarello – sell some of the damn tastiest curry in town. Plus, the packaging is biodegradable and a full meal runs $5 to $10. But how is one to find the Fojol foursome?

Well, they generally prowl Dupont Circle, Columbia Heights, Adams-Morgan, Georgetown and Chinatown – areas rich in their Gen Y-ish clientele base. But this being the 21st century and all, they can be tracked via Twitter @fojolbros (http://twitter.com/fojolbros). Updates on the Fojollocation are tweeted with the van's every movement.

The whole mobile food vendor thing is taking off in other directions in DC. As of press time, folks were raving about Sweetflow Mobile, the on-the-go version of Georgetown frozen yogurt purveyor Sweetgreen (p150). Sweetflow – yes, it's basically an ice-cream truck for yuppies and hipsters – usually stays in one spot for an hour at a time; you can twitter-stalk them @sweetflowmobile (http://twitter.com/Sweetflowmobile).

Follow @ontheflyDC to track down On the Fly (www.dconthefly.com), which is owned by perhaps the best named limited-liability firm in the world: Home Slice LLC. On the Fly vends the food of over a dozen local restaurants out of electrical, zero-emission 'smartkarts.' These guys have been around since 2007 and stake out around 13 regular sites in the District; see www.dconthefly.com/locations.php for a map.

grace. But the vibe is great for a night out; margaritas flow fast and are made strong, and a young and beautiful crowd tends to gather here, especially when the weather gets warm and the rooftop terrace opens up. See also p179.

AFTERWORDS CAFÉ & KRAMERBOOKS Map p96   American $$
☎ 202-387-1462; www.kramers.com; 1517 Connecticut Ave; mains $9-19; ⏰ 7:30am-1am; Ⓜ Dupont Circle

Generations of DC intelligentsia swear by this combination awesome bookstore and awesome squared brunch spot. Food is simple but very pleasing stuff, stick to your bones but pleasingly innovative – pecan-crusted catfish with hollandaise, anyone? Browsing the stacks (see p135) before stuffing our guts is a favorite way to spend Washington weekends.

BISTROT DU COIN Map p96   French $$
☎ 202-234-6969; www.bistrotducoin.com; 1738 Connecticut Ave; mains from $15; ⏰ lunch & dinner; Ⓜ Dupont Circle

How do you know if a French bistro is the real thing? The decor? Du Coin does up its dining rooms with a lovely tricolour spread come Bastille Day. Resistance to smoking bans? Du Coin held the line longer than

any DC restaurant we know of. But really, it's the food, and this is still our favorite spot for roll-up-your-sleeves, working-class French fare: steak frites, moules, cassoulet and the like. Not because it's necessarily the best (although it's quite good), but because the atmosphere feels plucked out of Orwell's Down and Out descriptions of Paris, the clientele is a fun mix of Dupont yuppies and nostalgic Euros and the prices are very reasonable. Nous t'aimons, du Coin.

HANK'S OYSTER BAR Map p96   Seafood $$
☎ 202-462 4265; www.hanksdc.com; 1624 Q St NW; mains $15-23; ⏰ dinner Wed-Mon, brunch Sat & Sun

There are a fair few oyster bars in Washington (slurping raw boys is good for political puffery, apparently) and Hank's is our favorite of the bunch. It's got the right testosterone combination, a bit of power-player muscle mixed with good-old-boy ambiance, which isn't to say women won't love it here. Just that guys really do. Needless to say, the oyster menu is extensive and excellent; there are always at least four varieties on hand. Quarters are cramped, and you often have to wait for a table – nothing a saki oyster bomb won't fix.

BLUE DUCK TAVERN Map p96 American $$

☎ 202-419-6755; 1201 24th St NW; www.blue
ducktavern.com; mains $16-28; ☯ breakfast, lunch
& dinner; Ⓜ Dupont Circle

The Blue Duck tries to create a rustic
kitchen ambience in the midst of one of
M St's uber-urbanized concrete corridors.
Design-wise, it doesn't quite work for us;
the Amish quilts and hand-crafted wood
accents seem to clash with the modernist
clean lines and art-gallery interior. Food-
wise, the experiment is a smashing success:
the menu sources off of farms across the
country, bringing diners lovely mains like
a pork terrine and trotter croquette made
from pigs in Virginia, crab cakes sourced
from the waters of Louisiana, and sturgeon
caviar plucked from the Columbia River in
Washington State.

ANNIE'S PARAMOUNT STEAKHOUSE
Map p96 Steakhouse $$

☎ 202-32-0395; 1609 17th St NW; meals $16-30;
☯ 10am-11pm Mon, to midnight Tue & Wed, to
1am Thu, 24hr Fri-Sun; Ⓜ Dupont Circle

There's always a great crowd at this neigh-
borhood steakhouse on Sundays, a mix of
families loving the excellent brunch and
gay club-hoppers eating off the headache-
inducing activities of the previous night.
After hours on weekends the place is at
its best, hopping with clubbers grabbing
a burger or breakfast on their way home.
Waitstaff are friendly, making this one of
the best places to meet and greet the gay
community.

WESTEND BISTRO Map p96 French $$

☎ 202-974-4900; www.westendbistrodc.com;
1190 22nd St NW; mains $16-35; ☯ dinner;
Ⓜ Dupont Circle

There's some intimidating talent behind
Westend's kitchen: the restaurant was
founded by Eric Ripert, who has a small
constellation of Michelin stars under his
belt, and the chef de cuisine is Joe Palma,
who has come up through some of the
best kitchens in DC and New York, including Citronelle (p152) and Le Bernardin. Those
sort of names attract some gushing hype,
attention which is pretty justified in this
gem of wood and warm tones. The French-
American menu is a mix of rich haute
cuisine and a playful wink; you can snack
on truffled popcorn at the bar, then enjoy
a fish burger dressed with a delicate saffron

aioli that hits like a delicious whisper – and
at $16, that burger isn't costing you much
more than a night at Red Lobster. Good
food, good deals – what's keeping you?

TABARD INN Map p96 American $$

☎ 202-331-8528; www.tabardinn.com/restau
rant; 1739 N St NW; mains $23-32; brunch $11-15;
☯ breakfast, lunch & dinner; Ⓜ Dupont Circle

In a city that loves its brunches, it's unfair
Dupont gets two standouts of the genre
(the other's Afterwords Café, p159), but the
gods put the Tabard here and we mortals
must contend. Dinners are great, but it's
the deceptively normal weekend brunch
menu – poached eggs, pecan waffles,
etc – that stands out. The ingredients
(including oysters caught specifically for
the inn) are just so good it's like brunch
enlightened.

NORA Map p96 American $$$

☎ 202-462-5143; www.noras.com; 2132 Florida
Ave; mains $26-35; ☯ dinner; Ⓜ Dupont Circle

Nora Pouillon remains the queen of the
Washington food scene. She made her
reputation serving food from farmers and
ranchers – this was by many accounts the
first organic restaurant in the country – and
a list of the farms that provided your food
is included on the menu. The way these
fresh ingredients are combined is in the
New American style, and while this school
of cooking has been done to death, Nora
was one of the originals and still executes
it so well that each bite is like rediscovering
what the nation can do with its ingredients:
Alaskan halibut arrives on a bed of corn
succotash, while Amish chicken livers soak
deliciously in their own jus. All this happens
in a quaint carriage house on one of Dupont's loveliest corners.

VIDALIA Map p96 Southern $$$

☎ 202-659-1990; 1990 M St NW; www.vidaliadc
.com; mains $30-34; ☯ dinner; Ⓜ Dupont Circle

Is it fair to call Vidalia 'Southern?' Chef Jeff
Buben, who also runs the kitchen in Bistro
Bis (p155), is a man who likes his French
influences. But there's clear Southern roots
in his focus on mixing the rich with the
filling – 'Southern' ain't just grits, after all.
Although with that said, the shrimp and
grits here are something else, a sort of Pla-
tonic ideal of the shrimp and grits concept.
Fare that's a bit more unique-sounding but

just as accessible to the everyman palette (and just as appreciable to a hard-core foodie) includes a cold cucumber soup of sea trout, squid ink and roe – pretty much like a spoonful of winter ocean – and rabbit loin and leg served under smoked bacon and a ginger-ale reduction (really?!) named, wait for it, 'What's Up, Doc?' The subterranean dining room, wallpapered in sultry-sweet magnolia, is exquisitely lovely. The signature side is a slow-cooked version of the titular onion, but we opt for the silly-expensive ($6.75!) sweet corn on the cob with truffled white butter. In terms of decadence, it's the culinary equivalent of a Roman orgy.

SUSHI TARO Map p96   Japanese $$$
☎ 202-462-8999; 1503 17th St NW; www.sushitaro.com; dinner from $50; ⊗ lunch & dinner Mon-Fri, dinner Sat; Ⓜ Dupont Circle

The argument over best sushi in town comes down to this place and Makoto (p151). In some ways, the issue boils down to aesthetics and service – both kitchens seem to (rightly) obsess over serving the finest, freshest fish possible arranged with beautiful sides and garnishes, presented with that attention to detail where the Japanese exist in a league of their own. A quivering bit of fatty tuna comes with a side of wasabi freshly grated from one long stem of Japanese horseradish into slivers of nose-tingling happiness. The tastes have almost mathematical layers of complexity, yet this intricacy is arrived at from the seemingly simple combination of a few fresh ingredients. The look and feel of the place is far more contemporary Japanese than Makoto, which looks like any Tokyo fish stand, and service is much more American. It comes down to a modernity vibe versus tradition, because at either joint you're going to eat very, very well.

OBELISK Map p96   Italian $$$
☎ 202-872-1180; 2029 P St NW; prix-fixe from $60; ⊗ dinner Tue-Sat; Ⓜ Dupont Circle

Oh the pleasure of dining at Obelisk. You need only do it once, but you need to do it, especially if you're a fan of pushing the boundaries of what can be done in an Italian *cucina*. The small and narrow dining room feels almost like eating at someone's kitchen table, and the set-course Italian feasts are lovingly prepared with first-rate

ingredients; the antipasti in particular is a revelation of just how powerful a start can be. The menu changes daily, but doesn't give you much selection (picky eaters should call ahead).

KOMI Map p96   Fusion $$$
☎ 202-332-9200; http://komirestaurant.com; 1509 17th St NW; set menu from $90; ⊗ dinner Tue-Sat; Ⓜ Dupont Circle

At the time of writing, the critical consensus was Komi was serving the best food in the capital. There's an admirable simplicity to the changing menu, which is rooted in Greece and influenced by everything, primarily genius. Suckling pig for two; scallops and truffles; a roasted baby goat. It all comes together, because here it's not just the food, but the incredible attention and measured pacing provided by the staff. You pay for Komi, but what you get is one of Washington's most knockout dining experiences. Komi's Venetian fairytale of a dining space doesn't take groups larger than four, and you need to reserve way in advance – like, now.

ADAMS-MORGAN

Adams-Morgan is Washington's international smorgasbord. Here you can dine on *mee goreng* (Indonesian noodles), shish kebabs, *yebeg alicha* (Ethiopian lamb stew), calzones, jerk chicken, seviche, *pupusas* (Salvadoran meat-stuffed pastry) and, of course, Happy Meals. Lots of people come here post-party on weekend nights to soak up the booze. Huge slices of pizza are a traditional DC post-bar snack; they're sold everywhere around here and are uniformly greasy and delicious when drunk. Or try Julia's empanadas at Julia's Empanadas (1001 18th St); we recommend the chorizo.

TRYST Map p103   American $
☎ 202-232-5500; www.trystdc.com; 2459 18th St NW; breakfast from $5, sandwiches from $6; ⊗ 6:30am-2am Mon-Thu, to 3am Fri & Sat, 7am-2am Sun; Ⓜ Woodley Park Zoo/Adams Morgan

This is where the yuppies roam. 'So-and-so is Trysting' is a perennial Facebook status/tweet in DC, which automatically tells you what to expect here: good coffee, good sandwiches, lots of Macs (no wi-fi on weekends, though). Come nightfall, baristas become bartenders, and rather good ones too. The next door Diner is the spot for more hearty fare of, imagine that, the diner school of cookery (eggs, burgers, the like, with mains priced $6 to $17). It's open 24 hours.

BARDIA'S Map p103 New Orleans $

☎ 202-234-0420; 2412 18th St NW; mains under $12; ⊙ lunch & dinner Tue-Fri, 10am-10pm Sat, 10am-9:30pm Sun; Ⓜ Woodley Park Zoo/Adams Morgan

We have it on good authority (a bunch of stoners stumbling out of B&K newsstand; the next door head shop that's one of DC's most notorious pipe shops) that this New Orleans–style cafe is the best cure for munchies in town. But that stereotype's a disservice; Bardia's food – the po' boys, the breakfasts and especially the beignets – is fantastic whatever your mental state. If you've lived in New Orleans (and yes, this author has) the stuff stacks up to the real thing: rich, silky luxurious, silly decadent, and while the setting isn't as attractive as Faubourg Marginy, it's pretty damn close.

MIXTEC Map p103 Mexican $

☎ 202-332-1011; 1792 Columbia Rd NW; mains $5-12; ⊙ breakfast, lunch & dinner; Ⓜ Woodley Park Zoo/Adams Morgan

Budget Mexican that eschews the taco/burrito/enchilada drabness of the genre, Mixtec is justifiably popular with Anglos and Latinos. The moles are freshly prepared, the meat authentically spiced (rumors say they use more than 200 seasonings) and the huevos rancheros are a great hangover cure.

PASTA MIA Map p103 Italian $

☎ 202-328-9114; 1790 Columbia Rd NW; mains $10-15; ⊙ dinner Mon-Sat; Ⓜ Woodley Park Zoo/Adams Morgan

Long lines, stiff waitstaff, crowded conditions, perfect pasta. This is the price of good, cheap Italian, friends. But that's OK. Sip your red, twirl one of 20-some types of flour/semolina/gram perfection and try not to break into operatic praise. It gets crowded inside, so this may not be the best place for romantic candlelight and Chianti, although it is grand for big groups and gregariousness. By the way, we mean it when we say 'long lines' – there's no reservations here, and if you're coming for dinner on a weekend night, you'll want to arrive early.

If you're in a big group, they won't seat you until everyone's arrived.

MESKEREM Map p103 Ethiopian $$

☎ 202-462-4100; http://meskeremethiopianfood.com; 2434 18th St NW; mains from $10; ⊙ 11am-midnight Mon-Thu, to 2am Fri & Sat; Ⓜ Woodley Park Zoo/Adams Morgan

As you make your way across DC, you'll see loads of places offering Ethiopian food, but Meskerem, named for the first month of the Ethiopian calendar, remains one of our favorites. This spot is a stalwart of quality despite many years on the block. It's the just-seared lamb served in spicy sauce, the *wat* (stew) scooped with spongy *injera* (pancake-like bread) and the vegetables, all deliciously spiced, not hot but rich, complex and savory. This is remarkably easy food for the most conservative palette, best washed down with some imported honey wine.

RUMBA CAFÉ Map p103 Brazilian $$

☎ 202-588-5501; www.rumbacafe.com; 2443 18th St NW; tapas $6-10, mains $18-28; ⊙ 5:30pm-2am; Ⓜ Woodley Park Zoo/Adams Morgan

Sit outside on the sidewalk and watch life pass you by while sipping some of the mintiest mojitos in the city and munching on mouthwatering morsels from South America. This tiny, eclectic restaurant's menu is mainly Brazilian, although it pops around the rest of the continent. We love the empanadas and, as is the Brazilian wont, anything steak-based is usually delicious. After dinner Rumba hosts live Latin bands in its shabby-chic, red-and-mirror-clad interior.

PERRYS Map p103 Asian $$

☎ 202-234-6218; www.perrysadamsmorgan.com; 1811 Columbia Rd NW; ⊙ dinner Sun-Thu, brunch Sat & Sun; mains $15-30; Ⓜ Woodley Park Zoo/Adams Morgan

Three words: drag queen brunch. What, you need more? *Drag queen brunch,* people! Fine; in addition to the above, you can also munch sushi at Perry's, but the creative fusion fare really deserves your tongue's attention. The only problem is deciding whether to dine in the attractive lounge or under the stars. This place can be hard to spot because there's no real sign – the doorway canopy uses rebus symbols (like a pear) to spell out the name.

CASHION'S EAT PLACE

Map p103   American $$

☎ 202-797-1819; www.cashionseatplace.com; 1819 Columbia Rd NW; mains $19-32; 🕑 dinner Tue-Sun, brunch Sun; Ⓜ Woodley Park Zoo/Adams Morgan

Restaurateur and chef Ann Cashion is a local celebrity for the original menu and inviting decor she has invented at this little bistro, lauded as one of the city's very best. Cashion's serves food that can be light and rich at the same time (or just rich and rich, as in duck breast served with foie gras). The mismatched furniture and flower boxes create an unpretentious setting to enjoy her work. The bar serves fancy late-night fare, like pork cheek and goat cheese quesadilla, till 2am on Friday and Saturday.

COLUMBIA HEIGHTS & NORTHEAST

This being the gentrification line, you'll find a lot of the most interesting restaurants in the city opening up across this enormous area. Some are quite *haute* in their approach to food, some are neighborhood soul-food joints and ethnic diners, and some are *haute-ed* up versions of soul-food joints and ethnic diners. For quick eats, Pupuseria San Miguel (Map p106–7; ☎ 202-387-5140; 3110 Mt Pleasant Ave NW) does some great, very cheap *pupusas*. Enjoy.

U STREET & SHAW

BEN'S CHILI BOWL Map pp106-7   American $

☎ 202-667-0909; www.benschilibowl.com; 1213 U St; dogs from $5; 🕑 lunch & dinner daily, to 4am Fri & Sat; Ⓜ U Street-Cardozo

Ben's is to DC dining what the White House and Capitol are to sightseeing: a must-visit. To take that analogy a little further, while the White House and Capitol are the most recognizably important symbols of DC as capital, Ben's holds the same status as regards DC, the place where people live. Opened and operated by Ben and Virginia Ali and family (it's now adjacent to Ben Ali Lane; Ben Ali died during the research for this book, which left a large hole in the U St business community), the Bowl has been around since 1958. It's one of the only businesses on U St to have survived the 1968 riots and the disruption that accompanied construction of the U Street Metro stop. The main

stock in trade is half smokes, DC's meatier, smokier (duh) version of the hot dog, usually slathered in mustard and the namesake chili. Until recently, Bill Cosby was the only person who ate here for free, but Michelle Obama and first daughters Sasha and Malia get the nod too – though apparently, not their presidential dad. That's a short list, as a *lot* of famous faces have passed through these doors, from Bono to both Bushes. Next door is Ben's Next Door, which offers a more upscale American menu (steak, trout, etc) at more upscale costs (mains $17 to $28). We have to admit we weren't able to try this place during our research, but readers have sent us good reviews.

SANKOFA Map pp106-7   Vegetarian $

☎ 202-234-4755; www.sankofa.com/sankofacafe .html; 2714 Georgia Ave; mains $6.50; 🕑 10:30am-10pm Tue-Sat; Ⓜ Columbia Heights

Good for your soul and your body, Sankofa is basically a black intellectual cafe expounding the old school Pan-African ideal. In the 21st century it still fronts an excellent African/African American–themed bookstore and video place, but don't miss the sandwiches, salads and wraps; the wraps constitute some of the best vegan fare in town. We're all about the Gaston Kaboré garlic hummus, honey Dijon, olives etc served in an excellent tortilla.

CHIX Map pp106-7   Chicken $

☎ 202-234-2449; http://chixdc.com; 2019 11th St NW; mains $7.50-12; 🕑 11:30am-10pm Mon-Fri, from 12:30pm Sat; Ⓜ U Street-Cardozo

The DC area takes its Peruvian chicken seriously. If you haven't had the stuff, it's slow-roasted, rotisserie style, and god is it good: succulent, juicy, the savory skin complementing the comforting pillowy meat. Most of the best Peruvian chicken (*pollo a la brasa*) in the area is actually outside of the city in the Maryland and Virginia 'burbs, but Chix is about as good as it gets in the District itself. Plus, Chix is green and good: it was built with sustainable materials and the cups are made out of fast-degrading corn.

CORK WINE BAR Map pp106-7   Wine Bar $$

☎ 202-265-2675; www.corkdc.com; 1720 14th St NW; small plates $7-14; 🕑 5pm-midnight Tue, Wed & Sun, to 1am Thu-Sat; Ⓜ U Street-Cardozo

This dark 'n' cozy wine bar manages to come off as foodie magnet and friendly neighborhood hangout all at once, which is a feat. Smart wine choices plus small plates equals culinary bliss – a brioche of prosciutto is graced by fontina cheese and a smiling, sunny-side-up egg, while chicken livers arrive on a rosemary bruschetta accompanied by a dollop of intriguing shallot marmalade. With this innovative menu (and excellent cheese selection) you generally can't go wrong, although those little dishes do add up on the wallet.

RESTAURANT JUDY
Map pp106-7   Latin American $$
☎ 202-265-2519; 2212 14th St; mains $7-15; ⏰ breakfast, lunch & dinner; Ⓜ U Street-Cardozo
When we asked a Honduran friend where to get good Central American food, her unhesitating answer was: 'Judy's.' Everything's good, but the breakfasts, consisting of tamales, white cheese and other odds and ends, are tops. Come at night for the best Spanish-language karaoke in town; if you don't speak Spanish, work on your hand gesturing.

BUSBOYS & POETS
Map pp106-7   American $$
☎ 202-387-7638; www.busboysandpoets.com; 2021 14th St; mains $7-15; ⏰ 8am-midnight Mon-Thu, to 2am Fri, 9am-2am Sat, 9am-midnight Sun; Ⓜ U Street-Cardozo
Busboys (named for a Langston Hughes poem) has, dare we say, become as much of a keystone of the U St scene as Ben's Chili Bowl. It's one of the first places this author takes all newcomers to the city, in the sense that is seems to capture that sense of what DC really *is* better than almost any one business. So what is DC? Intellectual, multiracial, opinionated, creative, takes itself just a little too seriously (just perhaps), supportive of its local community, but sometimes a bit too obsessed by its own laptop. Everything we've just described? Pretty much the daily scene inside B&P, the sort of place where everyone seems to gather for coffee, wi-fi and a progressive vibe (and attached bookstore) that makes San Francisco feel conservative. Oh, the food? Upscale diner stuff: sandwiches, burgers, pizzas and the like, all quite tasty and reasonably priced.

FLORIDA AVENUE GRILL
Map pp106-7   Diner $
☎ 202-265-1586; 1100 Florida Ave NW; mains from $10; ⏰ breakfast, lunch & dinner Tue-Thu, to 4am Fri & Sat, 8am-4:30pm Sun; Ⓜ U Street-Cardozo

Besides the Hitching Post (p166), we deem the Grill DC's quintessential diner. Be they president, Harlem globetrotter or college student, they've all come here for almost 70 years to eat turkey legs, catfish and meatloaf served with sides of sweet tea and more character than Shakespeare's collected works.

OOHH'S & AAHH'S
Map pp106-7   Soul $$
☎ 202-667-7142; 1005 U St NW; mains $8-25; ⏰ 4-11pm; Ⓜ U Street-Cardozo
Some of DC's best soul food is on offer at this barebones U St joint popular with everyone from the homeless to sports superstars. The down-home southern cooking comes in plentiful portions; it's hard to walk away from the fish platter with some mac 'n' cheese and greens without being filled up, unless you're some kind of human trash compactor, and the clientele is very much made up of the U St that was before this part of town gentrified.

CRÈME
Map pp106-7   Soul $$
☎ 202-234-1884; www.cremedc.com; 1322 U St; mains $10-25; ⏰ dinner Mon-Fri, brunch & dinner Sat, 10am-6pm Sun; Ⓜ U Street-Cardozo
Crème's upscale soul attracts a multi-culti crowd and is particularly popular with buppies (black yuppies), who enjoy a stick-to-your-ribs menu served in a slick dining room of soft beiges and buffed metal. Fight for seats at Sunday brunch; the chicken and waffles might be our favorite night-after nosh in DC, and based on the lines out the door, we're not the only folks sharing that opinion.

EATONVILLE
Map pp106-7   Soul $$
☎ 202-332-9672; http://eatonvillerestaurant.com; 2121 U St NW; mains $12-22; ⏰ lunch & dinner Mon-Fri, dinner Sat, brunch & dinner Sun; Ⓜ U Street-Cardozo
One of our favorite news restaurants in DC has an unconventional theme by culinary standards: novelist Zora Neal Hurston (Eatonville was her home town; we're not sure if the easy pun 'Eating-ville' was another source of the name). Well, what do you expect of the guys who opened next-door Busboys & Poets? The atmosphere and setting is superb, a sort of bayou dripped through impressionist-style murals of the South, then resurrected upon a modernist, cavernous dining hall that looks like

nothing less than a cathedral to black intelligentsia. And the food? Fine. Very fine. Catfish come correct with cheese grits, and the andouille-and-sweet-potato hash… don't get us started. Wash it down with lavender lemonade, which, on hot summer days, is sort of like drinking sex.

COPPI'S ORGANIC Map pp106-7 Italian $$
☎ 202-319-7773; www.coppisorganic.com; 1414 U St NW; pizza from $16, mains $19-27; ☺ dinner; Ⓜ U Street-Cardozo

An old-school U St restaurant that fires up the wood-burning oven nightly to serve perfectly crusted, crispy pizzas along with other seasonal and traditional Italian delicacies. The owner is crazy about bicycles and the cozy restaurant is jammed with cycling memorabilia. More importantly, the owner obsesses over fresh, high-quality ingredients, a consuming passion that shines through in the Italian fare. Coppi's gets packed on weekends, when locals flock in to partake of all of the above, plus some good cheap wine.

COLUMBIA HEIGHTS & MOUNT PLEASANT

DOS GRINGOS Map pp106-7 Latin American $
☎ 202-462-1159; www.dosgringoscafe.com; 3116 Mt Pleasant St NW; mains $4-7.50; ☺ 7:30am-8pm Tue-Thu, to 9pm Fri; 9am-9pm Sat, 9am-4pm Sun; Ⓜ Columbia Heights

You gotta chuckle at both the *cajones* and self-deprecation of putting this, well, gringo (white) owned cafe in the middle of Mt Pleasant and naming it as such. Not that anyone resents Dos Gringos' presence; Latinos and Anglos alike line up to order off a bilingual menu that includes fresh veg burritos, cheap cups of coffee, curry chicken salads and portabello sandwiches served in an Ikea-chic interior.

RED ROCKS PIZZA Map pp106-7 Pizza $
☎ 202-332-7383; www.firebrickpizza.com; 1400 Irving St NW; pizza from $10; ☺ 5-11pm Mon, 11am-11pm Tue-Thu & Sun, 11am-1am Fri & Sat; Ⓜ Columbia Heights

Red Rocks has been voted best pizza in the city in a glut of DC publications since its opening. That's testament to the unswerving excellence of their irregularly shaped, brick-fired pies, all of which feel like they

were individually crafted – because they have been. You're not gonna be shocked by any of the ingredients, except when it comes to their quality, which is impeccable: screamingly fresh basil and flour, tomatoes and cheese all imported from Italy.

W DOMKU Map pp106-7 Scandinavian $
☎ 202-722-7475; www.domkucafe.com; 821 Upshur St NW; mains $7-18; ☺ dinner Tue & Wed, 10am-11pm Thu, to midnight Fri & Sat, 10am-10pm Sun; Ⓜ Georgia Ave-Petworth

As unexpected as…well, a hip, artsy coffee shop in the middle of a very local strip of churches, funeral homes and Caribbean takeouts, Domku is a gem. The interior is like Ikea on good drugs, and the food is an intriguing execution on Polish, Norwegian and Russian fare; 'gypsy sandwiches,' poached eggs topped with caviar and pancakes baked on clouds dappled with lavender compote.

PETE'S APIZZA Map pp106-7 Pizza $
☎ 202-332-7383; www.petesapizza.com; 1400 Irving St NW; pizza $19-25, per slice around $5; ☺ lunch & dinner; Ⓜ Columbia Heights

The specialty pizza here is New Haven–style. No, that doesn't mean it comes dressed with Yale flair, that's a white pizza (ie no tomato sauce) with olive oil and clams, with an NYC-style thin crust. Take our word on this: it's really good. There's dozens of other combinations on the menu, but we'll opt for the white pizza with clams most days.

THE HEIGHTS Map pp106-7 American $
☎ 202-797-7227; www.theheightsdc.com; 3115 14th St NW; mains $9-15; ☺ lunch & dinner; Ⓜ Columbia Heights

They don't keep on reaching for such great heights at the Heights – they've seized them (sorry – Postal Service reference). The food is excellent Americana stuff – the fried chicken and mash potatoes is wonderful, and wasabi-crusted fish is gorgeous, but whatever you do, come on a weekend and order off the greatest Bloody Mary menu on Earth. Select from 10 different types of vodka, or tequila, or gin, then add from a glut of options, including beef broth, clam juice, Old Bay seasoning, lump crabmeat, bacon – well, we could go on. By the way, you can order all of the above *together*. Of course, then time would stop and the universe would implode upon itself, so you probably shouldn't.

HITCHING POST Map pp106-7   Diner $

☎ 202-726-1511; 200 Upshur St NW; mains $11-18 ◴ 10:30am-10pm Tue-Sat; Ⓜ Georgia Ave-Petworth

'This is East Coast jazz,' says the owner behind the counter. 'No one listens to this anymore.' Another song comes up; The Drifters. Really? The Drifters and jazz in a diner so neighborly it should put on a cardigan and loafers when it comes inside? Let's try the fried chicken…which, ohmygod, is seriously like a whole, freaking fried chicken. Served with two sides. And another man comes in and the owner calls him by name and the customer asks, 'This the Chi-lites?' and we know we're in love.

UPPER NORTHWEST DC

Despite its distance from the city center, Upper Northwest DC has its fair share of excellent eateries. Most are clustered around the Metro stops in Cleveland Park, Tenleytown and Woodley Park Zoo/Adams Morgan, although several are in Glover Park, just north of Georgetown.

VACE DELI Map p114   Self-catering $

☎ 202-363-1999; www.vaceitaliandeli.com; 3315 Connecticut Ave NW; whole pizza $8; ◴ 9am-9pm Mon-Fri, to 8pm Sat, 10am-5pm Sun; Ⓜ Cleveland Park

If you're going on a picnic in Rock Creek Park, may we suggest getting a bit of meat, a parcel of cheese and some bread and olives and wine and general happiness from Vace, perhaps the best deli in DC? Treat yourself to some of their pizza, too; it's divine.

ROCKLANDS BARBECUE
Map p114   Southern $

☎ 202-333-2558; www.rocklands.com; 2418 Wisconsin Ave; mains $7-22; ◴ lunch & dinner ◻ 30, 32, 34, 36 from Tenleytown-AU or Foggy Bottom-GWU Metro

We say Southern, but really, it's just about the barbeque here: slow smoked, red oak and hickory, no electricity, no gas, Texas-style and pretty good for the East Coast. The ribs, as you might guess, are the way to go – or if you wanna splurge, shell out $600 for a 120lb whole barbecued pig.

While you wait for your order, check out the huge selection of hot sauces ('From the Depths of Hell'). Then take a seat at the wooden counter in the window and watch the passers-by drool.

COMET PING PONG Map p114   Pizza $

☎ 202-364-0404; www.cometpingpong.com; 5037 Connecticut Ave NW; mains $12-17; ◴ 5-9:30pm, to 10:30pm Fri, 11am-10:30pm Sat, to 8pm Sun; Ⓜ Van Ness-UDC

Dinner time and the kids are as restless as your spirit, which longs to sit on a stool that's too high for you. To satisfy all nostalgic parties involved, may we suggest: Comet. A round of ping pong on the tables in the back is perfectly complimented by the Smoky – smoked bacon, gouda, mushrooms and…oh yeah (drool). It's possibly the most fun restaurant in the city, a sort of Chuck E. Cheese's that's been beat over the head with an awesome stick several times.

NAM VIET Map p114   Vietnamese $

☎ 202-237-1015; www.namviet1.com; 3419 Connecticut Ave NW; mains $11-19; ◴ lunch & dinner; Ⓜ Cleveland Park

Probably the best Vietnamese within the city lines is served here. The cooking is uncomplicated, but that doesn't mean it isn't excellent, especially the rich pho. The layout is from the 'every-Vietnamese-restaurant-you've-ever-been-in' cookie cutter, but the quality of the food elevates Nam Viet several notches above the pack.

BLUE RIDGE Map p114   American $$

☎ 202-333-4004; www.blueridgerestaurant.com; 2340 Wisconsin Ave NW; mains $10-21; ◴ lunch & dinner; ◻ 31, 35, N6 bus from Tenleytown or Dupont Circle Metro

We'll give you a few guesses as to what part of the country the menu at Blue Ridge is sourced from. Give up? Ah, you're not from around here. Makes sense; you bought the Lonely Planet after all. Well, the food here comes from the Blue Ridge Mountains, which form the western spine of Virginia. This is Americana stuff done up with superb attention to detail, served in a dining room that's a little too spare to feel as rustic as it wants to be (the waitstaff wear plaid, which comes off as more hipster than the intended country-fried). The mains are lovely, but we especially love the

FARMERS MARKETS

If you live in DC, it's possible to buy all of your foodstuffs from farmers markets. In addition to Eastern Market (p152; the granddaddy of DC open-air markets), try these options:

- **14th & U Farmers' Market** (Map pp106–7; 14th & U Sts NW; ☉ 9am-1pm Sat May-Nov; Ⓜ U St-Cardozo/ African American Civil War Memorial)
- **Adams-Morgan Farmers Market** (Map p103; Crestar Bank Plaza, cnr Columbia Rd & 18th St NW; ☉ 8am-1pm Sat May-Dec; Ⓜ Woodley Park Zoo/Adams Morgan, U Street-Cardozo)
- **Arlington Farmers' Market** (Map p122; www.arlingtonfarmersmarket.com; cnr N Courthouse Rd & N 14th St; ☉ 8am-noon Sat; Ⓜ Rosslyn, Clarendon)
- **Bloomingdale Farmers' Market** (Map pp106–7; 102 R St NW; ☉ 10am-2pm Sun May 18–Nov 23; Ⓜ Shaw-Howard University)
- **Chevy Chase Farmers' Market** (Map p114; Lafayette Elementary School, cnr Broad Branch Rd & Northampton St NW; ☉ 9am-1pm Sat Apr 25-Nov; 🚌 E2, E4 or E6 bus from Friendship Heights Metro)
- **Florida Ave Farmers' Market** (off Map pp78–9; 1309 5th St NE, Neal Place NE; ☉ 7am-2pm Sun, to 5.30pm Tue-Thu, to 6pm Fri & Sat; Ⓜ New York Ave)
- **Georgetown Farmers' Market** (Map p72; cnr 26th & O Sts NW; ☉ 4-7pm Wed Apr-Oct; 🚌 Georgetown shuttle, DC Circulator)
- **Historic Brookland Farmers Market** (off Map pp106–7; cnr 10th & Otis Sts NE; ☉ 4-7pm Tue, 10am-2pm Sun May-Nov; Ⓜ CUA-Brookland)
- **Mt Pleasant Farmers' Market** (Map pp106–7; www.mtpfm.org; Lamont Park, cnr 17th & Lamont Sts NW; ☉ 9am-1pm Sat; Ⓜ Columbia Heights)
- **Old Town Farmers Market** (Map p125; 301 King St, Old Town, Alexandria; http://alexandriava.gov/farmersmar ket; ☉ 5am-10:30am Sat; Ⓜ King St Metro)
- **USDA Farmers Market** (Map p54; Department of Agriculture Building, cnr 12th St & Independence Ave NW; ☉ 10am-2pm Fri; Ⓜ Smithsonian)

In addition, Fresh Farm Market (☎ 202-362-8889; www.freshfarmmarket.org) holds four regular markets in the city; they're one of the leaders of the Chesapeake Bay region local food movement, so more power to 'em. See their calendar at www.freshfarmmarket.org/calendar.php, or just go directly to:

- **Dupont Circle Market** (Map p96; 1560 20th St NW; ☉ 9am-1pm Apr-Jan, from 10am Dec-Mar; Ⓜ Dupont Circle)
- **Foggy Bottom Market** (Map p64; cnr I St & New Hampshire Ave; ☉ 2:30-7pm Wed Apr-Nov 25; Ⓜ Foggy Bottom-GWU)
- **H St Market** (Map pp78–9; 625 H St NE; ☉ 9am-noon Sat May-Nov 21; Ⓜ Foggy Bottom-GWU)
- **Penn Quarter Market** (Map p88; 450 8th St NW; ☉ 3-7pm Thu Apr-Dec 17; Ⓜ Gallery Pl-Chinatown, Archives-Navy Memorial)

charcuterie and cheese plates, filled with meat and fermented milk sourced from the area.

ARDEO'S Map p114 Wine Bar $$

☎ 202-244-6750; www.ardeorestaurant.com; 3311 Connecticut Ave NW; mains $12-26, small plates $9-14; ☉ dinner daily, brunch Sun; Ⓜ Cleveland Park

Ardeo's is one of the original small plates/ wine bars in the city, and still one of the best. There's a lot of rich pastas, fresh fish and juicy meat selections, plus a few salads and sandwiches. Try a local specialty like succulent, pan-roasted rockfish served with a ragout of prosciutto, sweet corn and plantains. The combo selections of wine and saki are excellent, and a good way of starting a long night.

BUCK'S FISHING & CAMPING
Map p114 American $$

☎ 202-364-0777; www.bucksfishingandcamping .com; 5031 Connecticut Ave; mains $14-26; ☉ dinner Tue-Sun; Ⓜ Tenley Town

We love Buck's for its vibe: haute lakeside fishing camp. Really? Yep – modern banquettes, canoes on the walls. The food is American comfort cooking at its best, with the kitchen cranking out chicken livers on toast and wood-grilled snapper. The no-reservations policy means you'll be waiting ages for a seat on weekend evenings, but when you do score one of the chairs at the communal tables you could be sharing it with your state's senator and the guy selling books at the coffee shop across the street.

PALENA Map p114 American $$$

☎ 202-537-9250; www.palenarestaurant
.com; 3529 Connecticut Ave NW; mains from $30;
🕑 5:30pm-10pm Tue-Sat; Ⓜ Cleveland Park

Set a night aside with a loved one or a
good friend and get ready for a culinary
ride past the limits of taste into innovative
gastro-orgasm land. Palena's menu defies
our conventions, deliciously; Swiss chard
served in ink ravioli, sturgeon wrapped in
pancetta, a guinea hen with pomerol and
foie fras, chestnut soup dressed with celery
and, yes, octopus (?!). The approach, as you
may have sussed out, is often unexpected;
the rewards are uniformly delicious. The
interior is warm but oddly modern in its
crafted rusticity, but to see or eat any of the
above, book early.

NORTHERN VIRGINIA

Northern Virginia offers two kinds of eating
experiences: cheap ethnic eateries, mainly in
Arlington, and more upscale, traditional sit-
down fare, plus a fair few pub-grub type spots,
in Alexandria. Of course genres aren't limited
to specific towns, and there's some good food
in the long strips of development between
NoVa's two main towns.

ARLINGTON

RAY'S HELL BURGER Map p122 Burgers $

☎ 703-841-0001; 1713 Wilson Blvd; burgers from
$7; 🕑 lunch Tue-Sun, dinner daily; Ⓜ Rosslyn

Do Ray's burgers taste as good as they
sound? Hell yes. What makes them
hellish(ly good)? The free jalapenos, and
the massive amounts of meat, and the way
the meat drip kinda melts the bun the way
your dad's burgers did, and any of the stu-
pendous cheeses you can melt on that bad
boy. Barack Obama and Joe Biden came
here for impromptu burgers right after they
got into office; needless to say, everyone
who was just kinda waiting at the counter
sort of had the meal of their lives.

WEENIE BEENIE off Map p122 American $

☎ 703-671-6661; 2680 S Shirlington Rd; under
$10; 🕑 6am-6pm

Ah Weenie, thy half-smokes descend upon
mine tongue like a benediction of sausage-y
grace from on high, melting upon the
mouth of the hungry with thy spicy chili top-
ping and onions – so sweet! – and mustard

and cheese – so greasy! – leaving upon the
memory naught but sweet remembrance,
until next I hold you, piping fresh buns and
all, 'twixt my fingers, which even now long
for thy half-smoky goodness. Your barbecue
ain't half bad either, to come to think of it.

MYANMAR off Map p122 Burmese $

☎ 703-289-0013; 7810 Lee Hwy; mains under $10;
🕑 11am-10pm

Myanmar's decor is barebones; the service
is slow; the portions are small; and the food
is delicious. This is home-cooked Burmese:
curries cooked with lots of garlic, turmeric
and oil, chili fish, mango salads and chicken
swimming in rich gravies. Try the *mohingar*,
the Burmese take on Southeast Asian noodle soup: thin noodles, plump bits of fish
and a garlicky, in-depth complexity that
will have you smiling into the bottom of
your soon-to-be-empty bowl. For an ethnic
eating experience, it doesn't get much
more authentic.

EL POLLO RICO Map p122 Chicken $

☎ 703-522-3220; www.ilovethischicken.com; 932
N Kenmore St; chicken with sides $5-12; 🕑 11am-
10pm; Ⓜ Clarendon, Virginia Sq-GMU

Drooling locals have flocked to this Peruvian chicken joint for decades now in
search of tender, juicy, flavor-packed birds
served with succulent (highly addictive)
dipping sauces, crunchy fries and sloppy
'slaw – lines form outside the door come
dinnertime. EPR is one of the first purveyors
of Peruvian chicken in the metro area, and
age hasn't hurt quality at one of the original kings of *polla a la brasa*.

FOUR SISTERS off Map p122 Vietnamese $

☎ 703-539-8566; www.foursistersrestaurant.com;
8190 Strawberry Lane; mains $8-14; 🕑 11am-
10pm; Ⓜ Dunn Loring-Merrifield

Four Sisters is, and has been for some time,
the best Vietnamese food in the DC metro
area. Originally located in the Eden Center
strip mall, the business this joint raked in
has allowed it to open new digs in a stand-
alone location. That says something about
their confidence, by the way – shutting
down your business and building a new location isn't an easy move, but the clientele
have roared back to the new Four Sisters.
The food is a trek through the endless varieties of Vietnamese cuisine, from Northern-
style *bun cha* (pork with rice noodles) to

clay pot fish to rice-paper crepes. The food is deceptively simple and the execution is flawless; eat here, and you will not leave disappointed. It's about a mile from the nearest Metro, so you may want to drive.

ABAY MARKET off Map p122   Ethiopian $

☎ 703-998-5322; 3811 S George Mason Dr, Falls Church; mains from $13; ☽ lunch & dinner

Tucked into a strip mall between a bunch of hideous apartment blocks and corporate towers is the best Ethiopian food we've had in the metro area. Abay is the real deal, run by an Ethiopian former air-force officer, with clientele straight out of Addis and food that will no doubt blow your mind – if you're adventurous. Because this ain't for the faint of heart. Abay specializes in raw or barely cooked meat, either ground up and cooked with spices (and, according to the owner, a bit of Coca-Cola), *kifto* style, or served in intimidating, chewy, and for our money, delicious slabs, yellow fat still definitely attached. The above comes with a very soft cheese that adds a nice, creamy complement, and should be sopped up with spongy *injera* bread. You'll need to drive to get out here, but it's cheaper than flying to the Horn of Africa, which is about the only way to beat Abay for authenticity.

YECHON off Map p122   Korean $

☎ 703-914-4646; www.yechonrestaurant.com; 4121 Hummer Rd, Annandale; mains $10-15; ☽ 24hr; Ⓜ Rosslyn

Annandale, a suburb on the edge of the beltway west of Arlington and Alexandria, is the center of the Washington, DC Korean community – and as you'd guess, the Korean culinary scene. Debates over who does the best Korean in the DC area have been the source of much gastronomic bickering; we like Yechon. It's an oldie but a goodie, always packed with Koreans (good sign) and curious Westerners. The *kalbi* is rich, smoky and, well, *meaty* – it's fantastic stuff, true stick-to-your-ribs Seoul food (get it? Ha ha). Contrast it with the complex seaweed and searing kimchi and this is a Korean feast that is affordable, delicious and (important point coming) *open 24/7*. Nothing works off the *soju* like 3am tofu and chili, after all…

ALEXANDRIA

MISHA'S COFFEE ROASTER
Map p125   Cafe $

☎ 703-548-4089; 102 S. Patrick St; ☽ 6am-8pm, from 6:30am Sun; pastries $3; Ⓜ King St Metro

Sip a lovely latte next to jars of strong-smelling beans imported from Indonesia and Ethiopia, bang out your play on your laptop (or procrastinate with the free wi-fi), check out the cute nerds at the other tables and reach caffeinated Nirvana at this very hip hangout.

EAMONN'S DUBLIN CHIPPER
Map p125   British $

☎ 703-299-8384; www.eamonnsdublinchipper .com; 728 King St; mains under $10; ☽ 11:30am-11pm, to 1am Fri & Sat; Ⓜ King St Metro

Right; we know it's a 'Dublin' chipper, but it serves fish and chips and we say that's

---

I JUST HAD FIVE GUYS AND IT WAS FANTASTIC!!!

No, that's not the first chapter of a nymphomaniac's confessional – it's a Facebook status posted by a friend of a friend of this author. Everyone who read it laughed, then nodded sagely.

Five Guys is arguably the best fast-food chain the DC area has ever produced. The Guys serve, in short, burgers, hot dogs and shakes, proof that KISS – keep it simple, stupid – is a good philosophy. That goes for the decor too, by the way: the barren white walls and boxes of (free!) peanuts that are the Five Guys trademark are oddly comforting in their sterility.

The chain got its start in Arlington back in 1986 (the original location is no more), but they didn't start expanding and franchising until 2001. Quantity usually hurts quality, and this writer will admit he never had Five Guys before they became a chain, but like many others he believes they're still slinging some quality product. The chain has been voted 'best burger' in town by too many publications to list here. There are now over 400 locations across the Eastern seaboard, and the chain is ubiquitous in DC, Maryland and Virginia.

The Five Guys philosophy is DIY: you order your meat, then choose your toppings (we like jalapenos, hot sauce, mushrooms and grilled onions). It's hard to get a better burger, drink and fries (cooked in glorious peanut oil) in these parts for under $10, so in conclusion, we say to our California friends: In-N-Out, eat your heart out.

British cuisine. And you'll find no better execution of the genre than at this upscale temple to battered and fried potato. How authentic is it? Folks: they import the mushy peas and deep-fried Mars Bars (and Milky Way and Snickers!) on request. Like many resto-pubs in this part of Old Town, Eamonn's is a good place for a drink on weekend nights.

KING STREET BLUES Map p125 Southern $

☎ 703-836-8800; www.kingstreetblues.com; 112 N Saint Asaph St; early bird special $7, mains from $10; Ⓜ King St Metro

King Street Blues is a crazy Southern 'roadhouse' diner that serves really good baked meatloaf, country-fried steak, Southern fried catfish and other diner favorites. The interior is strewn with colorful papier-mâché figures floating across its three levels, while shiny chrome furniture and multicolored tablecloths lend an attractive retro air. Live blues is played on Thursday nights.

TIFFANY TAVERN Map p125 Bar-Restaurant $

☎ 703-739-4265; www.tiffanytavern.com; 1116 King St; mains from $10; 🕓 5pm-midnight Mon-Thu, to 2am Fri & Sat; Ⓜ King St Metro

Besides serving excellent pub grub, Tiffany's is one of the best bluegrass venues around. It gets a little rough and a lot raucous on the best nights, when Yuengling on tap, mandolin and fiddle equal hours of roots music magic.

GADSBY'S TAVERN RESTAURANT

Map p125 American $$$

☎ 703-548-1288; www.gadsbystavernrestaurant.com; 138 N Royal St; mains $22-30; 🕓 lunch & dinner; Ⓜ King St Metro

Set in the building of an 18th-century tavern, Gadsby's is named after the Englishman who operated the tavern from 1796 to 1808 (when it was the center of Alexandria's social life). This place tries to emulate an 18th-century hostelry; the overall effect is rather kitsch, but it's good, clean, historical fun. Besides, who wouldn't want to try 'George Washington's Favorite' (duck stuffed with tart fruit and topped with Madeira gravy)?

RESTAURANT EVE Map p125 American $$$

☎ 703-706-0450; 110 S Pitt St; www.restauranteve.com; mains from $35, tasting menus from $105; Ⓜ King St Metro

While 'fusion' may be an overused adjective when it comes to describing restaurants, the best kitchens always fuse. Innovation and tradition, regional and international influences, comfort and class. Eve contains everything we have described, a combination of great American ingredients, precise French technique and some of the highest levels of service we've encountered in the area. Splurge here and opt for the tasting menus, which are simply on another level of gastronomic experience. This is one of the few vegan-friendly high-end restaurants in the DC metro area; just make sure to call a day ahead and chef-owner Cathal Armstrong's team will be happy to accommodate you.

NIGHTLIFE

top picks

For a city of its size, DC has a surfeit of nightspots. It's that damned work ethic, which translates into a stronger play ethic once the lights go down. This is a city that knows how to enjoy itself.

There's a lot of variety for your going-out experience these days, an incredible amount really, given DC's diminutive dimensions. Megaclubs? '*Thumpa-thumpa-thumpa* What? I can't hear you!' – er, yeah. We got those, especially near Penn Quarter. Smaller but just as pretentious lounges filled with just as beautiful people? Try Georgetown, or parts of Adams-Morgan and U St. Many of the city's best restaurants host the capital's best bars, so it's easy to kill two birds with one establishment if you're planning a dinner and drinks kind of night.

Neighborhood bars and cozy pubs? Well, they're all around the city's neighborhoods (imagine that), but we reckon the best ones are in Columbia Heights and Capitol Hill. Some are locals-type joints for an older crowd, some are frat-boy-style keg-o-ramas, and some sleek newcomers serve the discerning, hip DC drinker who wants a touch of sophistication accenting their local watering hole.

Dives and live-music venues are admittedly an area where some improvement could be called for. That's why we should all send a thank you note to the folks working the Black Cat and the Atlas District, a strip of fun joints all along H St NE. Some of the city's grungier neighborhood bars and pubs can also probably claim 'dive' status – hell, they'd be proud of it. There are some excellent jazz clubs in this town as well; most people can't go wrong looking for them in the U St area.

The different scenes here remain distinct in their DC clique-y way – think punk versus disco crowds in the 1970s – but they're integrating more and more. Most Democrats and Republicans seem able to recognize the true enemy isn't the other party, but their boss, who just saddled them with so much damn paperwork for the evening. In turn, they find common cause in sinking a few frosty ones together in low-lit pubs.

The drinking age in DC – as in the rest of the US – is 21. There are a lot of young foreigners here traveling, studying and working for embassies and international institutions. If you count yourself among these ranks, don't forget to take your passport out at night – you will get carded (asked for ID).

The best place to find out what's happening is the free weekly *Washington City Paper* (issued Thursday) or the monthly *On Tap,* both available in heaps at the entrances of stores and clubs. A more mainstream resource is the Weekend section of the Friday *Washington Post.* The free *Washington Blade,* available at stores and clubs, gives the scoop on gay and lesbian happenings.

OPENING HOURS

DC is a city that likes its drinking, but it doesn't stay out particularly late. Nor does it go home unreasonably early. Most bars open between 5pm and 6pm and stay open till 2am on weekdays, 3am on Friday and Saturday and 1am on Sunday. Some places – the ones that double as restaurants – open at 11:30am (if you *really* need to get your drink on). We've included hours in our reviews if they differ from this template.

WHAT TO WEAR

Washingtonian night dress code jukes it out between ultra laid-back, surreptitiously flashy and boringly conservative. In most of the bars we've reviewed you can come as you are – although you might feel out of place, we've seen folks rock into swish Poste (p177) in shorts, sandals and a T-shirt. In some bars and most clubs this look won't fly; closed-toed shoes and long pants are required, and *very* occasionally you have to leave the jeans at home. Some clubs also have rules about hats, which is as much of an antigang practice as playing fashion police. Women are rarely denied admission anywhere as long as they're not wearing a hoodie and sweatpants. For years (and this is a kind of depressing realization), the usual uniform of a DC guy out on the town has been a button-up shirt tucked into pants – even the most liberal activist ends up looking like Joe Young Republican at some stage. However, this rule isn't hard and fast, and there's more daring dress in edgier bars.

WHITE HOUSE AREA & FOGGY BOTTOM

College kids, doctors and journalists co-exist in this neighborhood. For the most part the vibe is sort of white-yuppie-meets-college-scruffy at the local pub, although there are some genuine wheeler-dealer bars in the bigger hotels.

FROGGY BOTTOM PUB
Map p64   Student Bar
☎ 202-338-3000; 2142 Pennsylvania Ave NW;
Ⓜ Foggy Bottom-GWU
This popular GWU hangout attracts students with grub-and-pub deals, a frat-boy-esque atmosphere and the sort of shot specials that make you want to down a lot of hard alcohol very quickly. As you might have guessed, things can get messy in here, but in a good, all-American college kinda way.

LE BAR Map p64   Hotel Bar
☎ 202-730-8800; Sofitel Lafayette Square, 806 15th St NW; Ⓨ 10am-midnight; Ⓜ McPherson Sq
Ah, Le Bar, *elle est si belle*. This is the kind of spot you should rightly enter in a trench coat in the midst of occupied Paris whilst delivering secret documents to a very attractive member of the Resistance…er, we're getting carried away again, aren't we? But seriously, that's kind of the vibe: all chandelier-like European glitz mixed with a bit of Washington power-player muscle, a heady combination that's as strong as the bourbon. The outdoor patio is wonderful on spring and humid summer nights.

MCFADDEN'S Map p64   Student Bar
☎ 202-223-2338; 2401 Pennsylvania Ave NW;
Ⓜ Foggy Bottom-GWU
There's a certain age when bars like McFadden's stop being fun – we reckon it's around 16. That doesn't stop loads *(loads)* of GWU students from swarming in here, making out in the corner, watching the female staff do *Coyote Ugly* dances on the bar, dancing on the bar themselves and spending their parents' college money on Jagerbombs. Needless to say, it's tons of fun if this is your scene.

OFF THE RECORD Map p64   Hotel Bar
☎ 202-638-6600; Hay-Adams Hotel, cnr H & 16th Sts NW; Ⓨ 11:30am-midnight Sun-Thu, to 12:30am Fri & Sat; Ⓜ McPherson Sq
Chintzy chairs, brass fixtures, Manhattan cocktails, location in the basement of one of the city's most prestigious hotels, the Hay-Adams (p203), and right across from the White House. If you came to DC to see important people get drunk, saunter on down to Off the Record (there's a reason it has the name – the politicos who imbibe here don't need the nearby reporters capturing their quotes). The on-site Steinway piano was a gift from the Kennedy family.

POV Map p64   Lounge
☎ 202-661-2400; W Hotel Washington, 515 15th St NW; Ⓜ Metro Center
The sky terrace of POV, which sits atop the W Hotel Washington (p204) is one of the best spots to watch the sunset on a hot summer night. From the rooftop the entire city stretches out in front of you, and the panoramic view is nothing short of spectacular. The actual drinks are great too (although do you ever pay for them) – there's a healthy respect for mixology here, and you won't find the sort of watered-down pre-mixes that occasionally rear their ugly heads in other bars around town.

ROUND ROBIN Map p64   Hotel Bar
☎ 202-628-9100; Willard Inter-Continental Hotel, 1401 Pennsylvania Ave NW; Ⓨ 4:30pm-1am Sun-Thu, from 3pm Fri, from noon Sat; Ⓜ Metro Center
The bar at the Willard Inter-Continental Hotel (p205) is likely the most famous drinking institution in the city. The word 'lobbyist' was invented here during the Grant administration, and too many politicians, heads of state, journalists and other bigwigs have passed through for this book to list. The small, circular drinking space is done up in Gilded Age accents, all dark wood and 19th-century flourishes, and while it's a bit tourist-y, you'll still see folks here likely determining your latest tax hike over a single-malt Scotch.

GEORGETOWN

M St is lined with all sorts of bars and pubs, many of which are close clones – British-style pubs with lots of heavy wood and dark nooks. Home to Georgetown University, this neighborhood attracts a young crowd with money to burn (drinks can be amazingly expensive). Tony & Joes Seafood Place (☎ 202-965-1789; Georgetown Waterfront; ☽ lunch-late; 🚌 shuttle from Foggy Bottom-GWU Metro) is meh for the seafood, but we like it as a spot for waterfront drinking.

BIRRERIA PARADISO Map p72 Bar
☎ 202-337-1245; 3282 M St NW; 🚌 Georgetown shuttle, DC Circulator

The basement of Pizzeria Paradiso (p150) is Birreria Paradiso, Italian for 'paradise of birreria.' OK, beer. Despite the low-level environs, the place gets lots of sunlight and has a warm Mediterranean vibe, but look, you're here for some hops, and you won't be disappointed: the menu feels something like an atlas for beer lovers who want to engage in some sudsy globetrotting.

BLUES ALLEY Map p72 Jazz Bar
☎ 202-337-4141; www.bluesalley.com; 1073 Rear Wisconsin Ave; admission from $15; ☽ shows 8pm & 10pm; 🚌 Georgetown shuttle, DC Circulator

Calling the Alley an establishment is like calling the Lincoln Memorial a landmark. If you grew up around the way, your parents likely went on dates here to watch greats like Dizzy Gillespie back in the day. The talent is just as sterling these days, and the setting just as sophisticated. If big names are playing, you'll want to reserve a ticket a fair bit in advance.

MIE N YU Map p72 Lounge
☎ 202-337-1245; 3282 M St NW; 🚌 Georgetown shuttle, DC Circulator

Georgetown's most popular lounge-bar is also an Asian-Mediterranean-Middle-Eastern-kitchen-sink fusion restaurant, but we come to see really, really good-looking people sip really, really expensive drinks. It can be a bit pretentious at times, but if you're into the slick lounge-itini scene, this will be right up your alley.

MR SMITH'S Map p72 Bar
☎ 202-333-3104; 3104 M St NW; 🚌 Georgetown shuttle, DC Circulator

This is as divey as they come in Georgetown – sawdust and dusky interior concealing patrons that only get more rowdy and roaring with the night. That said, Mr Smith's is as popular with Georgetown Jonathan as Average Joe, which makes for an intriguing and generally affable atmosphere.

RHINO BAR & PUMP HOUSE
Map p72 Sports Bar
☎ 202-333-3150; 3295 M St NW; 🚌 Georgetown shuttle, DC Circulator

This is a good spot to see Hoyas behaving badly – a college-age crowd checks its inhibitions at the door here most weekends. DJs play dance music on weekends, and the scene gets crazy in an undergrad kinda way, but for the rest of the week this is pretty much the bar for watching sports and downing wings in the Georgetown area.

SALOUN Map p72 Jazz Bar
☎ 202-965-4900; 3239 M St NW; admission from $5; 🚌 Georgetown shuttle, DC Circulator

More casual and cheaper than better-known Georgetown venue Blues Alley (left), the Saloun attracts patrons who are younger, less polished, but more fun. The mostly local acts play jazz during the week and blues and Motown on weekends. There are 18 beers on tap and Cajun food to soak up all the liquor swirling inside your tummy.

SEQUOIA Map p72 Bar
☎ 202-944-4200; Georgetown Harbor, 3000 K St; 🚌 Georgetown shuttle, DC Circulator

On a steamy summer night, Sequoia's patio is the spot to be. Plop down on a plastic chair on its cascading terrace overlooking the Potomac and check out the rich people messing around in boats. Or fight your way through the throng at the bar, grab an overpriced Corona, then start flirting and talking politics with the hottie of your choice. This bar attracts all types – from pretty gays to trustafarian college kids to 30-something lawyers – and has a reputation as a pick-up spot.

TOMBS Map p72 Student Bar
☎ 202-337-6668; 1226 36th St NW; ☽ 11:30am-2am Mon-Thu, to 3am Fri, 11am-3am Sat, 9:30am-1:15am Sun; 🚌 Georgetown shuttle, DC Circulator

Every school of a certain pedigree has 'that' bar – the one where faculty and students alike sip pints and play darts under athletic regalia of the old school. The Tombs are Georgetown's contribution to the genre, and also happened to be a shooting set for St Elmo's Fire. The house is usually filled with students, professors and the occasional Jesuit priest; walls are decked with rowing accoutrement and, oddly, WWI-era posters.

CAPITOL HILL & SOUTHEAST DC

You'd think the drinking here was all about acting the part of the power player, and to a degree, this is true. But the secret to the Capitol Hill scene is coming off as nonchalant; this is a result of the anti-elitism elitism demonstrated by so many DC residents, who don't like coming off as connected as they are. The atmosphere on Capitol Hill, still very much a residential neighborhood, is one of cozy pubs where policy talk gives way to Redskins predictions. H St NE, otherwise known as the Atlas District (p176), is a lovingly funky contrast to the Hill's red-brick conviviality.

18TH AMENDMENT Map pp78-9 Bar
☎ 202-543-3622; 613 Pennsylvania Ave SE;
Ⓜ Eastern Market, Capitol South

The amendment embraces a speakeasy theme – hence the name. Gangsters and bootleggers should head directly to the basement, where the furniture is made from beer barrels and whiskey crates, and there are pool tables on which to fight your duel. Upstairs there's a late-1920s art-deco air, reminiscent of prohibition-era Chicago. It has ample seating and eight beers on tap.

GRANVILLE MOORE'S Map pp78-9 Pub
☎ 202-399-2546; 1238 H St NE; Ⓜ Union Station

Besides being one of the best places to grab a steak sandwich in the District (p154), Granville Moore's has an extensive Belgian beer menu that should satisfy any fan of low-country boozing. With its raw, wooden fixtures and walls that look as if they were made from daub and mud, the interior resembles nothing so much as a medieval barracks; when they get the fire going in here, this is one of our favorite bars to repair into on a cold winter night.

H STREET COUNTRY CLUB
Map pp78-9 Bar
☎ 202-399-4722; 1335 H St NE; Ⓜ Union Station

The Country Club is two levels of fantasticness: the bottom floor is packed with pool tables, skeeball and shuffleboard, while the top contains (seriously) its own minigolf course ($7 to play), done up to resemble a tour of the city on a small scale. You putt-putt past a trio of Lego lobbyists, through Beltway traffic snarls and past a King Kong–

clad Washington monument. The whole vibe of the place just facilitates a relaxed atmosphere where it's very easy to strike up conversations with strangers – if you're shy and new to town, we'd highly recommend joining the Country Club, as it's hard to leave here without hitting up some random in conversation ('Nice chip, dude').

HAWK & DOVE Map pp78-9 Pub
☎ 202-543-3300; 329 Pennsylvania Ave SE;
Ⓜ Eastern Market

The quintessential Hillie (congressional staff) hangout is dark, intimate and funner than you think; there's political shoptalk, but also good beer, pool and, as the night wears on, the sort of fevered across-the-aisle hookups DC is famous for. Plainly put, it's a great neighborhood pub, the sort of place where people repair after work – it's just that in this neighborhood, the local place of employment is the United States Congress.

KELLY'S IRISH TIMES Map pp78-9 Irish Pub
☎ 202-543-5433; 14 F St NW; ⏰ 11am-2am Sun-Thu, later Fri & Sat; Ⓜ Union Station

Kelly's implores: 'Give me your tired, your hungry, your befuddled masses,' and the masses respond. Fans of the on-tap Guinness and Wednesday to Saturday live music tend to be younger than the patrons next door at the Dubliner – students and staffers and other suds-drinkers. The layout is like every Irish pub you've ever been in, but it's an exemplar of the genre.

LITTLE MISS WHISKEY'S GOLDEN DOLLAR Map pp78-9 Bar
1104 H St NE; Ⓜ Union Station

If Alice got back from Wonderland so traumatized by a near-beheading that she needed to start engaging in heavy drinking, we'd imagine she'd often pop down to Little Miss Whiskey's. She'd love the decor: somewhere between Wonderland's most whimsical moments of surrealism and the dark nightmares of a lost drug addict, all mixed with a heavy dose of Cure video *Goth-Glam*. And she'd probably go apepoo for the excellent beer and whiskey menu, served by savvy bartenders who are hand-picked veterans of the DC nightlife scene. These guys have specifically been selected to run this spot, and as such Little Miss Whiskey's feels like a bartender's bar, although to be fair it gets pretty fun for run-of-the-mill folk who enjoy a weirdly fantastic back patio and the thumping bass of an upstairs dance floor on weekends.

LOLA'S BARRACKS BAR & GRILL
Map pp78-9   Bar

☎ 202-547-5652; 711 8th St SE; ☉ 11am-2am Sun-Thu, to 3am Fri & Sat; Ⓜ Eastern Market

If the Ugly Mug (opposite) is the 20-something's bar of choice around this stretch of Eastern Market–adjacent Capitol Hill, Lola's is geared more toward 30-somethings and older. The mood is darker, a little more sophisticated – this is a spot to watch Cap Hill professionals drink wine instead of shots, although Lola's isn't sedate by any stretch. It's just that the buzz here is low and constant, compared with the roar at the spots next door.

PALACE OF WONDERS
Map pp78-9   Freak Show

☎ 202-398-7469; 1210 H St NE; Ⓜ Union Station

The Palace was one of the leaders of the charge that turned H St NE into one of the coolest parts of the capital. It is, frankly, what DC has always needed: a semipermanent freak show. Upstairs is a circus of oddities, local genius James Taylor's museum of the odd, twisted and awesome. Downstairs is a kickin' bar that attracts a pretty punk-ish crowd; on weekends, a cover charge (usually around $20) gets you in for all-night performances of sword-swallowing, flea circuses, fire eating and magic tricks. It's extremely fun, and what DC needed to offset its admittedly large preppie population.

PHASE ONE Map pp78–9   Lesbian Bar

☎ 202-544-6831; 525 8th St SE; ☉ 7pm-2am Wed-Sun; Ⓜ Eastern Market

'The Phase' claims to be the oldest lesbian bar in the country; it's certainly the best

lesbian dive in DC, not that there's much competition for the crown. It's great, friendly fun by any measure, chockablock with jelly wrestling, free pizza nights and an unpretentious but raucous enough atmosphere for ladies on the prowl. Come early to mingle in peace and quiet, or late to shake your booty on the packed dance floor. Line-dancing lessons and a pool tournament take place on Sundays.

RED AND BLACK Map pp78-9   Live Dive

☎ 202-399-3201; 1212 H St NE; Ⓜ Union Station

The Red and Black claims to be a New Orleans–style bar, and we'll accept that assessment. There are no brass bands rolling through, but if there were they wouldn't feel out of place in this wooden shack, which has all the dilapidated charm of the best parts of the Big Easy. This is first and foremost a live-music venue, where sets are played so up-close and personal you feel like you could kiss the singers (that's probably a bad idea, as they tend to be tatted graduates of the rock-and-roll school of hard knocks). Bartenders are friendly, and when the R&B isn't hosting a ripping show, it feels like a friendly-as-hell neighborhood joint.

ROCK & ROLL HOTEL Map pp78-9   Live Dive

☎ 202-388-7625; 1353 H St NE; Ⓜ Union Station

The Hilton this hotel ain't, unless the Hilton went to hell and came back on a screaming motorcycle while wailing on guitars made of fire. Right; that's a tad hyperbolic, but this is a great, grotty spot to catch rockin' live sets. Don't let the name fool you; this hotel hosts all kinds of music genres. This author is about to go catch an Afrofunk show there, and some of the city's freshest hip-hop acts grace the stage as well.

THE ATLAS DISTRICT ASCENDANT

H St NE between 12th and 14th Sts was once one of Washington's major shopping strips. That was before the race riots of 1968, which sadly gutted the area. No more – this is one of DC's interesting areas once again thanks to a rapid profusion of bars, restaurants and entertainment venues over the past few years. The quick rise is all the more interesting given that this was once, if not the ghetto, a poorer part of town that was rarely visited by outsiders. The whole thing is flanked by two Chinese takeout places – Danny's and Good Danny's (we can't tell you which one is better) – and anchored by the Atlas Performing Arts Center (p191). This beautiful deco structure has lent its name to what is now known as the Atlas District, or more commonly the H St Corridor (or just H St). The neighborhood is one of the best places for dinner and drinks in the city, a place where new and old DC seem to not so much collide as mesh – we just love it. The Atlas District is about a 25-minute walk from Union Station, but a free shuttle (☎ 301-751-1802) runs a few times per hour from Union Station to H St and there are plans to extend that service to the Chinatown Metro station.

ROSE'S DREAM BAR & LOUNGE

Map pp78-9   Club

☎ 202-398-5700; 1370 H St NE; Ⓜ Union Station

Go-go, the DC style of local music that's a cross between funk and an improvised drum line, occasionally dusted with a bit of hip-hop, has been a fading genre in the District. But Rose's keeps the beat alive. It's one of the few go-go clubs left where a white out-of-towner won't feel like they're interloping in someone else's territory; the clientele is primarily black, but this is a mixed crowd as these things go. Coming here is a DC cultural experience – go-go really is the city's own brand of music, re-sented in cities as close as Baltimore – but beyond that Rose's is plenty fun, with good bartenders working the line and karaoke, dance nights and live shows blowing up the house for the better part of the week.

UGLY MUG Map pp78-9   Sports Bar

☎ 202-547-8459; 723 8th St SE; ⏰ 11:30am-1:30am Sun-Thu, to 3am Fri & Sat; Ⓜ Eastern Market

The Mug's typical of the dives in this part of town: kinda grotty, but self-consciously so, attracting an interesting mix of preppie Hill-rats, Marines from the nearby barracks and Capitol Hill locals. The predominating crowd is usually pretty loud and raucous, making this the 8th St SE option for those wanting a bit more frattish ambience.

DOWNTOWN & PENN QUARTER

Downtown is mainly known for its VIP club scene, but a lot of these clubs are insuffer-able – long lines, aggressive bouncers, and expensive, watered-down drinks. Hit up some of the local bars instead. Penn Quarter and Chinatown are both good nightlife bets, easy transition spaces between sports-bar boozing and house-music-fueled cruising.

DA'S RFD WASHINGTON Map p88   Bar

☎ 202-289-2030; 810 7th St NW; ⏰ 11am-2am Sun-Thu, to 3am Fri & Sat; Ⓜ Gallery Pl-Chinatown

RFD – the initials stand for 'Real Food and Drink,' although the food is just greasy bar fare – has one of the most extensive beer menus in town. Compared with other bars of the 'hundreds of varieties' of booze genre, RFD has a slick, corporate feel, but the service is fast, it's rarely out of any one

brand and the actual drinking space is huge; if you've got a large group, this is a good spot to hit up.

GREEN LANTERN & TOOL SHED

Map p88   Gay Bar

☎ 202-347-4533; 1335 Green Ct NW; Ⓜ McPherson Sq

The gay Green Lantern is downstairs, with leather-lovers' Tool Shed on the 2nd floor. This place attracts a slightly older crowd, and there are all kinds of daily promotions – tea dances on Sundays, free beer for shirt-less men Thursday nights (10pm to 11pm), Monday karaoke etc. The Lantern has a nice, long happy hour too – from 4pm till at least 9pm, sometimes till close. All in all there's a hairier, bear-ier crowd here, so if you like 'em young and waxed, stick to Dupont.

POSTE Map p88   Lounge

☎ 202-783-6060; Hotel Monaco, 555 8th St NW; ⏰ to 10pm; Ⓜ Gallery Pl-Chinatown

Located in the back of the Hotel Monaco (p210), Poste is a fantastic spot for a strong cocktail and some eye candy. The bartenders take their trade seriously and they serve genuine absinthe, which is a sure method of getting yourself silly. The outdoor courtyard is an enormous, friendly space that's especially lovely on humid summer nights, while the interior resembles a mod-ish '60s bachelor pad done up with quite a bit of contempo-rary flash.

ROCKET BAR Map p88   Pool

☎ 202-628-7665; 714 7th St NW; Ⓜ Gallery Pl-Chinatown

Rocket Bar is an almost inexplicably popu-lar pool hall, although there's lots more going on than some stick – shuffle board, Golden Tee, all the oldies and goodies. It's a good spot on the singles' circuit, especially if you're looking for a place to check out members of the opposite sex without all the pomp, circumstance and dressing up that comes with a night of clubbing.

DUPONT CIRCLE & KALORAMA

DC's gay and lesbian nightlife Mecca, this neighborhood is packed with bars ranging from raunchy to ritzy. Regardless of your sexual orientation, there's something to keep you drinking around the circle. Chill coffee houses, super-sleek lounges and ramshackle joints known for cheap happy hours abound.

18TH STREET LOUNGE Map p96 Lounge
☎ 202-466-3922; 1212 18th St NW; admission free-$20; ⏰ 9:30pm-2am Tue & Wed, 5:30pm-2am Thu, 5:30pm-3am Fri, 9:30pm-3am Sat; Ⓜ Dupont Circle

The lack of a sign on the door proclaims the exclusivity of this swanky yet cozy club. In a beautiful mansion that once housed Teddy Roosevelt, its sleek dance floors are ruled by hip-hop and dub and ridiculously good-looking people. The decor ranges from gold upholstered couches and candelabras to blue walls, gilded mirrors, marble tables and flickering candles. The club is famed for bouncers leaving lesser patrons waiting in the cold, and was founded by local legends Thievery Corporation. Boys, leave the denim and sneakers behind.

APEX Map p96 Gay Club
☎ 202-296-0505; 1415 22nd St NW; admission from $10; ⏰ 9pm-2am Tue, to 3am Thu, to 4am Fri & Sat; Ⓜ Dupont Circle

One of the crown jewels of the gay P St dance-club scene, Apex brings out the college kids and buff boys in droves, especially on Friday. Apex is a meat market and everyone here knows it, so it's pretty fun for those just wanting to dance and those looking to cruise in about equal measure.

BEACON MARTINI SKY-BAR
Map p96 Lounge
☎ 202-872-1126; Beacon Hotel & Corporate Quarters, 1615 Rhode Island Ave NW; ⏰ May-Oct; Ⓜ Dupont Circle

On top of the swank Beacon Hotel, this patio on the roof offers ample sky-high (well, for DC) city views and an opportunity to mingle with new friends over signature martinis. Events are often held here, and while it can get crowded, this is a cool spot to listen to a DJ spin while surveying the greater capital area like the pimp you are.

BIG HUNT Map p96 Bar
☎ 202-785-2333; 1345 Connecticut Ave NW; Ⓜ Dupont Circle

If you just said the name of this bar and smiled a little inner smile (or turned red), well, that's kinda the point. The irreverence is carried on inside via two floors of general

tomfoolery, including one of the city's better rooftop patios and some pool, should you need to get some stick on.

BRICKSKELLER INN Map p96 Bar
☎ 202-293-1885; 1523 22nd St NW; Ⓜ Dupont Circle

The ambience is cavernous yet cozy and the staff friendly in the way of aficionados sharing a passion, that being for one of the largest beer menus in the world (over 1000 varieties. No, really). The booze menu runs from Sierra Nevada to brew from Sierra Leone (probably). Aim for a corner seat in the 'Skeller's cellar and soak up the pub-y atmosphere.

BUFFALO BILLIARDS Map p96 Pool
☎ 202-331-7665; 1330 19th St; ⏰ 4pm-2am Mon-Thu, to 3am Fri, 1pm-3am Sat, to 1am Sun; Ⓜ Dupont Circle

The 30 pool and snooker tables pull college kids and yuppies into this bright, below-street-level cave. There's usually a wait for a table, so trash yourself a bit before taking up some stick.

CAFE CITRON Map p96 Club
☎ 202-530-8844; 1343 Connecticut Ave NW; Ⓜ Dupont Circle

So here's the thing, ladies: when guys want to go out dancing, that's usually because they're trying to pick up girls. So here's the thing guys: when girls go out dancing and dress up really hot, they're usually just interested in dancing (or 'letting off steam,' 'chilling with my chicas' etc). Sociology lesson finished, nothing personifies this dichotomy of affairs more than Cafe Citron, one of DC's most popular Latin music bars (in fairness, it plays everything, but the focus is salsa, samba et al). Girls dance; guys watch; night goes on. Then guys come in who actually *can* dance, local guys grumble, girls get happy, realize their dancing partner is gay (not that all guys who can dance are gay, just sayin' it happens a lot, this being Dupont Circle), girls grumble. That whole saga wasn't a knock, by the way; nights out here are really fun, if only to observe the above unfolding epic.

COBALT Map p96 Gay Club
☎ 202-232-4416; 1639 R St NW; Sun-Thu free, Fri & Sat $5; ⏰ 5pm-2am; Ⓜ Dupont Circle

Cobalt pretty much rules the roost of the DC club scene. The music is great, the bartenders are ripped and sufficiently shirtless and the scene is equal parts all about the hook-up and getting down to some good (if pounding) dance music. Honestly, this place is such an epitome of a gay club it ought to come with its own five-piece costume ensemble of an Indian, a cop, a motorcycle rider etc. If you're in the mood for that sort of thing, this is pretty much a guaranteed good time.

HALO Map p96 Gay Bar
☎ 202-797-9730; 1435 P St NW; Ⓜ Dupont Circle
The funny thing about Halo is it looks like it should be a total den of douche-baggery, what with its super-sleek spaceship-style furniture and Euro I'm-too-cool-for-school vibe, but then you go inside and it's a totally friendly, even laid-back gay bar. The crowd is older and accommodating, and generally a joy to be around. This is a great bar for gay meet-and-greet early in the evening, although things definitely get a bit more cruise-y as the night wears on.

FIREFLY Map p96 Bar
☎ 202-861-1310; 1343 Connecticut Ave NW; Ⓨ to 10pm Sun-Thu, to 10:30pm Fri & Sat; Ⓜ Dupont Circle
Firefly is a restaurant first, but we haven't eaten here yet and can't judge it by those merits (other reviews seem to indicate it's quite good on the culinary front). We can say it's one of the coolest bars in Dupont, decked out with its surreal, magically happy 'firefly trees,' all candle-lit and reminiscent of childhood summer evenings, and romantic as hell to boot. The cocktail menu is a glorious thing; knock back an Opal (rum, chai spices and cream) and see if the world doesn't just glow a little more…wait, that's the firefly trees. Whatever – still happy!

JR'S Map p96 Gay Bar
☎ 202-328-0090; 1519 17th St NW; Ⓜ Dupont Circle
At JR's weekday happy hour you might think you've stepped into a living Banana Republic ad: chinos and button-downs are de rigueur at this popular gay hangout frequented by the 20- and 30-something, work-hard and play-hard set. Some DC residents claim that the crowd at JR's epitomizes the conservative nature of the capital's gay scene; but even if you love to hate it, as many do, JR's is the happy-hour spot in town and is packed more often than not.

LAURIOL PLAZA Map p96 Bar
☎ 202-387-0035; 1835 18th St NW; Ⓨ 11:30am-11pm Sun-Thu, to midnight Fri & Sat; Ⓜ Dupont Circle
Lauriol doubles as a decent Mexican restaurant (p158) by day; by night, she's extremely popular with the young and the restless and the hot. The theme being south of the border, most folks go for multicolored margaritas. Y'know, the ones that don't taste like they've got any booze in them, and you really shouldn't have ordered another three but aw whatever man, there's nothing in these…(30 minutes later)…WOOH! YEAH! I LOVE YOU, BRO!

LUCKY BAR Map p96 Bar
☎ 202-331-3733; 1221 Connecticut Ave NW; Ⓜ Dupont Circle
Lucky's interior is nothing special – your standard double-decker dark wood and cozy chairs. It's the crowd that sets it apart: an amalgamation of capital subcultures ranging from politicos, Dupont gay couples, club kids needing a break from *thumpa-thumpa* and the occasional tourist, everyone enjoying each other over a happy booze-fueled drone.

SIGN OF THE WHALE Map p96 Student Bar
☎ 202-785-1110; 1825 M St; Ⓨ 11:30am-1am; Ⓜ Dupont Circle
'They should call this place the sign of the whale tail,' a friend once pithily remarked, commenting on the sartorial state of the female clientele (American slang break: 'whale tail' is a term for the classy sight of a girl's thong underwear peeking above her low-rise jeans). The Sign (which is next to strip club Camelot, speaking of G-strings) attracts a raucous GWU crowd, plus a fair few lawyers, on weekends; on other days of the week it comes off as a pub with low-level buzz.

ADAMS-MORGAN
Adams-Morgan is one of the epicenters of DC nightlife. Simply put, the city rocks to its multicultural beat. You'll find most of the Latino bars and clubs on Columbia Rd, while 18th St is basically the miracle mile of bad behavior in the city on weekend nights. If you're looking for a quiet night out, you'd do best to avoid this area; if you want screaming debauchery, welcome home.

THE BLAGUARD Map p103   Irish Pub
☎ 202-588-7180; 2003 18th St NW; Ⓜ Woodley Park Zoo/Adams Morgan, U Street-Cardozo
The Blaguard, in addition to having an awesome name, is a great bar to finish an Adams-Morgan night on. After you've had too much time dancing and screaming into someone's ear, you want a place that'll keep the party going, but is a few notches lower on the crazy scale than a club. Enter this seedy, sticky, superb Irish pub.

BOSSA Map p103   Lounge
☎ 202-667-0088; 2463 18th St NW; admission free–$10; ☑ 6pm-1am Sun-Thu, to 2am Fri & Sat; Ⓜ Woodley Park Zoo/Adams Morgan
Dark, intimate, close and sexy – that's the scene in this Adams-Morgan watering hole. The soundtrack, if you couldn't guess, grooves: jazz, flamenco and bossa nova played in the candlelit lounge. Come drink mojitos and martinis, and taste the delectable tapas during happy hour.

BUKOM Map p103   Club
☎ 202-265-4600; 2442 18th St NW; ☑ shows 9pm Mon-Thu, 10pm Fri & Sat; Ⓜ Woodley Park Zoo/Adams Morgan
Come see DC's West African expats get their weekend going, and be prepared for sore but happy hips the next morning, 'cause these cats can move. There's an interesting vibe here when the African clientele gets joined by ex–Peace Corps types who've learned their dancing chops in the continent; this is one of those very DC moments when immigrants plus an internationally experienced population merge into one happy scene of dancing goodness.

CHI-CHA LOUNGE Map p103   Lounge
☎ 202-234-8400; 1624 U St NW; ☑ 5:30pm-2am Sun-Thu, to 3am Fri & Sat; Ⓜ U Street-Cardozo
On first thought, Arabic *arguilehs* (hookahs) and Andean food don't seem a felicitous combination, but Chi-Cha makes it work. Curl into velvet settees, nibble Ecuadorian tapas and order a pipe of Bahrainian fruit-and-honey-cured tobacco. A sort of double dose of swarthy clientele pays its respects as a result: Middle Eastern and South American accents are in evidence. Hookahs are available weekdays only.

CHIEF IKE'S MAMBO ROOM
Map p103   Club
☎ 202-332-2211; 1725 Columbia Rd NW; admission downstairs free–$4, upstairs free–$8; ☑ 9pm-2am; Ⓜ Woodley Park Zoo/Adams Morgan
What we love about Ike's is how it's a place to get a good Latin groove going…while surrounded by leering Evil Dead–esque murals of psychedelic voodoo zombies and assorted other undead. There are punk and hip-hop clubs upstairs if you tire of monster movie mambo, but they don't quite match the awesomeness of the whole Mexican Day of the Dead funfest on the bottom floor.

COLUMBIA STATION Map p103   Jazz Bar
☎ 202-462-6040; 2325 18th St NW; admission free; Ⓜ Woodley Park Zoo/Adams Morgan
Columbia Station is an intimate spot to listen to nightly jazz and blues, and if you're on a budget it's especially appealing – it doesn't have a cover charge. It's a good date spot (well, assuming your date likes jazz), with lots of low light and, natch, romantic music.

DAN'S CAFE Map p103   Dive
☎ 202-265-9241; 2315 18th St NW; Ⓜ U Street-Cardozo
Dan's dive is all the more grotty for its location: smack in the middle of the 18th St skimpy-skirt parade. Inside this barely signed bar is dim lighting, old locals, J Crew–looking types slumming it and flasks of whiskey, coke and a bucket of ice on sale for under $12(!). This is one of DC's great dives; the interior looks like the sort of place an evil Elks Club would have designed, all un-ironically old school 'art,' cheap paneling and dim lights barely illuminating the unapologetic sluminess.

FELIX Map p103   Club
☎ 202-483-3549; 2406 18th St; Ⓜ Woodley Park Zoo/Adams Morgan
Lines form early on weekend nights when the beautiful people flock to this beautiful lounge to drown beautiful sorrows in beautifully constructed martinis. Yes, Felix is a swank place where the attitude has attitude and the bouncer behind the velvet ropes can be a little too selective in his entrance policy for some people's patience. Plate-glass windows, neon letters and super-sleek decor give it serious character. Live jazz and funk bands set up on a stage against the front windows on Fridays and Saturdays.

HABANA VILLAGE Map p103　　Club

☎ 202-462-6310; 1834 Columbia Rd NW; admission from $5; ⏰ 6:30pm-3am Wed-Sat; Ⓜ Woodley Park Zoo/Adams Morgan

Squeezed into an old townhouse with a cosmopolitan bar and romantic back room is the Village, which is as close as the capital gets to Cuba. That's not particularly close, but you do get some good, stiff mojitos here, and the music – salsa, meringue, mambo, tango and bossa nova – could make you imagine you were in Miami when the dance floor gets packed, which happens every now and then.

HEAVEN & HELL Map p103　　Club

☎ 202-667-4355; 2327 18th St NW; admission from $5; ⏰ 7:30pm-2am Sun-Thu, to 3am Fri & Sat; Ⓜ Woodley Park Zoo/Adams Morgan, U Street-Cardozo

A perennial favorite with the college crowd, this hot spot hosts Heaven (upstairs), with thematic dance parties to flashing disco lights and a cool, airy interior; and Hell (downstairs), grittier, darker, hotter and packed with hard drinkers. The large outdoor patio in Heaven overlooks the 18th St strip and is popular on steamy nights.

LEFT BANK Map p103　　Club

☎ 202-464-2100; 2424 18th St NW; Ⓜ Woodley Park Zoo/Adams Morgan

The Left Bank is a hip, modern lounge with stark-white walls and orange chairs and booths. It's the perfect dark cave in which to escape a hot summer afternoon's mounting heat. The prime location, smack in the middle of 18th St, is perfect for people-watching from open windows if the place is quiet; which often is not the case. Left Bank attracts a sophisticated, international crowd that comes to sip martinis and listen to DJs spin mellow vibes. There's a menu, but the food is only OK.

LOCAL 16 Map p103　　Bar

☎ 202-265-2828; 1602 U St NW; Ⓜ U Street-Cardozo

Local 16 has such a great layout – the feel of a hip, semi-Victorian mansion that happens to have been crossed with a slamming bar and sweaty dance club. The problem is it gets too damn sweaty – this is one of those places where you have to elbow someone just to get to the bathroom on weekends, although with that said, the person you elbow is probably pretty attractive.

MADAM'S ORGAN Map p103　　Live Dive

☎ 202-667-5370; 2461 18th St NW; admission $1-10; ⏰ shows 9:30pm Mon-Thu, 10pm Fri & Sat; Ⓜ Woodley Park Zoo/Adams Morgan

'Where the beautiful people go to get ugly,' according to the T-shirt. It's not far off the mark – this is the kind of perfect dive where you'll see a beautiful girl shaking her ass on the bar one minute and puking in the bathroom the next. An enigmatic ramshackle place that's been around forever, Madam's Organ was once named one of *Playboy* magazine's favorite bars in America. The live jazz, blues and bluegrass can be downright riot-inducing. There is a roving magician, a raunchy bar-dancing scene, and funky decor with stuffed animals and bizarre paintings on the 1st floor. God bless you, you weird and wonderful Organ – keep DC strange.

MILLIE & AL'S Map p103　　Bar

☎ 202-387-8131; 2440 18th St NW; ⏰ 4pm-2am Mon-Thu, to 3am Fri & Sat; Ⓜ Woodley Park Zoo/Adams Morgan

This comfortably worn dive is an Adams-Morgan institution, famous for its $2 drafts, jelly shots and hit-the-spot pizza (best consumed in that order). Two TVs show a constant stream of sports. M&A has always been, and probably will always be, a yuppie bar with a frat-house flavor – the kind of place where you can expect to be hit on and have beer spilled on you in the same night.

REEF Map p103　　Bar

☎ 202-518-3800; 2446 18th St NW; Ⓜ Woodley Park Zoo/Adams Morgan

We mainly come to Reef for the roof, which is heavenly on hot capital nights, but somehow, everyone always ends up in the aquarium-studded main lounge. That's probably because the roof of the Reef, despite (or because of) it being an amazing space, is often too crowded to really enjoy, at least on weekends. Wherever you end up, every floor is usually packed with the hot and hot-to-trot, so sink a pint and, if you can't make it outside, make a friend next to the fishies.

SAKI Map p103　　Lounge

☎ 202-232-5005; www.sakidc.com; 2477 18th St NW; admission $5; ⏰ 5pm-1am; Ⓜ Woodley Park Zoo/Adams Morgan

At first Saki's basement lounge gives the impression of being a little like a psychiatric institution: low white ceilings, white walls, white floor and tables. But after a while your eyes adjust and you realize that creatively placed rectangular panels are bouncing constantly changing rainbows of light around the room, bathing the trendy couples sipping cocktails at the corner table in a wash of fire-engine red and dusty orange. Light shows aside, Saki is best known for its DJs. The space is small, but locals recommend it for the music, especially on Fridays when you get a mix of old-school funk and electro house. On other nights the DJ music ranges from acid rock to broken beat and hip-hop.

STETSON'S FAMOUS BAR & RESTAURANT Map p103 Bar
☎ 202-667-6295; 1610 U St NW; Ⓜ U Street-Cardozo

Famous? Maybe. But Stetson's is a great bar, period: the floors are scuffed, the outdoor courtyard is packed with smokers, the staff are friendly in that surly friendly way great bar staff can be and the shots come quick. It's popular with congressional Democratic staffers, although it attracts a mixed crowd of anyone you please on weekends.

TRYST Map p103 Cafe
☎ 202-232-5500; 2459 18th St NW; ☉ 6:30am-2am Mon-Thu, to 3am Fri & Sat, 8am-12:30am Sun; Ⓜ Woodley Park Zoo/Adams Morgan

This Greenwich Village–style place is a coffeehouse by day, cushy bar bordering on lounge by night. The couches, armchairs and bookshelves, and the light flooding through street-side windows, lure patrons so faithful they probably should pay rent. Sweet alcoholic concoctions flow along with caffeine (sometimes in the same glass), nice complements to the menu of waffles, muffins and cake. It's a great place to meet up with old friends or make new ones, hence the name.

COLUMBIA HEIGHTS & NORTHEAST

The U St Corridor has sort of evolved into one long strip of bars, plus a fair few jazz spots and concert halls. Further north, Columbia Heights and beyond – the periphery of DC development – has already become trendy among nighthawks. That kinda makes sense, as the first people to settle gentrification lines are the daring: the drinkers and dancers and DJs.

LOOKING GLASS LOUNGE
Map pp106-7 Bar
☎ 202-722-7669; 3634 Georgia Ave NW; Ⓜ Georgia Ave-Petworth

Here's who you expect to find when you look through the Looking Glass: an old guy, one who's owned his chair at the bar for decades, in a broad-brimmed cap and clutching a highball of Jameson as if to prove it. And that guy is here. But drinking next to him is a crowd of 20- and 30-somethings who respect his presence, even as they crank the music under dark chandelier-ish lighting and commiserate in the beer garden out back. If the scene in CoHi (Columbia Heights) is getting too raucous, this is a good alternative for a quiet tipple.

LOVE off Map pp106-7 Club
☎ 202-636-9030; www.lovetheclub.com; 1350 Okie St NE; admission $10-20; ☉ 9pm-4am Thu, 6pm-4am Fri, 9pm-4am Sat

Where does Beyoncé play when she's in DC? Yo, where is the Love? If you're going to go to a multifloor megaclub in DC, make it this gorgeous spot, where you're basically the star of your own Usher video. Dress to impress (the code is strict, no sneakers or baggy jeans allowed) as this club attracts thousands and lines form out the door. Friday nights see a predominantly hip-hop-heavy menu and African American crowd. Saturdays are more diverse, with international electronica pumped through the speakers and a mixed crowd. You need to drive or taxi out here.

RAVEN Map pp106-7 Dive
☎ 202-387-9274; 3125 Mt Pleasant St NW; ☉ from noon; Ⓜ Columbia Heights

The best jukebox in Washington, a dark interior crammed with locals and lovers, that neon lighting that casts you under a glow Edward Hopper should rightly paint and a tough but friendly bar staff are the ingredients in this shot, which, when slammed, hits you as DC's best dive by a mile. One of the greatest nightlife events that occurred over the course of this book's research happened here: a friend gave another friend a $20 bill, then told him, 'Make this alcohol.' Ten minutes later, second friend came back with roughly a case of Schlitz from the bar. That's quality, people. Quality.

RED DERBY Map pp106-7   Bar
☎ 202-291-5000; 3718 14th St NW; Ⓜ Columbia Heights

There's no sign – always a good sign – just the symbol of a red hat. Underneath that cap is a hipster-punk lounge where the 'tenders know the names, the sweet-potato fries soak up the beer ordered off an impressively long menu and – why yes, that is *The Princess Bride* – cult movies play on a projector screen. The lighting is blood red and sexy, natch; you can't help but look good under it.

ROOM 11 Map pp106-7   Bar
☎ 202-332-3234; 3234 11th St NW; Ⓜ Columbia Heights

Room 11 is a little too accurately named: this place really isn't much bigger than an ambitious living room, and as such it can get pretty crowded. On the plus side, everyone here is quite friendly, the intimacy is warmly inviting on chilly winter nights and there's a nice, spacious outdoor area for when it gets too hot inside. The crowd here is hip sans pretension, munching tapas off an evolving menu, sipping some excellent wines hand-selected by the management and enjoying some frankly kick-ass cocktails. There's beer too, of course, but we really recommend you order something that was once a grape, or order off the mixed-drink menu – that's where these cats excel.

WONDERLAND Map pp106-7   Bar
☎ 202-232-5263; 1101 Kenyon St NW; Ⓜ Columbia Heights

She's gotten almost too popular over the years, but Wonderland is still one of our favorite bars in DC. A sawdust-and-sweat mix of punk and hip-hop, this bar embodies the Columbia Heights vibe – kinda edgy, always eccentric and up for a good time. The interior is clapped out in vintage signs and found objects to the point it could be a folk-art museum, the outdoor patio is a good spot for meeting strangers and the upstairs dance floor is a good place to take said strangers for a bit of bump and grind. Trivia: this used to be Nob Hill, which was the longest-operating gay bar in the country (from 1953 to 2004), a major stop on the African American drag-queen circuit, and (of course) famous for its Sunday evening gospel concerts.

U STREET & SHAW

9:30 CLUB Map pp106-7   Live Music
☎ 202-265-0930; 815 V St NW; admission from $10; ⏱ from 7:30pm Sun-Thu; Ⓜ U Street-Cardozo

The 9:30, which can pack 1200 people into a surprisingly intimate venue, is the granddaddy of the live-music scene in DC. Pretty much every big name that comes through town ends up on this stage, and a concert here is the first-gig memory of many a DC-area teenager. The calendar is packed with a random assortment of big names – Justin Timberlake, The Violent Femmes, George Clinton, Wolfmother and the Yeah Yeah Yeahs, to name a few. Concerts usually include around three acts, with the headlining band taking the stage between 10:30pm and 11:30pm.

BAR PILAR Map pp106-7   Bar
☎ 202-265-1751; 1833 14th St NW; Ⓜ U Street-Cardozo

Just a stone's throw from Café Saint-Ex (p184), Bar Pilar is a laid-back option for those prowling the U St Corridor, although 'laid-back' is a relative term in these parts. The narrow drinking area doesn't accommodate too many guests, but those who can squeeze in are treated to a dark, intimate drinking space that is simultaneously buzzy come busy weekend nights. A good spot for those who want to have fun on U St minus the meat-market atmosphere you get in some spots.

BLACK CAT Map pp106-7   Live Music
☎ 202-667-7960; 1811 14th St NW; admission from $5; ⏱ box office from 8pm; Ⓜ U Street-Cardozo

Still one of the best places in town for rock or indie, the Cat always keeps something good going on the back stage, from soul-funk nights to heavy-metal dance-offs to big-band-era bashes. For DC, this is an iconic spot, the love child of Foo Fighter Dave Grohl, who cut his chops drumming in DC-area bands while still a Northern Virginia teenager.

BOHEMIAN CAVERNS Map pp106-7   Jazz Bar
☎ 202-299-0800; 2003 11th St NW; admission from $15; ⏱ 6pm-2am Wed-Sat; Ⓜ U Street-Cardozo

One of Washington's most pedigreed grand dames reopened in 2000; before, it hosted the likes of Miles, Coltrane, Ellington and

Ella. There are frequent open-mic nights and an increasing crop of names headlining to reestablish the title of this icon of American jazz.

CAFÉ SAINT-EX Map pp106-7 Bar
☎ 202-265-7839; 1847 14th St NW; admission free; ⏲ 5:30pm-1am Sun-Wed, to 2am Thu-Sat; Ⓜ U Street-Cardozo

Reminiscent of the Parisian Latin Quarter crossed with a U St lounge, Saint-Ex is always good for a night of sweaty flirting and heavy imbibing. Different DJs spin tunes every night and there's never a cover charge, although there's often a crowd. A bar salvaged from a 1930s Philadelphia pub, seats from an old movie theater and classic movies running on the TVs all lend a nostalgic air, but the folks inside are anything but: this is young, hip, popped-collar country. The downstairs lounge plays up the aeronautic theme with a wooden propeller from the owner's grandfather's WWI fighter plane.

DC9 Map pp106-7 Live Dive
☎ 202-483-5000; 1940 9th St NW; admission $12; ⏲ 5pm-3am Thu-Sat; Ⓜ U Street-Cardozo

DC9 is as intimate as DC's big-name venues get, and about as dive-y as well. Not that we're complaining; there's always a good edge on in this spot. Up-and-coming local bands, with an emphasis on indie rockers, play most nights of the week; when the live music finishes (often around 11pm) DJs keep the place spinning until about 3am. On the 2nd floor zodiac murals and diner booths set the mellow vibe; downstairs you'll find a narrow shotgun bar that's often packed wall to wall.

MARVIN Map pp106-7 Bar
☎ 202-797-7171; 2007 14th St NW; Ⓜ U Street-Cardozo

Named for native son Marvin Gaye, Marvin has gotten too damn popular of late, which is a shame. *Sigh*. This always seems to happen with great DC bars. Marvin has a great setting (in this case a clubby little back room and expansive porch that's one of the best alfresco drinking spaces in the city), an excellent Belgian beer menu and good DJs on weekends. But it gets *packed* some nights, with lines stretching around the block. Avoid on these evenings. Also, guys: no shorts or sandals on weekend nights.

REPUBLIC GARDENS Map pp106-7 Club
☎ 202-232-2710; 1355 U St NW; admission free-$20; Ⓜ U Street-Cardozo

This historic club (where Pearl Bailey waited tables in the 1940s) is one of the most attractive venues in town. Exposed brick walls, wood floors and modern leather furniture give it a sophisticated look, but the classy feel of the spot is old-school, jazz-era good times. You gotta come correct: no denim, no sneakers and definitely no T-shirts.

SALOON Map pp106-7 Bar
☎ 202-462-2640; 1207 U St NW; Ⓜ U Street-Cardozo

The Saloon takes a firm stand against packing patrons in like sardines, with posted rules against standing between tables. That's great, because the added elbow room better allows you to enjoy a brew ordered off one of the most extensive beer menus in town. For a casual drink or place to start the night in the U St area, it's arguably your best bet. Keep in mind the Saloon is usually closed for the month of August.

SOLLY'S Map pp106-7 Bar
☎ 202-232-6590; 1942 11th St NW; Ⓜ U Street-Cardozo

Solly's is always a good kick-off to the U St stumble: a neighborhood corner tavern on one floor and a meat market/hormone perfumery on the second. It's a beer and shot kinda place, but on weekends the clientele is as young and beautiful as anywhere else in the city (although all ages are well represented). This is a big rugby bar, so if you like to scrum, here's your spot.

TABAQ BISTRO Map pp106-7 Lounge
☎ 202-265-0965; 1336 U St NW; Ⓜ U Street-Cardozo

Ignore the restaurant downstairs and head for the top floors, all frosted glass, good views and a Middle Eastern/Asian/buppie (black professional) crowd getting down to R&B and stiff drinks. This author admits that he's never been to a super-posh sky club in Beirut, but he imagines that they'd have the look and feel of this sexily swish spot.

VELVET LOUNGE Map pp106-7 Live Dive
☎ 202-462-3213; 915 U St NW; admission $5; ⏲ 8pm-2am; Ⓜ U Street-Cardozo

Velvet is tiny, red and awesome. It's a hole in the wall, almost literally given its diminutive size, but that doesn't stop a steady stream of great rock and hip-hop artists taking the stage, or great DJs spinning house, funk and R&B on weekends.

UPPER NORTHWEST DC

This area is not particularly known for its nightlife, and most places tend to be of the quiet neighborhood pub variety where upper-middle-class couples linger over bottles of vintage Chardonnay.

The area exception is a cluster of rowdy Irish bars around Connecticut Ave in Cleveland Park, near the Uptown movie theater. This is probably Upper Northwest's most concentrated nightlife strip, and the crowd here is young, international and determined to party.

ARDEO'S Map p114   Wine Bar
☎ 202-244-7995; 3311 Connecticut Ave NW;
⏲ 5:30-10pm Mon-Thu, to 11:30pm Fri & Sat;
Ⓜ Cleveland Park
Besides being an excellent restaurant (p167), Ardeo's is one of our favorite spots for starting a night out on the town thanks to its excellent spirit samplers. We like to go with the Japanese saki variety packs; for around $13, one rack of three shots is enough to give you a pleasant edge and introduce you to new levels of rice-wine happiness.

AROMA Map p114   Bar
☎ 202-244-7995; 3417 Connecticut Ave NW;
⏲ 6pm-2am Sun-Thu, to 3am Fri & Sat; Ⓜ Cleveland Park
If you're a fan of the TV show *Mad Men*, you'll love this spot. There's a pronounced fascination with the 1950s: it's filled with those kidney-shaped coffee tables and old sofas; the tiled bar serves up the scotch and ciggies; and in general, whenever we come here we want to smooth out our suits and sexually harass our secretaries (that's a *Mad Men* reference – we'd never actually do that). That said, this is a politically incorrect bar in one important way: because Aroma does so much business in the cigar-selling trade, it's exempt from the smoking ban, so if you've got a thing against secondhand, you may want to steer clear.

ENOLOGY Map p114   Wine Bar
☎ 202-362-0362; 3238 Wisconsin Ave NW;
⏲ 5pm-1am Sun-Thu, to 2am Fri & Sat; Ⓜ Cleveland Park

Both as wine bar and cocktail corner, Enology rules. This isn't a spot to swill beer, which suits us fine; rather, swish some good wine in your glass and give a wink to the mature, booze-savvy clientele and bar staff, for Enology is for aficionados. The kaffir lime rickey is a perfect antidote to a hot DC summer day, to say nothing of your sobriety.

NANNY O'BRIEN'S IRISH PUB
Map p114   Irish Pub
☎ 202-686-9189; 3319 Connecticut Ave NW;
Ⓜ Cleveland Park
Washington's most authentic Irish pub, Nanny O'Brien's has been a favorite with real and wannabe Irish people for decades. You won't find any cheesy shamrock schlock or shameless promotions here; no, this bar would rather concentrate on serving stiff drinks along with fantastic music. The place is packed and gets pretty rowdy most nights.

NORTHERN VIRGINIA

It's often cheaper to sleep in Arlington than in the city, and if you do, you won't have to travel far to find a bar. The city has always had a lively nightlife scene. Head to Wilson and Clarendon Blvds in Arlington or King St in Alexandria for good bar-hopping with a crowd of folks who seem to be perpetually enrolled in the University of Virginia, Virginia Tech or George Mason University.

ARLINGTON

CLARENDON BALLROOM
Map p122   Live Music
☎ 703-469-2244; 3185 Wilson Blvd; cover varies;
Ⓜ Clarendon
A gorgeous ballroom done up to look like a big-band-era dance hall, the Ballroom is a NoVa cornerstone that attracts throngs of young professionals coming to hear emerging local artists, plus big names on national tours. The upstairs deck is perfect for lingering over a sunset Cosmopolitan.

CONTINENTAL Map p122   Pool
☎ 703-465-7675; 1911 N Fort Myer Dr; Ⓜ Rosslyn
A stone's throw from many Rosslyn hotels, this posh pool hall isn't your average billiards club. There's no stale-beer-and-cigarette stink here, where spaghetti lights form constellations on the ceiling and columns are painted like palm trees. Tiki heads

HOW TO HOOK UP HERE

Young, winsome interns flood DC with fresh faces and raging hormones every summer, but few realize there's an art to DC dating. You need to come off as connected but not trying to look connected; in with someone who matters but nonchalant; top of your class but unconcerned. Or as a friend puts it, 'Don't act like the douche bag you probably are.' Herein: some tips.

- Were you class president? Big deal. So was everyone else.
- Don't flash your ID badge unless you're absolutely sure it beats the one held by Mr Top Secret level clearance over by the jukebox.
- If hitting on Republicans: 'I work for the CIA/DoD (Department of Defense).' If hitting on Democrats: Obama transition team = Summer of Love!
- Need a fourth-quarter miracle? If it's 2am and you're flailing, try Wonderland (p183), Marvin's (p184) or anywhere on 18th St (p179).

and bars painted with silver glitter complete the picture. The owner says Disneyland was the inspiration for his style faux pas that somehow manages to epitomize cool.

IOTA Map p122   Live Music
☎ 703-522-8340; 2832 Wilson Blvd; tickets from $8; ◷ 11am-2am; Ⓜ Clarendon
With shows almost every night of the week, Iota is the best venue for live music in Clarendon's music strip. Tickets are available at the door only (no advance sales) and this place packs 'em in (the seating is first come, first served). Open-mic Wednesdays can be lots of fun or painfully self-important, as these things are wont to be.

IRELAND'S FOUR COURTS
Map p122   Irish Pub
☎ 703-525-3600; 2051 Wilson Blvd; ◷ 11am-2am Mon-Sat, 10am-2am Sun; Ⓜ Courthouse
Buckets of Guinness lubricate the O'Connors and McDonoughs at Arlington's favorite Irish pub. The sidewalk seating draws a lunchtime crowd for shepherd's pie and fish and chips, while the verdant Irish grass-green interior attracts an evening crowd for cold drafts and live tunes.

WHITLOW'S ON WILSON Map p122   Bar
☎ 703-276-9693; 2854 Wilson Blvd; ◷ 11:30am-2am Mon-Fri, 9am-2am Sat & Sun; Ⓜ Clarendon
Occupying almost an entire block just east of Clarendon Metro, Whitlow's has something for everyone: burgers, brunch and comfort food on the menu; happening happy hours and positive pick-up potential; plus 12 brews on tap, a pool table, jukebox, live music and an easygoing atmosphere. It's a favorite with singles.

ALEXANDRIA

BASIN STREET LOUNGE Map p125   Jazz Bar
☎ 703-549-1141; 219 King St; admission Fri & Sat $5; ◷ shows 8pm Tue-Thu, 9pm Fri & Sat; Ⓜ King Street
Wire-rimmed glasses and black turtlenecks may be the uniform at this sophisticated jazz venue, located in the back of the 219 restaurant. The downstairs lounge boasts quaint French Quarter Victorian decor, which is appropriate for the swinging piano, saxophone and bluesy jazz performances. The crowd is a bit older and if the music is good, the scene is pleasantly sedate.

BIRCHMERE off Map p125   Live Music
☎ 703-549-7500; www.birchmere.com; 3701 Mt Vernon Ave; admission $15-35; ◷ box office 5-9pm, shows 7:30pm; ▤ 10A from Pentagon City
Known as 'America's Legendary Music Hall,' this is the DC area's premier venue for folk, country, Celtic and bluegrass music. The talent that graces the stage is reason enough to come, but the venue is pretty great too: it sort of looks like a warehouse that collided with an army of LSD-savvy muralists. Located north of Old Town Alexandria off Glebe Rd.

UNION STREET PUBLIC HOUSE
Map p125   Pub
☎ 703-548-1785; 121 S Union St; ◷ 11:30am-1am Mon-Sat, 11am-1am Sun; Ⓜ King Street
Gas lamps out front welcome tourists and locals into this spacious taproom for frosty brews, raw-bar delights and nightly dinner specials. Inside, the atmosphere is equally inviting: a wide bar, heavy wooden furniture and exposed brick provide equal parts retro-and-warm atmosphere.

top picks

The arts scene in Washington has benefited enormously from the city's continuing gentrification. Between the influx of young professionals, the already-present large population of students and the growing cultural savvy of an increasingly prosperous local residential class, there's been a lot of room for the city's creative side to shine through. The city government has been encouraging the placement of arts districts in areas such as Downtown and the U St Corridor, which has drawn in lots of artists looking to exhibit for all those yuppies with their disposable cash.

Gentrification is a double-edged sword, though, and the high cost of living in the capital makes it a difficult place for artists to set up permanent shop – many are being drawn north to Baltimore, where the rents are quite a bit lower. In addition, the local arts scene draws its inspiration from the experience of the city's population, a population that has been trying to adjust to the pressures of the city's rapid growth and development. On the bright side, the local arts community has been trying to incorporate the city's local voices into its gallery work, readings and especially, performances.

The other side of the Washington arts scene is the showcasing of national and international talent – and historical masterpieces – within the grand halls of the Smithsonian and private institutions such as the Corcoran. Of course, other great cities contain this sort of culture as well – London, New York, Paris et al – but the District is such a small place that it all feels, well, a bit *intimate*. And, if we're talking about the Smithsonian, it's free.

Much of the American literary canon has been written in the nation's capital, a product of the wordsmiths who have been drawn here, from journalists to judges, professors and politicos. Good stories come out of the streets of the city, documenting the lives and loves of Washingtonians, and are written within the halls of power, telling the dream and vision of the nation's leaders. Most of the seminal tracts on American governance have been written in DC, or at least been inspired by a politician or journalist's time here.

Performance has always been an integral part of DC's creativity. The streets contain an urban rhythm that has sustained the local African American community from the time of emancipation to the modern day, and Washington's immigrants have often found one of the strongest links to their home culture is dance and theater. And everyone in this town loves theater. It's really the hometown industry. The drama and acting and artistry that constitutes politics is, at its base, the most fundamental theater around: convincing people you feel a certain way about something. District citizens are the subject of daily political theater, ranging from federal sleight of hand to promises from local police to step up patrols in their wards.

Come see our artsy side. It may not be the Washington you were expecting, but it's the side of the city that keeps the population breathing, that allows it to make sense of the contradictions of the capital. At the end of the day, all the political chicanery and clogged traffic don't seem like such a hassle if you're able to kick back with a bit of wine, a good show and the collected creativity of this major world capital.

ART GALLERIES

There are two sides of the visual arts coin in DC: independent art galleries, and the 'museum' scene to be found in the Smithsonian and smaller, independent institutions. We'll focus on the latter scene first. From the vast holdings of the National Gallery of Art (p58) and the rest of the Smithsonian Institution (p61), to the private collections and special exhibits at the Corcoran Gallery of Art (p66) and the Phillips Collection (p95), Washington contains enough recognized 'establishment' art for a city several times its size.

This is actually the main criticism levied at the museum scene: some citizens say the pieces selected for display at the Smithsonian are too conservative. This isn't very fair; the Smithsonian's mission is to educate Americans on art rather than just the avant-garde. And in any case, some Smithsonian exhibitions can be risqué; the National Portrait Gallery's (p90) works from the modern era, for example.

Less known, but no less important, DC is riddled with grassroots art galleries. Many are owned or operated by the artists themselves. This scene has blossomed since the 1990s, fuelled by DC's reinvigorated neighborhoods and increasingly cosmopolitan population. It is no longer a given that a talented artist will flee to New York to make it big. Some names to look out for on the DC art scene include Colby Caldwell, Steve Cushner, Sam Gilliam, Ryan Hackett, Jae Ko and Nancy Sansom Reynolds. DC can boast bona fide art districts in Dupont Circle and Downtown. The Old Torpedo Factory (p124) in Old Town Alexandria is also an incredible conglomeration of creative minds. These are the places to see the face of DC art at its most pure.

Attending a Friday evening gallery opening in Washington, DC can be a great way to experience the city's creative face in a more fun, less museum-structured environment. Downtown, Dupont Circle, Georgetown and the U St Corridor area are all thick with gallery talent these days. Many studios hold openings between 6pm and 8pm on the first Friday of each month; these are festive occasions, and Washingtonians use them as an excuse to dress up and socialize. Drinks (often wine or champagne) and some kind of cheese-and-cracker snack are served and the artist whose work is showcased is on hand for ego stoking and Q&A sessions. If you like what you see, this is a good time to buy – although you'll have to be satisfied with a sales receipt and letting the painting stay on the wall for the duration of the exhibit.

The *Washington Post's* Weekend section lists current shows. Also check out www.artlineplus .com/gallerymagazine. The website http://art -collecting.com/galleries_dc.htm provides a pretty thorough list of local galleries as well.

AARON GALLERY Map p96

☎ 202-387-0203; www.aarongallerydc.com; 1717 Connecticut Ave NW; ☽ 11am-5pm Tue-Sat; Ⓜ Dupont Circle
One of Dupont Circle's more established galleries, this place is a cornerstone of first Friday evening gallery walks.

CIVILIAN ART PROJECTS Map p88

☎ 202-347-0022; www.civilianartprojects.com; 406 7th St NW; Ⓜ Archives-Navy Memorial
One of the flasher new galleries holding together the Penn Quarter gallery scene. Features contemporary work and hosts tango classes run by local troupe Tango Mercurio (p192).

FLASHPOINT GALLERY Map p88

☎ 202-315-1310; www.flashpointdc.org; 916 G St NW; Ⓜ Metro Center, Gallery Pl-Chinatown

This large space focuses on providing a venue for emerging artists and local cultural organizations. There's visual arts space here, as well as a theater lab and dance studio.

FOUNDRY GALLERY Map p96

☎ 202-387-0203; www.foundrygallery.org; 9 Hillyer Ct NW; ☽ 11am-5pm Tue-Sat, 1-5pm Sun; Ⓜ Dupont Circle
A nonprofit member-run organization, this gallery features a diverse range of super-contemporary art made in the last decade – mediums include painting, sculpture and drawings – all created by local artists. Openings are held the first Friday of the month.

KATHLEEN EWING GALLERY Map p96

☎ 202-328-0955; www.kathleenewinggallery .com; 1609 Connecticut Ave NW; Ⓜ Dupont Circle
Photography is the focus at this gallery, which is renowned for its collection of 19th- and 20th-century photos. It also offers more contemporary pictures and multimedia works. Openings are held the first Friday of the month.

PRIMIMODA Map p96

☎ 202-232-7011; http://primimoda.com; 2010 R St NW; ☽ 11am-7pm Tue-Sat; Ⓜ Dupont Circle
Exhibits paintings and design work by the 'Africanistes,' an attempt by white artists to record the African continent and diaspora.

PROJECT 4 Map pp106-7

☎ 202-232-4340; www.project4gallery.com; 1353 U St NW; ☽ noon-6pm Wed-Sat; Ⓜ U Street-Cardozo
An extremely hip U St gallery that showcases some of the best of the contemporary ad pop art scene.

STUDIO GALLERY Map p96

☎ 202-232-8734; www.studiogallerydc.com; 2108 R St NW; ☺ 1-7pm Wed & Thu, 1-8pm Fri, 1-6pm Sat; Ⓜ Dupont Circle

A 30-artist cooperative featuring canvases and sculpture, it is the longest running artist-owned gallery in the area. There are both solo and group exhibits in all mediums. Openings are held the first Friday of the month.

TROYER GALLERY Map p96

☎ 202-328-7189; 1710 Connecticut Ave NW; ☺ 11am-5pm Tue-Sat; Ⓜ Dupont Circle

Among DC's better-known galleries, especially for emerging artists, it features a lot of home-grown paintings and sculptures, along with a large photography collection. Openings are held the first Friday of the month.

THEATER

The Washington, DC theater scene is divided into three distinct camps: the renowned Kennedy Center, presenting world-famous companies and productions; a second string of well-established theaters, which often host Broadway national runs; and a third group of adventurous small stages, presenting cutting-edge works whose quality ranges from totally fabulous to sophomoric.

ARENA STAGE Map pp78-9

☎ 202-488-3300; www.arenastage.org; 1101 6th St SW; tickets from $35; Ⓜ Waterfront-SEU

The three theaters at Arena Stage (including a theater-in-the-round) are top venues for traditional and experimental theatrical works, especially American classics, premieres of new plays and contemporary stories. Arena Stage was the city's first racially integrated theater and has continued its progressive tradition through performances addressing African American history.

CARTER BARRON AMPHITHEATER
off Map p114

☎ 202-426-0486; www.nps.gov/rocr/cbarron; cnr 16th St & Colorado Ave NW, Rock Creek Park; tickets free or $18; ☺ box office noon-9pm show days; ▣ S2, S4 from McPherson Sq

The outdoor Carter Barron Amphitheater in Rock Creek Park is the venue for Shakespeare Free for All (www.shakespearetheatre.org/about/ffa), a free series staged by the Shakespeare

Theatre. It also hosts music festivals and concerts throughout the summer. For free shows, tickets are distributed from 4pm on the day of the performance. For more information on the park, see Rock Creek Park (p117).

FOLGER SHAKESPEARE LIBRARY & THEATRE Map pp78-9

☎ 202-544-7077; www.folger.edu; 210 E Capitol St SE; tickets from $30; Ⓜ Capitol South

The magnificent Globe-style theater attached to the Folger Shakespeare Library stages classic and modern interpretations of the bard's plays. Exhibitions, poetry readings and great programs for children are all part of the repertoire at this venue, in addition to world-class Shakespearean theater.

FORD'S THEATRE Map p88

☎ 202-218-6500, 800-955-5566; www.fordsthea tre.org; 511 10th St NW; tickets $25-40; ☺ box office 10am-6pm Mon-Fri; Ⓜ Gallery Pl-Chinatown

The historical theater – where John Wilkes Booth killed Abraham Lincoln – has staged world-premiere musicals, mostly about Lincoln's life and times. It also hosts a series on American Originals: influential individuals who have played significant cultural roles. For more information see the Neighborhoods chapter, p91.

KENNEDY CENTER Map p64

☎ 202-467-4600; www.kennedy-center.org; 2700 F St NW; Ⓜ Foggy Bottom-GWU

Washington's main cultural jewel is given credit for transforming DC from a cultural backwater to an artistic contender in the late 20th century. The stately white-marble building overlooking the Potomac River opened to the public in 1971. It holds two big theaters, a theater lab (where new or experimental theater is staged), cinema, opera house and concert hall (and the fine Roof Terrace Restaurant to boot). It is home to the National Symphony Orchestra (p192) and the Washington Chamber Symphony, both directed by Leonard Slatkin, the Washington Opera (p193), directed by Placido Domingo, and the Washington Ballet (p192). Film festivals and cultural events are frequent highlights. About 3000 performances are held here annually.

Orchestra seats cost about $40 for concerts, $60 for theater, $140 for opera. On

SMALL DC THEATERS

There are lots of small theater venues and troupes in DC.

- **Atlas Theater** (Map pp78–9; ☎ 202-399-7993; 1333 H St SE) Art-deco theater that is the backbone of the H St NE revival.
- **DCAC** (Map p103; ☎ 202-462-7833; www.dcartscenter.org; 2438 18th St NW; Ⓜ Woodley Park Zoo/Adams Morgan) A 50-seat black-box theater hosting the improvisational interactive Playback.
- **Discovery Theatre** (Map p54; ☎ 202-633-8700; www.discoverytheater.org; Smithsonian Arts & Industries Bldg; Ⓜ Smithsonian) Stages delightful productions for kids, such as puppet shows.
- **Gala Hispanic Theatre** (Map pp106–7; ☎ 202-234-7174; www.galatheatre.org; 1625 Park Rd NW; Ⓜ Columbia Heights) Maintains a 30-year tradition of annual Spanish-language productions.
- **Lincoln Theatre** (Map pp106–7; ☎ 202-328-6000; www.thelincolntheatre.org; 1215 U St NW; Ⓜ U Street-Cardozo) Historic cinema recently renovated to host music and theater.
- **Source Theatre Company** (Map pp106–7; ☎ 202-204-7800; www.sourcedc.org; 1835 14th St NW; Ⓜ U Street-Cardozo) In the heart of the new U district, this theater hosts the Annual Washington Theatre Festival.
- **Studio Theatre** (Map p88; ☎ 202-332-3300; www.studiotheatre.org; 1333 P St NW; 🚍 G2 from Dupont Circle) Twenty-five years of producing Pulitzer Prize–winning and premiere plays.
- **Theater J** (Map p96; ☎ 202-777-3210; www.washingtondcjcc.org/center-for-arts/theater-j; 1529 16th St NW; Ⓜ Dupont Circle) Addresses urban American Jewish experience.
- **Woolly Mammoth Theatre Co** (Map p88; ☎ 202-393-3939; www.woollymammoth.net; 641 D St; Ⓜ Archives-Navy Memorial) The edgiest of the experimental groups.

the day of the performance, reduced-rate tickets are sometimes available for students and for obstructed-view seats. Order tickets by phone or purchase them at the box office.

The Kennedy Center also hosts the Millennium Stage, a series of first-rate music and dance performances that take place every day at 6pm in the Grand Foyer and cost absolutely nothing. Pick up a schedule at the Kennedy Center, or check the website for details.

A free shuttle bus runs between Foggy Bottom-GWU Metro station and the Kennedy Center every 15 minutes from 9:45am to midnight Monday to Saturday, noon to 8pm Sunday. There's also paid parking underneath the Kennedy Center.

NATIONAL THEATRE Map p88

☎ 202-628-6161, 800-447-7400; www.nationaltheatre.org; 1321 Pennsylvania Ave NW; ☯ box office 10am-9pm Mon-Sat, noon-8pm Sun; Ⓜ Federal Triangle

Established in 1835 and renovated in 1984, the National is Washington's oldest continually operating theater. This is where you would catch *Les Misérables* and *Rent*. Half-price tickets are available for students and seniors. Monday nights at the National are good value as they feature free performances at 6pm and 7:30pm.

SHAKESPEARE THEATRE Map p88

☎ 202-547-1122; www.shakespearetheatre.org; 450 7th St NW; tickets from $20; ☯ box office 10am-6pm Mon-Sat, noon-6pm Sun; Ⓜ Archives-Navy Memorial

Under artistic director Michael Kahn, this little theater on Gallery Row has been called 'one of the world's three great Shakespearean theaters' by the *Economist*. Its home company stages a half-dozen works annually, plus a free summer Shakespeare series in Rock Creek Park (see Carter Barron Amphitheater, opposite).

WARNER THEATRE Map p88

☎ 202-783-4000; www.warnertheatre.com; 1299 Pennsylvania Ave NW; tickets from $25; ☯ box office 10am-4pm Mon-Fri, noon-3pm Sat; Ⓜ Federal Triangle

The beautifully restored 1924 art-deco theater was originally built for vaudeville and silent films, but it now stages headliner concerts, comedians and national runs of Broadway musicals.

CLASSICAL MUSIC, OPERA & DANCE

The capital's most visible musicians are the big boys – those from the weighty cultural landmarks such as the National Symphony Orchestra and the Washington Opera. At the

NSO, directed by Leonard Slatkin, classical means classical. Placido Domingo directs the Washington Opera. Repertoire and productions tend to air on the traditional side but are technically sound – highlighted by special occasions when Domingo conducts or sings. Diva Denyce Graves, graduate of the local Duke Ellington School of Performing Arts, occasionally graces its stage and thrills her hometown audiences.

A national orchestra of sorts is the Marine Corps Marching Band, based at the Marine Barracks (p84) in Southeast DC. Back in the late 19th century, military marching-band music reached its apotheosis (such as it was) in the work of John Philip Sousa, who directed the Marine Corps Marching Band for many years (and was born and buried nearby). In this era of amped-up patriotism, this genre remains alive and well: the band still performs his work today.

A great resource for information about the contemporary local music scene is the DC Music Network (www.dcmusicnet.com).

The Kennedy Center is the premier venue for classical music and opera, but performances also take place at venues around town, including the National Gallery of Art, National Building Museum, Corcoran Gallery and Library of Congress, as well as at local universities and churches.

Performance dance in Washington, DC is surprisingly limited. The premier dance venue is the Kennedy Center, home of the Washington Ballet, but the lesser-known, and oddly located, Dance Place experiments with some more daring choreography.

DAKSHINA
☎ 202-247-1292; www.dakshina.org
Dance troupe that performs traditional Indian dance from across the subcontinent, as well as modern dance inspired by the second-generation Indian American experience. Performances are usually held in the Lincoln Theatre (p191).

DANA TAI SOON BURGESS & COMPANY
☎ 202-467-4600; www.dtsbco.com
One of the premier Asian American dance troupes in the country, Dana Tai's performances tend to blend Asian themes with modern dance trends in ways that have been critically acclaimed by local and national media. The company regularly tours both domestically and internationally, but also holds performances at various venues across town.

DANCE PLACE Map pp106-7
☎ 202-269-1600; www.danceplace.org; 3225 8th St NE; Ⓜ Brookland
The only truly cutting-edge dance space in the capital is tucked away up in Northeast DC. It's run by five resident modern-dance companies offering a year-round calendar of new work, which includes festivals featuring African dance, tap dancing, step dancing and other genres. It also hosts the work of top-notch national companies, such as the Joe Goode Performance Group.

KANKOURAN DANCE COMPANY
☎ 202-518-1213; www.kankouran.org
West African drum and dance troupe that holds community classes and local performances in different venues across the city. Currently, classes are held Monday and Wednesday from 7pm to 8:30pm and noon to 1:30pm on Saturday in the Randall Recreation Center (Map pp78–9; cnr I St & S Capitol St SW), by the Navy Yard Metro station.

NATIONAL SYMPHONY ORCHESTRA
☎ 202-467-4600; www.kennedy-center.org
Directed by Christoph Eschenbach, this is the affiliate orchestra of the Kennedy Center (p190) and one of the best chamber symphonies in the nation.

TANGO MERCURIO
www.tangomercurio.com
This nonprofit organization runs tango classes, holds performances around town and hosts *milongas* (tango dance evenings) in various clubs and art galleries around town. At the time of writing, *milongas* were held at Civilian Art Projects (p189) and the 18th Street Lounge (p178). Check its website for more details.

WASHINGTON BALLET
☎ 202-467-4600; www.kennedy-center.org
Housed at the Kennedy Center (p190), the Washington Ballet hasn't been known for any groundbreaking productions, although its reputation is beginning to change as it explores the work of younger choreographers. The center also hosts fine visiting groups such as Merce Cunningham and Alvin Ailey.

WASHINGTON OPERA

☎ 202-295-2400; www.dc-opera.org
The Washington Opera is housed at the Kennedy Center (p190) and puts on a varied showcase throughout the year. Previous choices have included *La Traviata* and *A Streetcar Named Desire*.

COMEDY

Washington, DC is not exactly Comedy Central, but the follies of the federal government provide fodder for some serious fun.

CAPITOL STEPS POLITICAL SATIRE
Map p64

☎ 202-312-1427; www.capsteps.com; Ronald Reagan Bldg & International Trade Center Amphitheater; tickets $35; ⏰ shows 7:30pm Fri & Sat; Ⓜ Federal Triangle
This troupe claims to be the only group in America that tries to be funnier than Congress. It's actually composed of current and former congressional staffers, so they know their stuff, although sometimes it can be a little overtly corny. The best of political comedy, this DC tradition pokes satirical bipartisan fun at both sides of the spectrum.

DC IMPROV Map p96

☎ 202-296-7008; www.dcimprov.com; 1140 Connecticut Ave; tickets from $10; ⏰ shows 8:30pm Tue-Thu, 8pm & 10:30pm Fri & Sat, 8pm Sun; Ⓜ Farragut North
This is comedy in the more traditional sense, featuring stand-up by comics from Comedy Central, Mad TV and HBO, among others. The Improv also offers workshops for those of us who think we're pretty funny. Six two-hour weekly workshop sessions cost $180.

READINGS & LECTURES

Check the *City Paper* and the *Washington Post* Weekend section for upcoming readings by local, national and international authors, lectures, poetry slams and open-mic nights. DC has hundreds of these things, held everywhere from brightly colored bookstores to dingy church basements. This type of event is hot with Washington singles, especially those who consider finding a match over shots at the local dive an appalling concept.

BUSBOYS & POETS Map pp106-7

☎ 202-387-7638; www.busboysandpoets.com; 2021 14th St; ⏰ 8am-midnight Mon-Thu, from 9am Sat & Sun
In just a few years, Busboys (named for a Langston Hughes poem) has become a U St stalwart, a black-owned business where everyone seems to gather for coffee, wi-fi, cafe fare and a progressive vibe (and attached bookstore) that makes San Francisco feel conservative.

POLITICS & PROSE BOOKSTORE
Map p114

☎ 202-364-1919; www.politics-prose.com; 5015 Connecticut Ave NW; Ⓜ Van Ness-UDC
Tucked away in a quiet corner of Northwest, Politics & Prose is famous with the literary set. Selling thousands of titles along with steaming mugs of chai, this independent bookstore is known for hosting brain-food readings and discussions on a regular basis.

CINEMA

Washington offers a few excellent opportunities for film buffs to see some unusual work. The Smithsonian, the Library of Congress and other museums round out the programming by offering a great variety of international, historical and educational films. Of course, Hollywood's finest are on view here, too.

AMC 9 THEATRES Map pp78-9

☎ 703-998-4AMC; www.amctheatres.com; 50 Massachusetts Ave; Ⓜ Union Station
This giant theater center shows the latest and greatest movies from Hollywood, from action-adventure to romantic comedy flicks. You can enter the cinema from inside Union Station. Other AMC branches include AMC Loews Uptown 1 (Map p114; ☎ 202-966-5401; 3426 Connecticut Ave NW) and AMC Loews Georgetown (Map p72; ☎ 202-342-6033; 3111 K St NW).

ARLINGTON CINEMA & DRAFTHOUSE off Map p122

☎ 703-486-2345; www.arlingtondrafthouse.com; 2903 Columbia Pike; Ⓜ Clarendon
Ice-cold beers and second-run films at bargain-basement prices? Who could resist that? Not many people. You need to be 21

WASHINGTON'S CHANGING FACE

The City Paper once said Washington is too divided for there to ever be a great DC novel? Do you agree? It is DC's divisions that ultimately make it fertile ground for great novels. Great is subjective and usually measured decades away from the novel's epicenter, but there are some DC-based novels that I think could be eventually considered: Marita Golden's *A Long Distance Life, Edge of Heaven* and *After,* Percival Everette's *Erasure,* Stephen Carter's *Emperor of Ocean Park,* Patricia Browning Griffith's *Supporting the Sky* and Edward P Jones' *Lost In the City* and *Hagar's Children,* both critically acclaimed short-story collections.

As a lifelong resident, where would you take a visitor who wanted to look past the Mall? I'd take them to the African American Civil War Museum (p107) on U St or over to Southeast to the Anacostia Museum (p83). I'd have them check out the city's two most beautiful vistas: Malcolm X Park (p103; Meridian Park to nonresidents and squares) and the overlook at Our Lady of Perpetual Help, next to the Panorama Room in Southeast DC. I'd also take them, weather permitting, to Haines Point and up to McKinley Technology High School to check out the view from the famous plaza. Of course I'd take them to U St for self-absorbed poetry readings, hip-hop performances, and a half-smoke from Ben's Chili Bowl (p163).

What neighborhood do you live in, and why? I live in a neighborhood called Michigan Park, near Brookland and Catholic University, in Northeast DC. I grew up in a public housing complex a couple miles from my home. As a youth I used to walk through this neighborhood on the way to the movies and often wished I lived in one of its quiet brick homes. I love the neighborhood. It's full of young families and retirees, and it's far away enough to avoid some of the problems of the city, but close enough to everything so that I don't feel isolated. The neighborhood, according to the woman who sold me the house, was desegregated in the late '40s, early '50s and has somehow managed to resist the lure of gentrifiers. My neighbors are retired African American teachers, government workers and black professionals. One of my favorite spots is Dance Place (p192), a performance venue in Brookland that brings in dancers from around the world and around the way.

DC is a demographically changing city. Where, neighborhoodwise, do you see the biggest shifts occurring? And what do you think are the negatives and positives of these changes? As I wrote in a piece for the *Washington Post,* change happens to most American cities. Shifting demographics is what gives cities their character. Most of the major changes I see are in the U St/Shaw/Columbia Heights neighborhood, where young, primarily white home and condo owners have moved in over the past decade or so. However, there are also major shifts elsewhere, including in Southeast beyond Capitol Hill, in places like Anacostia where both whites and Latinos are beginning to move into neighborhoods that have been almost exclusively black since the 1950s. I think the positive aspects of gentrification are that there is an increased diversity and a return to the neighborhood of services like grocery stores, arts, clubs, and increased police patrols and usually improved schools. The negatives are the displacement of lifelong neighborhood folks who can't afford rising taxes. Gentrifiers – not all are white – are more like postmodern pioneers less interested in being part of a neighborhood than seizing land and watching their property values increase. They often come armed with an arrogant ignorance of the culture of the neighborhoods they have moved into and a reluctance to learn and exchange. But overall, I think the movement is good for DC. The myth of Chocolate City somehow presupposes that black residents can't absorb diverse populations without losing their identity. That's an insult to the strength of the people and culture and fails to recognize a long history of mutual respect and exchange that has existed in many DC neighborhoods. I think we can manage to expand our palette to include *pupusas,* sushi and half smokes!

Kenny Carroll is the executive director of DC WritersCorp and a literature teacher at Duke Ellington High School of the Arts.

to enter (or with a parent), but once inside you will find comfy chairs for flick-viewing, a menu of sandwiches, pizzas and, of course, popcorn, as well as a selection of alcoholic drinks (this is one of the few places in DC where you can drink and catch a movie at the same time). Some nights the theater skips the movies and hosts stand-up comedy instead. Check the website. There are also family oriented programs some weekends.

MARY PICKFORD THEATER Map pp78-9
☎ 202-707-5677; www.loc.gov/rr/mopic/pickford; 101 Independence Ave SE, 3rd fl, Madison Bldg; admission free; ☺ shows 7pm Tue, Thu & Fri; Ⓜ Capitol South
The Mary Pickford Theater at the Library of Congress screens films on historical or cultural themes, relevant to current events. Seating is limited to only 64 people, but reservations can be made by telephone up to one week in advance.

SPORTS & ACTIVITIES

top picks

- Redskins game at FedEx Field (p199)
- Cycling the C&O Canal & Towpath (p197)
- Kayaking on the Chesapeake Bay (p198)
- Sunday strolls in Rock Creek Park (p198)
- Summer days in Francis Pool (p196)
- Hitting the Capital Crescent Trail (p197)
- Paddling the Potomac (p198)
- Gooooal! Checking out DC United (p200)
- Hot dogs at a Nats game (p200)

In a city where everyone seems to be from somewhere else and no one can agree on politics, sports are like social super glue. Besides beer, food and a good protest, one of the few things that can bring together all the elements of the DC area – Democrat, Republican, white kids from Arlington, Asian Americans from Bethesda, African Americans from Hyattsville, old timers in a Petworth corner shop, interns laying into a Capitol Hill pub – is a Redskins game. If you prick us, we shall bleed – red, but gold as well (ie the 'Skins team colors).

The old American sports saw – that baseball is embraced by the Northeast, football by the South and basketball by African Americans – could apply to several different slices of this city's population. For locals who resent the way New Yorkers, Baltimoreans and Philadelphians categorize their town as a city of transplants, game days are a reminder that competitive – and community – roots here run deep. For immigrants, a day at the games is an introduction to their new homeland's strange traditions. Or a chance to introduce some of their own – one of the larger cricket leagues in America (yes, we play) recruits heavily from the large local West Indies and South Asian population.

DC doesn't just watch sports, it plays them as well – from fast-paced Ultimate games in front of the Smithsonian Castle to competitive two-on-two volleyball near the Lincoln Memorial, league softball on the Mall and bocce ball in Capitol Hill. And there are a lot of outdoor resources here. This is partly attributable to the excellent urban planning idea that an ideal Republic's ideal capital required lots of green space. Planners from L'Enfant to Adrian Fenty have considered the inclusion of nature integral to the Washington experience. We're not just talking about preserving the outdoors in the midst of the city, although DC does so, most notably in enormous Rock Creek Park. But there's also the desire to collect and preserve America's flora in her capital and broker coexistence, and even a mutual synergy between two seemingly opposing energies: urban and natural.

If you want to see what we're driving at, check out Malcolm X Park spilling over the Fall Line and almost onto 16th St, the National Arboretum's gardens clumping like green hands pawing through Northeast's residential blocks, or the natural marsh that is the Kenilworth Aquatic Gardens. Have a howl at the local coyotes for us – this city is so deceptively wild it supports a coyote population – and when that's done, we can all meet on the Mall for some league kickball.

HEALTH & FITNESS

When in DC, there is no need to forego your regular routine of running or reflexology. The city has plenty of fitness centers and health spas to meet the calisthenics and chill-out needs of any visitor.

SWIMMING POOLS

When air-conditioning is not enough, get relief from the summer heat at one of these facilities.

Francis Pool (Map p72; ☎ 202-727-3285; 2500 N St NW; adult/child $7/4; ⊙ 1-8pm Mon & Wed-Fri, noon-6pm Sat & Sun Jun-Aug; Ⓜ Dupont Circle) Outdoor pool.

Georgetown Pool (Map p72; ☎ 202-282-0381; 3400 Volta Pl; adult/child $7/4; ⊙ 1-8pm Tue-Fri, noon-6pm Sat & Sun Jun-Aug; Ⓠ Georgetown shuttle, DC Circulator from Foggy Bottom-GWU Metro) Outdoor pool crowded with kids.

William H Rumsey Aquatic Center (Map pp78–9; ☎ 202-724-4495; 635 N Carolina Ave SE; adult/child $7/4; ⊙ 6:30am-9pm Mon-Fri, 10am-5pm Sat & Sun; Ⓜ Eastern Market) Indoor 25m facility.

GYMS & FITNESS CENTERS

DC has so many visitors and transient residents that most gyms allow for short-term (as short as one-day) memberships.

National Capital YMCA (Map p96; ☎ 202-862-9622; www.ymcadc.org; 1711 Rhode Island Ave NW; day pass/steam room $15/20; ⊙ 5:30am-10:30pm Mon-Fri, 8am-6:30pm Sat, 9am-5:30pm Sun; Ⓜ Farragut North) Seven floors of fitness and fun, including squash courts, basketball courts, indoor track, rock-climbing wall, free weights, cardio machines and classes.

Results the Gym (Map p103; ☎ 202-518-0600; 1612 U St NW; ⊙ 4am-midnight Mon-Fri, 6am-10pm Sat, 7am-9pm Sun; Ⓜ U Street-Cardozo, Dupont Circle)

Spiral Flight (Map p114; ☎ 202-965-1645; www
.spiralflightyoga.com; 1726 Wisconsin Ave NW; 60/90min
class $15/18; ☺ classes vary seasonally; 🚌 Georgetown
shuttle, DC Circulator from Foggy Bottom-GWU Metro)
Center for yoga and tai chi, in art-gallery setting.

MASSAGE & DAY SPAS

Every now and then, everyone needs to indulge. Hair gets frizzy, feet get sore, minds
grow weary and nothing but a little pricey
self-indulgence can fix matters. Here's a list of
good day spas where you can spoil yourself:

Andre Chreky Salon (Map p64; ☎ 202-293-9393; www
.andrechreky.com; 1604 K St NW; ☺ 9am-7pm Mon,
7am-8pm Tue-Fri, 7am-7pm Sat, 9am-5pm Sun;
Ⓜ McPherson Sq) Sleek business-district spa.

Aveda Georgetown (Map p72; ☎ 202-965-1325;
www.avedageorgetown.com; 1325 Wisconsin Ave NW;
☺ 10am-7pm Mon & Sun, to 8pm Tue, to 9pm Wed
& Thu, 8:30am-8pm Fri & Sat; 🚌 Georgetown shuttle,
DC Circulator from Foggy Bottom-GWU Metro) Does nice
herbal things to skin, body and hair.

Four Seasons Fitness Club/Spa (Map p72; ☎ 202-944-
2022; 2800 Pennsylvania Ave NW; 🚌 Georgetown, DC
Circulator shuttle from Foggy Bottom-GWU Metro) Part of
the luxurious Four Seasons Hotel. You can't use the gym
itself unless you stay overnight, but exercise classes and
spa treatments are available to nonguests.

ACTIVITIES

Washington, DC has an ideal climate for outdoor activities, although it can be muggy or
may rain often in the warmer months. The
city's geography, focused on the Potomac
River, and covered with parks and green space,
allows plenty of opportunities to take advantage of the outdoors. Whether your thing is
hiking, cycling, running, sunning, canoeing,
kayaking, equestrian outings or rock climbing,
you will find a place to do it in DC.

In summer, Harpers Ferry West Virginia,
1½ hours northwest of DC, becomes something like Adams-Morgan North as hundreds
of cityfolk go tubing down the Shenandoah
River – see p226.

CYCLING

Acres of parkland along the Potomac and
around the National Mall and a relatively flat
landscape make for great bike touring around
DC. The kicker is the miles and miles of off-
road bike trails, many of which became a part
of Rails to Trails. Now that Metro allows bicycles on trains and buses, there is almost no
place in DC that cannot be reached by bike.

In Rock Creek Park (p117) Beach Dr, between Military and Broad Branch Rds, closes
to traffic on weekends. South of Broad Branch,
a paved trail parallels the parkway past the zoo
and all the way to the Potomac. The trail is
narrow in spots and gets crowded on weekends, but it's an easy way to traverse the city
by bike. Access the trail at 27th and P Sts NW,
or at Connecticut Ave and Calvert St NW.

From Georgetown, take the 10-mile Capi-
tal Crescent Trail (Map p72; www.cctrail.org) along the
Potomac and into downtown Bethesda, Maryland. This paved trail is one of the best maintained in the city. It has beautiful lookouts
over the river, and winds through woodsy
areas and upscale neighborhoods. The southern trailhead is at the east end of K St (called
Water St here) under the Francis Scott Key
Bridge. From downtown Bethesda, the trail
continues for another 2 miles to northern
Rock Creek Park, but it is not paved. For
maps, call the Coalition for the Capital Crescent Trail
(☎ 202-234-4874).

The C&O Canal & Towpath (p73) starts in
Georgetown and stretches 185 miles northwest to Cumberland, Maryland. This wide
dusty path parallels the Capital Crescent
Trail for a few miles. The latter turns west,
while the towpath continues 14 miles north
to Great Falls National Park (p218) and beyond
to West Virginia. The towpath is not paved,
so all-terrain tires are an asset.

Ohio Dr starts at the Tidal Basin and cir-
cumnavigates the peninsula that contains East
Potomac Park (p84). A wide, paved sidewalk
runs parallel for cyclists who are not at ease
sharing the road with cars. The 5-mile loop
runs along the Washington Channel on one
side and the Potomac River on the other.

Across the Potomac, the Mt Vernon Trail
(Map p122) is a paved riverside path that is a
favorite with local cyclists. From the Francis
Scott Key Bridge, it follows the river south
past Roosevelt Island, Arlington Cemetery
and National Airport, through Old Town
Alexandria, all the way to Mount Vernon (18
miles). The course is mostly flat, except the
long climb up the hill to George Washington's
house at the end. The scenery is magnificent –
DC skylines and all – and the historical component is certainly unique.

Also in Virginia, the Washington & Old Dominion
Trail (W&OD; off Map p122; www.wodfriends.org) starts
in southern Arlington and follows the old

OUR BALLS ARE HARDER

Two separate amateur sports leagues are all the rage among DC's 20- and 30-somethings these days: the DC Bocce League (www.dcbocceleague.com) – their motto is the title of this box – and DC Kickball (http://dckickball.org). If you're not familiar with these sports, bocce is essentially lawn bowling, while kickball is an odd combination of soccer and baseball. Neither league requires experience or even skill to join. For the many young transient professionals in the capital, DC Bocce and Kickball are easy ways of meeting up with folks of a similar demographic, enjoying some sport and then (generally) getting wasted at bars for the post-game.

railway bed through historic Leesburg and on to Purcellville, in the Allegheny foothills. Its 45 miles are paved and spacious, winding their way through the Virginia suburbs. The easiest place to pick up the trail is outside the East Falls Church Metro station: exit right and turn right again onto Tuckahoe St, then follow the signs.

If you would like a guide, Bike the Sites (Map p88; ☎ 202-842-2453; www.bikethesites.com; Old Post Office Pavilion, 1100 Pennsylvania Ave; adult/child $40/30; ⏱ tours 9am & 1pm; Ⓜ Federal Triangle) offers professionally guided tours of the Capital, the monuments, and even a Sites@Nite tour. The price includes bike, equipment, bottled water and a snack. For more information, pick up *25 Bicycle Tours in and Around Washington D.C.: From the Capitol Steps to Country Roads*, by Anne H Oman, or *ADC's Washington Area Bike Map*.

HIKING & RUNNING

Besides the trails mentioned under Cycling (p197), many miles of unpaved trails provide walkers and runners a softer terrain and uninterrupted time on their feet. Rock Creek Park (p117) has 15 miles of unpaved trails. On the west side of Rock Creek, the 4.5-mile green-blazed Western Ridge Trail winds through the forest; pick it up at Beach Dr near the intersection with Porter St NW (take the Metro to Cleveland Park). On the east side, the 5.5-mile blue-blazed Valley Creek Trail runs closer to the creek; pick it up at Park Rd near the tennis courts (Ⓜ Cleveland Park). The trails are lightly trafficked and clearly blazed. Maps are available at the Nature Center & Planetarium (Map p114; ☎ 202-895-6070; off Military Rd; ⏱ 9am-5pm Wed-Sun Sep-May, daily Jun-Aug). There is also a 1.5-mile exercise

trail behind the Omni Shoreham Hotel (Map p114; 2500 Calvert St NW; Ⓜ Woodley Park Zoo/Adams Morgan), with 18 exercise station stops.

Extensive trail networks connect Rock Creek Park to the other northwestern DC parks – Normanstone, Montrose, Dumbarton Oaks, Whitehaven, Glover Archbold and Battery Kemble – so you can take a terrific cross-city parkland ramble. A good map is *Trails in the Rock Creek Park Area*, published by the Potomac Appalachian Trail Club.

Other good books include *60 Hikes within 60 Miles: Washington DC*, by Paul Elliot, and the *Washington, DC, Running Guide*, by Don Carter. For organized road races, check out www.runwashington.com or www.dcfront runners.org.

KAYAKING & CANOEING

Kayaks and canoes can cruise on the waters of both the Potomac River and the C&O Canal. The canal is ideal for canoeing between Georgetown and Violettes Lock (Mile 22); canoeists must portage around each lock. The Potomac has a great vantage point from which to admire the city skyline, but be careful – the river has some dangerous currents. North of Georgetown, white-water areas can be dangerous, especially between Great Falls and Chain Bridge.

Atlantic Kayak (off Map pp78–9; ☎ 301-292-6455; www.atlantickayak.com; 13600 King Charles Tce, Fort Washington, MD; ⏱ 10am-5pm Thu-Mon Jun & Jul, 10am-5pm Sat & Sun May & Aug) Atlantic Kayak offers beginners' kayaking classes, as well as tours of the waterways of the Chesapeake Bay. Its main office is located in Fort Washington, MD, about 15 miles south of Washington, DC.

Fletcher's Boathouse (off Map p114; ☎ 202-244-0461; www.fletchersboathouse.com; 4940 Canal Rd NW; canoe per hr/day $12/23; ⏱ 9am-7:30pm Mar-Nov; 🚌 Georgetown shuttle, DC Circulator) This boathouse is a few miles upriver from Georgetown (accessible by bike from the C&O Canal & Towpath or by car from Canal Rd). Canoes, rowboats and bicycles are available.

Potomac Paddlesports (off Map p114; ☎ 301-881-2626; www.potomacpaddlesports.com; 11917 Maple Ave, Rockville, MD; ⏱ 10am-9pm Mon-Fri, 9am-8pm Sat, 9am-6pm Sun) White-water and sea-kayaking lessons are the focus here, but there are also flat-water trips, such as fall foliage tours, moonlight tours of the Potomac and nature-lovers' tours through a wildlife refuge. Potomac Paddlesports' office is in Rockville, 21 miles north of the city center.

Thompson Boat Center (Map p72; ☎ 202-333-9543; www.thompsonboatcenter.com; 2900 Virginia Ave NW; watercraft per hr $8-13, per day $24-30; ☒ 6am-8pm; Ⓜ Foggy Bottom-GWU) Just across the street from the Kennedy Center, Thompson Boat Center rents canoes and kayaks and offers rowing classes. This is also a convenient place to rent bicycles.

GOLF

DC's three public golf courses are all fine places to enjoy a few rounds in the city. See www.golfdc.com for more information.

East Potomac Park (Map pp78–9; ☎ 202-554-7660; Ohio Dr SW; 18 holes weekday/weekend $26/30, 9 holes from $9/12; ☒ dawn-dusk; Ⓜ Smithsonian) A bit scrubby, with three courses.

Langston (Map pp78–9; ☎ 202-397-8638; 26th St NE & Benning Rd NE; 18 holes weekday/weekend $22/30, 9 holes $15/20; ☒ dawn-dusk; ☒ X1, X2 or X3 from Union Station) Fairways are flat, with lots of trees on the back nine.

Rock Creek Park Golf Course (off Map pp106–7; ☎ 202-723-8499; 1600 Rittenhouse St NW; 18 holes weekday/weekend $20/25, 9 holes $15/20; ☒ 6am-9pm Apr-Oct, 7am-5:30pm Nov-Mar; ☒ S1, S2, S4) Hilly and narrow fairways with large elevation changes – dense woods on either side replace water hazards.

HORSE RIDING

Thirteen miles of wide dirt trails crisscross the northern part of Rock Creek Park, with an Equitation Field nearby. The Rock Creek Horse Center (Map p114; ☎ 202-362-0117; www.rockcreekhorse center.com; 5100 Glover Rd NW; per hr $38; ☒ 6pm Tue-Thu, 9:30am & 11am Sat, 11am & 12:30pm Sun) offers guided trail rides, lessons and pony rides. Reservations required. Weekday rides are only available during summer; weekend rides run from April to October.

If you are interested in longer-term options, head out on River Rd towards and then past Potomac, MD. There are numerous horse farms out here offering everything from lessons to full board.

ROCK CLIMBING

In DC, climbers head for Rock Creek Park (p117). The bouldering area underneath the bridge at Massachusetts Ave and Whitehaven Rd is 20ft high and 50ft wide, large enough for four defined routes and the potential for more. Other climbing spots are at Carderock Recrea-

tion Area on the C&O Canal & Towpath (p73) and Great Falls National Park (p218). Indoor climbing walls are at the National Capital YMCA (p196), Results the Gym (p196) and an amazing wall at Sportsrock (off Map p125; ☎ 703-212-7265; www.nps.gov/grfa; 5308 Eisenhower Rd; gear & climb $27, without gear $18; ☒ noon-11pm Mon-Fri, 10am-6pm Sat & Sun) in Alexandria.

TENNIS

The city maintains over 50 free public courts, including Montrose Park (Map p114; cnr 31st & R Sts NW) and Rock Creek Park (off Map pp106–7; cnr 24th & N Sts NW). Call the DC Dept of Parks and Recreation (☎ 202-673-7647; http://dpr.dc.gov; ☒ 8am-6pm Mon-Fri) for information, schedules and a calendar of events.

SPECTATOR SPORTS

Offensive choreography, defensive policy and stiff competition: politics and sports have a lot in common. Watching sport in Washington, DC may come second to following politics, but it is still a popular pastime. Professional baseball, football, basketball, hockey and soccer teams, as well as competitive college basketball, keep DC sports fans active year-round.

You can try to buy tickets to games for all of the following teams direct from arenas and stadiums, or from scalpers outside, but usually you'll find yourself trying to score them online beforehand. Here's a list of providers, most of which will charge you an inconvenient 'convenience' charge (Ticketmaster is particularly egregious). You should also try Craigslist (www.craigslist.com), which serves as an online scalping service.

Dream Tix! (☎ 703-931-0916; www.dreamtix.com)

StubHub! (☎ 866-788-2482; www.stubhub.com)

TicketExchange by Ticketmaster (☎ 202-397-7328, 800-551-7328; www.ticketexchangebyticketmaster.com)

Tickets-Redskins (☎ 301-953-1163, 800-250-2525; www.tickets-redskins.com)

FOOTBALL

The Washington Redskins are a populist religion in DC, no matter whether they are winning or losing. 'Skins games empty the city, drawing streams of people into sports bars and living rooms to cheer on the tackles, turnovers and touchdowns.

The Redskins play September through January at FedEx Field (off Map pp78–9; ☎ 301-276-6000; www.redskins.com; 1600 Fedex Way, Landover, MD; tickets $40-500), but rare is the opportunity to actually see them play here.

There is a miles-long waiting list to buy season tickets, so there are never tickets left for individual games. The only exception is when some are returned to the box office by the opposing team, which you can find out about by calling the stadium two or three days before the game. If you have your heart set on seeing the 'Skins in person, online agents (see p199) will be pleased to sell you tickets with a hefty markup.

To get here, drive to FedEx Field by taking the Central Ave exit from I-495, or walk to the field from Morgan Blvd Metro station (1 mile). Or just watch the game in a local bar – everyone else in the city will be doing it.

BASKETBALL

All of DC's basketball teams – including the National Basketball Association's (NBA) Washington Wizards, the women's Washington Mystics (WNBA) and the Georgetown University Hoyas – play at the Verizon Center (Map p88; ☎ 202-639-0220; www.verizoncenter.com; 601 F St NW; ❤ box office 10am-5:30pm Mon-Sat; Ⓜ Gallery Pl-Chinatown).

The Washington Wizards (www.nba.com/wizards) play November through April. Tickets are as cheap as $10 for the nosebleed section; $50 for decent seats in the upper concourse; $80 to $90 for the club concourse; and higher and higher.

The Washington Mystics (www.wnba.com/mystics) play May through September and ticket prices are cheaper. The Georgetown Hoyas (hoyasaxa.com/sports/bball.htm) are part of the National College Athletic Association (NCAA), which plays during the same season as the NBA, ending with the NCAA tournament in March.

Also in the NCAA, the University of Maryland Terrapins has a consistently strong basketball team. Season ticket–holders buy up all the seats at the sleek, new Comcast Center (off Map pp106–7; ☎ 301-314-7070; www.umterps.com/facilities/md-comcast-center.html; Terrapin Tri, College Park, MD) on campus at the University of Maryland. If students don't pick up their entire allotment, single-game tickets may go on sale about two weeks before the game, but phone the ticket office to find out for sure.

BASEBALL

The Washington Nationals play at Nationals Stadium (Map pp78–9; ☎ 888-632-6287; http://washington.nationals.mlb.com; 1500 S Capitol St SE; Ⓜ Navy Yard). Games, with their 'running of the president' (an odd race between caricatures of George Washington, Abraham Lincoln, Thomas Jefferson and Teddy Roosevelt) are fun, more so in the rare event the Nationals win. Grandstand seats start at $5; infield boxes go for $63.

HOCKEY

The Verizon Center (Map p88; ☎ 202-639-0220; www.verizoncenter.com; 601 F St NW; ❤ box office 10am-5:30pm Mon-Sat; Ⓜ Gallery Pl-Chinatown) turns to ice when DC's National Hockey League team, the Washington Capitals (http://capitals.nhl.com), are playing. Tickets start from around $35.

SOCCER

Multiple-time Major League Soccer champions DC United (www.dcunited.com) play April through October at RFK Stadium (off Map pp78–9; ☎ 800-664-5056; 2400 East Capitol St; Ⓜ Stadium-Armory). Tickets start around $15.

The women's team, Washington Freedom (www.womensprosoccer.com/dc), whose roster has included US national team stars such as Mia Hamm and Abby Wambach, also plays at RFK.

SLEEPING

top picks

- Mansion on O Street (p212)
- Willard Inter-Continental Hotel (p205)
- Chester Arthur House (p209)
- St Regis Washington (p204)
- Tabard Inn (p210)
- Hotel Monaco (p210)
- Intown Uptown Inn (p214)
- Hay-Adams Hotel (p203)
- Dupont at the Circle (p211)
- DC Guesthouse (p209)

DC has always been a good town for accommodations. Before there was even a city here there was Suter's tavern, where George Washington himself sank some beers with local landowners and persuaded the latter to sell their holdings to Congress for $66 an acre, thus forming the core of the new capital.

Since then the city has done a good job of defining much of itself via providing places to stay. This is, after all, a town full of two 'T's – transients and tourists – and both groups require a place to lay their head. Visiting heads of state, politicos, journalists and the rest of the pack that comes here to participate, plan or cover important events are also a key target for local hoteliers. That said, the city has also learned to cater to Joe Travelpack and family, who've always been drawn to DC's sights, and Jacques Hipster and girlfriend, who are just now being drawn to its emerging cultural scene. Almost all of the hotels reviewed in this chapter are kitted out with wireless internet, and most luxury hotels also come with fitness rooms, 24-hour concierge services and the like.

Hotels are so crucial to Washington's identity they've become an indispensable part of our architectural heritage. Some of the city's classic accommodations (or new hotels in classic buildings) are monuments of Victorian, beaux arts and jazz-era opulence – exemplars include the Hay-Adams St Regis and Hotel Washington (now the W Hotel Washington), located near the White House. All of these hotels are fine in their own right, and we're sure your city also has some grande dame institutions similar to the above, but the historical scope of DC accommodations is tough to bear. When we call rooms the Roosevelt suite, we mean it: Teddy slept here.

Over the past two decades folks in need of a Washington bed have become more demanding and (ostensibly) more hip, to the general benefit of capital hotel hounds (the addition of the massive Convention Center to Downtown also helped in this regard). As a result, some digs don't have the sterile sense of ruthless similarity you get in your run-of-the-mill garden/comfort/executive by [insert chain here]. There is a bit of edge – nothing too racy, just pleasantly funky – to boutique sleeps like the Rouge, the Helix and to a lesser extent, the Palomar.

Bed and breakfasts often occupy any one of the gorgeous renovated Victorian mansions spattered about town. The character here is usually redolent of Old Washington, a place to flaunt cigars and brandy and ridiculous moustaches in baroquely appointed sitting rooms. The better B&Bs in town capture the dignity of the old days minus their pretension; the best ones, like DC Guesthouse DC, take it a step further, livening the chintz with a playful bit of kitsch and eclectic design. B&Bs are also usually cheap compared with the bigger luxury hotels, yet come with more personalized service. Their drawback is less of a sense of privacy and the creaks that come with operating businesses in some of the city's older houses – rooms are often small, and you occasionally have to deal with the odd grotty bathroom or musty smell.

If you're in DC for a while and need a roof over your head, your first option is, of course, the *Post* or *City Paper* classifieds, but you also might try websites like www.roomster.com, www.easyroomate.com, www.apartmentsearch.com and Craigslist (www.craigslist.com). The latter in particular is also useful if you're looking for rent swapping or short-term subletting deals.

Most of the following sleeping places offer parking. However, it's rarely free. Expect to pay from $15 to $40 (!) per day to keep your car in the city.

ROOM RATES

Sleeping options are organized here by budget, with the cheapest rooms listed first. Prices in Washington, DC fluctuate widely according to season and availability. Peak seasons are spring (late March to June) and autumn (September to October). Hotels that cater mainly to business and government travelers drop their prices significantly – by as much as 25% – on weekends. The best rates are usually available by reserving on the internet or through a booking agent. Many small B&B options do not advertise or book rooms *except* through a booking agent. See opposite for more information on web-based hotel deals. Check-in/check-out time is normally 3pm/noon. Many places will

BOOK ONLINE

Most of the rates we've included in this chapter are 'rack' rates, quoted to walk-in customers at the front desk. You can often find much cheaper rates by booking your accommodations online and scouring the web for travel deals – a $500 room can drop to $250 after 10 minutes of solid Google time. There are lots of travel websites to list here, but some of our favorites include www.kayak.com (which is a nice clearing house that gathers results from several discount sites, then directs you to the parent site of your choice), www.orbitz.com, www.priceline.com, www.expedia.com, www.cheaprooms.com, www.travelocity.com – the list goes on. See also p212.

Boutique hotels are hot in DC and there seems to be a new one opening every day. Calling ahead is rarely the best way to score a room. Instead, try an internet booking agent, which purchases blocks of rooms at a discounted rate and then passes a portion of this discount on to the consumer. We like www.hoteldiscounts.com, www.hotels.com and www.lonelyplanet.com. Two other booking agents we recommend are Capitol Reservations (www.capitolreservations.com) and DC Hotels (☎ 703-875-8711; www.dchotels.com).

allow early check-in as long as the room is available, or will provide temporary luggage storage if it is not.

WHITE HOUSE AREA & FOGGY BOTTOM

Sleeping in the president's 'hood has lots of perks even if the areas themselves don't have much 'neighborhood' feeling. The White House Area and Foggy Bottom are full of luxurious, often historic, hotels that usually cater to visiting dignitaries, movie stars and high-profile politicians. If you can afford it, this is a great place to lay your head, as the central location means it's just minutes from some of DC's most popular attractions. Foggy Bottom is slightly cheaper than the White House Area, and has some fun boutique options.

WHITE HOUSE AREA
SOFITEL LAFAYETTE SQUARE

Map p64   Business $$

☎ 202-730-8800, 800-763-4835; www.sofitel.com; 806 15th St NW; r from $210; Ⓜ McPherson Sq; ⊠ 🛜

In a fabulous corner location with lots of windows, the Sofitel's airy rooms let in loads of natural sunlight (try to reserve one of the 2nd- or 3rd-floor rooms facing 15th or H Sts; they are the brightest). Rooms in the historic building, erected in 1880, have a whiff of Parisian art deco about them; embroidered armchairs and marble fireplaces are fanciful embellishments in otherwise modern rooms done up in geometric design schemes that impart a pleasing feng shui.

HAY-ADAMS HOTEL Map p64   Business $$$

☎ 202-638-6600, 800-853-6807; www.hayadams.com; 1 Lafayette Sq; r from $430; Ⓜ McPherson Sq; Ⓟ ⊠ 🛜

Italian Renaissance exterior, English Renaissance interior – well, you can never get too much Renaissance, right? The Hay is a beautiful old building, where 'nothing is overlooked but the White House,' named for two mansions that once stood on the site (owned by secretary of state John Hay and historian Henry Adams). In their day they hosted the political and intellectual elite at Washington's leading salons. Today the hotel has a palazzo-style lobby and probably the best rooms of the old-school luxury genre in the city, all puffy mattresses like clouds shaded by four-poster canopies and gold-braid tassels, the sort of chamber you call a *chambre* and drink champagne

PRICE GUIDE

Most DC hotels, particularly upscale chains, have no set rates. Instead, prices vary from week to week and even day to day, depending on season and availability. Hotel rates are generally lower on weekends (Friday and Saturday) than on weekdays. Rates often vary seasonally as well, with peak seasons being late March through June and September through October. Discounts are often available for seniors, children and just about anybody if business is slow, so don't be shy about asking.

$	under $150
$$	$150-300
$$$	more than $300

To make your life simpler, we've included DC's 14.5% room tax in these rates.

from a crystal shoe and light cigars with $100 bills – oh. Damn. Non-smoking. There's a tasteful soupçon of Washington scandal on top of all this: back in the 1980s, this hotel was a site where Oliver North wooed contributors to his illegal contra-funding scheme.

ST REGIS WASHINGTON

Map p64   Business $$$

☎ 202-638-2626; www.starwoodhotels.com; 923 16th St NW; r from $500; Ⓜ McPherson Sq; 🖵 📶
The American Institute of Architects de-scribes the St Regis as 'indisputably one of the grandest hotels in the city' – and those guys don't throw such praise about lightly. But hell, what else can you say about a freestanding building designed to resemble nothing less than an Italian grand palace? Seriously, they shouldn't let cars pull up to the front of the St Regis – only horse-drawn buggies. The palatial exuberance carries inside: with crystal chandeliers hanging from coffered ceilings and oriental rugs on the parquet floor, the lobby of the St Regis Washington reflects the grandeur of a Renaissance palace. The rooms are a bit understated after all that – cheaper ones too much so, with boring sheets, over-furnishing and barebones carpets – al-though suites, with their antique furniture, feel plucked from the Gilded Age. And in general the service is suitably obsequious, although there are hitches, as anywhere. Room 1012 is famed for being the place where Monica Lewinsky spilled details of her now infamous shenanigans with Presi-dent Clinton to Ken Starr's investigators.

W HOTEL WASHINGTON

Map p64   Business $$$

☎ 202-661-2400; www.starwoodhotels.com/ whotels/index.html; cnr 15th St & Pennsylvania Ave; r from $550; Ⓜ McPherson Sq; 🖵 📶
When the oldest continuously operating hotel in Washington, DC was bought out by the W Hotel chain, everyone connected to the DC accommodations scene had a small heart attack. Would the famously hip W brand do away with the class, tradition and storied sense of history that has sat around the corner from the White House since 1918? Sadly, they kinda did. Yes, the old rooms were a bit antiquarian but – well, it was the freaking *Hotel Washington*! It was supposed to be stuffy. Now rooms

and suites are decked out in a sort of *Mad Men* meets *Wallpaper* magazine blend of retro/futuristic, all smooth lines and pared down furnishings, polished and occasion-ally playful. This look works well in some suites, but in smaller normal guest rooms the effect falls flat. And frankly, given the hotel's stately early-20th-century exterior (it was designed by the same firm that built the main branch of the New York Public Library, and it shows), we'd like a little more classicism on the inside. Ah well; the roof still has some of the best views of the city.

FOGGY BOTTOM

ONE WASHINGTON CIRCLE

Map p64   Suites $$

☎ 202-872-1680; www.thecirclehotel.com; 1 Washington Circle; ste from $150; Ⓜ Foggy Bottom-GWU; 🖵 📶 📺
At its eponymous address, this sleek, mod-ern all-suite hotel has always attracted high-profile guests; for example, Nixon maintained offices here after the Watergate scandal totaled his presidency. On-site kitchens make for easy self-catering, and the rooms themselves are actually a good deal, all shimmering sheets and spaces that look like a swinging (but tasteful) '60s bachelor pad – you know, the one Bond seduces the Russian spy in (come to think of it, that sort of thing has probably happened here…).

DOUBLETREE GUEST SUITES

WASHINGTON DC Map p64   Suites $$

☎ 202-785-2000; www.doubletree.com; 801 New Hampshire Ave NW; ste from $169; Ⓜ Foggy Bottom-GWU; 🅿 ✗ 🖵 💻 📺
Doubletree may mean bland corporatism to some, but in this case all that money has translated into an all-suites extrava-ganza. This is a good choice for families or small groups – the one- and two-bedroom digs are large enough to comfortably ac-commodate both, especially if you're self-catering. That said, you are trading style for size; there's not much to distinguish these rooms from a Holiday Inn but the extra space. Pets are allowed.

HOTEL LOMBARDY Map p64   Boutique $$

☎ 202-828-2600, 800-424-5486; www.hotellom bardy.com; 2019 I St NW; r from $175; Ⓜ Foggy Bottom-GWU; 🅿 ✗ 🖵 💻

Done up in Venetian decor (shuttered doors, warm gold walls), and beloved by World Bank and State Department types, this European boutique has multilingual staff and an international vibe – you hear French and Spanish as often as English in its halls. This attitude carries into rooms decorated with original artwork, and Chinese and European antiques.

GEORGE WASHINGTON UNIVERSITY INN Map p64 — Family $$

☎ 800-426-4455; www.gwuinn.com; 824 New Hampshire Ave NW; r from $180; Ⓜ Foggy Bottom-GWU; ✖ ☞

As you might guess, a lot of parents (of GWU students) find themselves staying in this pleasant hotel, situated on a quiet tree-lined street in the midst of tweedy academics and the occasional drunken undergrad. A little bit of colonial furnishing brightens up rooms that are fine if not particularly memorable; ask the staff to show you a few, as some have good views out onto the Potomac.

MELROSE HOTEL Map p64 — Boutique $$

☎ 202-955-6400; www.melrosehotelwashington dc.com; 2430 Pennsylvania Ave NW; r from $200; Ⓜ Foggy Bottom-GWU; ✖ ☞

For that chintzy, European luxury boudoir feel, you can't go wrong with the Melrose, which also boasts a fine, fine location: a few blocks from the Metro, steps from Rock Creek Park, just over the bridge from Georgetown and a plush spot overlooking a happening span of Pennsylvania Ave. Rooms are all terry-cloth soft and dark-wood elegance; the latter sense of style is very evident in the lobby and grand, on-site library.

RIVER INN Map p64 — Boutique $$

☎ 888-874-0100; www.theriverinn.com; 924 25th St NW; r from $250; Ⓜ Foggy Bottom-GWU; ✖ ☞

On a quiet residential street (despite the name, it's not actually on the river) a block away from the Kennedy Center, this building looks like a generic bit o' brick. Rooms are a little more exciting on the inside, which has a mostly modern layout with neutral tones offset by dark-wood accents. The real reason to stay here is easy access to Georgetown on one end, the White House on the other. Internet deals available through the website run as low as $100 per night.

RITZ-CARLTON Map p64 — Luxury $$$

☎ 800-241-3333; www.ritzcarlton.com; 1150 22nd St NW; r incl breakfast from $280; Ⓜ Farragut North; ✖ ☞

DC's first Ritz-Carlton offers lots of excellent little perks: goose-down pillows, marble bathrooms, and all the corporate amenities you would expect from the famous chain. The wood and marble lobby is the sort of spot where you'd split a cigar with Ulysses Grant; conference rooms could host a multinational corporation's most extravagant teleconference; and the fitness room could train the Olympic team of a small country. Rooms have a 1950s luxury vibe, with geometric patterns offset by beaux arts flourishes adding a little individuality to each chamber.

WILLARD INTER-CONTINENTAL HOTEL Map p64 — Luxury $$$

☎ 202-628-9100; http://washington.interconti nental.com/washa/index.shtml; 1401 Pennsylvania Ave NW; r from $349; Ⓜ Federal Triangle

You can't sleep much closer to DC history than here. This is where MLK wrote his 'I Have a Dream' speech; the term 'lobbyist' was coined (by President Grant to describe political wranglers trolling the lobby); and Lincoln, Coolidge and Harding have all lain their heads. Nathaniel Hawthorne observed that it could 'much more justly [be] called the center of Washington…than either the Capitol, the White House, or the State Department.' Which is all well and good, but damn if this isn't an amazing building on its own merits. The building is a masterpiece of the beaux arts movement, all fancy crenellations and soaring, dignity-laden elegance – upon entering the marble lobby, you'd be forgiven for expecting Jay Gatsby to stumble down the stairs clutching a bourbon. The chandelier-hung hallways are still thick with lobbyists and corporate aristocrats buffing their loafers on the dense carpets. The actual rooms are just as opulent: flowy curtains framed by potted palms, power-player views over the city and beds that kinda scream at you to engage in some high-class scandal (just sayin'). The stunning presidential suites are often utilized by visiting heads of state and start at around the trifling rate of $2300 a night. Don't miss the Round Robin bar (p173), which claims to be the birthplace of the mint julep.

RENAISSANCE MAYFLOWER HOTEL
Map p64   Luxury $$$
☎ 202-347-3000; www.renaissancehotels.com; 1127 Connecticut Ave NW; r from $350; Ⓜ Farragut North; ⊠ 🛜

J Edgar Hoover dined here; Richard Nixon resided here; and there are rumors that John F Kennedy sampled the charms of the fairer sex here. Although not the exclusive enclave it once was, this hotel remains regal with lots of frills and marble, and a beautiful grand ballroom. The actual rooms are a little more contemporary than classical, which we reckon doesn't quite jive with the grand ball theme of the building. High tea in the lounge-like hotel restaurant is great.

GEORGETOWN

Georgetown is one of DC's loveliest neighborhoods and its accommodations match its character: elegant and expensive. Keep in mind that staying in Georgetown is not convenient to visiting other parts of the city, as there's no Metro service out here.

HOTEL MONTICELLO
Map p72   Boutique $
☎ 202-337-0900, 800-388-2410; www.monticello hotel.com; 1075 Thomas Jefferson St NW; r $120; 🚌 Georgetown shuttle from Foggy Bottom-GWU Metro; ⊠ 🛜

An attractive boutique hotel popular with European visitors, Hotel Monticello is just off M St near the C&O Canal. It's one of the better deals in Washington; the rooms, with their brass-and-crystal chandeliers, colonial-reproduction furniture and tasteful flower arrangements, have a Euro-townhouse feel, like those cramped but cozy hotels you get in central London. This is honestly the same room you'll find in a dozen other DC hotels, but much cheaper – when did Georgetown ever get so budget-friendly?

LATHAM HOTEL
Map p72   Boutique $$
☎ 202-726-5000; www.thelatham.com; 3000 M St NW; r from $200; 🚌 Georgetown shuttle, DC Circulator; ⊠ 🛜 📱

Hot with visiting celebrities and European jet setters, this chic redbrick boutique hotel in the midst of the M St scene exudes European charm. The two-story Carriage House suites are luxe in a 19th-century kinda way; standard rooms possess a white

and off-white monochrome look overlaid by antique charm. One of DC's finest restaurants, Citronelle (p152) is on site. The rooftop sundeck by the pool is good for a chillax.

GEORGETOWN INN
Map p72   Romantic $$
☎ 888-587-2388; www.georgetowninn.com; 1310 Wisconsin Ave NW; r from $200; 🚌 Georgetown shuttle, DC Circulator; Ⓟ 🛜

The blue-blooded Georgetown Inn with a Revolutionary War–period look (think old Europe meets American colonial) is a gorgeous property favored by Georgetown University alumni and parents on college weekends. The inn spreads rooms through a collection of restored 18th-century townhouses and its stately decor (four-post beds, furniture with feet) is matched by stately service.

RITZ-CARLTON GEORGETOWN
Map p72   Luxury $$$
☎ 202-912-4100; www.ritzcarlton.com; 3100 South St NW; r from $380; 🚌 Georgetown shuttle, DC Circulator; ⊠ 🛜

Discreetly tucked into the revitalized waterfront of the harbor, the Ritz-Carlton reeks of swankness. Its slick design incorporates the surrounding industrial buildings, including a towering incinerator smokestack and several historic houses; the result is a modern, luxurious but understated setting. Rooms have feather duvets, goose-down pillows and oversized marble bathrooms; many also offer fabulous views of the Potomac. The hotel bar, Degrees, crawls with white-collars from area offices during happy hour.

FOUR SEASONS HOTEL
Map p72   Boutique $$$
☎ 202-342-0444; www.fourseasons.com; 2800 Pennsylvania Ave NW; r from $650; 🚌 Georgetown shuttle, DC Circulator; ⊠ 🛜

The local Four Seasons Hotel is perched atop Rock Creek Park's south end. It looks boxy and plain on the outside, but on the inside, you'll find even low-end rooms offer more space than most DC digs. Suites in particular have the feel of a nice studio apartment; other rooms are attractive enough, and many have good views over the C&O (ask to see a few), although we could do without the mauve color scheme.

CAPITOL HILL & SOUTHEAST

Capitol Hill can be easily divided into two accommodations areas. The northwest side of the Capitol, bordering Downtown, is an area in which the accommodations options are mainly upscale hotels – most of them large chain hotels with hundreds of rooms. By contrast, Capitol Hill itself (east of the Capitol building) is a residential area where accommodations include small guesthouses and B&Bs. There is one large hotel of note in Southwest DC as well.

CAPITOL CITY GUESTHOUSE
off Map pp78-9   Hostel $

☎ 202-328-3210; 2411 Benning Rd NE; dm from $24; 🚌 X2 bus from Union Station; 🖧 🛜

This is a cheap and cheerful hostel with decently clean dorms that tend to have a good communal vibe if there are enough people around. The real pleasure here is the staff and management; we've found them to be unfailingly helpful and considerate, going out of their way to make guests feel at home – often a rarity in budget digs. You are a bit out of the center here and will be relying on buses, but they are reliable, and you are close to the excellent nightlife action on H St NE.

WILLIAM PENN HOUSE
Map pp78-9   Hostel $

☎ 202-543-5560; www.quaker.org/pennhouse; 515 E Capitol St SE; r per person $35; Ⓜ Capitol South, Eastern Market; 🖧 ♿

No drugs or booze allowed, but this is not only one of the cheapest places to stay in the city (and in a prime location at that), it's also clean, and breakfast is included. Family rooms (up to four people) are available for $100 per night. The Quaker-run facility doesn't require religious observance, but there is a religious theme throughout, and it prefers guests be active in progressive causes.

THOMPSON-MARKWARD HALL
Map pp78-9   Long-term $

☎ 202-546-3255; www.ywch.org; 235 2nd St NE; r $900 per month; Ⓜ Union Station

Young women staying at least two weeks might consider this communal option, which is open to women 18 to 34 who are working or studying in Washington. (In summer, 90% of its guests are Hill interns.) The rates include two meals a day plus Sunday brunch, which is good value considering the average price of a sublet apartment in Washington. All rooms are small, furnished singles with phones, computer hookups and shared bathroom. The mood is like that of an upscale dorm, with a spacious courtyard, sundeck, pretty dining room and sitting areas. Coin laundry is available. Drawbacks: you can't drink, smoke or bring male guests above lobby level. (Thompson-Markward's second name is The Young Woman's Christian Home but, apart from these rules, you'd never know it.) If you start missing the Y-chromosome set, the Capitol Hill bar scene is just a couple of blocks away.

MAISON ORLEANS
Map pp78-9   B&B $$

☎ 202-328-3510, 877-893-3233; 414 5th St SE; r $140-180; Ⓜ Eastern Market, Capitol South; 🖧 🛜

The Maison is within excellent walking distance of the Capitol, Eastern Market and the Mall; you'd be hard pressed to find a better-located B&B. Or a prettier one: the look of the place is marvelous, a great example of the sturdy, elegant architecture that characterizes Capitol Hill row houses. The owner has tried to infuse a bit of French Quarter sensibility into the rooms (note the name), which are decked out in chintzy antique chic; the end effect comes off as somewhere between old school New Orleans and DC, which suits our nostalgic hearts fine.

CAPITOL HILL SUITES
Map pp78-9   Suites $$

☎ 202-543-6000; www.capitolhillsuites.com; 200 C St SE; ste incl breakfast from $170; Ⓜ Capitol South; 🖧 🛜

This all-suite property is ideally located in the heart of Hill legislative action. It's the only hotel that is actually *on* the Hill and heavily favored by congressional interns (even a few congresspeople and senators rent suites). And no wonder: the place is good value, especially since weekly and monthly rates are available. Thanks to expansive renovation work, rooms are a fair deal larger than the shoe boxes you often find in smaller DC properties, and they're attractive too, all clean lines, soft blue walls and subtle chocolate embellishments that add a bit of warmth to otherwise contemporary chambers.

PHOENIX PARK HOTEL

Map pp78-9   Business $$

☎ 202-638-6900, 800-824-5419; www.phoenix
parkhotel.com; 520 N Capitol St; r from $180;
Ⓜ Union Station; Ⓟ ⊠ 🐕 💻 ♿

It may look like a corporate bland-block
from the outside, but you could host a wake,
or a meeting of the Dail (Irish parliament), or
at least a rowdy Guinness-downing session
here. Right, enough Irish stereotyping, but
really, the rooms, upstairs from the Dubliner
pub, do have the feel of a Trinity College
reading room that Joyce could have penned
an unreadable novel in. Plus, this spot has
been home away from home for visiting
Irish politicians like Gerry Adams, so when
they lay on the Emerald Isle kitsch, it's genu-
ine. Kids under 16 stay free.

HOTEL GEORGE Map pp78-9   Boutique $$

☎ 202-347-4200; www.hotelgeorge.com; 15 E St
NW; r from $300; Ⓜ Union Station; 🐕 📶

George was the first DC hotel to take the
term 'boutique' to a daring, ultramodern
level. The stylish interior is framed by clean
lines, chrome-and-glass furniture and
modern art, with rooms that exude a cool,
frosty Zen. The pop-art presidential accents
(paintings of American currency, artfully
rearranged and diced up) are a little over-
done, but that's a minor complaint about
what is otherwise the hippest lodging on
the Hill.

SOUTHWEST DC

MANDARIN ORIENTAL

Map pp78-9   Luxury $$$

☎ 202-554-8588, 888-526-6567; www.mandarin
oriental.com; 1330 Maryland Ave SW; r from $600;
Ⓜ Smithsonian; 🐕 📶 🅿

The Mandarin delivers about everything
you'd expect: big-box swank, ridiculous
levels of amenities, service that's appropri-
ate for a Roman emperor, more amenities,
one of the city's best restaurants, City Zen
(p155), another amenity, rooms plucked
from a contemporary designer's dream
offset with comfy chaises and small Asian
touches, throw in an amenity etc. The only
drawback is the location: the massive Man-
darin grounds essentially form an isolated
island that can be difficult to access and
emerge from if you plan to explore the city
by foot, although plenty of shuttle services
are available.

DOWNTOWN & PENN QUARTER

With the revitalization of the Penn Quarter
and its trendy bars and restaurants, Down-
town is becoming a hip sleeping option. The
construction of the Convention Center also
means it has become hotel central for business
travelers. The obvious result is that accom-
modations are expensive in this area, although
there is certainly no shortage of choice.

HOSTELLING INTERNATIONAL – WASHINGTON DC Map p88   Hostel $

☎ 202-737-2333, 800-909-4776; www.hiwash
ingtondc.org; 1009 11th St NW; dm incl breakfast
members/nonmembers from $25/28; Ⓜ Metro
Center; 🐕 💻

If you're looking for an enormous (ie 270-
room) friendly hostel full of fun, young
international types, look no further than
this budget institution. The dorms are clean
and well-kept, although rowdy guests can
change this equation quickly. A program-
ming office organizes often free and always
unique outings: night tours of the monu-
ments, political panel discussions, concerts
at the Kennedy Center and the like. Res-
ervations highly recommended March to
October.

LOFTY INN Map p88   Hostel $

☎ 202-506-7106; www.dclofty.com; 1333 11th
St NW; dm from $33; Ⓜ Mt Vernon Sq/7th St-
Convention Center; 🐕 📶

Located in a crisp, clean house near the
Convention Center, Lofty, with its brick walls
and smooth wood floors vaguely delivers
on the implied hipness and semiluxury its
name suggests. The dorms are just dorms –
nothing to go wild over – but this is a good
central location for backpackers wanting to
explore the District on the cheap.

DISTRICT HOTEL Map p88   Business $

☎ 800-350-5759; www.thedistricthotel.com; 1440
Rhode Island Ave NW; r $80-100; Ⓜ Dupont Circle

Cheap and functional, the District is not for
those who want large rooms or quiet. What
it does provide is your own, small spartan
room, comfy enough if you're low mainte-
nance, for $100 or under (sometimes as low
as $50 online). That's as cheap as you'll find
this close to Dupont and Downtown DC,
unless you want to go with dorms.

HOTEL HARRINGTON Map p88   Family $

☎ 202-628-8140, 800-424-8532; www.hotel-harrington.com; 436 11th St NW; r from $120; Ⓜ Federal Triangle; ⊠ 🛜 ♿

As one of the most affordable options near the Mall, this hotel is popular among school groups, families and international guests. The rooms are basic and not particularly pretty, but considering the price, service is pretty spot on in this centrally located spot. We can think of other places that cost thrice as much where we've been treated with half the consideration shown by the Harrington staff. The budget-minded won't be disappointed, but if you're more comfort minded, look elsewhere.

CHESTER ARTHUR HOUSE
Map p88   B&B $$

☎ 877-893-3233; www.chesterarthurhouse.com; 1339 14th St NW; r $115-275; Ⓜ U Street-Cardozo, Shaw/Howard University; ⊠

Run by a delightful journalist couple with quite a bit of travel experience under their belts – they've both got *National Geographic* credentials – this is a good B&B option for those who want to explore under Washington's skin. Named for an obscure president primarily known for great sideburns (he also started the civil service), your accommodations are in one of three rooms in a beautiful Logan Circle row house. The house is Victorian in character, filled with antiques, the collected bric-a-brac of your hosts' global expeditions and a general sense of cozy conviviality. You're a 10-minute walk from the U St Corridor and some of the best nightlife and dining in the city.

MORRISON-CLARK INN
Map p88   Boutique $$

☎ 202-898-1200; www.morrisonclark.com; 1015 L St NW; r incl breakfast $150-300; Ⓜ Mt Vernon Sq/7th St-Convention Center; Ⓟ ✕ ⊠ 💻

The only hotel in town on the Register of Historic Places, this elegant inn has rooms ranging from Victorian to neoclassical, and embellishments from private balconies to marble fireplaces. All chambers conjure up the spirit of the antebellum South. Combining two 1864 Victorian residences, the boutique is thick with fine antiques, lace and chintz, but beware this is a *historic* home, and rooms are rather smaller than what you may be used to.

HOTEL HELIX Map p88   Boutique $$

☎ 202-462-9001, 866-508-0658; www.hotelhelix.com; 1430 Rhode Island Ave NW; r from $230; Ⓜ McPherson Sq; ⊠ 🛜

Modish and highlighter bright, the Helix is playfully cool – the perfect hotel for the bouncy international set that makes up the surrounding neighborhood of Dupont Circle. Little touches suggest a youthful energy (Pop Rocks in the minibar) balanced with worldly cool, like the pop-punk decor – just camp enough to be endearing. From the pink neon lights and sliding doors at the entrance, to the sign in the gym commanding 'Burn, baby, burn,' to the orange Barbie-doll throw pillows decorating the rooms, this is a decidedly eccentric Kimpton stand-out. Specialty rooms include Bunk (that's right, bunk beds) and the more enticing Zone, which features lounge seating and a loaded entertainment center.

HENLEY PARK HOTEL Map p88   Boutique $$

☎ 202-638-5200, 800-222-8474; www.henleypark.com; 926 Massachusetts Ave; r from $250; Ⓜ Mt Vernon Sq/7th St-Convention Center; ⊠ 🛜

A beautiful Tudor building with gargoyles and stained glass makes a fine setting for this historic hotel. The rooms – decked in prints and brass furniture – are as elegant as the edifice; some look like a piece of Delft porcelain given bedroom form. Others are slightly more understated, with solid color wallpaper worked over with flowery patterns; they're just as beautiful.

DC GUESTHOUSE Map p88   B&B $$

☎ 202-332-2502; www.dcguesthouse.com; 1337 10th St NW; r $200-300; Ⓜ Mt Vernon Sq-Convention Center, Shaw-Howard University; ⊠ 🛜

DC Guesthouse, you are just a big building full of win. Gosh, where do we start? Well, there's the house itself, a gorgeous old mansion, and its main common areas, which look like they were smashed through every interesting exhibit in the Smithsonian, then tastefully tidied up by a combination brilliant-curator-cum-interior-designer. That same genius had a go at the seven highly individualized rooms; the 'Red Room' has a sexy, contemporary Euro-aesthetic; the 'Chocolate' could be Dorothy Parker's boudoir; the 'Blue' is just hip, full stop. Original art, an off-center collection of global kitsch and lovely owners are the frosting on the cake of one of our favorite small places to stay in the capital.

HOTEL MONACO Map p88 Boutique $$
☎ 202-628-7177; www.monaco-dc.com; 700 F St NW; r from $240; Ⓜ Gallery Pl-Chinatown; Ⓟ ⊠ Ⓧ ⌷

The neoclassical facade has aged with considerable grace at this marble temple to stylish glamour. Free goldfish on request and a geometric, deco-inspired interior help polish the 1930s, cool-daddy-o vibe, all set in the historic, grand Corinthian-columned, all-marble 1839 Tariff Building. Bold artwork and modern furniture blend masterfully in the wood-paneled lobby; funky prints and jewel tones add new life to the arched ceilings and wood molding in the guestrooms. The on-site restaurant Poste (p157) is one of DC's hottest.

DONOVAN HOUSE Map p88 Luxury $$$
☎ 202-737-1200; www.donovanhousedc.com; 1155 14th St NW; r from $350; Ⓜ Mt Vernon Sq/7th St-Convention Center, McPherson Sq; Ⓧ ⌷ Ⓔ

With flat-screen TVs, molded club chairs, stainless-steel lamps, icy Sferra linens and geometric swirls throughout the plush rooms, plus the sort of lobby that should rightly become a nightclub come evenings, Donovan House is the brash, ultramodern new pretty girl in the DC accommodations scene. One gets the sense this place is the flag bearer, as hotels go, of the demographic shift that is evolving parts of DC into Manhattan south, which should either totally put you off it or have you booking before you finish the sentence. The rooftop pool/patio is suitably full of beautiful people on warm nights.

DUPONT CIRCLE & KALORAMA

Convenient transportation, lively nightlife and endless options make Dupont Circle the ideal destination for sleeping in DC. Shops, restaurants, museums and galleries are all at the doorstep of most hotels and B&Bs in this vicinity. The Metro, too, is easily accessible, as there are several stations in the neighborhood. Kalorama is not quite as convenient, as it lies in the northern part of the neighborhood and further from the Dupont Circle Metro.

EMBASSY INN Map p96 Family $
☎ 202-234-7800, 800-423-9111; www.embassy -inn.com; 1627 16th St NW; r from $90; Ⓜ Dupont Circle; Ⓧ ⌷

The Embassy is not quite as elegant as the Windsor, trading in the antique ambience for mostly tasteful reproductions of early-20th-century period furniture. The mosaic at the entrance and the marble stairway are originals from 1910. This is very good value for money, considering how central you are to some of the city's best eating and nightlife.

TABARD INN Map p96 Boutique $
☎ 202-785-1277; www.tabardinn.com; 1739 N St NW; r incl breakfast from $158, with shared bathroom from $113; Ⓜ Dupont Circle; Ⓧ

Named for the inn in *Canterbury Tales*, this delightful, historic hotel is set in a trio of Victorian-era row houses. The rooms are hard to generalize: all come with vintage quirks like iron bedsteads, overstuffed sofas and wing-backed armchairs, but little accents distinguish – a Matisse-like painted headboard here, Amish-looking quilts there. Downstairs the parlor, beautiful courtyard restaurant (p160) and bar have low ceilings and old furniture, highly conducive to curling up with a vintage port and the *Sunday Post*. The Wife of Bath never had it so good.

INN AT DUPONT CIRCLE Map p96 B&B $
☎ 202-467-6777; www.theinnatdupontcircle .com; 1312 19th St NW; r incl breakfast $95-230; Ⓜ Dupont Circle; Ⓧ

If you're craving a good range of B&B coziness in the heart of the capital, check out the four excellent heritage properties run by the Dupont Collection. Perhaps the two most convenient for the visitor are this one at Dupont South, evoking a chintz and lacy linen sensibility, and the Inn at Dupont Circle – Dupont North (1620 T St NW), which feels like the modern appointed home of a wealthy friend.

CARLYLE SUITES Map p96 Suites $
☎ 202-234-3200, 800-944-5377; www.carlyle suites.com; 1731 New Hampshire Ave NW; r from $129; Ⓜ Dupont Circle; Ⓧ ⌷

The art deco decor lends a retro air to this all-suite hotel, but its facilities are modern. The rooms live up to the promise implied by the impressive facade, all frosty white linens and carpets offset by little red accents, like an interior candy stripe. This is a great place for families: kids under 18 stay free. Head to the bar to check email (free) and have a martini (definitely not free but damn delicious). Book online.

AKWAABA Map p96 B&B $$

☎ 877-893-3233; www.akwaaba.com; 1708 16th St NW; r $150-265; M Dupont Circle; 🐾

Akwaaba is a small chain of B&Bs that puts an emphasis on African and African American heritage in its properties. Its DC outpost is ensconced in a fine, late-19th-century Dupont mansion; rooms are themed from abstractions ('Inspiration,' which has fine, airy ceilings and a slanting skylight) to authors ('Zora,' an all-red room that's romantic as all hell, perfect for a romantic weekend). The cooking gets rave reviews, and the Dupont vibe is literally at your doorstep.

SWANN HOUSE Map p96 B&B $$

☎ 202-265-4414; www.swannhouse.com; 1808 New Hampshire Ave NW; r incl breakfast $175-395; M Dupont Circle; 🐾 🛜

A dozen rooms are peppered around an exquisite 1883 Romanesque mansion, all just set off enough from Dupont to be quiet, but close enough to the action for you to get raucous, if you so choose. The rooms are highly individualized; some are too frilly for our tastes (although if you like doilies and porcelain, check out the Blue Sky suite), but others we just love. The Parisienne suite, with its fireplace and modern paintings, has a feeling of set-off seclusion; the hip Shanghai'away has rich colors and is overlaid with a well-executed Asian theme.

HOTEL PALOMAR Map p96 Boutique $$

☎ 202-448-1800, 877-866-8030; www.hotelpalomar-dc.com; 2121 P St NW; r from $200; M Dupont Circle; 🐾 🛜

Palomar has an 'art in motion' theme inspired by the 1930s French Modernist movement. The rooms look like multimedia galleries, with furniture that resembles modern art and geometric marble floors. Colors are bold, objets d'art, like floaty Lucite busts, grace the walls, and hip accents like animal-print sheets funk up the vibe. We just love how pet-friendly this hotel (and fellows in the Kimpton chain) is. Not only does your pooch get pampered each night with gourmet treats at turndown, he can also get a doggie massage. If he wants

to socialize, head to the Bark Bar, a three-tiered water bar for thirsty pets just outside the hotel. Humans will dig the complimentary evening wine reception in the hotel living room, but there's no reason to leave Fido upstairs. Drop him off at the Dish, the hotel's pet lounging area.

HOTEL MADERA Map p96 Boutique $$

☎ 202-296-7600, 800-368-5691; www.hotelmadera.com; 1310 New Hampshire Ave NW; r from $250; M Dupont Circle; 🐾 🛜

Cozy yet cosmopolitan, this hotel is another Kimpton property, the focus here being more of an intimate, small boutique than large funk-da-house hipster haunt. It's a little more staid than fellows such as Helix, Rouge and the Palomar, but more romantic for that, as well as classier. Here the modern art doesn't feel fun so much as tasteful. Rooms are outfitted in dark earth tones, colors as smooth as the thick, silky sheets.

ROUGE HOTEL Map p96 Boutique $$

☎ 202-939-6421; www.rougehotel.com; 1315 16th St NW; r from $250; M McPherson Sq; 🐾 🛜

Rouge is another playful Kimpton winner. Appropriately, the decor is definitively red, with bold designs, funky furniture and hip posters decorating the rooms. Specialty rooms include Chat Rooms with Pentium computers, Chow Rooms with kitchenettes, and Chill Rooms with Sony PlayStations and DVD players. As funky as the hotel, Bar Rouge attracts a regular stream of locals, especially for its Thursday happy hours.

DUPONT AT THE CIRCLE Map p96 B&B $$

☎ 202-332-5251; www.dupontatthecircle.com; 1604 19th St NW; r/ste incl breakfast from $250/350; M Dupont Circle

This upscale inn is housed in a stately brick Victorian row house, one block north of the circle. Its seven fully equipped guestrooms and two suites are furnished differently with tasteful antiques from varying periods – room two is named after Lincoln, another after Cuba – but all have private bathrooms with claw-foot tubs or Jacuzzis. Breakfasts are modest affairs: muffins, granola and fruit. Check out the Pinnacle for a special romantic evening: the inn's poshest suite boasts 22ft ceilings, a stained-glass window, a giant Jacuzzi for two and flat-screen plasma TV on a private floor perched at the very top of the inn.

BOOKING A B&B

DC has its fair share of B&Bs from the simple room in a private home to private homes turned exclusively into eccentric guesthouses (try the Mansion on O Street – below – our personal favorite). Many are clustered around Dupont Circle and Adams-Morgan as well as in Upper Northwest.

The following B&B agencies offer rooms in small inns, private homes or apartments starting from around $75 per night. Prices at the luxury guesthouses, however, can be as high as $300. Bed & Breakfast Accommodations Ltd (☎ 202-328-3510, 877-893-3233; www.bbonline.com/dc/washington.html) handles the bookings for many B&Bs in town; you'll note its phone number is the listing for quite a few of the smaller properties listed in this chapter. A good online starting point is Capitol Reservations (www.capitolreservations.com).

MADISON Map p96   Luxury $$$
☎ 202-862-1600; www.loewshotels.com; 1177 15th St NW; r $350; Ⓜ Farragut North; ⊠ ⊜
Having hosted every US president since JFK, this is a luxury hotel trying to be a family home – there's a whole floor dedicated to folks traveling with pets (and no deposit or size limit either). Rooms are attractive in a Washington power player kinda way, all warm chocolates, leather furniture and 300-thread count sheets that are screaming for you to don a smoking jacket. As a side note, the Madison is supposedly the first hotel in the world to have introduced the minibar – thanks, guys.

JEFFERSON HOTEL Map p96   Boutique $$$
☎ 866-270-8118; www.thejeffersonwashingtondc .com; 1200 16th St NW; r from $450; Ⓜ Farragut North; ⊠ ⊜
This luxury boutique is regularly near the top of Washington's best hotel lists. The elegant, two-winged 1923 mansion has an ornate porte cochere, beaux-arts architecture and a luxurious interior full of crystal and velvet. Favored by diplomatic visitors, its antique-furnished rooms are all silk sheets, four-poster luxury, tobacco and earth tones and Gilded Age class. The best praise we can give: the suites live up to the name presidential, which *means* something in this town.

MANSION ON O STREET Map p96   B&B $$$
☎ 202-496-2020; www.omansion.com; 2020 O St NW; r incl breakfast from $550; Ⓜ Dupont Circle; ⊠ ⊜
It doesn't advertise. It doesn't even have a sign or a brochure. But this place has quite a reputation anyway – it's just about the most flamboyant, original B&B around. Housed in a 100-room 1892 mansion (a remnant of the days when Dupont was a millionaires' neighborhood), it is part inn, part gallery performance space and part private club. In this latter incarnation, the Mansion has hosted Hollywood celebrities and Chelsea Clinton's sweet-16 party. Its owner, grande dame HH Leonards, has done the place up like a wedding at Castle Dracula: swags of velvet drapery, ornate chandeliers and lampshades, candelabras and concealed doorways. No two rooms, from the Russian Tea Room to the Log Cabin to the Billiards Suite, are alike, and everything from the bedstead to the pictures is for sale.

ADAMS-MORGAN

This colorful neighborhood offers its temporary residents an endless array of nightlife options, including restaurants and bars, music and dancing. Since the area is primarily residential, accommodations are all B&Bs, and they are set on quiet tree-lined streets with friendly neighbors. The disadvantage is the lack of public transport – it's a 15-minute walk to the nearest Metro.

WASHINGTON INTERNATIONAL STUDENT CENTER Map p103   Hostel $
☎ 202-667-7681; www.washingtondchostel .com; 2451 18th St NW; dm/s incl breakfast $23/56; Ⓜ Woodley Park Zoo/Adams Morgan; ⊠ ⊜
Well-located in the heart of Adams Morgan, you can basically stumble out of the club directly into your bed here. Dorms are decent, and the requisite rude receptionist works the counter, for that true backpacker experience.

KALORAMA GUEST HOUSE Map p103   B&B $
☎ 202-667-6369; 1854 Mintwood Place NW; s/d incl breakfast from $95/120, with shared bathroom from $90; Ⓜ Woodley Park Zoo/Adams Morgan; ⊠ ⊠

This Victorian townhouse is a couple of blocks west of 18th St and was among Washington's first B&Bs. It doesn't look like it, though – the owners have done a fine job of keeping accommodations clean and welcoming. Rooms have oriental rugs, down comforters and turn-of-the-century art, and because of the friendly atmosphere, there's a devoted band of return guests.

WINDSOR INN Map p103   Family $
☎ 202-667-0300, 800-423-9111; www.windsor -inn-dc.com; 1842 16th St NW; r from $120; Ⓜ Dupont Circle; ⊠ 🛜

Operated by the same management as the Embassy Inn (p210) up the street, this pleasant inn has an art-deco lobby, and original 1920s moldings and floor tiles. The rooms are decorated in spare, colonial style – nothing too grand (or large), but good value for the price. In the European tradition, guests receive continental breakfast, and evening snacks and sherry are included.

ADAM'S INN Map p103   B&B $
☎ 202-745-3600; www.adamsinn.com; 1744 Lanier Place NW; r incl breakfast $109-159; Ⓜ Woodley Park Zoo/Adams Morgan; ⊠ 🛜

It can be a struggle to get eye contact, let alone one-on-one service in Washington, but this townhouse B&B provides all of the above, along with fluffy linens and a central location. The owner (and yes, his name really is Adam) converted two adjacent townhouses and a carriage house on a shady residential street into an inviting and homey guesthouse. The pleasant common areas have a nice garden patio, and there's a general sense of sherry-scented chintz.

TAFT BRIDGE INN Map p103   B&B $$
☎ 202-387-2007; www.taftbridgeinn.com; 2007 Wyoming Ave NW; s incl breakfast $175-180, d $195-200, with shared bathroom s $90-95, d $115-135; Ⓜ Dupont Circle; Ⓟ ⊠ 🛜

Named for the bridge that leaps over Rock Creek Park just to the north, this beautiful 19th-century Georgian mansion is an easy walk to Adams-Morgan or Dupont Circle. The inn has a paneled drawing room, classy antiques, six fireplaces and a garden. Some rooms have a colonial Americana theme, accentuated by Amish quilts and the like;

others are more tweedy, exuding a Euro-renaissance in their decor.

BED & BREAKFAST ON U STREET
Map p103   B&B $$
☎ 202-328-3510, 877-893-3233; www.bedand breakfastonustreet.com; cnr 17th & U Sts NW; r $90-250, ste $125-275; Ⓜ Dupont Circle; ⊠

With hardwood floors, carved-wood trim, decorative fireplaces and high ceilings, this Victorian-era B&B is comfortable, just minutes' walk from Dupont Circle and by the heart of the U St Corridor. The 2nd-floor suite, with a sleeper sofa and sitting room, is a good choice for families – mom and dad even get their own space. The cheapest rooms share bathrooms.

MERIDIAN MANOR Map p103   B&B $$
☎ 202-328-3510, 877-893-3233; www.meridian manordc.com; U & 16th St NW; r $100-250; Ⓜ Dupont Circle; ⊠ 🛜

Unlike in many similar B&Bs, the six rooms here have a more contemporary vibe. They're all decked out with designer furniture and monochrome color schemes, which stands in nice contrast to the 'manor' itself, a lovely old DC residence that blends in easily with nearby embassies. You're within minutes of Dupont Circle and a stone's throw from Malcolm X Park (p103), one of our favorite outdoor spaces in the city.

AMERICAN GUEST HOUSE
Map p103   B&B $$
☎ 703-768-0335; www.americanguesthouse.com; 2005 Columbia Rd NW; r from $184; Ⓜ Woodley Park Zoo/Adams Morgan, Dupont Circle

With a dozen rooms, this property is technically more of a boutique than a B&B, but the intimate sense of service and individualized digs push it into the more cozy B&B column. Rooms run the gamut from Victorian vibe (Room 203) to New England cottage (Room 304) to colonial love nest (Room 303).

WASHINGTON HILTON & TOWERS
Map p103   Business $$
☎ 202-483-3000; www.hilton.com; 1919 Connecticut Ave NW; r from $195; Ⓜ Dupont Circle; ⊠ 🛜

This 1960s-style semicircular structure is a giant hotel with all the amenities you would expect from a Hilton. It is famed as the site of John Hinckley's attempt to assassinate President Ronald Reagan, on March 30, 1981. Hoping to impress the actor Jodie Foster, the disturbed young man shot Reagan, his press secretary and an FBI agent near the T St NW entrance. The rooms here are corporate, but considering the full weight of the service you get at a Hilton and the superb location, you're actually making out on quite a deal.

COLUMBIA HEIGHTS & NORTHEAST

The sleeping options out this way are growing as the neighborhoods of Northeast and Near-Northeast gentrify. Don't expect any chains coming this way (maybe on U St); otherwise, lodging remains of the small, charming B&B sort, plus some good hostels.

HILLTOP HOSTEL off Map pp106-7   Hostel $
☎ 202-291-9591; www.hosteldc.com; 300 Carroll St; dm $24; Ⓜ Takoma; 🏠 🖥
Laid-back and super-friendly, this hostel is in the bohemian, politically leftist neighborhood of Takoma Park, in far northeast DC. Set in a century-old Victorian mansion, this spot is frequented by crowds of backpackers from all over the world. The backyard BBQ and hammock inspire frequent impromptu parties. Don't be frightened off by the hostel's distance from downtown: it's across the street from the Metro, which gets you to Capitol Hill in about 15 minutes. Besides, Takoma has its own strip of antique shops and vegetarian restaurants to explore.

INTOWN UPTOWN INN
off Map pp106-7   B&B $$
☎ 202-541-9400; www.meridianmanordc.com; 4907 14th St NW; r $125-200; Ⓜ Columbia Heights; 🏠 🖥
The Intown is one of the better urban B&Bs out there. We love it for its ability to combine crucial, sometimes disparate elements of an intimate stay in a city: owners who are knowledgeable about town, a design aesthetic that combines the best of the area's traditional aesthetic (the main sitting and dining rooms) with its more cutting-edge style (most of the guest rooms, especially the red-and-white 'Room With a View' and airy 'Soho' chamber), plus a good host of mod-cons. The only drawback is you're

not near much of anything here; talk with the owners about connections to the city center on the 14th St bus.

MONUMENT MAISON Map pp106-7   B&B $$
☎ 301-637-4540; www.suite34.us.com/mansion .html; cnr N Capitol St & Rhode Island Ave; r from $150; Ⓜ Shaw-Howard University; 🏠 🖥
The interior of this spot has the feel of a contemporary apartment, with brick walls and wooden floors; the rooms themselves are Ikea-chic, which is to say comfy if not overwhelmingly memorable. The house itself is a beautiful, turreted example of the best of row house architecture in this corner of town, which is a little removed from the city center but charming in its own, on-the-edge-of-gentrification way.

UPPER NORTHWEST DC

The accommodations options in Upper Northwest DC are clustered around Woodley Park. This area offers easy access to transport. There are also many restaurants, as well as some good nightlife, in the immediate vicinity.

KALORAMA GUEST HOUSE AT
WOODLEY PARK Map p114   B&B $
☎ 202-328-0860; 2700 Cathedral Ave NW; r incl breakfast $95-15, with shared bathroom $90; Ⓜ Woodley Park Zoo/Adams Morgan; ✕ 🏠
This sister to the Kalorama Guest House (p212) in Adams-Morgan, this is a cozy 1910 Victorian row house with 19 antique-furnished rooms. Additional facilities are in another property down the street. In winter guests are served sherry in the evenings; in summer fresh lemonade is poured throughout the day.

WOODLEY PARK GUEST HOUSE
Map p114   B&B $
☎ 202-667-0218, 866-667-0218; www.woodley parkguesthouse.com; 2647 Woodley Rd NW; r incl breakfast $165-205, with shared bathroom $100; Ⓜ Woodley Park Zoo/Adams Morgan; Ⓟ ✕ 🏠
This elegant 1920s-era home is a beautiful, historic B&B that is excellent value. Seventeen sunny rooms have antique furniture, hardwood floors and white coverlets. The front porch is a wonderful perch for a summer afternoon. The owners are incredibly friendly, and many guests are faithful regulars.

NORTHERN VIRGINIA

There are loads of big-box hotel chains in Arlington, which may not have much character, but they're cheaper than sleeping in the District. Pick one near a Metro and it's almost as convenient as staying in the city (especially true if you have a car – parking in the city costs upwards of $30 per day at hotels, while most here offer it for free). The best – and they're almost interchangeable, but for their prices – are Key Bridge Marriott (☎ 703-524-6400; www.marriott.com; 1401 Lee Hwy; r from $80; Ⓜ Rosslyn; 🕸 🛜) and Ritz-Carlton Pentagon City (☎ 703-415-5000; www.ritz-carlton.com; 1250 S Hayes St; r from $140; Ⓜ Pentagon City; 🕸 🛜).

Old Town Alexandria offers a trade-off: the Metro is not as immediate and prices are higher, but the neighborhood is way more charming. Virginia room tax is about 10%.

ALEXANDRIA

ALEXANDRIA TRAVEL LODGE
Map p125   Motel $

☎ 703-836-5100; 702 N Washington St, Alexandria; r $60-150; Ⓜ King St Metro; 🕸

This motel – on a busy section of Washington St – is about a mile north of Old Town's historic district. It is a good bet for budget travelers who have their own car; parking is free. Basic clean rooms have TVs, telephones and full bathrooms. Amenities are otherwise limited, but you can't beat the price.

MORRISON HOUSE Map p125   Boutique $$

☎ 703-838-8000; www.morrisonhouse.com; 116 S Alfred St; r from $175; Ⓜ King St Metro; 🕸

In the heart of Old Town Alexandria, Morrison House captures the neighborhood's charm with its Georgian-style building and the Federal-style reproduction furniture. This boutique hotel offers the service and amenities of a luxury hotel: you'll find terrycloth bathrobes and high-speed internet access in every room. Rooms are beautifully decorated, especially the elegant library, where afternoon tea is served. The kicker here is the service of a butler to cater to your every whim, any time of the day or night. The on-site restaurant is well respected.

DAY TRIPS & EXCURSIONS

DAY TRIPS & EXCURSIONS

After a few days of taking in Washington's charms, allow some time to explore the fascinating region just beyond the city's borders. Here you'll find a blend of historic sites, beautifully preserved national parks, and sweet little villages amid idyllic surrounds.

North and east of the capital, Maryland provides an enticing array of attractions, from the revitalized streets of Baltimore to the picturesque towns along the Chesapeake Bay. You can stroll the historic harbor of Annapolis, swim in the refreshing waters off Atlantic beaches and feast on Maryland's famous blue crabs.

Virginia, lying to the south and west of Washington, offers a completely different landscape – not to mention culture and history. Here you'll find the immaculately preserved presidential home of America's first (and some say greatest) president, one of the Civil War's most evocative battlefields, and Colonial-era towns well placed for outdoor adventures such as hiking and rafting.

Wherever you go there is much to discover, including the surprising riches of Virginia wine country and the windswept beaches of Assateague Island, where wild ponies still roam.

AMERICAN HISTORY

The outskirts of DC have no shortage of historic sites in the near vicinity. George Washington's magnificent estate at Mount Vernon (p220) is an easy half-day trip from the city, as is Manassas (p222), the site of the first major Civil War battle and a shining example of old-fashioned America. The Colonial town of Leesburg (p223) is one of the oldest settlements in the area – the old town is still an easy charmer, but avoid it during rush hour when the roads are clogged with commuters. The towns on the Chesapeake (p229) – such as Annapolis and St Michaels – preserve their maritime histories with harbors that have been bustling for hundreds of years, and the picture-book lanes are sprinkled with old mansions overlooking the bay.

BEACHES

Nothing relieves the heat and humidity of DC summers like a trip to the beach. Fortunately, the Atlantic coast of Virginia, Maryland and Delaware offers numerous options. Pristine Assateague Island (p233) is protected by the National Park Service and offers a beautiful sweep of Atlantic coastline. It is accessible from quiet Chincoteague in the south and party-loving Ocean City (p232) in the north. Delaware's beach resorts fall somewhere in the middle of this spectrum. Rehoboth (p233) and Dewey (p233) are fun family towns with a lively bar and club scene and a built-up beach. Rehoboth is also the local gay beach. The protected Delaware Seashore State Park (p233) is also nearby.

PARKS & WILDLIFE

Your choice here will be determined by the time you have available. If you can only spare a few hours, Great Falls (below) is a wonderful waterside getaway, less than 20 miles northwest of the city. It stretches across both sides of the Potomac, but on the Maryland side the falls are part of C&O Canal National Historical Park (p220), which is fabulous for easy hiking and cycling. If you have a day or more, head west to the forested hills of Shenandoah National Park (p225) with its rolling mountains of purple and blue, making sure to linger along the fantastic Skyline Dr. Further afield there are outdoor adventures, including mountain biking and white-water rafting, in Harpers Ferry (p226).

GREAT FALLS

Fourteen miles upriver from DC's Georgetown, where the central Piedmont meets the coastal plain, the normally placid Potomac cascades 77ft down a series of beautiful, treacherous rapids known as Great Falls. The Chesapeake & Ohio (C&O) Canal was constructed to allow barges to bypass the falls. Today there are parks on both sides of the river providing glorious views of the falls, as well as hiking, cycling and picnicking spots. (The entry fee is good for three days at both parks.) The Maryland side hooks up to Georgetown via the C&O Canal Towpath (p73), which is an excellent route for a cycling trip (it's not paved).

On the Virginia side, the falls lie in the 800-acre Great Falls National Park (☎ 703-285-2965;

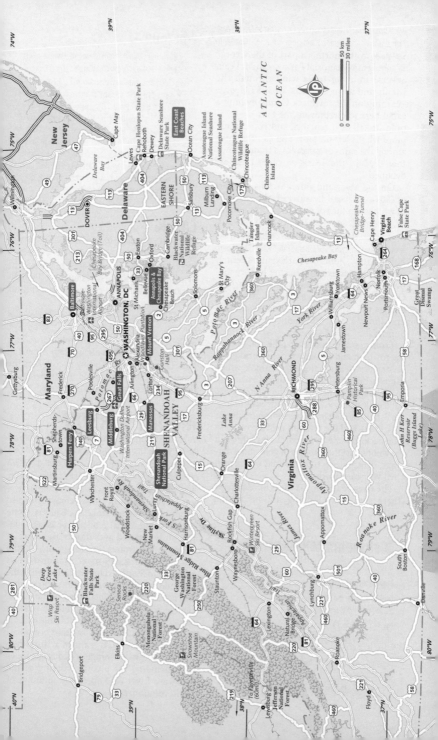

www.nps.gov/grfa; admission per car/cyclist $5/3; ☾ park 7am-dusk, visitors center 10am-5pm Jun-Aug, 10am-4pm Sep-May), in the northern part of the George Washington Memorial Parkway in McLean. Several miles of trails wind through the woods and along the falls. In 1785 George Washington's Patowmack Company built a canal here to circumvent the falls – a 0.75-mile stretch of it remains, and you can explore what's left on foot. You can also hike among the ruins of Matildaville, a trading town that died in the 1820s as canal business declined.

On the Maryland side, the falls are part of C&O Canal National Historical Park, the entrance of which is in the sprawling, wealthy suburb of Potomac. Great Falls Tavern (☎ 301-767-3714; www.nps.gov/choh; 11710 MacArthur Blvd, Potomac, MD; admission per car/cyclist $5/3, barge ride $5; ☾ 9am-5pm), built in 1828, holds the park visitors center, which features exhibits on the history and design of the canal locks. From April to October, the *Clipper*, a mule-drawn barge, cruises the canal, departing from here several times a day, on Wednesday through Sunday.

From the tavern, a half-mile walk down the towpath and across a series of bridges to Olmstead Island leads to the falls overlook, which offers a beautiful view of rugged rock and roaring rapids. (The white-water is dangerous, so keep kids close.) For serious scramblers, the 2-mile Billy Goat Trail traverses mountainous rock crags, and the towpath provides an easy loop back. Other easy loop trails lead through the woods past the remains of gold-mine diggings, prospector's trenches and overgrown Civil War earthworks.

The Great Falls area is ideal for day trips (there aren't any lodging options in the area).

TRANSPORTATION: GREAT FALLS

Direction 14 miles north.

Travel time 20 minutes by car.

Bicycle Pick up the C&O canal path anywhere in Georgetown and head north.

Car To reach the C&O Canal National Historical Park on the Maryland side, take Canal Rd out of Georgetown, then MacArthur Blvd to its end. For Great Falls National Park in Virginia, from I-495 take exit 13 to Georgetown Pike. Drive 4 miles to Old Dominion Dr and turn right to enter the park.

DETOUR

Twenty miles upriver from Great Falls, White's Ferry (☎ 301-349-5200; 24801 White's Ferry Rd, Dickerson, MD; cars one way/round-trip $4/7, cyclists $1; ☾ 5am-11pm) is the last of the many ferries that once plied the Potomac. It's a nice way to hop from the Maryland to the Virginia shore, particularly if you're headed for historic Leesburg, which is just 4 miles west of here. A general store on the premises rents out canoes (call for prices) and there are shady, grassy picnic places by the Potomac. The river here is safe for swimming; however, the current is quite strong, so don't venture out too far.

EATING

L'Auberge Chez Francois (☎ 703-759-3800; 332 Springvale Rd, Great Falls, VA; 4-course lunch $32, 6-course dinner $62-74; ☾ 5:30-9:30pm Tue-Sat, 5:30-8pm Sun) One of the Washington area's best restaurants. French-Alsatian cuisine is served. Reservations required.

Old Angler's Inn (☎ 301-365-2425; 10801 MacArthur Blvd, MD; mains lunch $13-22, dinner $27-38; ☾ noon-2:30pm & 5:30-10pm Tue-Sun) This beautifully set restaurant serves delicious contemporary American fare. There's outdoor seating overlooking the canal, and a cozy dining room complete with fireplace. Reservations recommended.

MOUNT VERNON

A visit to George Washington's Virginia home, Mount Vernon (☎ 703-780-2000; www.mountvernon.org; 3200 George Washington Memorial Parkway; adult/child $15/7, audio tour $6; ☾ 8am-5pm Apr-Aug, 9am-5pm Mar, Sep & Oct, 9am-4pm Nov-Feb), is an easy escape from the city – one that the president himself enjoyed. It's also a journey through history: the country estate of this quintessential gentleman has been meticulously restored and affords a glimpse of rural gentility from a time long gone. On the Potomac banks, the 19-room mansion displays George and Martha's colonial tastes, while the outbuildings and slave quarters show what was needed for the functioning of the estate. George and Martha are both buried here, as requested by the first president in his will.

The modern Ford Orientation Center is a must-see on the grounds. It features a 20-minute film that shows Washington's courage under fire, including his pivotal crossing of the Delaware River (the do-or-die moment of the Revolutionary War).

Another highlight is the sleek **Reynolds Museum and Education Center**. Home to galleries and theaters, it gives more insight into Washington's life using interactive displays, short films produced by the cable TV History Channel and three life-size models of Washington himself. The museum also features period furnishings, clothing and jewelry (Martha was quite taken with finery) and George's unusual dentures.

In the town of Mount Vernon, **Woodlawn Plantation** (☎ 703-780-4000; www.woodlawn1805 .org; 9000 Richmond Hwy, Mount Vernon; adult/child $9/4; 10am-5pm Thu-Mon Apr-Dec) has two very different houses that are both splendid examples of their architectural times. The plantation home itself once belonged to Eleanor 'Nelly' Custis, granddaughter of Martha Washington, and her husband, Major Lawrence Lewis, George Washington's nephew. The house contains period antiques and a stunning rose garden.

Also on the grounds, architect Frank Lloyd Wright's **Pope-Leighey House** (☎ 703-780-4000; www.popeleighey1940.org; 9000 Richmond Hwy, Mount Vernon; adult/child $9/4; 10am-5pm Thu-Mon Apr-Dec) is a 1940s Usonian dwelling of cypress, brick and glass. Originally intended as low-cost housing for the middle class, Wright's Usonian dwellings featured aesthetically elegant designs made from durable, inexpensive materials. It was moved to Woodlawn in 1964 from Falls Church to rescue it from destruction. Furnished with Wright pieces, the house is utilitarian in structure, but quite beautiful. Combination tickets to visit both Woodlawn Plantation and the Pope-Leighey House are available (adult/child $15/5).

Three miles south of Mount Vernon, on Rte 235, you'll find **George Washington's Distillery & Gristmill** (☎ 703-780-2000; www.mountvernon.org; adult/child $4/2, with Mount Vernon tickets $2/1; 10am-5pm Apr-Oct), which was also part of the president's estate. Although Washington's leadership skills were well known, his prowess at farming and making whiskey were less discussed. He also patented a milling system – and you can purchase stone-ground cornmeal from the shop. The museum has exhibits, a film on Washington's whiskey, and actors in period costume demonstrating how it all worked.

Southwest of Mount Vernon, on a bend in the Potomac River, is the 1775 brick mansion **Gunston Hall** (☎ 703-550-9220; www.gunstonhall.org; 10709 Gunston Rd, Mason Neck, VA; admission & tour adult/child $9/5; 9:30am-5pm), which belonged to a statesman and contemporary of George Washington, George Mason. Mason penned the lines 'all men are by nature equally free and independent, and have certain inherent rights' – words adapted by Thomas Jefferson for the Declaration of Independence. Dating from 1755, the mansion is an architectural masterpiece, with elegantly carved wooden interiors and meticulously kept formal gardens.

EATING & SLEEPING

The food court is in the visitors center, with pizzas, premade sandwiches and the like.

Mount Vernon Inn (☎ 703-780-0011; 3200 George Washington Memorial Parkway; lunch $9-12, dinner $16-22; lunch & dinner Mon-Sat) A Colonial-style restaurant on the grounds of Mount Vernon serving traditional lunches and candlelit dinners, including roast turkey with cranberry sauce year-round.

TRANSPORTATION: MOUNT VERNON

Direction Mount Vernon and Woodlawn Plantation 18 miles south of DC; Gunston Hall 23 miles south.

Travel time 30 minutes by car.

Bicycle From the Key Bridge or Arlington Cemetery, take the George Washington Memorial Parkway trail south.

Boat The cruise ship Spirit of Mount Vernon (Map pp78–9; ☎ 866-302-2469; www.spiritofwashington.com; round-trip $42; Ⓜ Waterfront) departs for Mount Vernon from Pier 4, at 6th & Water Sts SW.

Car From DC, cross Memorial Bridge and at the roundabout, veer right and take the first left, heading south on the George Washington Memorial Parkway, which ends at Mount Vernon. At the traffic circle at Mount Vernon, head south on Rte 235 to reach Woodlawn, which lies at the intersection of Rte 235 with Rte 1. To reach Gunston Hall, turn left on Rte 1 and left on Gunston Rd (Rte 242).

Metro Take a Yellow Line to Huntington, then board the Fairfax Connector (☎ 703-339-7200) bus 101 to Mount Vernon.

Comfort Inn Gunston Corner (☎ 703-643-3100; www.ci gunston.com; 8180 Silverbrook Rd, Lorton, VA; r incl continental breakfast from $120; **P** 🐾 🛎️) A comfortable suburban hotel with an outdoor pool and exercise facility; provides convenient shuttle to Metro. Lorton is about 5 miles southeast of Mount Vernon (from Rte 1 turn right on Lorton Rd and right on Silverbrook Rd).

MANASSAS & MANASSAS NATIONAL BATTLEFIELD PARK

A visit to the Manassas National Battlefield Park (☎ 703-361-1339; www.nps.gov/mana; 12521 Lee Hwy; adult/child $3/free, film $3; 🕑 8:30am-5pm, tours 11:15am, 12:15pm, 2:15pm Jun-Aug) is a must for Civil War buffs. The battles that took place at Manassas (known as Bull Run in the north) were not the most significant, but the grassy hills tell a dramatic tale of two unexpected Confederate victories. Manassas I, the war's first major battle, shocked soldiers and spectators alike by its bloody outcome – see The Battles of Manassas (1861 & 1862), opposite. Start at the visitors center, which has a small exhibit and an excellent film about the battles. You can also pick up a pamphlet, which outlines a walking tour around the points of interest in the battlefields. Note the reconstructed Henry House in the middle of the battlefield where 85-year-old Judith Henry was killed when Union troops fired on Confederate soldiers inside the house. Her grave lies near the house. Guided walking tours are offered several times daily. In August, reenactments of the two Civil War battles are staged.

The town of Manassas lies 5 miles south of the battlefield along Rte 234. Don't be fooled by the heavily trafficked, strip-mall-lined highway: the old center of town is a quaint area with antique shops and galleries, and a keen sense of history. The Manassas Railroad Depot, built in 1914, also houses the visitors center (below). Across the tracks, the Manassas Museum (☎ 703-368-1873; www.manassascity.org; 9101 Prince William St; adult/child $5/4; 🕑 10am-5pm Tue-Sun) emphasizes Civil War history, but also displays photographs, artifacts and videos about the community. The Center for the Arts at the Candy Factory (☎ 703-330-2787; www.center-for-the-arts.org; 9419 Battle St; admission by donation; 🕑 10am-5pm Mon-Fri, 1-5pm Sat) is a spacious, light-filled gallery housed in a reconverted candy factory that offers theatrical performances throughout the year and free summer concerts on alternate Saturday evenings (call for specifics).

There are other Civil War sights to explore in the area. The Ben Lomond Manor House (☎ 703-367-7872; 10311 Sudley Manor Dr) was used as a hospital for Union and Confederate soldiers during the war, and today is famous for its antique rose gardens. Signal Hill was an integral Confederate observation post during the Civil War (and you'll understand why when you see the view it provides). It directly contributed to the Confederate victory at the first Battle of Bull Run. Signal Hill is located just off Signal Hill Rd across from the entrance to Signal Hill Park. Ask at the Manassas Museum or Manassas National Battlefield Park for directions.

INFORMATION

Manassas Visitors Center (Visitors Center; ☎ 703-361-6599; 9431 West St; 🕑 9am-5pm) Located inside the historic Manassas Railroad Depot (and working Amtrak station), this center distributes maps and walking tour information.

EATING

City Square Café (☎ 703-369-6022; 9428 Battle St; mains lunch $8-12, dinner $19-24; 🕑 11am-9pm Mon-Fri, 8:30am-10pm Sat, 8:30am-3pm Sun) Nicely set across from the train depot, this cafe serves fresh-tasting sandwiches and salads for lunch and heartier bistro fare for dinner (Maryland crab cakes, NY strip steak, pesto chicken with gnocchi). Pleasant outdoor seating.

Okra's Louisiana Bistro (☎ 703-330-2729; 9110 Center St; mains $13-20; 🕑 11am-midnight Mon-Thu, 11am-2am Fri & Sat, 11am-10pm Sun) Okra's whips up satisfying Cajun dishes, including jambalaya, shrimp

---

TRANSPORTATION: MANASSAS

Direction 26 miles west.

Travel time 40 minutes by car.

Car Take Rte 66 to Rte 234, exit 47: the battlefield is half a mile north; the town of Manassas is 5 miles south.

Train A commuter service runs between Washington, DC's Union Station and downtown Manassas on weekdays. There's no public transport from Manassas to the battlefield; a taxi with Manassas Cab Co (☎ 703-257-0222) to the park will cost about $15.

THE BATTLES OF MANASSAS (1861 & 1862)

Not long after the first shots were fired at Fort Sumter, SC, on April 12, 1861, sizable armies of both Union and Confederate troops began to gather around the capitals of Richmond and Washington, DC.

The first significant battle of the Civil War occurred after Confederate soldiers, commanded by PGT Beauregard, camped near the rail junction of Manassas, perilously close to the national capital. The battle that Northerners hoped would end the war, Manassas I (Bull Run), started with an air of ebullience. Under orders from Abraham Lincoln, Brigadier General Irvin McDowell roused his 32,000 poorly trained troops on the afternoon of July 16 and marched to Centreville, 20 miles west of DC. McDowell's men skirmished and scouted near Bull Run, gathering scanty intelligence and, on July 21, the general committed two divisions, including cavalry and artillery, against the Confederate lines.

McDowell's first assault on the right flank was checked by Confederate General Stonewall Jackson's soldiers and driven back. Then, what was meant to be an organized retreat turned into a rout. The Union troops knew tactical drilling techniques well enough, but they had not been taught the essentials of withdrawal under fire.

On the supposedly 'safe' side of Bull Run, there had been a macabre picnic in progress, with civilians from Washington, DC coming down to witness the fray. As the soldiers fled in panic, they intermingled with this now-befuddled crowd of onlookers, and there was a melee, especially when a strategic bridge across Cub Run collapsed. When the counting ended, the Confederates, who incurred about 2000 casualties as opposed to McDowell's 3000, could claim victory. Both groups were so ill trained at this early stage of the war, however, that any advantage could not be followed up.

More than a year later, the war returned to Manassas. Following Major General McClellan's Peninsula Campaign and the Seven Days Battles, Union troops had withdrawn to the safety of DC, and many of McClellan's soldiers were handed over to a new commander, John Pope. By the time Pope was ordered to move against Richmond, Robert E Lee was in command of the Confederates.

Pope advanced south toward the Rappahannock River, and Lee advanced north to confront Pope's troops before they could be reinforced by McClellan. Lee brilliantly split his force and consigned an attack on Pope's supply base at Manassas to stonewall Jackson's men. Jackson's force came up against a numerically inferior force commanded by Nathaniel Banks at Cedar Mountain and, after a seesawing battle, the Union troops were forced back with heavy losses.

Pope's main body came up the next day, and Manassas II (Bull Run) commenced on August 29, with Pope making heavy but futile attacks on Jackson's troops, who were in defense behind the bed of an unfinished railroad.

The following day, Lee unexpectedly arrived in force with the 30,000-strong force of James Longstreet, which in a devastating flank assault on the Union's left (combined with Jackson's attacks on the other flank) caused a repeat of Manassas I, with the Northerners fleeing back across Bull Run to the security of Washington, DC. At this stage, almost all of Virginia had been returned to the hands of the Confederates.

Pope lost his job when it was revealed that he had lost about a quarter of his force of 70,000 (the remainder of which was then incorporated into the Army of the Potomac), while Lee had lost only 10,000 of his 60,000.

Creole and red beans and rice. Live music on Friday and Saturday nights.

City Tavern (☎ 703-330-0076; 9405 Main St; mains $6-14; ◷ 11am-2am) This well-known spot has a dining room filled with memorabilia (old black-and-white photos, pin-up-girl posters) and serves classic pub fare, including sirloin steaks, broiled salmon and burgers.

SLEEPING

Bennett House (☎ 800-354-7060; www.virginia-bennethouse.com; 9252 Bennett Dr; r $115-150; ✷ ◌) A genteel Victorian B&B with charming rooms that offers a full Virginia-style country breakfast.

Old Towne Inn (☎ 703-368-9191; 9403 Main St; r $70-80; ◌) This motel in the center of town has basic rooms in need of an update; it's rumored to be haunted.

LEESBURG & MIDDLEBURG

Leesburg is one of Northern Virginia's oldest towns and its colonial-era center is lined with historic sites, plus antique shops, galleries and restaurants. Leesburg also has a less alluring modern side, with shopping malls and traffic-filled highways. Many people commute from here to work in the city, so avoid traveling around rush hour. Leesburg sits along the Washington & Old Dominion Trail (see Cycling, p197), and makes an excellent destination for cyclists.

For historical sights, start at the Loudoun Museum (☎ 703-777-7427; www.loudounmuseum.org; 16 Loudoun St, Leesburg; admission free, guided city tours adult/child $10/3; ◷ 10am-5pm Mon & Wed-Sat, 1-5pm Sun), which

TRANSPORTATION: LEESBURG & MIDDLEBURG

Direction 35 miles northwest.

Travel time 40 minutes by car.

Bicycle Pick up the Washington & Old Dominion Trail just outside the East Falls Church Metro in Arlington and head west.

Car Take I-495 or Rte 66 to the Dulles Toll Rd exit (Rte 267) – look for signs to Dulles International Airport. When it turns into the Dulles Greenway, continue 13 miles to the end. Exit left and take the first right exit to Leesburg Business. Follow King St to Loudoun St, the center of historic Leesburg. Middleburg is 19 miles southwest of Leesburg. Take US-15 south and turn right on US-50.

narrates the history of northern Virginia from the first Native American settlements to the present day. You can also arrange walking tours of historic Leesburg here. On the first Friday of every month, you can join in for the Leesburg's First Friday (www.leesburgfirstfriday.com; ☿ 6-9pm), when shops and galleries stay open till 9pm and offer drinks and special sales.

Morven Park (☎ 703-777-2414; www.morvenpark.org; 17263 Southern Planter Lane; admission to grounds free, mansion tours adult/child $7/1; ☿ grounds 7am-6pm daily, tours 11am-4pm Mon, Fri & Sat, 1-4pm Sun) is a 1000-acre property that was once the home of Virginia Governor Westmoreland Davis. The Greek Revival mansion, with its manicured boxwood gardens, resembles a transplanted White House, and its antique carriage museum includes more than 100 horse-drawn vehicles. Morven Park is 1 mile west of Leesburg off Rte 7 (Market St). Heading west, turn right onto Morven Park Rd and follow it to the property.

Six miles south of Leesburg, Oatlands Plantation (☎ 703-777-3174; 20850 Oatlands Plantation Lane, Leesburg; adult/child $10/7, grounds only $7; ☿ 10am-5pm Mon-Sat, 1-5pm Sun Apr-Dec) was established in 1803 by a great-grandson of Robert 'King' Carter, a wealthy pre-Revolutionary planter. The carefully restored Greek Revival mansion is surrounded by 4 acres of formal gardens and connecting terraces. It's located on US-15, about 5 miles south of Leesburg.

Lying 19 miles southwest of Leesburg, smaller Middleburg is another quaint Northern Virginia town, with colonial buildings that hide some enticing restaurants and shops. Either town makes a fine base for visiting the wineries in the area.

INFORMATION

Leesburg Tourist Office (☎ 703-669-2002; www .visitloudoun.org; 112G South St, Market Station, Leesburg; ☿ 9am-5pm) Friendly and helpful office with loads of regional information, including a useful wine-country guide.

EATING

Lightfoot (☎ 703-771-2233; 11 N King St, Leesburg; mains lunch $9-18, dinner $22-30; ☿ 11:30am-2:30pm & 5:30-10pm Sun, to 11pm Mon-Thu, to midnight Fri & Sat) Lightfoot is an award-winning restaurant featuring delicious, progressive American fare such as slow-braised pork shank, swordfish *au poivre* and artichoke gratin-crusted salmon.

Tuscarora Mill (☎ 703-771-9300; 203 Harrison St, Leesburg; mains $19-28; ☿ 11am-11pm Mon-Sat, 11am-9pm Sun) In the Market Station complex (where the tourist office is), Tuscarora Mill serves market-fresh fare, including rack of lamb, ahi tuna steak with roasted portobello mushrooms and a delectable seafood stew.

La Chocita (☎ 703-443-2319; 210 Loudoun St SE, Leesburg; mains $5-12; ☿ 11am-10pm) This casual welcoming spot serves Latin American food, including satisfying enchiladas, tacos and *pupusas* (maize flatbreads), although its rotisserie chicken is famous. Outside seating in back.

Market Salamander (☎ 540-687-8011; 200 W Washington St, Middleburg; mains $7-13; ☿ 11am-5pm Sun, to 6pm Mon-Thu, to 7pm Fri & Sat) Well worth the trip to Middleburg, Market Salamander is a small gourmet food shop with a low-key restaurant serving delicious market fare such as roasted chicken, crab cakes, mac 'n' cheese and bourbon pecan chicken salad. Save room for dessert.

SLEEPING

Norris House Inn (☎ 703-777-1806; www.norrishouse.com; 108 Loudoun St SW, Leesburg; d $115-150) A renovated 1760 redbrick Colonial; tea is served in the lovely Stone House Tearoom. The rate here is for weekends; weekday rates are cheaper.

Best Western Leesburg Dulles (☎ 703-777-9400; www.bestwestern.com; 726 E Market St, Leesburg; r $100; ✷ ⧉ ⧇) The rooms boast green carpeting and orange bedspreads, but friendly service and all the extras (pool, free hot breakfast and wi-fi, in-room fridge and microwave) make up for aesthetic shortcomings.

Welbourne B&B (☎ 540-687-3201; www.welbour neinn.com; 22314 Welbourne Farm Lane, Middleburg; r $143; ✷ ⧉ ⧇) Located 6 miles west of Mid-

VINEYARDS OF VIRGINIA

Back in the 1980s, when a single vineyard operated in Loudoun County, a Virginian bottle of wine was likely to earn about as much respect as a convicted felon running for office. Much has changed in the last generation, and today this rich farming region has become one of the country's fastest-growing wine regions – with more than 20 vineyards at last count. While largely unknown outside Virginia, Loudoun County wines are garnering critical attention after winning awards at international competitions.

For the traveler, going wine tasting makes a fine day's outing from DC. You can explore the rolling hills and leafy lanes of this pretty countryside, stopping at excellent restaurants and local farmers' markets en route. Both Leesburg and Middleburg are fine bases to begin the viticultural journey.

A useful guide to the vineyards, with detailed information on the wineries, is the *Touring Guide to DC's Wine Country*, available free at the Leesburg Tourist Office (opposite).

Here are a few favorites from the wine country:

- Bluemont Vineyard (☎ 540-554-8439; www.bluemontvineyard.com; 18755 Foggy Bottom Rd, Bluemont; tasting $5; ☒ noon-6pm Fri-Sun) Bluemont produces ruby red Nortons and crisp Viogniers, though it's equally famous for its spectacular location – at a 950ft elevation with sweeping views over the countryside. It's open outside hours by appointment.

- Breaux Vineyards (☎ 540-668-6299; www.breauxvineyards.com; 36888 Breaux Vineyards Lane, Hillsborough; tasting $10; ☒ 11am-6pm) One of Virginia's largest vineyards, with over 17 varietals, Breaux produces award-winning reds including an exceptional Merlot Reserve. Breaux hosts three culinary festivals throughout the summer.

- Chrysalis Vineyards (☎ 540-687-8222; www.chrysaliswine.com; 23876 Champe Ford Rd, Middleburg; tasting $5-10; ☒ 10am-5pm) Proudly using the native Norton grape (which dates back to 1820), Chrysalis produces highly drinkable reds and whites – including a refreshing Viognier. The pretty estate hosts a bluegrass fest in October.

- Fabbioli Cellars (☎ 703-771-1197; www.fabbioliwines.com; 15669 Limestone School Rd, Leesburg; tasting $5; ☒ 11am-5pm Fri-Sun) This eco-friendly winery provides an intimate but informal tasting experience, where you can learn about the wines from the innovative winemaker Doug Fabbioli himself. It's open outside hours by appointment.

- Tarara Vineyard (☎ 703-771-7100; www.tarara.com; 13648 Tarara Lane, Leesburg; tasting $5-10; ☒ 11am-5pm) On a bluff overlooking the Potomac, this 475-acre estate provides guided tours showing the grape's journey from vine to glass. The winery is located in a 6000-sq-ft cave, and visitors can pick fruit in the orchard or hike the 6 miles of trails through rolling countryside. Tarara also hosts summertime Saturday evening concerts and three major wine festivals.

dleburg, the Welbourne is set in a historic landmark house (c 1770), surrounded by 520 acres. Guests stay in one of five heritage rooms with wood-burning fireplaces. Hearty Southern-style breakfast included.

SHENANDOAH NATIONAL PARK

Shenandoah National Park (☎ 540-999-3500; www.nps .gov/shen; 3655 US-211 E, Luray; 7-day entry car $15, walker & cyclist $8) is easy on the eyes, set against a backdrop of the dreamy Blue Ridge Mountains, ancient granite and metamorphic formations that are more than one billion years old. The park itself is almost 70 years old, founded in 1935 as a retreat for East Coast urban populations. It is an accessible day-trip destination from DC, but stay longer if you can. The 500 miles of hiking trails, 75 scenic overlooks, 30 fishing streams, seven picnic areas and four campgrounds are sure to keep you entertained.

Skyline Drive is the breathtaking road that follows the main ridge of the Blue Ridge Mountains and winds 105 miles through the center of the park. It begins in Front Royal near the western end of I-66, and ends in the southern part of the range near Rockfish Gap near I-64. Mile markers at the side of the road provide a reference.

Your first stop should be the Dickey Ridge Visitors Center (☎ 540-635-3566; Skyline Dr, Mile 4.6; ☒ 9am-5pm Apr-Nov) at Mile 4.6, close to the northern end of Skyline Dr, or Byrd Visitors Center (☎ 540-999-3283; Skyline Dr, Mile 50; ☒ 9am-5pm Apr-Nov) at Mile 50. Both places have exhibits on flora and fauna, as well as maps and information about hiking trails and activities. Miles and miles of blazed trails wander through the park.

The most famous trail in the park is the stretch of Appalachian Trail (AT), which travels 101 miles through Shenandoah from south to north, and is part of the 2175-mile Appalachian Trail crossing through 14 states. Access the trail from Skyline Dr, which roughly parallels the trail.

Aside from the AT, Shenandoah has over 400 miles of hiking trails in the park. Options for shorter hikes include the following:

Compton Peak Mile 10.4, 2.4 miles, easy to moderate.

Traces Mile 22.2, 1.7 miles, easy.

Overall Run Mile 22.2, 6 miles, moderate.

White Oak Canyon Mile 42.6, 4.6 miles, strenuous.

Hawksbill Mountain Summit Mile 46.7, 2.1 miles, moderate. This is the park's highest peak.

Horseback riding is allowed on designated trails: pick up your pony at Skyland Stables (☎ 540-999-2210; guided group rides 1/2½hr $30/50; ☺ 9am-5pm May-Oct), near Mile 41.7. Cycling is allowed on Skyline Dr only – not off-road. Backcountry camping is allowed but requires a permit, which you can pick up at the visitors centers.

The town of Front Royal, at the northern end of Skyline Dr, is a convenient jumping-off point for the park. It's a good place to pack your picnic before heading into the wilderness. If you have some free time here, visit the Oasis Winery (☎ 540-635-9933; www.oasiswine.com; 14141 Hume Rd; wine tasting $5-10; ☺ 10am-5pm), off Rte 635 near Front Royal. The sparkling wines produced here have a solid reputation. The town is also home to the Skyline Caverns (☎ 800-296-4545; www.skylinecaverns.com; entrance to Skyline Dr; adult/child $16/8; ☺ 9am-5pm), whose interiors are decked with unusual anthodites ('cave flowers'). Unlike stalactites and stalagmites, these spiky nodes defy gravity and grow in all directions, one inch every 7000 years.

TRANSPORTATION: SHENANDOAH NATIONAL PARK

Direction Front Royal 70 miles west; Luray 90 miles west.

Travel time Ninety minutes to the northern entrance at Front Royal.

Car From Washington, DC, take I-66 west to Rte 340. Front Royal is 3 miles south; Luray is 27 miles south.

The small town of Luray sits snug between Massanutten Mountain, in George Washington National Forest, and Shenandoah National Park. The eastern US's largest and most popular caves, Luray Caverns (☎ 540-743-6551; www.luraycaverns.com; Rte 211; adult/child $21/10; ☺ 9am-7pm Jun-Aug, 9am-6pm Sep-Nov, Apr & May, 9am-4pm Mon-Fri Dec-Mar), are 9 miles west of here on Rte 211.

EATING & SLEEPING

Elkwallow Wayside (☎ 540-999-2253; Skyline Dr, Mile 24.1; ☺ 9am-5:30pm Apr-Oct) Camp store with supplies and ice, plus a counter serving sandwiches and grilled items.

Big Meadows Lodge (☎ 540-999-2255; www.nps.gov/shen; Skyline Dr, Mile 51.2; r $85-150, cabins $100-110; ☺ late May-Oct) The historic Big Meadows Lodge has 29 cozy wood-paneled rooms and several rustic cabins. The on-site Spotswood Dining Room serves three hearty meals a day; reserve well in advance.

Skyland Resort (☎ 540-743-5108, 800-999-4714; Skyline Dr, Mile 41.7; r $90-152, cabins $75-140; ☺ Apr-Oct) Founded in 1888, this beautifully set resort has fantastic views over the countryside. You'll find simple, wood-finished rooms and a full-service dining room, and you can arrange horseback rides from here.

Lewis Mountain Cabins (☎ 540-999-2255; www.nps.gov/shen; Skyline Dr, Mile 57.6; cabins $90-100, campsites $16; ☺ Apr-Oct) Lewis Mountain has several suitably rustic but pleasantly furnished cabins complete with private baths for a hot shower after a day's hiking. Lewis Mountain also has a campground with a store, laundry and showers.

Potomac Appalachian Trail Club Cabins (☎ 703-242-0315; www.patc.net; cabins per weekday/weekend $25/40) Six primitive cabins have bunk beds and wood stoves, but you need to bring everything else – water, wood for fuel, sleeping bags and, of course, food. The cabins are set in lovely backcountry. Reservations mandatory.

HARPERS FERRY

Rich history and wild recreation are packed onto a scenic spit of land where the Shenandoah and Potomac Rivers meet to form the boundaries of three states in Harpers Ferry. The federal armory here was the target of abolitionist John Brown's raid in 1859 and, though Brown's ambition to arm slaves and spark a national rebellion against slavery died once he was caught and hanged, the incident incited slaveholders'

TRANSPORTATION: HARPERS FERRY

Direction 66 miles northwest.

Travel time 90 minutes.

Car From Washington take I-495 north to the I-270. I-270 turns into I-70. Merge onto US-340 west and follow the signs for downtown Harpers Ferry.

worst fears and helped precipitate the Civil War. Union and Confederate forces soon fought for control of the armory and town.

The most fun to be had in Harpers Ferry takes place on foot, bicycle and boat. The 2175-mile Appalachian Trail (AT) not only passes through town, it has headquarters at the Appalachian Trail Conference (below), which is a tremendous resource for local hikers as well as backpackers. Day hikers can scale the Maryland Heights Trail past Civil War fortifications or the Loudoun Heights Trail for scenic river views.

River Riders (☎ 800-326-7238; www.riverriders.com; 408 Alstadts Hill Rd) is a one-stop shop for adventure sports, and rental bikes (half-day $20 to $30) to explore the C&O Canal Towpath (also see p73). The scenic path follows the Potomac River. It's not exactly technical mountain biking stuff, but it's a beautiful ride. Or take a raft or kayak trip down the Shenandoah River (Class I-III). The rafting costs $55 to $75, the kayaking $65. Try the kayaking if you're looking for more of an adrenaline rush. A cheaper (and equally fun) option is tubing. For $27 to $35 the company will give you a tube, life jacket and shuttle transport to and from the Potomac River. You're then on your own to negotiate the Class I-III rapids.

INFORMATION

Appalachian Trail Conference (☎ 304-535-6331; www.appalachiantrail.org; 799 Washington St; ☉ Apr-Oct) A nonprofit organization devoted to protecting and maintaining the Appalachian Trail.

Visitors Center (☎ 304-535-6029; 171 Shoreline Dr; vehicle/pedestrian passes $6/4)

EATING

Anvil (☎ 304-535-2582; 1290 Washington St; mains lunch $6-9, dinner $15-18; ☉ 11am-9pm Wed-Sun) Chicken quesadillas, vegetarian pasta and pan-seared trout taste mighty fine here after a day's outing.

Country Café (☎ 304-535-2327; 1715 W Washington St; dishes $5; ☉ 7am-3pm) A charmingly old-fashioned restaurant serving hearty breakfasts as well as fresh-made chili, soups and sandwiches.

SLEEPING

Harpers Ferry KOA (☎ 304-535-6895; www.harpersferrykoa.com; campsites/cabins from $40/80; ☉ year-round; ☒) Two miles southwest on Hwy 340, Harpers Ferry KOA has camping and a range of cabins. The heated Olympic-sized swimming pool is an added bonus for travelers year-round.

HI Harpers Ferry Lodge (☎ 301-834-7652; www.harpersferryhostel.org; 19123 Sandy Hook Rd; dm/d from $18/55; ☉ mid-Mar–Oct; ☐ ☎) Located 2.5 miles from the train station in Knoxville, MD. It has the usual hostel amenities, as well as an outdoor campfire.

Anglers Inn (☎ 304-535-1239; www.theanglersinn.com; 867 W Washington St; r weekday/weekend $120/155; ☎) An 1880 Victorian with spacious, comfortably furnished rooms. Gourmet breakfast included.

BALTIMORE

Baltimore's dramatic and continuing redevelopment has transformed the gritty city into an exciting historical and modern destination. The Inner Harbor's waterfront promenade and distinct neighborhoods bursting with personality are the main draws. The city's undeniable importance in shaping American history – from the birthplace of the national anthem to Underground Railroad hideaways for fugitive slaves – is highlighted in numerous attractions, and there's plenty of nightlife if you're looking to stay up late. It's a great hardworking, ball-playing, no-nonsense US city where citizens welcome visitors with a friendly 'Hey Hon.'

Thanks to major revitalization projects, the Inner Harbor is packed with renovated attractions and is a great place to spend the afternoon. The area is dominated by Harborplace, two complexes that house restaurants, shops and the Inner Harbor Visitors Center (p229).

The National Aquarium in Baltimore (☎ 410-576-3800; www.aqua.org; Piers 3-4, 501 E Pratt St; adult/child $25/15; ☉ 9am-5pm Sat-Thu, 9am-8pm Fri) put the city on the map as a tourist destination when it opened in 1981. Stretching seven stories high over two piers, its tanks house more than 10,000 marine animals, including sharks, rays

TRANSPORTATION: BALTIMORE

Direction 45 miles northeast.

Travel time 45 to 60 minutes by car.

Car Take I-95 or I-295 (Baltimore–Washington Parkway) north to Russell St, which terminates west of the Inner Harbor. Or take I-95 north to I-395, which spills out downtown as Howard St. Beware of this drive during rush hour.

Train Both Amtrak (☎ 800-872-7245; www.amtrak.com) and the Maryland Rail Commuter (MARC; ☎ 866-743-3682; www.mtamaryland.com; ⏱ 6:30am-10:30pm Mon-Fri) travel between Washington, DC's Union Station and Baltimore's Penn Station. MARC is cheaper but it runs only on weekdays. Buses 3 and 11 travel up Charles St past Penn Station at 1515 N Charles St.

and porpoises, plus dolphins in the Marine Mammal Pavilion.

For manufactured aquatic wonders, visit the Baltimore Maritime Museum (☎ 410-396-3453; www.baltomaritimemuseum.org; Piers 3 & 5, 301 E Pratt St; admission 1/2/4 ships $10/13/16; ⏱ 10am-5:30pm), which consists of a lighthouse (admission free) and four US Naval vessels that visitors can tour. These include a 1930s double-masted lightship, a submarine, a warship that saw action in Pearl Harbor and, most impressive of all, the three-masted 1854 USS *Constellation*.

One of the most distinctive museums around here is the American Visionary Art Museum (☎ 410-244-1900; www.avam.org; 800 Key Hwy; adult/child $14/8; ⏱ 10am-6pm Tue-Sun), on the south side of the harbor. This avant-garde gallery showcases the raw genius of 'outsider' artists: broken mirror collages, a maniacally embroidered last will, a giant model ship constructed from toothpicks, and other oddities.

Baltimore boasts two top stops for kids, both within a few blocks of the Inner Harbor. The Maryland Science Center (☎ 410-685-5225; www.mdsci.org; 601 Light St; adult/child $15/11, IMAX film $12; ⏱ 10am-5pm Wed-Fri, 10am-6pm Sat, 11am-5pm Sun) sits at the harbor's southeast corner. The excellent rotating exhibits and IMAX films are the highlight. Two blocks north, Port Discovery (☎ 410-727-8120; www.portdiscovery.org; 35 Market Pl; admission $13; ⏱ 10am-4:30pm Tue-Sat, noon-5pm Sun) is a converted fish market, which has a playhouse, laboratory, TV studio and even Pharaoh's tomb. Wear your kids out here.

The Orioles' baseball park, Camden Yards (☎ 888-848-2473; www.theorioles.com; 333 W Camden St, Baltimore; tickets $15-80; ⏱ box office 10am-5pm Mon-Sat, noon-5pm Sun), occupies an entire city block west of the Inner Harbor. It was the first 'retro' ball park, which reconciled Major League Baseball's need for more space with fans' nostalgia. Painted baseballs on the sidewalk lead

two blocks northwest to the birthplace of a baseball legend; it's now the Babe Ruth Museum (☎ 410-727-1539; www.baberuthmuseum.com; 216 Emory St; adult/child $6/3; ⏱ 10am-5pm), which pays homage to one of the sport's all-time greats. It's open to 7pm on Orioles' game days.

Four blocks north of Camden Yards is Lexington Market. A city market has thrived on this site since 1782. More than 140 merchants hawk everything from homemade kielbasa to Korean barbecue. Around the corner, Edgar Allan Poe is buried in Westminster Cemetery. If you are here around his birthday, January 19, you may see roses and cognac decorating the gravesite.

Behind the power plant is the delightful Little Italy neighborhood, packed with exquisite restaurants, a bocce ball court and a giant brick wall that doubles as an outdoor movie screen in summer. For a dose of American nostalgia head to the Star-Spangled Banner Flag House & 1812 Museum (☎ 410-837-1793; www.flaghouse.org; 844 E Pratt St; adult/child $7/5; ⏱ 10am-4pm Tue-Sat). It opens the home where Mary Pickersgill sewed the flag that inspired Francis Scott Key's *Star-Spangled Banner* poem. On Mount Vernon Sq you'll find Walters Art Museum (☎ 410-547-9000; www.thewalters.org; 600 N Charles St; admission free; ⏱ 10am-5pm Wed-Sun), the city's finest museum. Its art collection spans 55 centuries, from ancient to contemporary, with excellent displays of Asian treasures, rare and ornate manuscripts and books, and a comprehensive collection of French paintings; there's also a great atrium cafe.

The Fort McHenry National Monument & Historic Shrine (☎ 410-962-4290; 2400 E Fort Ave; adult/child $7/free; ⏱ 8am-5pm) is one of the most-visited sites in Baltimore, and was instrumental in saving the city from the British attack during the War of 1812.

Cobblestones fill Market Sq between the Broadway Market and the harbor in the historic maritime neighborhood of Fells Point. Here, you'll find the city's liveliest restaurants and nightlife. Further east, the slightly more sophisticated streets of Canton fan out around a grassy square surrounded by more great restaurants and bars.

The 'Hon' expression of affection, an often imitated but never quite duplicated Baltimorese peculiarity, was born from Hampden, an urban neighborhood just reaching its pinnacle of hipness. Spend a long afternoon browsing kitsch, antiques and eclectic clothing along the avenue (aka 36th St).

INFORMATION

Inner Harbor Visitors Center (☎ 800-282-6632; www .baltimore.org; 100 Light St; ⏱ 9am-6pm) A useful first stop, this modern center is conveniently located in Inner Harbor.

EATING

Miss Shirley's (☎ 410-528-5373; 750 E Pratt St; mains $9-17; ⏱ 7am-3pm Mon-Fri, 8am-4pm Sat & Sun) Serves some of Baltimore's most decadent breakfasts, including smoked salmon eggs Benedict, crabmeat omelettes and German apple pancakes. Delicious soups, salads and sandwiches bring in the lunch crowds.

John Steven (☎ 410-327-5561; 1800 Thames St; mains $16-28; ⏱ 11am-midnight) In the heart of Fells Point, John Steven is known for delicious, reasonably priced seafood, including scrumptious bouillabaisse, seared ahi tuna and the famed crab cakes. Dine in the casual pub or in the open-air patio in back.

Harborplace (☎ 410-332-4191, 800-427-2671; www .harborplace.com; cnr Pratt & Light Sts; ⏱ 10am-9pm Mon-Sat, 11am-7pm Sun) Two waterfront pavilions are sprinkled with restaurants catering to all budgets. The best have outdoor seating opening onto the waterfront.

La Scala (☎ 410-783-9209; 1012 Eastern Ave; mains $15-32; ⏱ 5-10pm Mon-Thu, 5-11pm Sat, 2-10pm Sun) Well worth the price for Little Italy's best. Here you'll find creamy risotto with shrimp and porcini mushrooms, angel-hair pasta with lobster tail, and rich gnocchi with pesto. There's also a good wine list and an indoor bocce court that sees a fair bit of action.

Brewer's Art (☎ 410-547-6925; 1106 N Charles St; sandwiches $9-12, mains $19-26; ⏱ 4pm-2am Mon-Sat, 5pm-2am Sun) In a lovely early-20th-century townhouse, Brewer's Art serves delicious Belgian-style microbrews to a laid-back Mount Vernon crowd. You can enjoy tasty pub fare in the bar or enter the heritage dining room in back for innovative grilled meat and seafood dishes. Head downstairs for a more raucous atmosphere.

SLEEPING

Mount Vernon Hotel (☎ 410-727-2000; www.mountvernon baltimore.com; 24 W Franklin St; s/d from $80/90; P ✗) One of the best values in town, the Mount Vernon Hotel has handsomely furnished rooms in a good location near the restaurant scene along Charles St. Hearty cooked breakfasts sweeten the deal.

Admiral Fell Inn (☎ 410-522-7377, 800-292-4667; www .admiralfell.com; 888 S Broadway; r from $200) An old Fells Point sailors' hotel that has been converted into a lovely inn with Federal-style furniture and four-post beds.

Blue Door on Baltimore (☎ 410-732-0191; www.blue doorbaltimore.com; 2023 E Baltimore St; r $150-180; ✗) In an early 1900s row house, this spotless inn has elegantly furnished rooms, each with a king-sized bed, claw-foot bathtub (and separate shower) and thoughtful extras like an in-room fountain and fresh flowers. It lies north of Fells Point near Johns Hopkins University.

Hostel International Baltimore (☎ 410-576-8880; www.baltimorehostel.org; 17 W Mulberry St; dm/d $28/63) Across the street from the basilica, this hostel has single-sex dorm rooms as well as two much-in-demand private rooms with a shared bathroom. There's a good traveler-friendly vibe and the usual hostel amenities.

ANNAPOLIS & CHESAPEAKE BAY

Sailors and seafood-lovers will relish exploring the coves and waterways of the Chesapeake Bay. A day trip to endearing Annapolis is the easiest way to get a dose of both treats, but if you have time to spare, check out the Eastern Shore. Here you'll find ancestral farms, working waterways and small towns to explore by bike or boat.

Boasting some of the tastiest seafood in the region, Maryland's capital city, Annapolis, is a tribute to the Colonial era. The historic landmark is a perfectly preserved tableau of narrow lanes, brick houses and original 18th-century architecture (one of the largest concentrations of such buildings in the country).

Home of the US Naval Academy since 1845, Annapolis Harbor and its connecting tidal creeks shelter dozens of marinas where thousands of cruising and racing sailboats tie up, earning the city the title Sailing Capital – it has 17 miles of waterfront and there are more than 2500 craft docked here.

The lovely Navy Campus is northwest of the Annapolis historic district; enter via Gate 1 (at the intersection of King George, East and Randall Sts) and head to the US Naval Academy Armel Leftwich Visitors Center (☎ 410-293-8687; www .navyonline.com; 52 King George St, Annapolis; tours adult/child $9/7; ☼ 9am-3pm Mar-Dec, 9am-4pm Jan & Feb, tours 10am-3pm Mon-Sat, 12:30-3pm Sun), which features a film, some exhibits and guided tours. Preble Hall contains the US Naval Academy Museum (☎ 410-293-2108; www.usna.edu/museum; 118 Maryland Ave, Annapolis; admission free; ☼ 9am-5pm Mon-Sat, 11am-5pm Sun) with lots of artifacts, including remnants of the famed battleship USS *Maine*.

Annapolis' lively harbor, City Dock, is the center of its nightlife and – obviously – its nautical life. There are many opportunities to experience it firsthand. Schooner Woodwind (☎ 410-263-7837; www.schoonerwoodwind.com; adult/child cruise $37/22) offers daily two-hour sailing cruises aboard a 74ft schooner. Watermark (☎ 410-268-7600; www.watermarkjourney.com; 40min cruise adult/child $12/7) offers a wide variety of motorized cruises around the harbor. If you have a weekend to spare, you can sign up for an intensive sailing class from Annapolis Sailing School (☎ 800-638-9192; www.annapolissailing.com; 601 6th St, Annapolis). When visiting the harbor, note the Kunta Kinte-Alex Haley Memorial, which marks the spot where the enslaved African arrived in the USA, as told by Alex Haley's novel *Roots*.

The heart of Annapolis is the Maryland State House (☎ 410-974-3400; 91 State Circle, Annapolis; admission free; ☼ 9am-5pm Mon-Fri, 10am-4pm Sat & Sun, tours 11am & 3pm). A dignified domed building built in 1792, it served as the first capitol of the fledgling United States and as a meeting place for the Continental Congress from 1783 to 1784. The period artwork and furnishings are worth a peek around; guided tours are also available.

The collection of historic homes and buildings clustered on Cornhill and Fleet Sts between the State House and the harbor is extraordinary. Guided walking and bus tours abound, or you can pick up a free brochure at the Annapolis & Anne Arundel County Conference & Visitors Bureau (opposite). Some of the highlights that are open to the public include

TRANSPORTATION: ANNAPOLIS & CHESAPEAKE BAY

Direction Annapolis 35 miles east; Easton 73 miles east; St Michaels 79 miles east; Oxford 79 miles east.

Travel time Annapolis 50 minutes; Easton, St Michaels and Oxford 90 minutes.

Car Rte 50 east goes straight into downtown Annapolis. To Easton, continue east over the Chesapeake Bay Bridge and stay on Rte 50 (east) to Rte 33 west.

the jewel Hammond Harwood House (☎ 410-263-4683; www.hammondharwoodhouse.org; 19 Maryland Ave, Annapolis; adult/child $6/3; ☼ noon-5pm Tue-Sun Apr-Oct) and the William Paca House & Garden (☎ 410-990-4543; www .annapolis.org; 186 Prince George St, Annapolis; adult/child $8/5; ☼ 10am-5pm Mon-Sat, noon-5pm Sun Apr-Dec, 10am-4pm Sat, noon-4pm Sun Jan-Mar).

On the Eastern Shore of the Chesapeake Bay, Easton is known more as a gateway to the nearby town of St Michaels, but it is also the commercial and cultural center of surrounding Talbot County. Travelers will discover a town with an 18th-century center that has all the tradition and charm of Annapolis. Stop by the Talbot County Chamber of Commerce (opposite) for information about the Eastern Shore.

The Historical Society of Talbot County (☎ 410-822-0773; www.hstc.org; 25 S Washington St, Easton; admission free; ☼ 10am-4pm Mon-Sat) runs a local history museum in its 19th-century headquarters and offers guided tours ($5) of three historic houses – call for tour times. Other old buildings that are open to the public include the 1794 Talbot County Courthouse (☎ 410-822-2401; 11 N Washington St, Easton; ☼ 9am-5pm Mon-Fri) and the 1682 Third Haven Meeting House (☎ 410-822-0293; 405 S Washington St, Easton; admission free; ☼ 9am-5pm). The Academy Art Museum (☎ 410-822-2787; www.art -academy.org; 106 South St, Easton; admission $3, Wed free; ☼ 10am-4pm Mon-Sat) houses a good collection of 19th- and 20th-century art in an oversized 1820s schoolhouse.

Bay Hundred Peninsula thrusts into the Chesapeake near Easton. Along the shores lie the sweeping manors and productive fishing ports that have typified Chesapeake life for three centuries. The highlight is St Michaels, a gem of a Colonial town with redbrick Georgian buildings, flowering gardens and historic watercraft tied at the wharf. It is a popular tourist spot and the harbor is packed with visiting yachts. Despite its tourist allure, the place manages to retain traces of its not-so-distant maritime past, when many citizens earned a living harvesting the bay's oysters in winter and blue crabs in summer.

Overlooking the harbor from Navy Point, the 1879 Hooper Strait octagonal lighthouse has become the image most people associate with Chesapeake Bay. It is the focal point for the Chesapeake Bay Maritime Museum (☎ 410-745-2916; www.cbmm.org; St Michaels; adult/child $13/6; ⊗ 10am-5pm), a collection of historic buildings that surround the lighthouse on the water's edge. From here you can take a cruise around the bay with Patriot Cruises (☎ 410-745-3100; www.patriotcruises.com; St Michaels; 1hr cruise adult/child $25/13; ⊗ 10am-5pm Nov-Feb, 9am-5pm Oct & Mar-May, 9am-6pm Jun-Sep).

St Michaels is packed with shops and galleries, and a few historic houses. But the real reason to come here is to explore the maze of coves by boat, or to cycle around and admire the stately manor houses. Rent bikes and boats at St Michaels Marina (☎ 800-678-8980; www.stmichaelsmarina.com; 305 Mulberry St, St Michaels; bikes per hr/day $5/18; ⊗ May-Oct). Travelers come to Oxford to ride the village's historic Oxford-Bellevue Ferry (☎ 410-745-9023; www.oxfordferry.com; 27456 Oxford Rd, Oxford; car/passenger/bicycle/pedestrian one-way $10/1/4/3; ⊗ 9am-dusk Apr-Nov), which has been operating since 1683. The car ferry crosses the Tred Avon River from Oxford to Bellevue in 10 minutes; from Bellevue you can drive or cycle 7 miles to St Michaels. There is always a cooling breeze and a lovely view of the pastoral peace surrounding Oxford.

INFORMATION

Annapolis & Anne Arundel County Conference & Visitors Bureau (☎ 410-263-9591; 26 West St, Annapolis; ⊗ 9am-5pm)

Talbot County Chamber of Commerce (☎ 410-822-4653; www.talbotchamber.org; 210 Marlboro Rd, Easton; ⊗ 8:30am-5pm Mon-Fri)

EATING

Middleton Tavern (☎ 410-263-3323; www.middletontavern.com; 2 Market Space, Annapolis; sandwiches $7-10, dinners $15-20; ⊗ 11am-midnight Sun-Thu, 11am-1am Fri & Sat) A few steps from the city dock, the country's second-oldest tavern serves delectably fresh crab cakes, seafood platters and sliders (mini-crab or scallop sandwiches). Go early for a seat on the front patio.

49 West Cafe (☎ 410-626-9796; 49 West St, Annapolis; mains lunch $8-10, dinner $14-23; ⊗ 8am-11pm) This inviting cafe serves eclectic fare – gourmet sandwiches and salads at lunch, handsomely prepared seafood and grills at dinner – with live music most nights.

Carpenter St Saloon (☎ 410-745-5111; 113 S Talbot St, St Michaels; mains $10-18; ⊗ 11:30am-9pm) Atmospheric corner bar for oysters and beers, with an airy dining room for families next door.

Chick & Ruth's Delly (☎ 410-269-6737; 165 Main St, Annapolis; mains $8-16; ⊗ 6:30am-11:30pm Sun-Thu, to 12:30am Fri & Sat) A second-generation Annapolis institution serving up burgers, milkshakes, crab cakes and breakfast goodies all with a smile.

Crab Claw Restaurant (☎ 410-745-2900; 2 Market Space, St Michaels; mains $15-25; ⊗ 11am-9pm) Next door to the maritime museum, the Crab Claw serves up tasty Maryland blue crabs to splendid views over the harbor. Avoid the seafood sampler, unless you're a fan of deep-fried seafood.

Out of the Fire (☎ 410-770-4777; 22 Goldsborough St, Easton; mains $19-26; ⊗ 11:30am-2pm & 5-9pm Tue-Sat) One of Easton's best, with tasty paella, oak-planked arctic char, spiced pork tenderloin and a reputable crab cake, served in an elegant dining room.

DETOUR: BLACKWATER NATIONAL WILDLIFE REFUGE

This 17,000-acre refuge, 20 miles south of Easton, contains tidal marshes protected for migrating waterfowl. It has large populations of bald eagles, snow geese, peregrine falcons, blue herons, ospreys and 20 species of duck. October through December is prime bird-watching time. You may also spot woodland creatures such as red foxes, fox squirrels and white-tailed deer.

A 5-mile nature drive cuts through the refuge; there are also four hiking trails, ranging in length from 0.3 miles to 2.7 miles. This is also a great spot for cyclists and kayakers to explore: biking and paddling maps are available at the Blackwater Refuge Visitors Center (☎ 410-228-2677; www.friendsofblackwater.org; 2145 Key Wallace Dr, Cambridge; car/walker & cyclist $3/1; ⊗ dawn-dusk). Take Rte 50 south to Cambridge, then Rte 16 south to State Road 335. Take a left at Key Wallace Dr.

If you come during the warmer months, be sure to bring insect repellent.

SLEEPING

Historic Inns of Annapolis (☎ 410-263-2641; www.histor icinnsofannapolis.com; 58 State Circle, Annapolis; r from $165) Three historic properties with period furnishings and modern conveniences.

Parsonage Inn (☎ 410-745-8383; www.parsonage-inn .com; 210 N Talbot St, St Michaels; r $140-185) A charming inn set in an 1883 brick Victorian. Rooms are florally decorated, with brass beds and oil paintings on the walls. The best have fireplaces.

ScotLaur Inn (☎ 410-268-5665; www.scotlaurinn.com; 165 Main St, Annapolis; r $95-125) Ten simple newly furnished B&B rooms in the heart of the historic district are found at this good-value inn.

Tidewater Inn (☎ 410-822-1300, 800-237-8775; www .tidewaterinn.com; 101 E Dover St, Easton; r from $150) Queen Anne replica with modern rooms and traditional mahogany furniture. The adjoining Restaurant Local serves creative American fare.

EASTERN SHORE

When the temperature soars, do as the locals do and hit the beach. From Virginia through Maryland and up to Delaware, the Eastern Shore comprises a string of protected marshland and preserved beaches, interspersed with resort towns. Chincoteague, Ocean City, Rehoboth and Dewey all offer a most welcome – even necessary – respite from the heat and humidity of Washington summers. The rewards are great if you can manage to squeeze in a trip here, but you'll need at least two days – these places are too far for a day trip from DC. A weekend will allow you to get your fill of surf, sun and, perhaps most importantly, all-you-can-eat crab.

With no contest, the loveliest destination town in the group is Chincoteague, Virginia. It's also the furthest from DC. The small beach town (population 4300) sits across an inlet from Assateague Island, which contains Chincoteague National Wildlife Refuge (opposite). Famous from the 1940s novel *Misty of Chincoteague*, the island is still home to wild ponies, which in truth are not really all that wild. In July they are herded across the channel in an annual celebratory festival.

Besides miles of pristine sandy beaches, the refuge contains marshland that attracts migrating waterfowl – a bird-watcher's paradise. Paved trails and roads provide various tours for walkers, cyclists and drivers to try to spot birds, ponies and other wildlife. Cycling or kayaking is the ideal way to explore the area. You can rent bikes at Bike Depot (☎ 757-336-5511; 7058 Maddox Blvd, Chincoteague; per hr/day from $3/14), next to the Refuge Inn. Kayaks and motorboats can be hired from Capt Bob's Marina (☎ 757-336-6654; www.captbobs-marina.com; 2477 Main St, Chincoteague; kayak rental per 3/8hr $25/40). In town, there is not much to keep you occupied in case of rain, only the mildly interesting Oyster & Maritime Museum (☎ 757-336-6117; www.chincoteague.com; 7125 Maddox Blvd, Chincoteague; adult/child $4/2; ⏰ 10am-5pm daily Jun-Aug, 10am-5pm Sat & Sun Apr, May, Sep & Oct), which has exhibits on the history of the area, marine life and seafood.

North of Chincoteague and closer to DC is Ocean City, Maryland, a mammoth Atlantic coast resort that swells in summer when Coppertone-slicked beachgoers crowd the boardwalk and cruise the Coastal Hwy, which is lined with budget motels. For most of its length, along 10 miles of barrier beach, you'll find side-by-side hotels and motels, thumping bars advertising bikini contests, and shops

---

TRANSPORTATION: EASTERN SHORE

Direction Chincoteague and Assateague 160 miles southeast; Ocean City 130 miles southeast; Rehoboth and Dewey 115 miles east.

Travel time Four hours by car to Chincoteague; three hours to Ocean City, Rehoboth and Lewes.

Boat The Cape May-Lewes ferry (☎ 800-643-3779; www.capemaylewesferry.com; one-way car & driver $30-44, passenger $8-10) travels year-round between Lewes and Cape May, the southern tip of the New Jersey shore. The ferry takes 70 minutes to transport cars and bikes across the open mouth of the Delaware Bay. On weekends, make reservations in advance.

Car Take Rte 50 south to Rte 13 in Salisbury, MD. To Chincoteague, take Rte 13 south to Rte 175, about 5 miles past Pocomoke City, MD. Travel east on Rte 175 to Chincoteague Island, then east on Maddox Blvd. To reach Ocean City, stay on Rte 50, which leads right to the inlet. For Rehoboth and Lewes, take Rte 50 to Rte 404 east. To Rehoboth, go south on Rte 1; to Lewes, head east on Rte 9.

selling airbrushed T-shirts, salt-water taffy and beachwear. If this whets your appetite, pick up more information on OC at the Ocean City Convention & Visitors Bureau (☎ 800-626-2326; www .ococean.com; 4001 Coastal Hwy, Convention Center, Ocean City; ☽ 9am-5pm Mon-Fri); if all this sounds like hell, keep driving.

The town originated at the southern tip of the Strand, now called the Inlet, which retains a tiny hint of Victorian flavor. Here, a 2.5-mile boardwalk provides a pedestrian promenade that is the heart of the Ocean City experience.

Across the Inlet is Assateague Island. This beautiful 37-mile-long barrier island preserves a rare stretch of undeveloped seashore, one of the most pristine and picture-perfect spots on the mid-Atlantic coast. As an undeveloped barrier island, it provides a sharp contrast to the overdeveloped beach resorts that dominate the coast. Besides its natural appeal, the island is home to a legendary herd of wild ponies, whose dramatic silhouettes race across the dunes.

The National Park Service manages most of the protected national seashore; the southern end of the island is Chincoteague National Wildlife Refuge (☎ 757-336-6122; http://chinco.fws.gov; Chincoteague, VA; daily/weekly car pass $15/5, walker & cyclist free; ☽ 5am-10pm May-Oct, 6am-6pm Dec-Mar, 6am-8pm Apr & Nov). A bridge accesses the northern portion of the island, but roads do not go further. To drive from the northern end near Ocean City to the southern end at Chincoteague requires a circuitous inland detour.

The island is a sanctuary where you can get away from the crowds of Ocean City and swim, cycle, hike, fish, canoe, kayak or camp, with nothing but the sound of the surf and the whir of the wind as your companions. Drive south on Rte 611 from Ocean City Dr to visit the Barrier Island Visitors Center (☎ 410-641-1441; Rte 11; ☽ 9am-5pm), near Verrazzano Bridge.

Flat, paved pathways along the island are ideal for cycling; the protected marshland shores make for adventurous canoeing; and conditions are ideal for swimming, hiking and watching birds. Rent bikes and boats from Coastal Bays (☎ 410-726-3217; kayak per hr/day $15/45, bike per hr/day $6/20; ☽ 9am-6pm daily Jun-Aug, 10-4pm Sat & Sun mid-Apr–May & Sep–mid-Oct), located at the end of Bayside Dr (second right after passing the national park toll booth). If you're searching for serenity, backcountry camping is the answer – inquire about regulations at the visitors center. Drive-up campsites fill up

quickly; reserve well ahead through Reserve America (☎ 877-444-6777; www.recreation.gov; campsites $20).

Further north up Rte 1, the Delaware Seashore State Park (www.destateparks.com; Rte 1; per in-state/out-of-state car $4/8), south of Dewey, DE, is a 10-mile-long, half-mile-wide peninsula with a long, straight clean beach. Stop at the park office (☎ 302-227-2800; ☽ 8am-4:30pm) to pick up information about pontoon boat tours, hiking trails and guarded swimming areas. The Indian River Inlet Marina (☎ 302-227-3071; Rte 1), west of the park office, charters fishing boats.

Long known as a fashionable gay resort, Rehoboth, Delaware, is a vibrant old seaside town tucked behind a tacky stretch of Hwy 1 (follow signs to the resort area). Beach houses trimmed in clapboard and cedar shingles sit among tree-lined streets and picturesque lagoons. Modern oceanfront resort motels and hotels spoil the magic a bit as you approach the waterfront.

Poodle beach, at the southern tip of the boardwalk, is primarily gay, while lesbians congregate at North Shores beach at the south end of Cape Henlopen State Park (☎ 302-645-8983; www .destateparks.com; 15099 Cape Henlopen Dr, Lewes, DE; per in-state/out-of-state car $4/8; ☽ park 8am-dusk, visitors center 8am-5pm). Straight folks shouldn't feel excluded – the beach attracts all types.

The main drag, Rehoboth Ave, is lined with restaurants, food stands and souvenir shops, as well as the mile-long beach boardwalk and the easy-to-miss Rehoboth Chamber of Commerce & Visitors Center (☎ 302-227-2233, 800-441-1329; www.beach-fun .com; 501 Rehoboth Ave, Rehoboth, DE; ☽ 9am-5pm Mon-Fri year-round, 9am-2pm Sat, 9am-1pm Sun summer). Look for the center just across the canal bridge in the restored 1879 railway station.

Travel further south along Hwy 1 and you'll reach Dewey Beach. Rehoboth's wild little sister, Dewey is best known for its frantic nightlife. When the sun goes down throngs of under-30s swarm the streets and quickly forget their sunburn after downing a couple at the numerous watering holes.

EATING

Dogfish Head Brewing & Eats (☎ 302-226-2739; 320 Rehoboth Ave, Rehoboth, DE; mains $10-23) Delaware's famous microbrewery also has a popular, family-friendly restaurant with a big menu featuring wood-grilled pizza, seafood and steaks. Catch live bands here on Friday and Saturday nights (at 10pm).

Liquid Assets (☎ 410-524-7037; cnr 94th St & Coastal Hwy, Ocean City, MD; mains $10-26) With lively ambience, a winning drink menu and nicely prepared seafood and bistro fare, this is a top OC choice.

Phillips Crab House (☎ 410-289-6821; 2004 Philadelphia Ave, Ocean City, MD; mains $12-28) Though now synonymous with crabs in the DC region (Phillips operates restaurants throughout the capital region), it all started in Ocean City. The restaurant is a casual place, with a huge menu emphasizing crabs, which is what you should order.

Seacrets (☎ 410-524-4900; 117 W 49th St, Ocean City, MD) A Jamaican-themed bar and club straight out of MTV's *Spring Break*, Seacrets has beach parties, spring-loaded indoor dance floors, and watery areas where you can drift in an inner tube while sipping your drink.

Steamers (☎ 757-336-5300; 6251 Maddox Blvd, Chincoteague, VA; mains $14-28; ☾ 5-10pm) This fun casual place is famous for its all-you-can-eat crabs.

Venus on the Half Shell (☎ 302-227-9292; Dagsworthy St, Dewey, DE; mains $14-26) Beautifully set on Dewey Beach, this is the place to come for a seafood feast at sunset before hitting the bars.

SLEEPING

Assateague Inn (☎ 757-336-3738; www.assateague-inn.com; cnr Maddox Blvd & Chicken City Rd, Chincoteague, VA; r/ste/apt $95/130/155; 🎇 🛜 🖳) Has clean, motel-style rooms with balconies overlooking the saltwater marsh. Suites with kitchenettes and roomier one-bedroom apartments, with full kitchens, are also available.

King Charles Hotel (☎ 410-289-6141; www.kingcharleshotel.com; 1209 Baltimore Ave, Ocean City, MD; r weekdays/weekends $105/150; 🎇) This place feels like a summer cottage and is a good deal for the high season. It's centrally located half a block from the beach in the heart of the boardwalk action.

Royal Rose Inn B&B (☎ 302-226-2535; www.royalroseinn.com; 41 Baltimore Ave, Ocean City, MD; r from $135; 🎇 🛜) This place is a great bang for your buck, with a rooftop hot tub, screened porch and sundeck. It's just a block from the boardwalk.

Rehoboth Guest House (☎ 302-227-4117; www.guesthse.com; 40 Maryland Ave; r $95-130; 🎇 🖳) Gay-owned and operated, this tidy guesthouse is wildly popular for its afternoon wine-and-cheese parties, private sunbathing decks and immaculate rooms, not to mention its five-minute walk to the boardwalk. Reservations recommended.

TRANSPORTATION

Flights, tours and rail tickets can be booked online at www.lonelyplanet.com/travel_services.

AIR

Washington, DC is a major international air hub, and all major airlines fly into the capital. The city is served by three airports.

Ronald Reagan Washington National Airport (DCA; ☎ 703-417-8000; www.metwashairports.com) is across the river in Arlington, VA. It is easily accessible by Metro (Yellow or Blue Line).

Washington Dulles International Airport (IAD; ☎ 703-572-2700; www.metwashairports.com) is in the Virginia suburbs 26 miles west of DC. Take I-66 west to the Dulles Toll Rd. Both domestic and international flights depart from here. Dulles is not on a Metro line, although Washington Flyer (☎ 888-927-4359; www

.washfly.com; one way/round-trip $10/18; ⏲ 6am-11pm) operates a shuttle from West Falls Church Metro station. The average length of shuttle trips is 20 to 30 minutes. Washington Flyer also operates a door-to-door taxi service (☎ 703-572-8294); rates depend on the distance

TRANSPORT FROM THE AIRPORTS

	Taxi	Metro	Train	SuperShuttle
Pick-up point	Outside arrivals	National Airport: concourse B or C	BWI: follow signs to MARC station	Follow signs from arrivals halls Dulles Airport: West Falls Church via Washington Flyer shuttle BWI: Greenbelt via express bus
Drop-off point	Anywhere	Anywhere on the DC metro system	Union Station	Anywhere
Duration (to city center)	Dulles Airport: 30-60min depending on traffic National Airport: 10-30min BWI: 45-60min	Dulles Airport: 60-90min National Airport: 15min BWI: 60-90min	BWI: 60-90min	Same as taxis; add time to account for shared-van services
Cost (to city center)	From Dulles Airport: $50-55 From National Airport: $12-20 From BWI: $90	Dulles: $12 (shuttle + metro fare) National: $1.35 BWI: around $5 (bus + metro fare)	$7	Dulles Airport: $29 National Airport: $14 BWI: $37
Other	Fares increase at night	Metro runs till midnight Sun-Thu, till 3am Fri & Sat	Reduced service and increased ticket price ($13) on weekends	Shared-van service
Contact	Dulles and National airports: ☎ 703-572-8294 BWI: ☎ 800-878-7743	Metro: ☎ 202-637-7000	☎ 410-672-6169; www.mtamary land.com	☎ 800-258-3826; www.supershuttle.com Washington Flyer: ☎ 703-572-8294

CLIMATE CHANGE & TRAVEL

Climate change is a serious threat to the ecosystems that humans rely upon, and air travel is the fastest-growing contributor to the problem. Lonely Planet regards travel, overall, as a global benefit, but believes we all have a responsibility to limit our personal impact on global warming.

Flying & Climate Change

Pretty much every form of motor transport generates CO_2 (the main cause of human-induced climate change) but planes are far and away the worst offenders, not just because of the sheer distances they allow us to travel, but because they release greenhouse gases high into the atmosphere. The statistics are frightening: two people taking a return flight between Europe and the US will contribute as much to climate change as an average household's gas and electricity consumption over a whole year.

Carbon Offset Schemes

Climatecare.org and other websites use 'carbon calculators' that allow jet-setters to offset the greenhouse gases they are responsible for with contributions to energy-saving projects and other climate-friendly initiatives in the developing world – including projects in India, Honduras, Kazakhstan and Uganda.

Lonely Planet, together with Rough Guides and other concerned partners in the travel industry, supports the carbon offset scheme run by climatecare.org. Lonely Planet offsets all of its staff and author travel.

For more information check out our website: www.lonelyplanet.com.

---

covered, with a one-way fare to Capitol Hill being $54 at the time of research.

Baltimore-Washington International Airport (BWI; ☎ 800-435-9294; www.bwiairport.com) is 30 miles, or about 45 minutes' drive, northeast of DC in Maryland. Get onto the Baltimore–Washington Parkway via New York Ave NE, and follow the parkway until you see the I-195/BWI exit. Often you will find that cheaper fares are available to/from BWI than to either National or Dulles; so despite its geographic inconvenience, this is a handy airport for those on a budget. Maryland Rail Commuter (MARC; ☎ 800-325-7245; www.mtamaryland.com) and Amtrak trains travel between DC's Union Station and a terminal near BWI, and an express (B30) bus operated by the Washington Metropolitan Area Transit Authority (☎ 202-637-7000; www.wmata.com/bus/b30_brochure.cfm) runs every 40 minutes between BWI and Greenbelt Metro station.

SuperShuttle (see Getting into Town, below), runs door-to-door van service from all three of the airports; call ahead or check the website for a quoted fare. An up-to-date list of transportation options from Washington's three airports can also be found at www.downtowndc.org/visit/get_around/airports.

BICYCLE

Cycling is one of the best ways to get around DC. In recent years, Metro has taken new measures to encourage bicycle commuting. Riders can take their bikes free of charge on trains, except during rush hour (7am to 10am and 4pm to 7pm Monday to Friday) and on busy holidays, such as July 4. Bikes are not permitted to use the center door of trains or the escalator. All buses are now equipped with bike racks, so riders can transport their bikes by bus, too. Here are some options for rental:

Better Bikes Inc (☎ 202-293-2080; per 24hr $38) Delivers and picks up bikes anywhere in the DC area. Price includes helmets, locks and assistance.

Big Wheel Bikes (Map p72; ☎ 202-337-0254; 1034 33rd St NW; per hr/day $7/35; Ⓜ Rosslyn) In Georgetown, just up the hill from the end of the Capital Crescent Trail. Just below M St, look for the bright-yellow building with a huge bicycle on it. There's a three-hour minimum with rentals.

Bike the Sites (Map p88; ☎ 202-842-2453; 1100 Pennsylvania Ave, Old Post Office Pavilion; per hr/day $7/35; Ⓜ Federal Triangle) Weekly rentals, plus guided tours also available.

GETTING INTO TOWN

If you fly into Ronald Reagan Washington National Airport, you can catch the Metro directly into the city. From Washington Dulles or BWI the options are more limited. The cheapest way is the SuperShuttle (☎ 800-258-3826; www.supershuttle.com; Dulles/National $25/12; ☙ 5:30am-12:30am), which provides door-to-door service to/from all three airports in a shared van.

BUS

DC's bus system (technically called 'Metrobus') is operated by the Washington Metropolitan Transit Authority (WMATA), or Metro. It provides a clean and efficient bus service throughout the city and to outlying suburbs. Stops are marked by red, white and blue signposts. The fare is $1.25 ($3 on express routes), or 35¢ with a Metrorail transfer. Kids under four ride free. Automatic fare machines accept paper dollars, but you must have exact change.

Useful bus routes include:

30, 32, 34, 36, Wisconsin Ave Runs from Friendship Heights down Wisconsin Ave (through Georgetown) to Foggy Bottom-GWU.

D2, P St NW Connects Georgetown to Dupont Circle.

L2, 18th St NW Connects Woodley Park Zoo to Foggy Bottom-GWU via Adams Morgan.

The DC Circulator (☎ 202-962-1423; www.dccirculator .com; fare $1), also operated by WMATA, is another good bus option that runs five lines operating at 10-minute intervals. Visit http://circulator .dc.gov to get schedule updates onto your mobile phone. The lines concentrate on linking downtown DC to major tourism areas; useful routes connect Georgetown to Union Station via K St and Massachusetts Ave, the Convention Center to the Waterfront, and Woodley Park and Adams-Morgan to the White House Area.

Interstate

The main bus company is Greyhound (Map pp78–9; ☎ 202-289-5141; www.greyhound.com; 1005 1st St NE), which provides nationwide service. Peter Pan Trailways (Map pp78–9; ☎ 800-343-9999; www.peterpanbus.com), which travels to the northeastern US, uses a terminal just opposite Greyhound's. This neighborhood is deserted after dark, and the nearest Metro station is several blocks south (via 1st St NE) at Union Station. Cabs are usually available at the bus station, and you should use one; don't walk across town from the bus station at night.

There are numerous cheap bus services to New York, Philadelphia and Richmond; most charge around $20 for a one-way trip (it takes about four to five hours). Pick-up locations are scattered around town, but are always Metro-accessible, and are included in the following listings. Tickets usually need to be bought online, but can also be purchased at the bus itself if there is room. Vamoose Bus runs to Arlington, VA and Bethesda, MD. Try any of the following, and note the following addresses are street pick-up points, not bus stations. Generally, buses show up 30 to 20 minutes prior to departure time. Confirm time and place of travel with your agency and ultimately, go where they tell you to go to catch your ride.

Apex (Map p88; ☎ 202-449-9758; www.apexbus.com; 622 I St NW)

Boltbus (Map p88; ☎ 877-265-8287; www.boltbus .com; 700 10th St NW)

DC2NY (☎ 202-332-2691; www.dc2ny.com; Map p96; cnr 20th St & Massachusetts Ave NW; Map p88; cnr 14th & I St NW)

New Century (Map p88; ☎ 202-789-8222; www.2000coach.com; 513 H St NW)

Vamoose Bus (☎ 877-393-2828; www.vamoosebus.com; Map p122; 1801 N Lynn St, Rosslyn, VA; off Map p114; 7490 Waverly St, Bethesda, MD)

WashNY (☎ 866-287-6932; www.washny.com; Map p96; 1333 19th St NW; Map pp78–9; 1015 15th St NW; Map p64; 441 New Jersey Ave NW)

CAR & MOTORCYCLE

Car Share

Zipcar (☎ 866-494-7227; www.zipcar.com), with its cute, eco-friendly Priuses and parking-friendly minis, is a popular commuting tool in this town. If you're on vacation, weekday rates run $9.25/60 hourly/daily and weekends $10.50/77 hourly/daily. That includes gas and insurance and good parking spaces around town.

Driving

In 2009, the Associated Press reported DC had the second-worst traffic congestion in the USA. The worst bottlenecks are in the suburbs, where the Capital Beltway (I-495) meets Maryland's I-270 and I-95, and Virginia's I-66 and I-95. Avoid the beltway during early morning and late-afternoon rush hours (about 6am to 9am and 3pm to 6pm). Clogged rush-hour streets in DC include the main access arteries from the suburbs: Massachusetts, Wisconsin, Connecticut and Georgia Aves NW, among others.

Certain lanes of some major traffic arteries change direction during rush hour, and some two-way streets become one-way. Signs indicate hours of these changes, so keep your eyes peeled. Except where otherwise posted, the speed limit on DC surface streets is 25mph (15mph in alleys and school zones). You must wear your seat belt and restrain kids under three years in child-safety seats.

For emergency road service and towing, members can call the American Automobile Association (☎ 800-222-4357). It has a branch: AAA travel agency (Map p64; ☎ 202-331-3000; 701 15th St NW, Suite 100; ⌚ 9am-5.30pm Mon-Fri).

Parking

Finding street parking is difficult Downtown and in popular neighborhoods (Georgetown, Adams-Morgan and the U St area are particularly nightmares), but it's reasonably easy in less-congested districts. Note that residential areas often have a two-hour limit on street parking. If you tempt the local traffic gods, you'll probably get ticketed. Parking garages in the city normally cost $15 to $30 per day.

Rental

All major car-rental agencies and many small local ones are represented in DC, especially at the airports. Many big agencies maintain offices downtown and at Union Station. Airport rates are often better than those at downtown offices. Car-rental rates do fluctuate radically, but weekly rates are often the best deal. An economy-sized car typically costs $150 to $200 per week. Expect to pay more during peak visitor times, such as the Cherry Blossom Festival (p13), and when big conventions and political demonstrations are in town. Gas is pricier inside the city than in Maryland and Virginia.

Most major agencies in DC won't rent to anyone under 25. Some local companies rent to drivers over 21 who have a major credit card, but their rates generally aren't competitive. Agencies in DC include the following:

Alamo (☎ 800-327-9633, 703-260-0182; Dulles airport)

Budget (Map pp78–9; ☎ 800-527-0700, 202-289-5373; Union Station); National airport (☎ 703-920-3360)

Enterprise (Map p64; ☎ 800-325-8007, 202-393-0900; 1029 Vermont Ave NW); National airport (☎ 703-553-7744); Dulles airport (☎ 703-661-8800)

Hertz (Map pp78–9; ☎ 202-289-5366; Union Station); National airport (☎ 703-419-6300)

National (Map pp78–9; ☎ 888-826-6890, 202-842-7454; Union Station); National airport (☎ 202-783-1590); Dulles airport (☎ 703-471-5278)

Thrifty (Map p88; ☎ 202-347-8266; Verizon Center); National and Dulles airports (☎ 877-283-0898)

METRO

DC's sleek modern subway network is the Metrorail, commonly called Metro (☎ 202-637-7000; www.wmata.com; fares from $1.35; ⌚ 5am-midnight Mon-Thu, 5am-3am Fri, 7am-3am Sat, 7am-midnight Sun). It is managed by DC, Maryland, Virginia and the federal government. Thanks to ample federal funding, its trains and stations are well marked, well maintained, well lit, climate controlled, reasonably priced, decently staffed, reliable and safe. Parking is available at certain outlying stations.

To ride Metro, buy a computerized fare-card from the self-service machines inside the station entrance. The minimum fare is $1.35, although it increases for longer distances and during rush hour. The posted station-to-station chart provides exact fares for each route. You must use the fare-card to enter *and* exit station turnstiles. Upon exit, the turnstile deducts the fare and returns the card. If the value of the card is insufficient, you need to use an 'Addfare' machine to add money. Other machines inside the gates dispense free bus transfers that enable you to pay just 35¢ on connecting bus routes.

A variety of passes are available, including a one-day pass ($6.50) or a weekly pass ($32.50). Special passes are available from the Sales & Information office (Map p88; Metro Center station, cnr 12th & F Sts NW), from the website, and from Safeway and Giant grocery stores.

If you're in DC for a week or more, you may want to get a SmarTrip card. This is basically a rechargeable fare-card that's easier to carry than disposable Metro tickets. They can be purchased at all Metro stations (you need to put a minimum of $30 on the card) or online at http://www.wmata.com/fares/purchase/store.

TAXI

Taxicabs are plentiful in central DC; hail them with a wave of the hand. Diamond (☎ 202-387-4410), Yellow (☎ 202-544-1212) and Capitol (☎ 202-546-2400) are three major companies. Fares generally start at $3.50 at flag drop and increase at roughly 75¢ per half-mile – it's a pricey way of getting around. Add at least 10% for a tip and keep in mind rates increase at night and for radio dispatches. Cabs are easy to hail along major streets and adjacent arteries, but expect a wait in nightlife hot spots on weekend nights and during major holidays.

TRAIN

Most trains departing Union Station (Map pp78–9) are bound for other East Coast destinations. The station is the southern terminus of the northeast rail corridor, which stops at Baltimore, Philadelphia, New York, New Haven (Connecticut), Boston and intermediate points. There is usually at least one departure per hour throughout the day. Regular (unreserved) trains are cheapest, but pokey. Express Metroliners (reserved) to New York are faster; fastest of all are the fewer-stop Acela trains that zing to New York and on to Boston at speeds in excess of 150mph.

Trains also depart for Virginia destinations (Richmond, Williamsburg, Virginia Beach), Montréal and southern destinations, including Florida and New Orleans, and also to Amtrak's national hub, Chicago, where you can connect to Midwest- and West Coast–bound trains. MARC and VRE commuter trains connect Union Station to Virginia and Maryland.

Fares vary according to type of seating (coach seats or sleeping compartments) and season. Amtrak also offers a variety of all-inclusive holiday tour packages along with regional rail passes and frequent specials.

DIRECTORY

BUSINESS HOURS

Most offices and government agencies in Washington are open 9am to 5pm Monday to Friday. Most shops are open 10am to 7pm Monday to Saturday, noon to 5pm Sunday. Smaller shops may be closed Sunday, Monday or both days. Restaurants are usually open 11:30am to 2:30pm for lunch and 5:30pm to 10pm for dinner Monday to Friday and later (until 11pm or midnight) on Friday and Saturday nights. Bars are open until 1am or 2am during the week and 3am on weekends. Banks, schools and offices are closed on all public holidays; most shops, museums and restaurants stay open on public holidays, except July 4, Thanksgiving (fourth Thursday in November), Christmas and New Year's Day.

CHILDREN

Washington may be the best big city in the US to travel with children: all major museums are oriented (in part or in total) toward kids; the monuments and historical sites are child friendly; and there's plenty of parkland and green space where kids can romp. Furthermore, a vacation to Washington is usually educational. Best of all, most attractions here are absolutely free.

The *Washington Post* Weekend section, published each Friday, features 'Saturday's Child,' which details upcoming family- and kid-oriented activities, exhibits and cultural events. See also the great website Our Kids (www .our-kids.com) for event listings and local kid-related news. Helpful books include *Going Places with Children in Washington, DC* by Pamela McDermott and *Travel with Children* published by Lonely Planet.

Babysitting

Many hotels offer babysitting services on site. If your lodge does not have a relationship with a childcare provider, a reputable organization is Mothers' Aides (☎ 703-250-0700, 800-526-2669; www.mothersaides.com), which will send a caregiver to a hotel for a minimum of four hours. Rates are generally $17 to $25 per hour depending on the number of children and the time of year.

CLIMATE

See p12 for information on the best seasons for travel. For weather conditions and forecasts, go to the Washington Post (www.washingtonpost .com) site and click on 'Weather.'

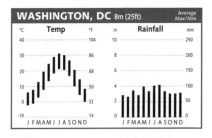

WASHINGTON, DC 8m (25ft) — Average Max/Min

CUSTOMS REGULATIONS

Everyone entering the US is required to fill out a customs declaration form. Visitors over 21 can bring in 200 cigarettes and 1L of alcohol. US citizens are allowed a $400 duty-free exemption; non-US citizens are allowed $100. Strict rules apply to fruit, flowers, meats and animals. There's no limit on the amount of cash, traveler's checks etc that you can bring in, but you must declare any amount over $10,000.

ELECTRICITY

Electric current in the USA is 110V to 115V, 60Hz AC. Outlets may accept flat two-prong or three-prong grounded plugs. Adapters are readily available at drugstores and anywhere that sells hardware. The Steve Kropla (www.kropla .com) website has useful information on electricity and plugs.

EMBASSIES

Nearly every country in the world has an embassy in DC, making this one of the US's most vibrant multinational cities. The handy Electronic Embassy (www.embassy.org) offers links to all DC embassy homepages. The hours listed represent the visa office.

Australia (Map p96; ☎ 202-797-3000; www.usa .embassy.gov.au; 1601 Massachusetts Ave NW, 20036; 🕗 8:30am-2:30pm; Ⓜ Dupont Circle)

Canada (Map p88; ☎ 202-682-1740; www.canadain ternational.gc.ca/washington; 501 Pennsylvania Ave NW, 20001; ⏱ 9am-noon; Ⓜ Archives-Navy Memorial)

China (Map p103; ☎ 202-328-2500; www.china-em bassy.org; 2300 Connecticut Ave NW, 20008; Ⓜ Wood-ley Park Zoo/Adams Morgan); visa office (Map p114; ☎ 202-338-6688; 2201 Wisconsin Ave NW, Suite 110; ⏱ 9:30am-12:30pm; 🚌 30, 32, 34 or 36 from Tenley-town station)

France (Map p114; ☎ 202-944-6000; www.ambafrance -us.org; 4101 Reservoir Rd NW, 20007; ⏱ 8:45am-12:45pm; 🚌 Georgetown Shuttle, DC Circulator)

Germany (Map p114; ☎ 202-298-4000; www.germany .info; 4645 Reservoir Rd NW, 20007; ⏱ 8:30-11:30am; 🚌 Georgetown Shuttle, DC Circulator)

India (Map p96; ☎ 202-939-7000; www.indianembassy .org; 2107 Massachusetts Ave NW, 20008); visa office (Map p96; 2536 Massachusetts Ave NW; ⏱ 9:30am-12:30pm; Ⓜ Dupont Circle)

Ireland (Map p96; ☎ 202-462-3939; www.irelandemb .org; 2234 Massachusetts Ave NW, 20008; ⏱ 9am-1pm & 2-4pm; Ⓜ Dupont Circle)

Israel (Map p114; ☎ 202-364-5500; www.israelemb.org; 3514 International Drive NW, 20008; ⏱ 9:30am-1pm; Ⓜ Van Ness-UDC)

Japan (Map p114; ☎ 202-238-6700; www.us.emb-japan .go.jp; 2520 Massachusetts Ave NW, 20008; ⏱ 10am-noon & 2-4pm; Ⓜ Dupont Circle)

Mexico (Map p64; ☎ 202-728-1600; http://portal.sre .gob.mx/usa; 1911 Pennsylvania Ave NW, 20006; ⏱ 8am-1pm; Ⓜ Farragut West)

Netherlands (Map p114; ☎ 202-244-5300; www.nether lands-embassy.org/homepage.asp; 4200 Linnean Ave NW, 20008; ⏱ 10am-noon; Ⓜ Van Ness-UDC)

New Zealand (Map p114; ☎ 202-328-4800; www.nzem bassy.com/home.cfm?c=31; 37 Observatory Circle, 20008; ⏱ 9am-5pm; 🚌 N6 from Farragut Sq downtown)

Russia (Map p114; ☎ 202-298-5700; www.russianem bassy.org; 2650 Wisconsin Ave NW, 20007); visa office (☎ 202-939-8907; 2641 Tunlaw Rd NW, behind main office; ⏱ 9am-12:30pm Mon-Fri; 🚌 30, 32, 34 or 36)

South Africa (Map p114; ☎ 202-232-4400; www .saembassy.org; 3051 Massachusetts Ave NW, 20008; ⏱ 9am-12:30pm; 🚌 N6)

Spain (Map p64; ☎ 202-452-0100; www.maec.es; 2375 Pennsylvania Ave NW, 20037; ⏱ 9am-12:30pm; Ⓜ Foggy Bottom-GWU)

UK (Map p114; ☎ 202-588-6500; http://ukinusa.fco.gov .uk; 3100 Massachusetts Ave NW, 20008; 🚌 N6)

EMERGENCY

Ambulance/police/fire	☎ 911
DC Rape Crisis Center	☎ 202-333-7273
Poison Control	☎ 800-222-1222
Travelers' Aid Society	☎ 202-546-3120

GAY & LESBIAN TRAVELERS

Home to more than 30 national gay and lesbian organizations and more than 300 social, athletic, religious and political support groups, DC is one of the most gay-friendly cities in the US. The community is most visible in the Dupont Circle and Capitol Hill neighborhoods, where there are many gay-friendly businesses, including the landmark bookstore Lambda Rising (p136). The Washington Blade (www.washing tonblade.com), a gay and lesbian weekly newspaper, offers coverage of politics, information about community resources, and lots and lots of nightlife and meeting-place listings. Other good sources include Metro Weekly (www .metroweekly.com), a publication with information about a slew of women's organizations in the Washington area, from the DC Lesbian Avengers to Older, Wiser Lesbians (OWLS). You can also check out the free *Gay & Lesbian Guide to Washington, DC*, available at the Washington, DC Convention & Visitors Association (www .washington.org) website.

AIDS Hotline (☎ 800-342-2437) A 24-hour help line.

Bi Women's Cultural Alliance (☎ 202-828-3065) Organizes casual get-togethers for lesbians and bisexual women.

Gay & Lesbian Hotline (☎ 202-833-3234) Phone counseling and referrals.

Whitman-Walker Clinic (Map pp106–7; ☎ 202-797-3500; www.wwc.org; 1407 S St NW; Ⓜ U Street-Cardozo) General health care and HIV/AIDS care.

Women in the Life (Map p96; ☎ 202-483-9818; www .womeninthelife.com; 1611 Connecticut Ave NW; Ⓜ Dupont Circle) An advocacy group for lesbians. Sponsors a variety of events during the summer.

HOLIDAYS

Much of Washington, DC shuts down over Christmas and New Year, but other holidays are bustling. The busiest times are in the spring, especially during the National Cherry Blossom Festival (p13) and Easter week, in early summer, during the week of Independence Day and over the Thanksgiving weekend. At these times, expect museums to be packed and prices to be high. Alternatively, during the month of August, and from mid-December to mid-January when Congress is not in session, crowds disappear and bargains abound.

Public Holidays

New Year's Day January 1

Martin Luther King Jr Day Third Monday in January

Inauguration Day January 20, every four years

Presidents' Day Third Monday in February

Memorial Day Last Monday in May

Independence Day July 4

Labor Day First Monday in September

Columbus Day Second Monday in October

Veterans Day November 11

Thanksgiving Day Fourth Thursday in November

Christmas Day December 25

INTERNET ACCESS

For travelers without a computer, the cheapest place to access the internet is at any branch of the DC public library. Fifteen-minute-limit terminals are available free to the public. If you wish to use the internet for longer than 15 minutes, you must sign up for a user's card, which is also free and allows access to computers at any DC public library. Wi-fi is available in many areas of the city, including most hotels. Check www.wififreespot.com/dc.html for up-to-date listings on other free wi-fi spots.

Martin Luther King Jr Memorial Library (Map p88; ☎ 202-727-1126; 901 G St NW; Ⓜ Metro Center)

Mt Pleasant Neighborhood Library (Map pp106–7; ☎ 202-671-0200; 3160 16th St NW; Ⓜ Columbia Heights)

Public Library – Cleveland Park Branch (Map p114; ☎ 202-282-3080; 3310 Connecticut Ave at Macomb St NW; Ⓜ Cleveland Park)

Public Library – Tenley-Friendship Branch (Map p114; ☎ 202-244-3212; 4450 Wisconsin Ave at Albemarle St NW; Ⓜ Tenleytown)

West End Neighborhood Library (Map p64; ☎ 202-724-8707; 1101 24th St at L St NW; Ⓜ Foggy Bottom-GWU)

LEGAL MATTERS

You must be 21 to buy or drink alcohol in DC. Club and bar bouncers are generally fastidious about seeing photo ID for proof of age.

Stiff fines, jail time and loss of your driver's license are the usual penalties for driving while intoxicated.

If you are arrested, you have the right to remain silent and the right to a lawyer. *There is no legal reason to speak to a police officer if you don't want to* – we can't stress this enough – but never walk away from an officer until given permission. If you're arrested, you are legally allowed one phone call. If you don't have a lawyer or a relative to help you, call your embassy. The police will give you the phone number upon request.

MAPS

Lonely Planet's *Washington, DC* street map is a laminated pocket-size guide that shows all major DC attractions. ADC's *Washington, DC* street atlas is a folio-size book that shows all city streets in detail. The best place to buy maps is the ADC Map & Travel Center (p129).

MEASUREMENTS

Like the rest of the country, DC uses the US measurement system. Distances are in feet, yards and miles; weights are in ounces and pounds. There's a conversion chart inside the front cover of this book.

MEDICAL SERVICES

Washington, DC has no unexpected health dangers and excellent medical facilities; the only real concern is that a collision with the US medical system might injure your wallet. Remember to buy health insurance before you travel. Recommended medical facilities:

George Washington University Hospital (Map p64; ☎ 202-715-4000; 900 23rd St NW; Ⓜ Foggy Bottom-GWU)

Howard University Hospital (Map pp106–7; ☎ 202-865-6100; 2041 Georgia Ave NW; Ⓜ Shaw-Howard University)

Institute of International Medicine (Map p64; ☎ 202-715-5100; 900 23rd St NW, Suite G-1094; Ⓜ Foggy Bottom-GWU) Offers immunizations and health advice for travelers going anywhere on the planet; it's housed inside GWU.

Pharmacies

The most prominent pharmacy chain is CVS, with locations all around the city. These convenient branches are open 24 hours:

CVS Dupont Circle (Map p96; ☎ 202-785-1466; 6-7 Dupont Circle; Ⓜ Dupont Circle)

CVS Thomas Circle (Map p64; ☎ 202-628-0720; 1199 Vermont Ave NW; Ⓜ McPherson Sq)

MONEY

Most DC businesses accept cash, credit and/or debit cards and traveler's checks; for security and convenience, it is useful to have all three. A credit card may be required for renting a car or making reservations at some hotels. For information on the costs involved in visiting the city, see p16; exchange rates are listed on the inside front cover.

ATMs

Most banks have 24-hour ATMs affiliated with various networks, including Exchange, Accel, Plus and Cirrus. If you use a credit card, however, you probably will be charged a small fee and incur interest on the withdrawal until you pay it back. Furthermore, if you use an ATM that doesn't belong to your own bank, you'll be charged for the withdrawal.

Changing Money

Although the airports have exchange bureaus, better rates can usually be obtained at banks in the city.

American Express (Map p96; ☎ 202-457-1300; 1150 Connecticut Ave NW; Ⓜ Farragut North)

Thomas Cook (☎ 202-237-2229; 5335 Wisconsin Ave NW; Ⓜ Friendship Heights)

Currency

The only currency accepted in DC is the US dollar ($), consisting of 100 cents (¢). Coins are the penny (1¢), nickel (5¢), dime (10¢), quarter (25¢), half-dollar and dollar (the gold-colored 'Sacajawea' coin). Keep a stash of quarters for use in vending machines, parking meters and laundromats. US bills can confuse the foreign visitor – they're all the same size and color – and exist in denominations of $1, $2 (rare), $5, $10, $20, $50 and $100. Lately, the United States Treasury has been introducing more color into paper bills in an effort to thwart counterfeits.

Traveler's Checks

Traveler's checks are generally as good as cash in the US. Their major advantage is that they are replaceable if stolen. American Express and Thomas Cook (see office locations, left) have efficient replacement policies. A record of the check numbers is vital should you need to replace them – note them carefully and keep the record separate from the checks themselves. Buy checks in US dollars and in large denominations to avoid excessive service fees.

NEWSPAPERS & MAGAZINES

The Washington Post (www.washingtonpost.com) is among the nation's top newspapers. Its competitor is the conservative and less-respected Washington Times (www.washingtontimes.com). The Washington Afro-American (www.afro.com) is the city's African American newspaper, the Washington Blade (www.washblade.com) serves the LGBT community and El Tiempo Latino (http://eltiempolatino.com) provides Spanish-language news. The Washington City Paper (www.washingtoncitypaper.com) is an alternative weekly, distributed free throughout the city. It scrutinizes DC politics and has great entertainment coverage. The Politico (www.politico.com) is an excellent peek into the city's major industry (ie politics), while the Onion (www.theonion.com) may be the nation's best satirical publication – hard copies of both web-based publications are distributed for gratis here. On Tap is another freebie, providing the scoop on local watering holes. Most DC neighborhoods have their own papers, such as the Georgetown Independent and the Hill Rag. The Washingtonian (www.washingtonian .com) is a gossipy lifestyle magazine. The Smithsonian (www.smithsonianmag.com) has articles about the institution – an enjoyable, less-slick National Geographic. For more background on the city's media, see p40.

ORGANIZED TOURS

Now – right now! – log on to Cultural Tourism DC (☎ 202-661-7581; www.culturaltourismdc.org) and check out the stunning range of neighborhood walking tours this admirable organization offers. Otherwise, there are plenty of other tours out there. The big companies are easy to spot, but we've listed some quirky favorites that often fall under the average tourist's radar.

A Tour de Force (☎ 703-525-2948; www.atourdeforce .com) Local historian and author Jeanne Fogle leads visitors on four- to eight-hour explorations of a city her family has called home for four generations. The list of themes is staggering – everything from your standard monument romp to a First Ladies' tour to the Civil War – or you can cater something to your individual tastes. Fogle arranges transportation by car, SUV, bus, limousine (and foot, of course); prices vary depending on size of group and length of tour.

Anecdotal History Tours (☎ 301-294-9514; www .dcsightseeing.com; tours $300) These private group tours, led by author and former Associated Press editor Anthony Pitch (great journalist name, by the way), come very highly recommended. Pitch can do custom tours, but his history stuff really shines; his Lincoln's Assassination tour and Burning of Washington in 1814 trip are fine ways to get under this city's very historic skin.

Bike the Sites (Map p88; ☎ 202-842-2543; www .bikethesites.com; 1100 Pennsylvania Ave, Old Post Office Pavilion; adult/child from $40/30; ☺ 9am & 1pm; Ⓜ Federal Triangle) Knowledgeable guides lead tours of DC's major landmarks, as well as offering more specialized options, such as tours over and under Washington bridges or to Civil War sites. Additional tours vary with the season. The price includes bikes and all necessary equipment.

City Segway Tours (Map p88; ☎ 877-734-8687, 202-626-0017; http://citysegwaytours.com/washington -dc; 624 9th St NW; tours $70; ☺ 10am, 2pm & 6pm; Ⓜ Chinatown, Metro Center) In case you don't know, Segways are essentially electronic two-wheeled scooters that move about by intuitive control (which basically means just about anyone can operate one). You may look a little ridiculous, but this is a great way of covering ground, getting a street view and never breaking a sweat. The City Segway tour takes in the major sites on the Mall and in Downtown, and is reliably considered one of the better operators in the District.

Tour DC (☎ 301-588-8999; www.tourdc.com; group walks from $350) These excellent tours are led by local historian and travel writer Mary Kay Ricks; to say she knows the city well is excessive understatement. Her walks concentrate on DC's neighborhoods, especially Georgetown and Dupont Circle, and explore themes like spies and scandal, black heritage, the Civil War, the Kennedys, gardens and mansions and Embassy Row. Only groups or those willing to join a group are accepted as of writing.

Tourmobile (☎ 202-554-5100, 888-868-7707; www .tourmobile.com; adult/child $27/13; ☺ 9:30am-4:30pm; Ⓜ Federal Triangle, Arlington Cemetery) Tourmobile's primary tour runs around the National Mall, Capitol, White House and out to Arlington National Cemetery. You can hop off and reboard free at any of its 40 stops, which is nice for those who aren't able to walk long distances. Tourmobile also does separate tours of Arlington National Cemetery (adult/child $7.50/3.75), Mount Vernon ($32/16) and some black heritage sites ($7/3.50). A twilight tour, See Washington by Night ($20/10), is offered in season – mid-June through Labor Day (first Monday in September).

PHOTOGRAPHY

There are hundreds of stores throughout the district that sell both film and digital cameras along with supplies. CVS pharmacy and Ritz Camera are just two of many chains that transfer digital images to CD or make prints from either digital or film.

You can photograph anything outdoors in DC, although video and still camera use is restricted in airports and other high-security areas. Depending on the terrorist-threat level in the United States at the time of your visit, photography and video use may be restricted in other public areas as well.

If you are interested in photography, check out Lonely Planet's *Travel Photography* book.

POST

The most convenient post offices are located in the Old Post Office Pavilion (Map p88; 1100 Pennsylvania Ave) and the National Postal Museum (Map pp78–9; 2 Massachusetts Ave NE). Branch post offices (☎ 800-275-8777) are found throughout the city.

The main post office (off Map pp106–7; ☎ 202-635-5300; 900 Brentwood Rd NE; ☺ 8am-6pm Mon-Fri, 7:30am-4pm Sat; Ⓜ Rhode Island Ave) is where you will receive poste restante. All poste restante items should be addressed to you c/o General Delivery, Main Post Office, 900 Brentwood Rd NE, Washington, DC, 20066, with 'Hold for Arrival' written on the front of the envelope. Mail is usually held for 10 days; a picture ID is required for collection of poste restante items. American Express (opposite) and Thomas Cook (opposite) provide mail services for their customers.

Priority & express mail service (www.usps.com) is available. You can buy stamps at post offices and ATMs around the city. If you have the correct postage, you can drop mail into any blue street mailbox. If your items require packaging, you might call on a local packaging service, such as UPS Store (☎ 202-371-0065; 1220 L St NW) or Fedex (see p246), which provide shipping services and sell packaging materials.

Item	Postal Rates
1st-class mail within USA	44¢ for letters up to 1oz, 17¢ each additional ounce
postcards within USA	28¢
letters to Canada/Mexico	75/79¢
international airmail	98¢ per 1oz letter, 98¢ per postcard

RADIO

National Public Radio programs and classical music can be found on WETA-FM90.9; more NPR and talk shows are on WAMU-FM88.5. WPFW-FM89.3 plays jazz, local news and world music, and broadcasts alternative media such as *Democracy Now!* Two of the most popular stations in Washington are WKYS-FM93.9 and WPGC-FM95.5; both play hip-hop and R&B. Album-oriented dinosaur rock is on the menu at WWDC-FM101.1, but if you can pick it up, opt for the edgier WRNR-FM103.1 instead, which broadcasts out of nearby Annapolis, MD. Radio heads will enjoy tours of DC-based National Public Radio (p93).

SAFETY

DC has a reputation for violent crimes, but it is worth noting the homicide rate has dropped considerably from the bad old days of the '80s and late '90s. Even then, violent crime was mainly localized, and tourists were not in much danger of deadly assault. With that said, you need to be cautious if you're walking on your own late at night, especially in nightlife hot spots such as U St and Adams-Morgan, where lonely side streets are popular hunting grounds for muggers. People are held up at night in areas as posh as Woodley Park. If you are with other people, you probably won't be a target. If you're on your own after the bars shut down, please consider taking a cab. If you are held up, just hand everything over.

TAXES

Some tax is charged on nearly everything you buy in the USA. It may be included in the price or added onto advertised prices. When inquiring about lodging rates, always ask whether taxes are included. Unless otherwise stated, prices given in this book don't include taxes.

DC restaurant tax 10%

DC room tax 14.5% (plus an additional $1.50 per-night surcharge)

DC sales tax 6%

Maryland room tax 5-8%

Maryland sales tax 6%

Virginia room tax 9.5-10%

Virginia sales tax 5%

TELEPHONE

Pay phones are generally coin operated and cost 50¢ to make a local call. Prepaid phone cards are sold at newsstands and pharmacies around town. Fax services are available at Fedex (☎ 202-898-1401; 1400 K St NW; ☒ 7am-11pm Mon-Fri, 9am-9pm Sat & Sun), UPS Store (p245) and many upscale hotel business centers.

When calling DC from abroad, first dial the US country code (1). To place an international call from DC, dial ☎ 011 + country code + area code (dropping the leading 0) + number. Numbers beginning with ☎ 800, 888, 866 or 87 are toll free. For useful numbers, see the inside front cover of this book.

TELEVISION

All of the national networks are represented on the DC dial: NBC is on Channel 4, Fox on Channel 5, ABC on Channel 7 and CBS on Channel 9. Each of these channels has its own Sunday-morning political talk show based in Washington that focuses on national events: *Meet the Press* on NBC, *Face the Nation* on CBS and *This Week* on ABC. The federally supported Public Broadcasting System, based in DC, is on WETA Channel 26. C-SPAN broadcasts live from the floor of Congress (aired in offices and bars across Capitol Hill).

TIME

DC is on Eastern Standard Time, five hours behind Greenwich Mean Time. Daylight Saving Time is observed between April and October. When it's noon in DC, it's 5pm in London, 6am the next day in Sydney and 8am the next day in Auckland.

TOURIST INFORMATION

Washington, DC operates several information centers in the city to help travelers arrange accommodations and develop itineraries.

DC Chamber of Commerce Visitor Information Center (Map p88; ☎ 202-328-4748; www.dcchamber.org; 1300 Pennsylvania Ave NW, Ronald Reagan Bldg; ☒ 8am-4:30pm Mon-Fri Sep 2-Mar 14, 8:30am-5:30pm Mon-Fri, 9am-4pm Sat Mar 15-Sep 1; Ⓜ Federal Triangle) Offers tours, maps, lodging brochures and events listings, and sells film, tickets and souvenirs.

NPS Ellipse Visitor Pavilion (Map p64; ☎ 202-208-1631; ☒ 8am-3pm) At the northeast corner of the Ellipse, south of the White House.

Smithsonian Visitors Center (Map p54; ☎ 202-663-1000, TTY 202-633-5285; www.si.edu/visit;1000 Jefferson Dr SW, Smithsonian Institution Bldg – The Castle; ☺ 8:30am-5:30pm Mon-Sat; Ⓜ Smithsonian) Everything you ever wanted to know about the museum programs.

Washington, DC Convention & Visitors Association (Map p88; ☎ 202-789-7000; www.washington.org; 901 7th St NW, 4th fl; ☺ 9am-5pm Mon-Fri; Ⓜ Gallery Pl-Chinatown) Distributes information on lodgings, restaurants and attractions by mail, or you can pick them up at its office.

TRAVELERS WITH DISABILITIES

DC is an excellent destination for disabled visitors. Most museums and major sights are wheelchair accessible, as are most large hotels and restaurants. The Smithsonian (☎ 202-633-1000, TTY 202-633-5285) and many museums arrange special tours for people with visual, auditory or other impairments.

All Metro trains and most buses are accessible to people in wheelchairs. All Metro stations have elevators, and guide dogs are allowed on trains and buses. Disabled people are eligible for a Metro Disability ID Card, which qualifies them for discounted fares. Apply through the Washington Metropolitan Area Transit Authority (☎ 202-962-1245, TTY 202-628-8973; www.wmata.com/accessibility/disability_id.cfm). If you cannot use public transit, you can use MetroAccess (☎ 202-962-2700), a door-to-door transport provider. Many large hotels have suites for disabled guests, but call the hotel itself – not the chain's 800 number – to check with it directly before you reserve. Larger car-rental agencies offer hand-controlled models at no extra charge. All major airlines, Greyhound buses and Amtrak trains allow service animals on board and frequently sell two-for-one packages if you need an attendant to accompany you.

Out of doors, hindrances to wheelchair users include buckled-brick sidewalks in the historic blocks of Georgetown and Capitol Hill, but sidewalks in most other parts of DC are in good shape and have dropped curbs. Unfortunately, only a handful of crosswalks, mostly near the Mall, have audible crossing signals.

The Washington, DC Convention & Visitors Association (Map p88; ☎ 202-789-7000; www.washington.org; 901 7th St NW, 4th fl; ☺ 9am-5pm Mon-Fri; Ⓜ Gallery Pl-Chinatown) provides a fact sheet with details regarding accessibility at local attractions, lodgings and restaurants.

Hearing-impaired visitors should check out Gallaudet University (☎ 202-651-5000; www.gallaudet.edu) in Northeast DC, which hosts lectures and cultural events especially for the deaf.

VISAS

A passport with an official visa is required for most visitors to the United States; contact the American embassy or consulate in your home country for more information on specific requirements. Visitors between the ages of 14 and 79 have to be interviewed before a visa is granted, and all applicants must pay fees that currently stand at $131. You'll also have to prove you're not trying to stay in the USA permanently. If you are traveling for 90 days or less you may qualify for the Visa Waiver Program (VWP); currently citizens of 43 countries are eligible for this program. Learn more at http://travel.state.gov/visa/temp/without/without_1990.html. The Electronic System for Travel Authorization (https://esta.cbp.dhs.gov) determines if you are eligible for the VWP. For general visa information, have a look at http://travel.state.gov/visa/visa_1750.html.

Visa Extensions

If you try to extend your time in the country, immigration authorities often assume you're working illegally – so hang on to evidence that shows you've been a model tourist (like receipts to demonstrate that you've spent money in the USA or ticket stubs to show that you've traveled extensively). You must apply for an extension *before* your visa has expired – four to six weeks is a good window. To extend your stay, you must file Form I-539, copies of your I-94 visa application, proof of financial support (ie bank statements), copies of your passport and copies of return tickets. Extensions can be obtained from the Bureau of Citizenship & Immigration Service (☎ 800-375-5283; www.uscis.gov; Washington District Office, 2675 Prosperity Ave, Fairfax, VA 20598; Ⓜ Dunn-Loring), but you need to schedule your appointment before visiting at http://infopass.uscis.gov.

WOMEN TRAVELERS

Washington is a safe and fascinating destination for women travelers, especially given that innumerable monuments and historic sites remember women's key roles in the nation and the city, including the National Museum of Women in the Arts (p91), the Women in Military Service for America Memorial (p121), and the Mary McLeod Bethune Council House (p93).

Women traveling alone might appreciate the all-women hostel Thompson-Markward Hall (p207) on Capitol Hill.

Other useful organizations:

Planned Parenthood (Map p64; ☎ 202-347-8500; 1108 16th St NW; Ⓜ Farragut North) Offers obstetric, gynecological and counseling services.

Washington Women Outdoors (☎ 301-864-3070; www.washingtonwomenoutdoors.org; 19450 Caravan Dr, Germantown, MD 20874) About 30 miles northwest of DC. A full calendar of hikes, climbs and cycling trips that are a great way to befriend local women.

WORK

Foreign visitors are not legally allowed to work in the USA without the appropriate working visa. But US citizens, especially young ones, flock here in summer to take up internships on Capitol Hill, at federal agencies and in think tanks. If you want an internship, it's important to start looking early – the fall of the preceding year is a good time to start. Find your congressional representatives' office addresses via the Capitol switchboard (☎ 202-224-3121).

Volunteering

If you want to volunteer in the DC metro area, check out www.volunteermatch.org, which offers hundreds of ways you can make a difference in the District.

BEHIND THE SCENES

THIS BOOK

This 4th edition of *Washington, DC* was written by Adam Karlin and Regis St. Louis. The third edition was written by Becca Blond and Aaron Anderson. Previous editions were written by Mara Vorhees and Laura Harger. This edition was commissioned in Lonely Planet's Oakland office and produced by the following:

Commissioning Editor Jennye Garibaldi

Coordinating Editors Michelle Bennett, Monique Choy

Coordinating Cartographers Anita Bahn, Enes Basic

Coordinating Layout Designer Frank Deim

Senior Editors Helen Christinis, Katie Lynch

Managing Cartographers Shahara Ahmed, Herman So

Managing Layout Designer Laura Jane

Assisting Editor Judith Bamber

Assisting Cartographers Xavier Di Toro, Andras Bogdanovits

Cover Designer Kate Slattery, lonelyplanetimages.com

Internal Image Research Sabrina Dalbesio, lonelyplanetimages.com

Project Managers Craig Kilburn, Chris Love

Thanks to Sasha Baskett, Lucy Birchley, Jessica Boland, Catherine Craddock-Carillo, Melanie Dankel, Sally Darmody, Heather Dickson, Ryan Evans, Indra Kilfoyle, Alison Lyall, Naomi Parker, Raphael Richards

Cover photographs Sleek Metro subway station, Izzy Schwartz/Photolibrary (top); Joggers silhouetted against the Washington Monument, Pete Miller/eStock Photo (bottom).

Internal photographs
All images are copyright of the photographer unless otherwise indicated. Many of the images in this guide are available for licensing from Lonely Planet Images: www .lonelyplanetimages.com.

THANKS
ADAM KARLIN

Huge thanks to John Groth, Nick Blumenthal, Dan Matthews, Drew Rawls, Jessie Nymeyer, Jordan Sauer, Matt Sheehan (and Max), and the Froveys, Mussemeyers and Brewingthews for providing insight, good companionship and places to crash and work. Thank you Emma for the calming presence of your purring as I write, and for scattering your fur on my laptop. Thanks also to Becca Blond for doing such a great job on the last DC guide, and Regis St. Louis for kicking ass on this one. Thanks mom and dad for being who you are, and everyone who's ever helped me act the fool in the nation's capital.

REGIS ST. LOUIS

Many thanks to Jennye Garibaldi, Craig Kilburn and other LP staff behind the scenes for their patience and dedication to the latest and greatest incarnation of *Washington, DC*. Big thanks to Adam Karlin and friends for useful tips on DC and the fashion scene. As always, thanks to Cassandra, Magdalena and Genevieve for continued love and support.

THE LONELY PLANET STORY

Fresh from an epic journey across Europe, Asia and Australia in 1972, Tony and Maureen Wheeler sat at their kitchen table stapling together notes. The first Lonely Planet guidebook, *Across Asia on the Cheap*, was born.

Travelers snapped up the guides. Inspired by their success, the Wheelers began publishing books to Southeast Asia, India and beyond. Demand was prodigious, and the Wheelers expanded the business rapidly to keep up. Over the years, Lonely Planet extended its coverage to every country and into the virtual world via lonelyplanet.com and the Thorn Tree message board.

As Lonely Planet became a globally loved brand, Tony and Maureen received several offers for the company. But it wasn't until 2007 that they found a partner whom they trusted to remain true to the company's principles of traveling widely, treading lightly and giving sustainably. In October of that year, BBC Worldwide acquired a 75% share in the company, pledging to uphold Lonely Planet's commitment to independent travel, trustworthy advice and editorial independence.

Today, Lonely Planet has offices in Melbourne, London and Oakland, with over 500 staff members and 300 authors. Tony and Maureen are still actively involved with Lonely Planet. They're traveling more often than ever, and they're devoting their spare time to charitable projects. And the company is still driven by the philosophy of *Across Asia on the Cheap*: 'All you've got to do is decide to go and the hardest part is over. So go!'

SEND US YOUR FEEDBACK

We love to hear from travelers – your comments keep us on our toes and help make our books better. Our well-traveled team reads every word on what you loved or loathed about this book. Although we cannot reply individually to postal submissions, we always guarantee that your feedback goes straight to the appropriate authors, in time for the next edition. Each person who sends us information is thanked in the next edition and the most useful submissions are rewarded with a free book.

To send us your updates – and find out about Lonely Planet events, newsletters and travel news – visit our award-winning website: lonelyplanet.com/contact.

Note: we may edit, reproduce and incorporate your comments in Lonely Planet products such as guidebooks, websites and digital products, so let us know if you don't want your comments reproduced or your name acknowledged. For a copy of our privacy policy visit lonelyplanet.com/privacy.

OUR READERS

Many thanks to the travelers who used the last edition and wrote to us with helpful hints, useful advice and interesting anecdotes:

Brooke Bennett, Seth Berger, Stefanie Bode, Edwin De Voogd, Jeruen Dery, Will Gibbons, Gina Gomez, Ben Hindman, Jong Hyun Jang, Irving Levinson, John Lockwood, Rebecca Menes, Rodney Miles, Heather Monell, Megan Peniston-Bird, Marcus Roper, Lillian Rosen, Tina Seashore, Craig Smith, Carolyn Stachowski, Paul Summers, Karen Vock, Tony Wheeler.

Notes

INDEX

A

accommodations 202-16, *see also* Sleeping *subindex*
  bookings 203, 212
activities 196-200, *see also* Sports & Activities *subindex & individual activities*
Adams, Henry 30, 203
Adams Morgan Festival 16
Adams-Morgan 102-4, **103**
  accommodations 212-14
  food 161-3
  internet resources 102
  nightlife 179-82
  orientation 102
  shopping 137-9
Advise & Consent 36
African American Civil War 107-8, 111
air travel 235-6
Alexandria 124-6, **125**, *see also* Northern Virginia
  accommodations 215
  food 169-70
  internet resources 121
  nightlife 186
All the President's Men 35
ambulance 242
Anderson, Marian 26-7, 55
Andres, Jose 156, 158
animals 39-40, 68
Annapolis 229-32
antiques, *see* Shopping *subindex*

000 map pages
000 photographs

Appalachian Trail 226, 227
aquariums 227
architecture 37-9, 67, *see also* Sights *subindex*
area codes, see *inside front cover*
Arlington 121-4, **122**, *see also* Northern Virginia
  accommodations 215
  food 168-9
  internet resources 121
  nightlife 185-6
Arlington National Cemetery 121
Armstrong, Louis 34, 111
art galleries 29-30, 188-90 *see also* Arts & Sights *subindexes*
Arthur M Sackler Gallery 38-9
arts 29-37, 188-94, *see also* Shopping *subindex & individual arts*
Assateague Island 233
Atlas District 176
ATMs 244

B

B&Bs 202, 212, *see also* Sleeping *subindex*
babysitting 241
Bacon, Henry 55
ballet 192
Baltimore 227-9
Baltimore-Washington International Airport 236
Banneker, Benjamin 21, 85
Barbecue Battle 14-15
Barry, Marion 28, 45
bars, *see* Nightlife *subindex*
baseball 200, 228
basketball 200
Battles of Manassas 223
beaches 218, 232-3
beaux arts 38, 81, 101
Ben's Chili Bowl 6, 17, 111, 146, 163, **6**
Bernstein, Carl 31, 35, 40, 45
Bethune, Mary McLeod 82, 93
bicycle travel, *see* cycling

Bill of Rights 62, 81, 89-90
birds 39-40, 231
bird-watching 123, 231, 233
Black History Month 12
Blackwater National Wildlife Refuge 231
boat travel, *see* Sports & Activities *subindex*
bocce 198
Bonus Army 44
books 20, 30-2, *see also* Shopping *subindex*
Booth, John Wilkes 23, 91
Brown, Dan 32
Brown, John 23, 226
Buben, Jeff 155, 160-1
buildings, *see* Sights *subindex*
Bunshaft, Gordon 38
bus travel 237
Bush, George W 28-9, 43
business hours 241, *see also inside front cover*
  bars 172
  restaurants 144-5
  shops 128

C

C&O Canal & Towpath 73, 197
C&O Canal National Historical Park 220
cafes, *see* Eating & Nightlife *subindexes*
canoeing 198-9
Cape Henlopen State Park 233
Capital Crescent Trail 197
Capital Jazz Fest 14
Capital Pride 14
Capitol 77, 80, 85, **3**
Capitol Hill & Southeast DC 76-86, **78-9**, **86**
  accommodations 207-8
  food 152-5
  internet resources 77
  nightlife 175-7
  orientation 76-7
  shopping 133-4
  walking tour 85-6
car travel 237-8
Cardina, Douglas 38

Carroll, Kenny 50, 194
Carter, Jimmy 28
Cashion, Ann 163
cathedrals, *see* Sights *subindex*
caving, *see* Sports & Activities *subindex*
cemeteries, *see* Sights *subindex*
chemists 243-4
Cherry Blossom 10-Mile Run 13
Cherry Blossom Festival 13
Chesapeake Bay 229-32, **8**
children, travel with 7, 116, 241, *see also* Shopping & Sleeping *subindexes*
Chinatown 86, 87, 92-3
Chincoteague 232
Chincoteague National Wildlife Refuge 233
Chinese New Year 12
churches, *see* Sights *subindex*
cinema 35-7, 193-4, *see also* Arts *subindex*
  film festivals 13, 14, 15, 16
civil rights 26-7, 55, 83, 91, 105, 107-8
Civil War 22-4, 107, 110, 111, 117, 124, 222-3, 226-7
Clancy, Tom 32
classical music 191-4, *see also* Arts *subindex*
climate 12, 241
climate change 236
Clooney, George 35
clothes, *see* Shopping *subindex*
clubs, *see* Nightlife *subindex*
Cold War 25-6
Columbia Heights & Northeast DC 105-12, **106-7**, **112**
  accommodations 214
  food 163-6
  internet resouces 108
  nightlife 182-5
  orientation 105-6
  shopping 139-40
  walking tour 111-12

INDEX

000 map pages
000 photographs

INDEX

000 map pages
000 photographs

MAP LEGEND
ROUTES

Tollway	Mall/Steps
Freeway	Tunnel
Primary	Pedestrian Overpass
Secondary	Walking Tour
Tertiary	Walking Trail
Lane	Walking Path

TRANSPORT

Metro
Rail (Underground)

HYDROGRAPHY

River
Water

BOUNDARIES

State

Marine Park

AREA FEATURES

Airport	Land
Beach	Mall
Building	Market
Campus	Park
Cemetery	Reservation
Forest	Sports

SYMBOLS

Information
- Bank, ATM
- Embassy
- Hospital
- Information
- Internet Facilities
- Police Station
- Post Office
- Telephone
- Toilets

Sights
- Beach
- Christian
- Monument
- Museum
- Point of Interest
- Ruin

Shopping
- Shopping

Eating
- Eating

Entertainment
- Entertainment

Drinking
- Drinking
- Cafe

Nightlife
- Nightlife

Arts
- Arts

Sports & Activities
- Pool
- Trail Head

Sleeping
- Sleeping

Transport
- Airport
- Bus Station
- Cycling
- General Transport
- Parking Area
- Petrol Station
- Taxi Rank

Geographic
- Lighthouse
- Lookout
- Mountain
- National Park
- River Flow

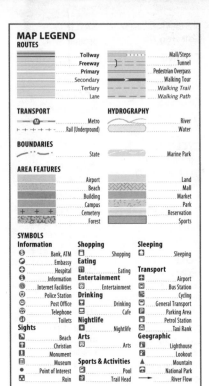

Published by Lonely Planet
ABN 36 005 607 983

Australia (Head Office)
Locked Bag 1, Footscray, Victoria 3011,
☎03 8379 8000, fax 03 8379 8111,
talk2us@lonelyplanet.com.au

USA 150 Linden St, Oakland, CA 94607,
☎510 250 6400, toll free 800 275 8555,
fax 510 893 8572, info@lonelyplanet.com

UK 2nd fl, 186 City Rd, London, EC1V 2NT,
☎020 7106 2100, fax 020 7106 2101,
go@lonelyplanet.co.uk

Mixed Sources
Product group from well-managed
forests and other controlled sources
www.fsc.org Cert no. SGS-COC-005002
© 1996 Forest Stewardship Council